FORTUNE FAVOURS THE BRAVE

FORTUNE FAVOURS THE BRAVE

Tales of Courage and Tenacity in Canadian Military History

Edited by Colonel Bernd Horn

Foreword by Senator Roméo Dallaire

DUNDURN PRESS
TORONTO

Editor: Michael Carroll
Copy-editor: Nigel Heseltine
Design: Jennifer Scott
Printer: Marquis

Library and Archives Canada Cataloguing in Publication

Fortune favours the brave : tales of courage and tenacity in Canadian military history / edited by Bernd Horn.

Includes index.
ISBN 978-1-55002-841-6

1. Canada--History, Military. 2. Battles--Canada. 3. Soldiers— Canada--History. I. Horn, Bernd, 1959-

FC226.F67 2009   355.00971   C2008-903965-3

1   2   3   4   5   13   12   11   10   09

Conseil des Arts du Canada   Canada Council for the Arts   ONTARIO ARTS COUNCIL   CONSEIL DES ARTS DE L'ONTARIO

Canada

We acknowledge the support of the **Canada Council for the Arts** and the **Ontario Arts Council** for our publishing program. We also acknowledge the financial support of the **Government of Canada** through the **Book Publishing Industry Development Program** and **The Association for the Export of Canadian Books**, and the **Government of Ontario** through the **Ontario Book Publishers Tax Credit program**, and the **Ontario Media Development Corporation.**

Printed and bound in Canada.
www.dundurn.com

Dundurn Press	Gazelle Book Services Limited	Dundurn Press
3 Church Street, Suite 500	White Cross Mills	2250 Military Road
Toronto, Ontario, Canada	High Town, Lancaster, England	Tonawanda, NY
M5E 1M2	LA1 4XS	U.S.A. 14150

CONTENTS

FOREWORD

I have always been impressed by the courage, dedication, and resilience of Canada's military personnel. As a small boy, I watched my father and his comrades, recently returned veterans from the cauldron of war in Europe, humbly soldier on in a peacetime army, seemingly ambivalent to their great contribution in shaping the world. I witnessed the same sense of duty and humility when I myself donned the uniform to serve my country. Quite simply, our men and women in uniform serve a greater cause, quietly and professionally, doing what is asked of them. They act in accordance with a yet unwritten social contract between the military and their fellow citizens that demands an unlimited liability on their part. They have never failed Canadians, and the ethos of soldiering in Canada will continue to guarantee that commitment now and into the future.

Consistently, our service members have ventured out fearlessly and helped shape the world in accordance with Canadian values and interests. Although peace-loving, regardless of the task assigned, this nation's soldiers, sailors, and air personnel have always demonstrated a tenacious warrior spirit. Ironically, the Canadian public, whose perception of peacekeeping is based on missions conducted during the Cold War and a misguided understanding of what the task entails, have always seen their Canadian Forces in a more benign light.

The war in Afghanistan, however, is changing some of this perception. But what Canadians must realize is that their military has always been combat capable and comprised of warriors. This is nothing new. *Fortune Favours the Brave* captures this reality. It showcases the indomitable spirit of Canadians who throughout our military history have gone into harm's way to serve their nation, their fellow Canadians, and the global community at large. This book demonstrates the bold, courageous, and unconquerable spirit of the average Canadian soldier, sailor, and airman/woman. It speaks to our military heritage as capable warriors, dependable allies, and a dreaded foe.

Throughout my 35-year career, I had the distinct honour of leading our nation's sons and daughters in peacetime and on operations. Their unrelenting professionalism, civility, and unrivalled tenacity to accomplish the mission were humbling.

This book captures that tradition. I highly recommend it to all Canadians, whether military or civilian. It captures the essence of our rich and colourful Canadian military history. It also speaks to the warrior ethos and warfighting tradition of our nation's military.

Roméo Dallaire
Senator
Lieutenant-General (Retired)

ACKNOWLEDGEMENTS

Bernd Horn

As always in an endeavour such as this, the completed project is never really the work of one individual. Many hands play their part. In that vein I wish to acknowledge, on my account and on behalf of all contributors, the assistance of others. Initially, I wish to thank the contributors themselves for putting in the time and enormous effort necessary to create the essays that appear in this book. The knowledge they bring to their subjects and their continued enthusiasm in sharing what they know is always inspiring.

In addition, I would like to thank once again Paramount Press, Susan Surgeson, and Gail Cariou of Parks Canada, as well as Robert Flacke Sr. and the Fort William Henry Corporation, who made possible the use of many of the graphics that are used in the first three chapters of the book. Similarly, I would also like to thank Silvia Pecota for the use of her outstanding artwork on the back cover. Thanks is also due to Lucie Ethier of the National Defence Imagery Library and Lieutenant-Colonel Joe Holland for their assistance in sourcing photographs of the Medak pocket and Captain (Retired) Robert M. Mahar for his photographs from Korea.

I also wish to acknowledge the outstanding contribution of Dr. Emily Spencer for her assistance in research, proofing, and editorial comment, as well as Michel Wyczynski for his consistently outstanding advice on research and archival matters.

Collectively, we would also like to thank a number of organizations and individuals for their expertise and invaluable assistance. We owe a debt of gratitude to the staff of the Fortress of Louisbourg, National Historic Site of Canada, specifically Sandy Balcom, Ruby Fougere, Heather Gillis, A.J.B. Johnston, Anne Marie Lane Jonah, and Heidi Moses, as well as Gerald Boulet of Parks Canada, Atlantic Service Centre, and George Vandervlugt, CRM Research and Analysis, Parks Canada.

I must also acknowledge the assistance of Dundurn editorial director Michael Carroll and copy-editor Nigel Heseltine whose efforts ensured a rough manuscript was massaged into the book you see before you. Finally, I must thank my wife, Kim, and my daughters, Calli and Katie, for their continued patience and tolerance.

INTRODUCTION

Bernd Horn

"Canadians are fierce fighters," observed U.S. Secretary of State Condoleezza Rice when speaking about Canada's role in the ongoing struggle for Afghanistan.[1] For those who know their Canadian military history this is not a surprising statement. For many Canadians, however, it is. They are surprised, if not somewhat aghast. For a multitude of Canadians the immediate response would be "My gosh, no — they are peacekeepers!" Canadians are seemingly reluctant to leave behind the Cold War notion that somehow its military is a benign force that only does humanitarian and peacekeeping operations.

The reality, is, and has always been, different. Canada's soldiers, sailors, and air personnel have always been courageous, professional, and technically competent military practitioners. When required they have always been tenacious warriors. The war in Afghanistan is only the most recent manifestation. Pitted against a brutal and unrelenting enemy the Canadian Forces (CF) has fought a bitter counterinsurgency in Kandahar Province since 2006. The scale of the fight is such that as of September 2008, the nation has suffered over 90 dead and hundreds of wounded.

Nonetheless, Canadians still have difficulty accepting this reality. Understandably, they lament the loss and suffering of their soldiers and the Afghan people. They proudly support their military, but are strongly opposed to the involvement of the CF in Afghanistan. At the heart of the Canadian philosophical and political discord is the lingering peacekeeper mythology.

Quite simply, many Canadians do not believe their military is a warfighting force. They wish to maintain the illusion that we are a a nation of peacekeepers who venture forth in the turbulent violent world and do good. They wish to hang-on to images of soldiers delivering humanitarian supplies, providing aid and infrastructure, and passing out teddy bears to children in impoverished war-torn or disaster-inflicted areas around the world. This expectation and myth grew out of the Cold War when Canada in many ways made its name in the United Nations (UN) as a reliable and effective peacekeeping force.

However, the reality is much different. Throughout this nation's history, Canadians have proven to be formidable warriors — dreaded foes and cherished allies. Although not a militaristic society or people, we have continually been capable soldiers — second to none. From Canada's first expeditionary force in the Boer War, through the two world wars, Korea, and then the myriad of Cold War peacekeeping missions, through the turbulent 1990s in the post–Cold War era in such places as Somalia, Bosnia-Hercegovina, East Timor, Cambodia, and now Afghanistan, this nation's soldiers have always shown courage, daring, and tenacity. Canada's allies, as well as the international community as a whole, have long realized that they can count on our soldiers, sailors, and air personnel to get the job done. "The men and women who wear our uniform — who wear the nation's flag on their left-hand shoulder are equal to the best in the world," asserted General Rick Hillier, the former Chief of the Defence Staff (CDS). "They are ready to serve wherever they are needed and in fact become our nation's very credentials throughout the world."[2]

This is exactly what our military has always done — accomplish the mission — wherever required. Moreover, they have often done this while showing a distinctive daring attitude. The nation's military forces have always had the courage to oppose and defy the odds against success, to boldly venture forth to accomplish the mission no matter how dangerous. They have always been prepared to take risks and display the necessary fearlessness to take on even the hardest tasks. In the end, our nation's military has always shown courage, tenacity, and daring — whether in thought, planning, or execution.

Clearly, these attributes apply to actions and deeds — the storming of an impregnable stronghold or position; an attack or spirited defence against insurmountable odds; or the conduct of an individual, group, or organization. However, courage, tenacity, and daring can also extend to planning or a mindset that operates on the fringes and constantly pushes the envelope of safe or conventionally accepted reasoned action. In the end, through bravery, courage, tenacity, and intellect — our military forces have always proved to be a capable fighting force respected by friend and foe alike.

This book captures that spirit. It recounts a number of formidable actions in Canadian military history where Canadians and their forbearers — the Natives who inhabited the North American wilderness and the Europeans who ventured forth to the New World as settlers, entrepreneurs, or soldiers — bravely fought the British Empire's and later the nation's wars, no matter how they may be defined. As such, this book begins with fascinating account of the bitter and deadly struggle for control of the wilderness in colonial North America. The first chapter, written by Bernd Horn, captures the savage contest between the French Canadian partisans and their Native allies against the English, specifically their arch-nemesis Major Robert Rogers, on the Lake Champlain frontier. On 8 August 1758, both sides collided at Wood Creek in what became a bitter struggle for survival.

The next chapter, by national archivist Michel Wyczynski, covers yet another engagement during the Seven Years' War in North America. It describes the daring amphibious assault of Brigadier James Wolfe as he led Highlanders and Grenadiers ashore in a raging surf during the siege of Louisbourg on 8 June 1758. His courage and tenacity won the British a foothold that would later result in the defeat of the great French fortress.

In chapter 3, John Grodzinski narrates the daring account of the British attack on Fort Niagara during the War of 1812. After setting the context of the often bitter, see-saw struggle on the Niagara frontier, Grodzinski examines the bold British strike on 18–19 December 1813, to wrest control of the key American strategic fortification that controlled access to Lake Ontario and the Niagara River. On that cold, dark night the British stealthily crossed the river and quietly approached the imposing fortified position that was held by a force of almost equal strength. Through guile and audacity the British forced their way into the fort and fought a vicious action to gain its control. Its daring capture triggered a subsequent campaign that turned 25 miles of the American Niagara frontier into wasteland, thus, securing for the British the vital Niagara theatre of operations.

The next chapter leaps forward to the First World War. Here Ken Reynolds describes a daring Canadian raid on 8–9 June 1917. In the aftermath of the great victory at Vimy Ridge several months earlier in April, further allied progress was stymied by a bitter war of attrition. Newly won ground was difficult to hold as a result of tenacious German counterattacks and bombardments. The shift of allied artillery to another front hampered the ability of the Canadians to hold ground that they subsequently gained or to provide counter-battery fire as a means of relief from the heavy German shelling. As a result, Canadian Corps Commander, Lieutenant-General Julian Byng, questioned why Canadian blood was required to be spent to attack and gain ground only to eventually withdraw in the face of unremitting enemy pressure and a lack of artillery support. As an alternative, he suggested that the objective desired might be achieved by "carrying out the operations in the form of a big raid."

In essence, he decided that "the attack would be carried out exactly as planned in full strength to ensure getting in to the German trenches, and that after killing and capturing all the German garrison, destroying dugouts [and] machine-gun emplacements" the troops would be withdrawn under cover of darkness and a rear guard.[3] This is exactly what the tenacious Canadian troops did. After meticulous planning and rehearsals the large raid was launched. Canadian troops fought tenaciously through the enemy lines and captured their objectives. However, as always, it came at great cost. Despite inflicting great punishment on the enemy, for some, the price exacted was too great.

In chapter 5 Andrew Godefroy remains with a First World War theme as he recounts the harrowing tale of the Canadian and German clash of wills as they fought for control of Mount Sorrel in early June 1916. In that short bitter struggle for the pock-marked slashed ground, 12,000 Canadians were killed, wounded, or missing. In the end, however, the Canadians emerged victorious and retained control of their objective.

The following action moves the reader into Second World War. Chapter 6 tells the exciting story of the 1st Canadian Parachute Battalion and their harrowing combat jump across the Rhine River to pierce Hitler's Third Reich as part of Operation Varsity on 24 March 1945. Pitted against a skilled and heavily entrenched enemy, the Canadian paratroopers jumped into a hail of fire and wrestled their objective from the German defenders in a bitter and costly struggle. The hard fought battle resulted in the award of a Victoria Cross, the only one the unit would earn during the war.

The next two chapters deal with the Korean conflict. In chapter 7, William Johnson tells the story of the Battle of Kap'yong, from 23–26 April 1951, when 2nd Battalion, Princess Patricia's Canadian Light Infantry (2 PPCLI) heroically held their ground against an unrelenting Chinese offensive. Newly arrived in the theatre in December 1950, just as Chinese troops began their intervention and pushed UN troops back to the 38th parallel, the battalion participated in several tough battles against the enemy rearguard during the UN counteroffensive. However, 2 PPCLI distinguished itself in April 1951, when it held a key feature along the Kap'yong River during another Chinese offensive. The brave "Patricias" (nickname for the PPCLI soldiers) held firm against wave after wave of attacking infantry and halted the drive of the Chinese 118th Division. For their heroic action 2 PPCLI was awarded a United States Presidential Unit Citation, the only Canadian unit ever to be so recognized until 2001.

Chapter 8, by Bernd Horn also recounts a tale of courage and tenacity from the Korean conflict. By the fall of 1952, the conflict had evolved into a war of patrols, with deadly raids and attacks designed more to inflict casualties and dominate ground than actually seize terrain. The conflict in the harsh, inhospitable Korean mountains seemed to teeter between overwhelming boredom and sheer terror. On the night of 23 October 1952 it was the latter as a prolonged period of shelling and bombardment of 1 RCR's position ended, giving way to a brutal assault by Chinese infantry. Brutal hand-to-hand combat ensued and the fortitude and bravery of the Canadian soldiers won the day.

The next chapter, "Doin' the Biz," by naval historian Michael Whitby provides a rare glimpse into the heretofore undisclosed world of Canadian submarine patrol operations against Soviet nuclear submarines during the Cold War. Using secret files that were specifically declassified for this chapter, Whitby describes operations and exercises conducted by the Canadian submarines in a deadly game of cat and mouse in the depths of the Atlantic Ocean.

Lee Windsor moves the volume out of the Cold War and into the stability campaigns of the 1990s. In fact, chapter 10, set in the vortex of the "decade of darkness,"[4] examines the actions of the 2nd Battalion, Princess Patricia's Canadian Light Infantry in September 1993, when they had to engage in combat with Croatian troops to complete their mission. In fact, the Canadians were purposely given the difficult and extremely dangerous task of enforcing a ceasefire and disarmament agreement because the French commander of the UN Protection Force in the former Yugoslavia needed a force he could count on to stop the fighting and regain credibility for UN forces in the region. In the end, the Canadians achieved his aims and developed a template for gathering evidence to bring those guilty of war crimes to justice.

In chapter 11, Bernd Horn captures the enduring theme of Canada's warrior spirit. He recounts in vivid detail Operation Medusa, which was conducted from 1–17 September 2006, in Kandahar Province in Afghanistan. Described as an operation that demonstrated NATO resolve and saved the nation of Afghanistan, it was largely a Canadian accomplishment paid for in Canadian blood. Fighting against a numerically superior, very determined enemy, soldiers of Task Force 3–06 fought a bitter battle that resulted in the defeat of the Taliban in their own heartland. The former CDS, General Rick Hillier, summed up the feat. "On labor day weekend 2006, that terrible weekend, Charles Company, 1st Battalion, The Royal Canadian Regiment, lost a company commander in action, lost a company sergeant-major, lost one out of three platoon commanders, lost all three platoon warrant officers, one wounded, two killed, lost five section commanders out of nine and lost all of the sections' second in command master-corporals — a total of 40-plus wounded and five killed in a 48-hour period. They all stepped up. A young sergeant, just promoted to sergeant last July, became the company sergeant-major. Young master-corporals became platoon commanders and platoon second in commands. And young soldiers became section commanders and they carried on the operation and the fight against the Taliban that gave NATO such an incredible boost right at the start of the mission. Now if that's not a Canadian epic, I don't know what is."[5]

The final chapter by Sean Maloney carries on the story of Afghanistan. He describes another Canadian action in the same region but a year later. Maloney describes how Canadian soldiers once again demonstrated élan, courage, and tenacity during Operation Intizaar Zmarey, in yet another battle to destroy Taliban influence in the Arghandab, from 30 October-1 November, 2007. Tactical ingenuity, professionalism, and an unconquerable warrior spirit once again prevailed to secure mission success.

In sum, the collection of essays in this volume, varied as they are in style and scope, capture the richness of Canadian military history. Although Canadians see their nation as a peaceable kingdom and themselves as an unmilitary people, the truth is that our nation has a proud military heritage. Moreover, its citizens and their forebearers share a legacy of courage, tenacity and warfighting prowess. As such, this book showcases our rich and distinct national military experience while capturing the indomitable spirit of the Canadian soldier.

NOTES

1. Michael Tutton, "Rice gives nod to military," *The Kingston-Whig Standard*, 13 September 2006, 11.

2. "Canadian Officer responsible for Regional Command South in Kandahar," CEFCOM News Release 06.003, 28 February 2006.

3. Library and Archives Canada [henceforth LAC], Record Group [henceforth RG] 9, III D 3, Vol. 4815, War Diary, Canadian Corps — General Staff, 4 June 1917.

4. The "Decade of Darkness" is a term used by senior military commanders, chiefs of the defence staff, scholars, and military analysts to describe the 1990s, which, despite many successes resulting from the actions of professional CF men and women, was marked by a large numbers of failings of the institution and its military and civilian leadership. Revisionists, however, often try to redefine the term to apply only to the resource constraints under which the CF was forced to operate.

5. General Rick Hillier, speech at Conference of Defence Associates Seminar, Ottawa, 15 February 2007.

1

DEADLY ENCOUNTER AT WOOD CREEK, 8 AUGUST 1758

Bernd Horn

*T*ha-boom! The musket shot reverberated through the Adirondack wilderness shattering the morning stillness. Within seconds two more shots rang out and echoed through the forest.[1] Captain Joseph Marin, the veteran French Canadian partisan leader froze immediately. The enemy was close — very close. He quickly, but quietly, arranged his war party of 500 Canadians, *coureur de bois*, and Natives into a crescent shaped ambush on the edge of the forest clearing. Within minutes the large force virtually vanished as it melted into the thick brush and awaited its unsuspecting prey.

Joseph Marin de la Malgue was well versed in *la petite guerre* — the savage guerrilla warfare that centered on the use of shock action and surprise to achieve limited objectives.[2] Daring raids and ambushes were the preferred methods of the French and their Native allies. They had used them to good effect terrorizing the New England frontiers and tying down large number of provincial soldiers in a desperate attempt to provide security.

Marin was no stranger to the English, particularly Rogers's Rangers. They had played a deadly game of cat and mouse for years — Marin usually the victor. He was once again leading a war party against the British hoping to further demoralize the English by striking them at Fort Edward and Albany. They were emboldened by the French victory at Fort Ticonderoga a month earlier, on 8 July 1758, when Major-General

Louis-Joseph de Montcalm's force of 3,600 turned away Major-General James Abercromby's army of 15,000. Although no immediate follow-up was taken by Montcalm at the time, the arrival of more Canadians and their Native allies allowed the French to mount an active raiding campaign to keep the English off balance.

For most of the war, the French owned the forests and their skilled Canadians and Native raiders bottled up garrisons and terrorized settlements tying down large forces in a defensive role.[3] Just days earlier on 28 July, another French Canadian, La Corne, with 300 Canadians and Natives massacred a convoy of 116 men and women between Fort Edward and Halfway Brook. Upon hearing of the outrage, Major-General Abercromby immediately ordered Major Robert Rogers[4] and Major Israel Putnam, with a combined force of 1,400 men, to run down the impertinent La Corne. Despite their haste they reached the narrow of Lake Champlain too late. La Corne just narrowly missed their noose. However, the stage was now set for yet another encounter between Marin and Rogers.

Three days later, 11 Rangers patrolling the Wood Creek approach from Fort Ticonderoga stumbled upon fresh tracks of a large Native war party. They pursued the trail for four miles where they decided to halt for a meal. Suddenly, the tables were turned — the hunter became the prey. They were surrounded and attacked by 50 Natives. In the desperate and savage struggle eight Rangers and 17 Natives were killed and two Rangers were captured. Only one Ranger, Sergeant Hackett escaped. Ominously, on his flight to Fort Edward, he discovered additional fresh tracks of an

Courtesy The Fort William Henry Corporation.

Rogers's Rangers were created to provide the British with a scouting/ reconnaissance capability similar to the French. However, they never achieved the same level of expertise or success.

Courtesy Parks Canada PD 161.

Rogers's Rangers achieved notoriety in the English press. During the initial years, the Rangers seemed to be the only body of troops conducting successful operations against the enemy. Major Robert Rogers was adept at providing colourful exploits to raise the morale of the terrorized population along the frontier.

even larger enemy war party apparently heading in the direction of Fort Edward and Albany.

Upon receiving the latest report Abercromby devised a plan to intercept and destroy the unidentified French raiding party. He sent a dispatch to Rogers and Putnam, who were still in the field, to take 700 chosen men and 10 days of provisions and "sweep all that back country" of South Bay and Wood Creek to Fort Edward.

On the night of 31 July, Rogers and Putnam and their force camped on Sloop Island. The next day was spent preparing the expedition and on 2 August, the two men set off with separate groups to set ambushes at the junction of Wood Creek and East Bay and South Bay, respectively. This proved to be unproductive. Four days later Rogers and Putnam rejoined forces and marched to the decaying ruins of Fort St. Anne where they camped on the night of 7 August 1758.

Little had been accomplished to date. Other than the near capture of an enemy canoe with six warriors there was no sign of enemy forces.[5] Vigilance began to slip. Already 170 soldiers were released and they returned to Fort Edward. Rogers's command now numbered approximately 530 as they settled in for the night.

As the sun began to rise over the hills, Rogers and Putnam prepared for the westward march to Fort Edward. Inexplicably Rogers, the author of the famous "Standing Orders of Rogers Rangers," which articulated rules on light infantry warfare in North America, demonstrated a lethal lapse of judgment. A friendly argument fuelled by strong egos developed between Rogers and Ensign William Irwin of Gage's Light Infantry

Regiment in regard to who was the more skilled marksman. Words soon led to action and then a series of what would prove to be fatal shots rang out as they fired at marks to prove who was the better shot.[6]

As the thunderclaps echoed through the forests, not too far away, Marin's reaction was instantaneous. His trained eye surveyed the ground and he quickly spotted an ideal ambush site. Equally swift, he developed a plan and deployed his forces. Between him and the unknown hostile force lay a clearing that was choked with alder and brush. It was dissected by a single narrow trail that led directly into the forest where Marin had positioned his men. The dense cover would allow the enemy to unwittingly walk right into Marin's ambush location, the jaws of death, without knowing it. By the time they realized the threat — it would be too late.

Major Putnam led the column with his 300 Connecticut Provincials in the van. Behind him followed Captain James Dalyell with detachments from the 80th and 44th Regiments. Rogers brought up the rear with his Rangers and the remaining Provincials. Putnam marched right into the ambush. Lieutenant Tracy and three soldiers were suddenly overwhelmed and dragged into the thick brush. Then the French Canadians and their Native allies unleashed a lethal volley on the unsuspecting English troops caught in the open clearing. "The enemy rose as a cloud and fired upon us," recorded one participant, "the tomahawks and bullets flying around my ears like hailstones."[7]

Putnam immediately ordered his men to return fire and a deadly melee began in the thick alder brush and forest. But the odds were against them. "The enemy discovering them," recounted Dr. Caleb Rea, "ambushed'm in form of a Semi Circle which gave the Enemy a great advantage of our men."[8] The Provincial troops quickly broke and fell back behind the Regulars who were led forward by Captain Dalyell.

The battle now centred around a huge fallen tree. Marin pounded the British with four volleys of fire before the "Red Coats" managed to flank the tree and engage the enemy in hand-to-hand combat. At this point, the momentum of the battle began to turn in favour of the British. Major Rogers was at the back of the column with his men. He quickly moved his forces to the sound of battle. The antagonists were now evenly matched and the action raged on for another hour.

The provincial militia.

The thick bush and alder at the edge of the forest turned the battle into a series of very personal fights as the close terrain prevented much group action. At one point, a monstrous Native chief who stood six feet, four inches tall, jumped upon the large fallen tree and killed two British Regulars who tried to oppose him. A British officer attempting to come to the aid of the stricken soldiers struck the giant with his musket to no avail. Although drawing blood, he only enraged the Native who was about to dispatch the officer with his tomahawk when Major Rogers proved his marksmanship and shot the Native chief dead.

Marin now tried to outflank the British, by turning their right flank. He made four valiant attempts, however, Rogers and his Rangers were obstinate and gave no ground. As the inferno raged around him, Rogers sensed the flow of battle and reversed the initiative. He now began to shift his Rangers right in a bid to outmanoeuvre the French Canadians. Some Canadians began to break. Then, the Rangers charged. Half the Rangers would fire, while the other half would reload — in this manner they kept up a constant fire and movement forward. Under this constant fire and pressure the remainder of the French Canadians gave way.

However, Marin was no novice in bush warfare. Realizing the situation he avoided a rout and destruction of his force by dividing the survivors into small parties and taking different withdrawal routes. The groups reunited later that night and made their bivouac in a secluded location surrounded by impenetrable swamp.

The British chose not to pursue. Rather they stayed on the battlefield and buried their dead. As always, the casualty figures vary. However, it appears that British losses added up to 53 killed, 50 wounded and four taken prisoner. The French suffered approximately 77 killed.[9]

Although, Rogers was partly responsible for creating the ambush because of his careless discharge of firearms, he received credit for driving the French Canadians away. One veteran believed that Rogers displayed "heroic good conduct" and that he "surrounded the enemy and obliged them to quit the field with the loss of their chief and 200 men killed and missing, 80 left upon the field and three prisoners."[10] Dr. Rea's account was similar in its praise of Rogers. "As soon as the Enemy

A French Canadian officer discusses the next course of action with his Native ally.

perceived Rogers Party flanking upon'm," Rea explained, "they [French and Natives] retreated carrying off their dead and wounded what they cou'd, our men pursued them not but took care of their Dead & wounded & came off so that it seems rather a Drawn Battle than either party victorious."[11] Captain Dalyell later informed Major-General Abercromby that Rogers "acted the whole time with great calmness and officer like."[12] The accolades continued as Abercromby reported back to British Prime Minister Pitt that "Rogers deserved much to be commended," thus, increasing the fame of Rogers and his Rangers in Europe.[13]

Once the dead were buried, Rogers and his party continued their march for Fort Edwards carrying their wounded on litters made of strong branches with blankets strung over them. En route, a relief force of 400 soldiers under Major Munster, which included an additional 40 Rangers, as well as a surgeon, met the column. Rogers then encamped for the night.

Although Rogers and his surviving force revelled in what they considered a victory that night, the encounter still proved potentially deadly for Major Putnam. After discharging his musket several times, his close proximity at the head of the column put him in a desperate position. Unable to reload, without support and confronted by the enemy, Putnam surrendered. He was unceremoniously tied to a tree, while his captors fought the remainder of Putnam's column. During the course of the battle as it surged to and fro, Putnam found himself in the line of fire — musket balls whistling through the air close to his body. Some thudded into the tree to which he was bound.

The errant musket balls were not his only concern. Behind the enemy's skirmish line Putnam became the centre of attention on a number of occasions. First, a young warrior took time from the battle to test Putnam's nerve or his own accuracy or perhaps both. Repeatedly, the Native threw his tomahawk attempting to get as close to Putnam as possible without actually hitting him. Escaping harm, just barely on a number of throws, Putnam next had to deal with a French officer who attempted to discharge his musket into the prisoner's chest. Fortuitously, the weapon misfired, and deaf to Putnam's pleas for quarter, the Frenchman struck Putnam across his jaw with the stock of his musket.

Friends Under Fire by Robert Griffing, Courtesy Paramount Press.

The Natives often proved to be fickle allies.

As the momentum of the battle began to swing in favour of the British, some Natives untied Putnam and dragged him along as they withdrew. A short distance away from the battlefield, the Natives stopped and stripped Putnam of his belongings. He lost his coat, vest, stockings and shoes. Then he was loaded with as many of the packs of the wounded as could be piled upon him. Strongly pinioned and with his wrists tied as closely and tightly as possible so that he could be led by a cord, he was marched off into the wilderness at a quick pace.

Putnam's agony was not hard to imagine. His hands swelled from the tightness of his ligature causing him great pain. His bare feet ripped and torn from the hard terrain and brush bled openly. Exhausted, in pain and succumbing to the weight thrust upon him, Putnam implored the Natives to kill and scalp him now and get done with it. A French officer intervened and ordered his hands untied and some of the weight removed. However, his respite was temporary.

As the march continued, Putnam was continuously abused, and at one point a deep wound was inflicted on Putnam's cheek with a tomahawk. Worse yet, upon reaching the site where the French would encamp for the night, Putnam recoiled in horror as he realized what was about to happen. The Natives now stripped him naked and tied him to a tree. Enraged by the day's events and their lost comrades, the Natives had decided to roast Putnam alive. As the rope bit into his flesh, he could feel the rough bark of the tree dig into his back. To the accompaniment of high pitched screams, the Natives piled dry brush and sticks in small piles at a short distant from Putnam. Then they set the piles alight.

Photo-Art by Silvia Pecota.

Natives allied to the French fire at the unsuspecting English as they stumble onto the ambush.

A sudden downpour doused the flames. Not to be cheated, however, the Natives quickly nursed the piles of kindling until a fierce fire raged. Putnam soon felt the scorching heat and he squirmed his body from side to side in a futile attempt to avoid the searing heat. His discomfort and impending doom fuelled the excitement of his antagonists.

Putnam had resigned himself to his fate when a sudden commotion caught his attention. A French Canadian officer, who turned out to be no-one other than Marin himself, bullied his way through the crowd and kicked the burning piles aside. He then untied Putnam and castigated Putnam's tormentors. Marin then stayed with Putnam until he could hand him over to the Native who had actually taken Putnam prisoner. The worst was over. Upon arrival at Fort Ticonderoga, Putnam was interviewed by Major-General, the Marquis de Montcalm and then escorted to Montreal by a French officer who "treated him with the greatest indulgence and humanity."[14]

Annex A: Robert Rogers "Rules or Plan of Discipline"[15]

I.   All Rangers are to be subject to the rules and articles of war; to appear at roll-call every evening on their own parade, equipped, each with a firelock, sixty rounds of powder and ball, and a hatchet, at which time an officer from each company is to inspect the same, to see they are in order, so as to be ready on any emergency to march at a minute's warning; and before they are dismissed the necessary guards are to be draughted, and scouts for the next day appointed.

II.   Whenever you are ordered out to the enemies forts or frontiers for discoveries, if your number be small, march in single file, keeping at such a distance from each other as to prevent one shot from killing two men, sending one man, or more, forward, and the like on each side, at the distance of twenty yards from the main body, if the ground you march over will admit of it, to give the signal to the officer of the approach of an enemy, and of their number, & c.

III.   If you march over marshes or soft ground change your position, and march abreast of each other to prevent the enemy from tracking you (as they would do if you marched in a single file) till you get over such ground, and then resume your former order, and march till it is quite dark before you encamp, which do, if possible, on a piece of ground that may afford your centries [sic] the advantage of seeing or hearing the enemy some considerable distance, keeping one half of your whole party awake alternately through the night.

IV.   Some time before you come to the place you would reconnoitre, make a stand, and send one or two men in whom you can confide, to look out the best ground for making your observations.

V.   If you have the good fortune to take any prisoners, keep them separate, till they are examine [sic], and in your return take a different route from that in which you went out, that you may the better discover any party in your rear, and have an opportunity, if their strength be superior to yours to alter your course, or disperse, as circumstances may require.

VI.   If you march in a large body of three or four hundred, with a design to attack the enemy, divide your party into three columns, each headed by a proper officer, and let those columns march in single files, the columns to the right and left keeping at twenty yards distance or more from that of the center, if the ground will admit, and let proper guards be kept in the front and rear, and suitable flanking parties at a due distance as before directed, with orders to halt on all eminences, to take a view of the surrounding ground, to prevent your being ambuscaded, and to notify the approach or retreat of the enemy, that proper dispositions may be made for attacking, defending, & c. And if the enemy approach in your front on level ground form a front of your three columns or main body with the advanced guard, keeping out your flanking parties, as if you were marching under the command of trusty officers, to prevent the enemy from pressing hard on either of your wings, or surrounding you, which is the usual method of the savages, if their number will admit of it, and be careful likewise to support and strengthen your rear-guard.

VII.   If you are obliged to receive the enemy's fire, fall, or squat down, till it is over, then rise and discharge at them. If their main body is equal to yours, extend yourself occasionally; but if superior, be careful to support and strengthen your flanking parties, to make them equal to theirs, that if possible you may repulse them to their main body, in which case push upon them with the greatest resolution with equal force in each flank and in the center, observing to keep at a due distance from each other, and advance from tree to tree with one half of the party before the other ten or twelve yards. If the enemy push upon you, let your front fire and fall down, and then let your rear advance thro' them and do the like, by which time those who before were in front will be ready to discharge again, and repeat the same alternately, as occasion shall require; by this means you will keep up such a constant fire, that the enemy will not be able easily to break your order, or gain your ground.

VIII.   If you oblige the enemy to retreat, be careful, in your pursuit of them, to keep out your flanking parties, and prevent them from gaining eminences, or rising grounds, in which case they would perhaps be able to rally and repulse you in turn.

IX.   If you are obliged to retreat, let the front of your whole party fire and fall back, till the rear hath done the same, making for the best ground you can; by this means you will oblige the enemy to pursue you, if they do it at all, in the face of a constant fire.

X.   If the enemy is so superior that you are in danger of being surrounded by them, let the whole body disperse, and every one take a different road to the place of rendezvous appointed for that evening, which must every morning be altered and fixed for the evening ensuing, in order to bring the whole party, or as many of them as possible, together after any separation that may happen in the day; but if you should happen to be actually surrounded, form yourselves into a square, or if in the woods, a circle is best, and if possible, make a stand till the darkness of the night favours your escape.

XI.   If your rear is attacked, the man body and flankers must face about to the right and left, as occasion shall require, and form themselves to oppose the enemy, as before directed; and the same method must be observed, if attacked in either of your flanks, by which means you will always make a rear of one of your flank-guards.

XII.   In general, when pushed upon by the enemy, reserve your fire till they approach very near, which will then put them into the greatest surprize [sic] and consternation, and give you an opportunity of rushing upon them with your hatchets and cutlasses to the better advantage.

XIII. When you encamp at night, fix your centries [*sic*] in such a manner as not to be relieved from main body till morning, profound secrecy and silence being often of the last importance in these cases. Each centry [*sic*] therefore should consist of six men, two of whom must be constantly alert, and when relieved by their fellows, it should be done without noise; and in case those on duty see or hear anything, which alarms them, they are not to speak, but one of them is silently to retreat, and acquaint the commanding officer thereof, that proper dispositions may be made; and all occasional centries [*sic*] should be fixe d in like manner.

XIV. At the first dawn of day, awake your whole detachment; that being the time when the savages chuse [*sic*] to fall upon their enemies, you should by all means be in readiness to receive them.

XV. If the enemy should be discovered by your detachments in the morning, and their numbers are superior to yours, and a victory doubtful, you should not attack them till the evening, as then they will not know your numbers, and if you are repulsed, your retreat will be favoured by the darkness of the night.

XVI. Before you leave your encampment, send out small parties to scout round it, to see if there be any appearance or track of an enemy that might have been near you during the night.

XVII. When you stop for refreshment, chuse [*sic*] some spring or rivulet if you can, and dispose your party so as not to be surprised, posting proper guards and centries [*sic*] at a due distance, and let a small party waylay the path you came in, lest the enemy should be pursuing.

XVIII. If, in your return, you have to cross rivers, avoid the usual fords as much as possible, lest the enemy should have discovered, and be there expecting you.

XIX. If you have to pass by lakes, keep at some distance from the edge of the water, lest, in case of an ambuscade or an attack from the enemy, when in that situation, your retreat should be cut off.

XX.   If the enemy pursue your rear, take a circle till you come to your own tracks, and there form an ambush to receive them, and give them the first fire.

XXI.   When you return from a scout, and come near our forts, avoid the usual roads, and avenues thereto, lest the enemy should have headed you and lay in ambush to receive you, when almost exhausted with fatigues.

XXII.   When you pursue any party that has been near our forts or encampments, follow not directly in their tracks, lest they should be discovered by their rear-guards, who, at such a time, would be most alert; but endeavour, by a different route, to head and meet them in some narrow pass, or lay in ambush to receive them when and where they least expect it.

XXIII.   If you are to embark in canoes, battoes, or otherwise, by water, chuse [sic] the evening for the time of our embarkation, as you will then have the whole night before you, to pass undiscovered by any parties of the enemy, on hills, or other places, which command a prospect of the lake or river you are upon.

XXIV.   In padling [sic] or rowing, give orders that the boat or canoe next the sternmost, wait for her, and the third for the second, and the fourth for the third, and so on, to prevent separation, and that you may be ready to assist each other on any of emergency.

XXV.   Appoint one man in each boat to look out for fires, on the adjacent shores, from the numbers and size of which you may form some judgement of the number that kindled them, and whether you are able to attack them or not.

XXVI.   If you find the enemy encamped near the banks of a river or lake, which you imagine they will attempt to cross for their security upon being attacked, leave a detachment of your party on the op-posite shore to receive them, while, with the remainder, you sur-prize [sic] them, having them between you and the lake or river.

XXVII.   If you cannot satisfy yourself as to the enemy's number and strength, from their fire, & c. conceal our boats at some distance, and ascertain their number by a reconnoitring party, when they embark, or march, in the morning, marking the course they steer, &c. When you may pursue, ambush, and attack them, or let them pass, as prudence shall direct you. In general, however, that you many not be discovered by the enemy on the lakes and rivers at a great distance, it is safest to lay by, with your boats and party concealed all day, without noise or shew [*sic*], and to pursue your intended route by night; and whether you go by land or water, give out parole and countersigns, in order to know one another in the dark, and likewise appoint a stations for every man to repair to, in case of any accident that may separate you.

Annex B: "Standing Orders Rogers Rangers"

A modernized abbreviated version captures a rustic charm and pragmatism and purveys useful advise to soldiers patrolling.[16] However, they are a modern creation and are not the original rules set by Rogers. Nonetheless, the current United Stated Rangers refer to them as titled and have them posted on their website. They are given as:

1. Don't forget nothing.
2. Have your musket clean as a whistle, hatchet scoured, sixty rounds powder and ball, and be ready to march at a minute's warning.
3. When you're on the march, act the way you would if you was sneaking up on a deer. See the enemy first.
4. Tell the truth about what you see and what you do. There is an army depending on us for correct information. You can lie all you please when you tell other folks about the Rangers, but don't ever lie to a Ranger or officer.
5. Don't never take a chance you don't have to.
6. When we're on the march we march single file, far enough apart so one shot can't go through two men.
7. If we strike swamps, or soft ground, we spread out abreast, so its hard to track us.

8. When we march, we keep moving till dark, so as to give the enemy the least possible chance at us.

9. When we camp, half the party stays awake while the other half sleeps.

10. If we take prisoners, we keep'em separate till we have had time to examine them, so they can't cook up a story between'em.

11. Don't ever march home the same way. Take a different route so you won't be ambushed.

12. No matter whether we travel in big parties or little ones, each party has to keep a scout 20 yards ahead, 20 yards on each flank, and 20 yards in the rear so the main body can't be surprised and wiped out.

13. Every night you'll be told where to meet if surrounded by a superior force.

14. Don't sit down to eat without posting sentries.

15. Don't sleep beyond dawn. Dawn's when the French and Indians attack.

16. Don't cross a river by a regular ford.

17. If somebody's trailing you, make a circle, come back onto your own tracks, and ambush the folks that aim to ambush you.

18. Don't stand up when the enemy's coming against you. Kneel down, lie down, hide behind a tree.

19. Let the enemy come till he's almost close enough to touch, then let him have it and jump out and finish him up with your hatchet.

NOTES

1. This account is based on the following sources: Pierre Pouchot, *Memoirs on the Late War in North America Between France and England* (originally Yverdon, 1781 — reprint Youngstown, NY: Old Fort Niagara Association,

Inc, 2004); Dr. Thomas Haynes, "Memorandum of Collonial French War a.d. 1758," *The Bulletin of the Fort Ticonderoga Museum*, September 1966, Vol. 12, No. 2, 150–157; Louis Antoine Bougainville (Edward P. Hamilton, editor and translator), *Adventure in the Wilderness* (Norman: University of Oklahoma Press, 1964); H.R. Casgrain, ed. *Journal du Marquis de Montcalm durant ses Campagnes en Canada de 1756–1759* (Québec: L.J. Demers & Frère, 1895); John R. Cuneo, *Robert Rogers of the Rangers* (New York: Oxford University Press, 1959), 88–90; John D. Lock, *To Fight with Intrepidity … The Complete History of the U.S. Army Rangers, 1622 to Present* (New York: Pocket Books, 1998), 74–76; Burt G. Loescher, *Genesis Rogers' Rangers. The First Green Berets* (1969, reprint Bowie, MD: Heritage Books, Inc., 2000), 12–20, 208–211; Francis Parkman, *Montcalm and Wolfe* (New York: The Modern Library, 1999), 222; Timothy J. Todish, *The Annotated and Illustrated Journals of Major Robert Rogers* (Fleischmanns, NY: Purple Mountain Press, 2002), 57–64; and *Warfare on the Colonial American Frontier: The Journals of Major Robert Rogers & An Historical Account of the Expedition Against the Ohio Indians in the Year 1764, Under the Command of Henry Bouquet, Esq.* [henceforth *Rogers Journals*].(1769, reprint Bargersville, IN: Dreslar Publishing, 2001), 35–41

2. Marin, because of his time spent in the fur trade in various outposts, was fluent in Sioux and several Algonquin dialects. See *Dictionary of Canadian Biography, Vol. 4, 1771–1800* (Toronto: University of Toronto Press, 1979), 512; and Bernd Horn, "Master Practitioners of *la petite guerre*," in Bernd Horn and Roch Legault, eds. *Loyal Service* (Toronto: CDA Press/Dundurn Press, 2006).

3. The Seven Years' War was arguably one of the first global conflicts. It was fought in Europe, North America, and India, with maritime operations reaching out over the Atlantic and Indian Oceans, as well as the Mediterranean and Caribbean Seas. At its core, Austria, France, Russia, Sweden, and Saxony, deeply concerned over Prussia's growing strength and territorial expansion under Frederick the Great, formed a coalition designed to defeat Prussia. Not surprisingly, England, already involved in a colonial and maritime struggle with France, entered into an alliance with Prussia. In North America, the conflict (often termed the French and Indian War) actually began two years earlier in the late spring of 1754. The growing competition for the rich lands of the Ohio Valley proved the catalyst for the latest round of conflict

between the French and English colonies. Robert Dinwiddie, the Governor of Virginia, concerned with the news that the French and Canadians were solidifying their claim to the Ohio by constructing a series of forts, dispatched Lieutenant-Colonel George Washington and a detachment of militia to build a fort of their own on the forks of the Ohio River. A confrontation soon followed. Washington and his party were subsequently defeated by the French at Great Meadows (Fort Necessity) and pushed back over the Allegheny Mountains. A second attempt by Major-General Braddock was made the following summer, but his force was ambushed near Fort Duquesne and virtually annihilated. The North American theatre eventually became part of the greater conflict. Initial French victories and English setbacks in the early years of the war were reversed by 1758, because the British decided to focus their strategy and resources on the wilderness campaign. A virtual naval blockade, in concert with an infusion of more than 20,000 British regulars, turned the tide. The capture of the Fortress of Louisbourg and Fort Frontenac in 1758, forced the French to adopt a defensive posture centered around Quebec and Montreal. The deteriorating French situation also caused many of their Native allies to defect. In 1759, the British began to roll up the remaining French forts on the frontier. One army captured Fort Niagara, and another marched up the Lake Champlain/Richelieu River corridor, while a third invested Quebec. The siege ended in September 1759, with the British victory on the Plains of Abraham. The remnants of the French Army, along with their Canadian militia and remaining Native allies, withdrew to Montreal in hopes of recapturing Quebec in the spring. Although almost successful, as a result of their victory in the Battle at Ste. Foy and subsequent siege of Quebec in April 1760, the appearance of the Royal Navy, forced the French to return to Montreal where they later surrendered on 8 September 1760. The war was formally ended by the Treaty of Paris which ceded most of New France to the British.

4. Robert Rogers remains one of the legendary colonial heroes to emerge from the French and Indian War. Born in Methuen, Massachusetts on 18 November 1731, Rogers moved to New Hampshire near present day Concord with his family in 1739. He spent his youth exploring the wilderness and the proximity of his home town on the frontier made him familiar with Natives and their ruthless raids in time of war. At the age of only 14 he served in the militia during the War of the Austrian Succession. From 1743–1755,

some historians suggest that Rogers was engaged in smuggling. In April 1754, he signed up 50 recruits and became a captain of "Company One" of the New Hampshire Regiment. At first Rogers and his men escorted supply wagons between Albany and Fort Edward. However, Rogers's knowledge and experience with the "haunts and passes of the enemy and the Native method of fighting" soon brought him to the attention of his superior, Major-General William Johnson. By the fall of 1755, he was conducting scouts behind enemy lines. By the winter of 1756, his bold forays behind enemy French lines were regularly reported in newspapers throughout the colonies and in March 1756, Major-General Shirley, commander-in-chief of the British forces in North America, ordered Rogers to raise a 60-man independent Ranger company that was separate from both the provincial and regular units.

5. See Loescher, *The First Green Berets*, 16.

6. Varied literature tends to try and excuse the colonial legend's carelessness by offering different versions of the cause of the shots or by playing down the seriousness of the misjudgment. Loescher does both. Cuneo clearly attempts to portray Rogers as the victim of jealousy. He simply states, "Vigilance relaxed: three muskets were discharged — some later said at game; others, at marks." Cuneo, 89. However, contemporary accounts describe the events in a very uncompromising manner depicting Rogers as careless. One participant wrote, "Rogers and one Lieut. of the light infantry laid a wager to shoot at a mark and discharged their pieces at an old tree." Dr. Thomas Haynes, "Memorandum of Collonial French War a.d. 1758," *The Bulletin of the Fort Ticonderoga Museum*, September 1966, Vol. 12, No. 2, 153. Similarly, another account stated, "it seems, at least Rogers' party, grew careless, some firing at Turkeys others at marks." "*The Journal of Dr. Caleb Rea, Written During the Expedition Against Ticonderoga in 1758* [henceforth *Rea Journal*]," in *Historical Collections of the Essex Institute*, Vol. 18, Nos. 4–6, April, May, June 1881, 179. Finally, two militia captains, Stephen Maynard and Andrew Giddings publicly stated that the carelessness that led to the ambush was the fault of the Rangers and the 80th Regiment. On the morning of the ambush they wrote, "the officers were so little apprehensive of an enemy near, that Major Rogers and a Lieutenant of the Light Infantry, upon a wager, fired their pieces several times at marks." Pouchot, 162, endnote 449.

7. Quoted in Cuneo, 89.

8. *Rea Journal*, 179.

9. See Loescher, *Genesis*, 18; Haynes, 154; *Rea Journal*, 180; and Extract of Colonel Humphrey's *Life of General Putnam*, in Archibald Loudon, ed. *Loudon's Indian Narratives* (Lewisburg, PA: Wennawoods Publishing, 1996), 114. The number was based on bodies supposedly found on the ground. Bougainville notes in his journal that they (French) suffered 13 dead (five of them Natives), and 10 wounded. Bougainville, *Adventure in the Wilderness*, 261. Captain Pouchot states in his journal that the English suffered 100 killed, while the French suffered only four Indians killed and six wounded, and six Canadians killed and six wounded. Pouchot, 162. Two militia captains who were participants admitted that the English losses were five captured, 49 killed, and 40 wounded. Pouchot, 162, editor's endnote 449. Another contemporary witness wrote, "at night mager Rogers came in: and Brought nues how it was: thay got fifty two scalps and two prisoners and thay killed a good menney more which thay did get: and thay reken that all the men of ouirs that was keld, wouned and twock was aBought ninty: and thay reken that thay keld two to won of the French and ingens: and mager putmun was taken and one Lt. Tennet which we have heard of and some more privets." *Amos Richardson's Journal*, 1758, reprinted in *The Bulletin of the Fort Ticonderoga Museum* (September 1968), Vol. 12, No. 4, 282.

10. Haynes, 153–154.

11. *Rea Journal*, 179.

12. Quoted in Loescher, *Genesis*, 20.

13. *Ibid.*, 20.

14. See "Extract of Colonel Humphrey's *Life of General Putnam*," 111–118. The British learned of Putnam's capture and safe arrival at Fort Ticonderoga on the evening of 11 August when Dr Stakes, captured by the French at Oswego earlier in the year, arrived at Fort Edward under a flag of truce. The initial message was an offer of an exchange of prisoners — Putnam for a French

officer taken during Abercromby's failed assault on Fort Ticonderoga earlier that summer. See *Rea Journal*, 180.

15. These rules are taken from his journal as reprinted in: *The Journals of Major Robert Rogers*, 55–64; and Todish, *The Annotated and Illustrated Journals of Major Robert Rogers*, 72–78. They have been grossly abbreviated, changed, and entitled "Standing Orders Rogers Rangers." The modern-day "version" is provided for comparison.

16. Taken from the 75th Ranger Regiment website at *http://www.soc.mil/75thrr/75thrrorders.shtml* (accessed 5 January 2001).

2

RENDEZVOUS WITH DESTINY: THE BRITISH AMPHIBIOUS ASSAULT — LANDING AT LOUISBOURG, ÎLE ROYALE, 8 JUNE 1758

Michel Wyczynski

By the end of 1757, British and French forces had been involved in multiple gruelling land and naval operations throughout various parts of North America. During the course of the previous three years the British found themselves mainly on the defensive, reacting largely to French military initiatives.[1] As a result, British government officials, and senior army and naval commanders agreed that it was now not only opportune, but necessary, to plan and initiate as rapidly as possible an aggressive and sustained combined naval and ground campaign to crush the French forces stationed throughout North America. The first step required to achieve this daunting objective was to capture the strategically located fortified port city of Louisbourg, in Île Royale, (Cape Breton).[2]

Originally built in 1713, the fortress of Louisbourg underwent many construction and expansion phases. By 1758, its extensive fortification system and buildings could accommodate a large garrison and population. More important, its natural harbour was a welcomed safe haven for naval commanders following their long and arduous trans-Atlantic voyages. This ideally situated port was capable of holding several squadrons as well as providing essential repair and refitting services. Ships of the line and frigates were revamped and their crews rested, so they could take part in naval operations. The French ship captains aggressively patrolled the waters at the entrance of the Gulf of St. Lawrence with their warships in order to keep a sharp eye on British commercial maritime and naval activities.

When opportunities presented themselves they actively pursued and engaged enemy warships and trading vessels sailing along the extensive eastern coastline, as well as those entering or exiting the sea lanes.

Consequently, Louisbourg presented a constant threat to British war efforts and commercial ventures in North America. From past experience, the British strategists realized that if they wished to launch and conduct unimpeded ground operations and limit the ability of French Army commanders to resupply their scattered forces stationed throughout New France, the Royal Navy had to gain and maintain absolute control over these waterways, and coastlines. To achieve this crucial objective meant that Louisbourg had to be initially isolated, weakened, and ultimately destroyed.[3]

The Royal Navy's operational superiority in these waters was greatly enhanced by the founding of the city and port of Halifax, Nova Scotia, in 1749. The long-awaited naval base provided British commanders with a much needed strategic harbour, on the Atlantic coast. This new location featured excellent facilities of the kind required to assemble, prepare, and launch large naval squadrons and ground forces against various parts of the French colony and especially Louisbourg.

This latest British military initiative against Louisbourg would be their third attempt since 1745 to capture New France's largest fortification.[4] This time, failure was not an option. George II, the English monarch, ordered that no effort be spared to seal the fortress's fate once and for all. Empowered with such a clear military directive, an eager William Pitt, Earl of Chatham, the British secretary of state, worked feverishly during the first months of 1758, to select new army and naval commanders to conduct three crucial operations in North America. These multiple offensive thrusts were designed to either overextend, split, or force French troops to remain in specific geographical locations.[5] To successfully achieve these important operational objectives, Pitt spared no efforts to locate competent and energetic senior officers currently serving in North America and in Europe.

Bitterly disappointed by the lack of aggressive planning and uninspired leadership displayed by Lord James Campbell, Earl of Loudoun, during the preparatory phases of the second campaign against

Louisbourg in 1757, Pitt relieved him of his command. In his stead, Pitt appointed Major-General James Abercromby, who had served in North America since early 1756, as the new commander-in-chief of His Majesty's Forces in North America.[6] Pitt ordered Abercromby to undertake, in earnest, the preparations necessary to invade Canada by way of Lake George (Lac du Saint-Sacrement) and the capture of Fort Carillon (Ticonderoga, New York).[7]

In addition, Brigadier-General John Forbes, also in North America since the summer of 1757, was ordered to plan an attack against Fort Duquesne (Pittsburgh, Pennsylvania).[8] Lastly, Pitt promoted Colonel Jeffrey Amherst, who had been serving in Germany, to the rank of major-general in America. He was named commander of all the British ground forces in North America. Amherst's objective was to capture the fortress of Louisbourg.[9]

To ensure that Amherst conducted a successful campaign the King authorized that a contingent of 14,000 men be committed to this significant enterprise.[10] The secretary of state then selected Brigadiers James Wolfe, Charles Lawrence, and Edward Whitemore to serve as Amherst's brigade commanders.[11] Furthermore, Colonel John Henry Bastide was chosen to oversee Amherst's engineer requirements, while Lieutenant-Colonel George Williamson was appointed to command the invasion force's artillery component.[12] Such a large army along with great quantities of ammunition, armaments, artillery, siege equipment, and stores required a substantial naval component capable of transporting this force, and providing continual and efficient administrative and logistical support during all phases of the campaign.

As such, the Admiralty ordered that all available ships of the line, frigates, transport vessels, and hospital ships be outfitted and assembled simultaneously in various British ports and in Halifax. Admiral Edward Boscawen, recently promoted Admiral of the Blue, a personal favourite of William Pitt who referred to him as "my great Admiral," was appointed to command this formidable invasion armada.[13] Pitt then selected Sir Charles Hardy to serve as Boscawen's second in command.[14] Concurrently, the secretary of state ordered that the War Office's administrative staff verify and report on the current status of all available regular force infantry units posted throughout England, Ireland, Scotland, and North America. Upon confirmation, arrangements were made to transport, as quickly as possible, all selected ground forces to Halifax. Time was now of the essence. Pitt ordered Boscawen to leave for Halifax without delay.

Concerned about the long and harsh seasons in North America, the King was adamant that he did not want to expose his soldiers and equipment to any unnecessary hardships. For this reason George II ordered that the Louisbourg campaign begin no later than 20 April 1758.[15] Issued with this inflexible deadline the proactive Boscawen weighed anchor, as directed on 19 February 1758, with only five ships of the line, two frigates, and two fire ships.[16] However, deep down, this veteran naval senior officer knew that it would be impossible to launch this substantial operation by the prescribed date.

After a long and uneventful voyage the admiral arrived in Halifax on 10 May 1758.[17] There, he met Brigadier Wolfe who had arrived two days earlier. Also in location were Brigadier Charles Lawrence and his staff.[18] Brigadier Edward Whitemore and his troops arrived a few days later from New York. Already three weeks behind schedule, the campaign's planning phase was further complicated by the absence of Major-General Amherst, who was still at sea. Not wanting to remain idle, and remembering the King's firm directives, Boscawen took it upon himself to oversee and monitor all aspects of the campaign's logistical preparations, while initiating and monitoring the efficiency of the Royal Navy's upcoming blockade against Louisbourg.[19]

This pre-invasion naval operation was a vital element of the invaders' strategy to ensure a successful ground campaign against the fortress of Louisbourg. The objective was to isolate the French defenders, by intercepting the arrival of much needed military supplies and reinforcements prior to the siege. This demanding task was conferred to Sir Charles Hardy who was in Halifax since 19 March 1758. Unfortunately, at that time, few ships were in port. Nevertheless, Boscawen's second-in-command proceeded to inspect the vessels that had wintered in Halifax. Wasting no time, the dutiful Hardy dispatched, without delay, a 50-gun ship of the line to cruise in the vicinity of Louisbourg.[20]

However, Hardy knew that the shortage of ships of the line, coupled with the current harsh climactic conditions and the dangerous ice flows in the North American coastal waters, made it next to impossible to conduct an effective blockade. Nevertheless, an upbeat Hardy welcomed this challenge and reassured Pitt by stating, "I shall use my utmost endeavors to Block up the Port of Louisbourg."[21] Realistically, this experienced naval officer was fully aware of the fact that one vessel alone could not block off the port. Conversely, observing and gathering intelligence could prove useful to the planning of the upcoming campaign. Shortly after, as vessels arrived from England, Hardy selected eight ships of the line, and a frigate for blockade duty. He sailed with this squadron for Louisbourg on 5 April 1758.[22]

During April and May, as Hardy cruised off the coast of Louisbourg, the number of vessels under his command gradually increased. Concurrently, vast quantities of supplies and armaments were delivered weekly to the busy port of Halifax. Moreover, a relieved Boscawen, was encouraged by the timely arrival of large contingents of British regular force infantry and Highland units hailing from various North American locations, as well as from Ireland and England. As these units set up encampments around the now congested city of Halifax, Wolfe made it a point to visit and inspect each unit. The young brigadier rated the soldiers as being "in fine order and healthy ... and the Highlanders are very useful serviceable soldiers, commanded by most manly corps of officers I ever saw."[23] However, Colonel Robert Monckton's troops were undermanned reported the concerned Wolfe, scarcely "exceeding 300 men a regiment."[24] As for the 500 Rangers raised in the colony, the critical brigadier described them "as being little better than *canaille*."[25] The British ground forces would eventually consist of 14 infantry regiments, engineers, and artillerymen totalling 13,200 men.[26]

Another issue of concern was the operational readiness and condition of all siege apparatus and supplies that had been gathered for the previous aborted 1757 campaign. Pitt ordered Abercromby to ensure that this equipment, "be constantly kept in most perfect repair and order, and fit for immediate service."[27] Abercromby conferred this challenging task to practitioner engineer John Montresor, who was one of the 11 engineers selected to take part in the upcoming siege. With little time to spare, Montresor tasks during May 1758, consisted of organizing work parties, inspecting, repairing, testing, preparing, and loading large numbers of siege machinery, tools, and supplies onto awaiting transport vessels.[28]

As the administrative and logistical preparatory phases were winding down Boscawen now focused his energies and attention on devising the invasion force's amphibious assault landing plan. To maximize the impact of this critical operation, the naval commander decided to conduct a series of landing exercises to ascertain how many soldiers could be transported and put ashore within the shortest possible time frame. On 22 May 1758, Boscawen convened the masters of all his transport vessels, and explained the aim of this first test landing exercise. The admiral elected to limit this initial trial landing drill to include only the soldiers that were on board his transport vessels. Furthermore, only the embarkations (cutters and other small boats) of these vessels were to be used to carry and land the troops.[29]

Orders in hand, the masters quickly returned to their vessels, and briefed their crews and soldiers. During this time all the designated embarkations were being lowered into the water. The selected sailors then went over the sides of their transport, descended rapidly, took up their stations, and verified their oars. As these small vessels then positioned themselves along the hulls of the respective transport ships, hesitant soldiers formed up in single files and lowered themselves cautiously into these awaiting bobbing vessels. When the last soldiers were seated, the sailors were ordered to push off and row to the predetermined assembly point. Upon the given signal the small flotilla cut through the waves, picked up speed, and headed swiftly towards the selected landing area. Meanwhile, Boscawen carefully observed its final approach. Suddenly, as the hulls scraped the bottom of the rocky shoreline orders to disembark were barked out. Simultaneously, oars were raised, in unison, enabling the soldiers to jump over the sides. Crashing into waist high cold water, the soldiers, ensuring that their muskets were kept well away from the water, battled the waves and waded ashore. "We landed 2,957 [soldiers]. They were formed in seven minutes," reported a pleased Boscawen.[30] However, despite the soldiers and sailors loud cheers the admiral knew that this assault landing exercise was conducted in the most favourable weather conditions and without the presence of a well-entrenched and hostile enemy force.

This prompted Boscawen to plan and conduct a second, and much larger, amphibious landing assault exercise. The apprehensive admiral knew that this was an important phase, if not the most crucial operation of the upcoming campaign. Brigadier Wolfe echoed Boscawen's concerns. "When the army is landed," remarked the young general, "the business is half done."[31] Failure to execute this demanding operation correctly could result in a terrible loss of lives. More important, it could severely affect the invasion force's morale, while enhancing the defenders' confidence, and resolve to fight. Three days later, on 25 May, Boscawen had revised his assault landing exercise. This time, the admiral ordered that all the fleet's embarkations be used for this second dry run.[32] The ensuing results proved much more encouraging. A total of 5,700 soldiers stormed ashore.[33] Once the beachhead was secured, the troops moved, "in the Woods," observed James Cunningham, a British officer, and practiced "the different maneuvers they were likely to act on the Island of Cape Breton."[34]

Later that day, with this latest rehearsal in hand, Boscawen reviewed once again Major-General James Abercromby's assault landing directives. Bearing in mind his superior's orders the admiral then proceeded to draft the invasion force's final amphibious assault landing plan and operational orders.[35] Meanwhile, in Louisbourg, the French defenders, under the command of Governor Augustin de Boschenry De Drucour were busily assessing the current state of their fortification and preparing their defensive plans.[36]

Having narrowly escaped the failed 1757 British invasion attempt to capture the fortress, the French governor knew as early as January 1758, from gathered intelligence, that it was now only a matter of time before the British would return in force. Accordingly, Drucour worked feverishly with his War Council to address all the pressing operational issues required to oblige the invaders to engage and conduct a lengthy siege. If the defenders' strategy proved successful it would provide Pierre de Rigaud de Vaudreuil de Cavagnial, the governor of New France, with valuable time to further consolidate his defensive positions in Quebec and Montreal.[37] However, if he was to keep such a large invasion force in check, Drucour required more experienced ground troops to defend the fortress and man the various coastal positions. He also needed the three promised naval squadrons to arrive soon. These ships of the line and frigates were essential to ensure the defence of the harbour and the city's open wharves against the inevitable British naval attacks.

Despite Admiral Hardy's blockade the much awaited French reinforcements reached Louisbourg, in small groups, between April and the beginning of June 1758. After a long and difficult trans-Atlantic voyage Commodore Marquis Jean-Antoine Charry Desgouttes, with three vessels, dropped anchor in Louisbourg harbour on 24 April 1758. Four days later, a large contingent of 660 men of the 2nd Battalion of the Volontaires Étrangers transported by Louis-Joseph Beaussier de Lisle arrived without incident from Brest aboard four ships of the line, and a frigate.[38] When all troops and supplies were unloaded, Commodore Desgouttes ordered his captains to immediately position their ships of the line in a defensive horseshoe formation extending from Lighthouse Point to Battery Island, thus sealing off the harbour's entrance.[39]

Reacting to the increasing number of British warships cruising in the vicinity of Louisbourg, Comte Du Chauffault de Besné, commanding officer of the third squadron, opted not to risk joining up with Desgouttes in Louisbourg. Instead, he moored his vessels, a few miles away, in Ste. Anne's Bay, on 29 May 1758.[40] Waiting impatiently aboard these ships of the line were 685 members of the 2nd Battalion of the Régiment de Cambis. Including these latest reinforcements, the garrison now totalled 3,234 regular force infantrymen, *troupes de la marine*, artillery personnel, bourgeois volunteers, Acadians, and a small group of aboriginal allies.[41] In anticipation of the upcoming campaign Governor Drucour instructed that all ground troops be placed under the command of Mathieu-Henri Marchant de La Houlière, the senior army officer in Louisbourg. Moreover, the naval component of 3,870 sailors and gunners remained under the command of Commodore Desgouttes. These two combined forces bolstered the total of the French defenders to 7,104 all ranks.[42] More important, these reinforcements also provided to the Governor and his chief engineer Louis Franquet a much-needed labour force that would be used to carry out multiple urgent repairs to the fortress.

A series of inspections conducted by French engineers and army officers during early spring 1758 revealed that overall the fortress was in poor shape. The defenders were now going to pay a heavy price for the lack of much needed maintenance and repairs that should have been conducted over the course of the past decade. There were other factors that contributed to the current decrepit state of the fortifications, foremost among them being the British occupation of Louisbourg from 1745 to 1749, following the first siege. During this period the commanding officer of the British garrison had purposely refrained from initiating any type of repair work, because the British commanders in North America were uncertain whether England would retain Louisbourg. Not surprisingly, concerned British colonial administrators were unwilling to invest materials, personnel, and large sums of money in work that in the end would only benefit a despised enemy. When the fortress was finally returned to France in 1749, indifferent French colonial administrators saw no urgency in overhauling or expanding Louisbourg. As a result, lack of realistic funding, administrative red tape, poor construction and repair planning and scheduling, shortage of proper building materials, unskilled labour, and unfavourable climactic conditions all conspired to contribute to the continuing disintegration of the fortress's large masonry structures, and gun platforms.[43] Chevalier James Johnstone, a Scottish Jacobite, serving with the French forces in Louisbourg provided the following insight into the state of the fortress before the British landing in 1758:

> But what is still more astonishing, the stupid negligence of the French in not repairing the fortifications; probably they had not the experience that the sea sand is not fit for mortar as it does not dry, bind and harden, as with river sand, which may be caused by the particles of salt it contains. All the walls of masonry, the embrasures, the counterscarp, and the parapets, were tumbled into the fosses, which were filled up with rubbish the palisades

were all of them rotten — in many parts of the covert way they were crumbled away on a level with the ground, and there was scare any vestige of glacis which had not been destroyed by grazing there; all the planks were entirely rotten, as the carriages of the cannons; in short, that the town had more the look of ancient ruins than of a modern fortification, since the treaty of Utrecht.[44]

Moreover, the surrounding heights overlooking the foredoomed fortress would ultimately assist the invaders in capturing Louisbourg. Regardless of the number of bastions, ramparts, and earthworks, none of these structures could protect the French forces or the inhabitants from the deadly fire of British batteries that would be positioned on these hills.[45] Many of the garrison's officers were concerned that they were hemmed into such an unfavourable location. "There cannot be a fortified town in a worse situation than Louisbourg," explained Johnstone. "It was commanded all round by heights," pointed out the apprehensive officer.[46] Even newly arrived Commodore Desgouttes was immediately alarmed by the unnerving proximity of these looming hills. "Since the navy was navy," expounded the commodore, "it was unheard of to subject war vessels to bear a siege in a closed harbour which now resembled to a mouse trap."[47] Despite his many detractors, an ailing Louis Franquet, worked feverishly to remedy this catastrophic situation.[48] A series of repair efforts conducted since 1754 did correct some of the most serious deficiencies.[49]

However, this gallant initiative was too little, too late. As the months passed, it became increasingly evident to the French high command that if Louisbourg was to survive another invasion attempt, then it was of the utmost importance that every effort be made to neutralize and defeat the invaders on the beachhead.[50] As the last snow melted away in the spring of 1758, regular patrols were sent out to monitor the coastline. Shortly after 500 soldiers were ordered to bivouac in various defensive positions along Gabarus Bay.[51]

As soon as the weather conditions improved, Drucour and Franquet toured and inspected, on 1 May 1758, the defensive coastal emplacements that had been built and manned during the previous year.[52] All had

Courtesy Bernd Horn.

The King's Bastion.

sustained various decrees of damage in the harsh winter. Work parties were immediately dispatched to repair gun platforms and artillery positions and consolidate the earthworks located along Louisbourg's eastern and western shorelines.[53] Upon being informed that the artillery positions had been repaired the governor requested Commodore Desgouttes to provide all the necessary guns, artillery supplies, shells, and gun crews and man the positions immediately.[54] Additionally, ammunition and food caches were set up in event that the defenders were cut off from the fortress and forced to operate on their own for a few days.

Despite the poor weather conditions throughout the month of May, work progressed well on all these coastal positions. Nevertheless, during these four weeks, heavy wet fogs, rain, and nightly frost sapped the morale and stamina of the work crews and gunners. Many soldiers became ill and were hospitalized. To counter this escalating crisis work shifts and sentry duties were shortened.[55]

As the French defenders continued to fortify their emplacements, Drucour met, on 14 May 1758, with his battalion commanders. During this meeting, the governor reviewed the proposed battle procedures and tactics, and confirmed the roles of each of his senior officers for the inevitable upcoming invasion. Lieutenant-Colonel Jean Mascle de St-Julhien, commanding officer of the 2nd Battalion of the Régiment D'Artois was selected to defend Cormorandière Cove (now Kennington Cove). He also had under his command a large group of reinforcements that were to be deployed, where required, once the initial enemy troops were attempting to land. Lieutenant-Colonel Michel Marin du Bourzt, commanding officer of the 2nd Battalion of the Régiment de Bourgogne was tasked to provide support to the defenders entrenched in Flat Point. Lastly, Lieutenant-Colonel Henri-Valentin-Jacques d'Anthonay, commanding officer of the 2nd Battalion of the Régiment des Volontaires Étrangers was assigned to support White Point.[56] At the conclusion of this briefing the governor emphasized that once the landing began, he expected them to apply their "experience in these matters and to utilize the best means of action to accomplish their missions."[57]

After the meeting, the confident senior French officers left the governor's residence and met with their officers to review their battalion-level tactical preparations. By the end of May, a total of 2,102 soldiers, sailors, and gunners were actively patrolling the coastlines and manning five major defensive positions.[58] As the days passed, bored French gunners gazed over the vast expanse of Gabarus Bay. There was nothing more they could do but wait. Inevitably, impatience now gave way to anxiety.

Meanwhile, within the dynamic port of Halifax, a poised and confident Admiral Boscawen and his invasion force were eagerly completing their final preparations. During the last two weeks in May, the senior British army and naval commanders ordered their staff to verify and confirm that all logistical requirements concerning the loading of rations, water, ammunition, and siege supplies aboard the transport vessels had been addressed and completed. Infantry units were then ordered to board their pre-assigned transport ships. The invasion fleet was now ready to sail as soon as the weather cleared. While the ships' captains impatiently awaited Boscawen's signal to hoist anchor, the admiral and the senior army officers studied the latest intelligence reports regarding French military activities along Gabarus Bay. These updates were in fact troubling. "The enemy we were told," reported Wolfe, "has entrenched the shoar of the bay of Gabarus and has planted his artillery upon the beach thereof. If we find him strong in that part, we must try him at a greater distance, and where perhaps he is less prepared," explained the concerned brigadier.[59]

To corroborate this information and obtain additional data regarding the exact locations of the French coastal defences, Boscawen ordered that Major Robinson, an infantry officer, be sent aboard the *Gramont* (18 guns) to carefully examine the coastline around Louisbourg. As well, the major was tasked to "discover the best landing place in Gabarus Bay."[60] For the moment, however, it was agreed that the assault landing plan not be altered. Nevertheless, Wolfe was not entirely comfortable with the existing plan devised by Boscawen. The young brigadier stated that he hoped that "Major-General Amherst may arrive in the meanwhile time enough to improve the present plan."[61]

To compel the French defenders to overextend their resources and personnel positioned outside the fortress, Boscawen favoured a three-prong landing around Louisbourg. Brigadier Wolfe commanding the 15th and 48th Fraser's Battalion of Highlanders supported by 1,100 Rangers was to land at Miré Bay, 15 miles from Gabarus Bay. From this point Wolf would march his troops and engage all encountered enemy forces. A second force commanded by Colonel Monckton comprising of two battalions would disembark at Lorembec. Upon landing, Monckton would secure the area and prepare a series of defensive entrenchments. The third force under the command of Colonel Lawrence was to storm onto a pre-determined landing point on the shores of Gabarus Bay. If French resistance along this coastline was too strong, Lawrence would be ordered to hold off his landing operations and await the arrival of Wolfe and Monckton. Once in position these two contingents were to conduct a series of diversions, thus facilitating Lawrence's assault landing.[62] Boscawen was confident in the successful execution of his plan. The admiral now waited impatiently for a break in the weather. The British invasion force was ready to leave Halifax at a moment's notice.[63]

Finally, on Sunday, 28 May 1758, Admiral Boscawen judged that the weather conditions were favoured launching the long awaited campaign. The order to sail came as a blessing to the 13,200 soldiers crammed into

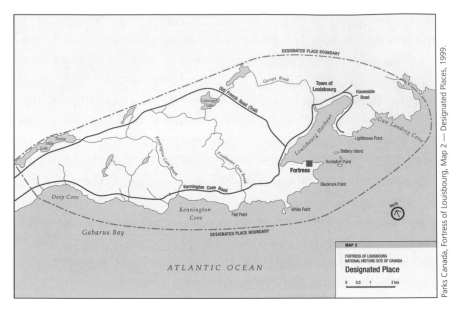

Louisbourg's eastern and western coastlines.

the tight confines of their transport vessels. All were anxious to leave and get on with the task at hand. Despite these uncomfortable temporary living quarters Brigadier Charles Lawrence described the soldiers as being, "in the highest health and spirits."[64] Signals were sent ordering the invasion fleet to weigh anchor. A total of 17 ships of the line and 127 transport vessels reacted in unison and commenced their voyage.[65] The following day the *Dublin* (74 guns), arriving from England, joined up with invasion fleet. Shortly after, Captain G.B. Rodney manoeuvred his ship of the line next to Boscawen's flag ship the *Namur* (90 guns).

Within a few minutes, General Jeffery Amherst had been safely transferred aboard Boscawen's vessel.[66] The invasion force's senior officer corps was now complete. After settling in, the commander-in-chief was immediately briefed on the current status of the upcoming operation. The infantry major who had left Halifax aboard the *Gramount* on 28 May, had returned and joined the fleet on 1 June. He reported that "he had seen five or six small encampments of a dozen tents," along the Gabarus Bay coastline. Captain Rous, of the *Sutherland* (50 guns), added that "there were 13 sails in the harbour."[67] As the British fleet approached the entrance of Gabarus Bay later that day, Amherst studied and reviewed

Boscawen's proposed amphibious assault landing plan. Meanwhile, in the distance, the French defenders sounded the alarm.

The sight of this impressive invasion fleet prompted a very concerned Drucour to send extra personnel to various coastal positions extending from the fortress to Cormorandière Cove. Furthermore, the French governor requested that Desgouttes dispatch supplementary work parties, over the course of the next few days, to haul additional guns and mortars overland and transport them by boat to predetermined coastal positions. This frustrating and backbreaking work was further complicated by poor conditions of the small earth beaten paths leading to these artillery emplacements. "This forced labor," reported the worried French commodore, "put many of my seamen in hospital." Desgouttes' manpower was already stretched to the limit.[68] Moreover, Drucour requested that all battalions send extra ammunition, tents, ropes, as well as changes of socks and shoes to the troops who were bivouacking along the coast. On 2 June, Boscawen ordered the vessels to drop anchor in the bottom part of Gabarus Bay. The remainder of the invasion fleet trickled in over the course of the next few days. While the various vessels took up their positions, Admiral Boscawen took great care to ensure that all his ship captains were safely anchored out of the range of the French coastal batteries.

As British seamen prepared their vessels for the impending assault Boscawen, observed with great interest the enemy's activities along the coast. The admiral wasted no time in initiating a series of naval actions to unnerve and confuse the coastal defenders. More important, these manoeuvres were intended to provide cover to ongoing naval coastal reconnaissance missions. Later that day, Boscawen dispatched a number of barges, and pinnaces at dusk. He ordered the sailors to row towards the harbour and, "to make an alarm, in order, thereby to discover where the strength of the enemy's forces was posted," disclosed the admiral.[69]

A few hours earlier unbeknownst to the French defenders, "the Generals went to reconnoiter different parts of the North Side of the Bay, and round the White Point," revealed a very pleased Boscawen.[70] During the course of this successful reconnaissance mission Major-General Amherst observed that "the enemy had a chain of posts from Cape Noir to Flat Point and irregulars from thence to the bottom of the bay, some works thrown up at the places which appeared practicable to land at, and some batteries."[71] Upon the return of all the barges and pinnaces, Boscawen then dispatched, at midnight, one of his officer's to sound the Cormorandière Cove and confirm the depths near the shoreline.[72] With the gathering and analysis of new intelligence, the urgency of getting this campaign finally underway, coupled with the ongoing assessment of the defenders' operational activities, and a better understanding of the coastal geographical layout, Amherst now re-examined the assault landing plan. He found that it was no longer valid.

Rather than sending Brigadier Wolf and Colonel Monckton on their original diversion operations, Amherst opted instead to concentrate all his available forces and have them land simultaneously, on 3 June 1758, on three selected objectives located along the Gabarus Bay coastline. However, high waves caused the operation to be cancelled. Despite this unforeseen postponement all was not lost. Sailors reported that Cormorandière Cove had considerable less surf than the other two objectives. Taking into account this latest information Amherst quickly revised his assault landing plan and informed his three brigadiers that they would now land in one location.[73]

Concurrently, Boscawen experimented with the positioning of six frigates along the shoreline to draw enemy fire.[74] The Admiral ordered their captains to find the best locations and engage the French defenders over the course of the next few days. One of the selected frigates, was the *Kennington* (20 guns). On 3 June, Captain Maxim Jacobs sailed towards the Cormorandière Cove, dropped anchor, and opened fire on the French entrenchments. The French gunners were not deterred by this bold action and replied with volleys of their own and musket fire.[75] This sporadic engagement lasted throughout the day and had little effect on either party. However, around six o'clock in the evening a British shell hit a French gunpowder depot. This triggered a violent explosion that killed two soldiers and wounded several others.[76]

Following this unexpected incident, Jacob's frigate sustained a few direct hits. Three British sailors were killed and another six were wounded.[77] Even though this action yielded limited results, Boscawen nevertheless found the information gathered during the course of these firefights useful. From this, the admiral was able to determine the enemy gunners' efficiency and range, and the calibre of their artillery. More important, he could confirm and identify the ideal distances and locations where the frigates could be repositioned to provide improved fire support for the upcoming assault landing.[78] Boscawen then ordered the captains of these frigates to continue to bombard the French coastal positions during the next four days.[79]

The enduring inclement weather, daily bombardments, and movements of vessels provided ideal cover that enabled senior British officers to further reconnoitre the coastline, confirm, uncover other enemy positions, and select the most appropriate landing site and finalize the assault landing plan.[80] However, all attempted assault landings from 3 to 6 June were repeatedly foiled by thick fogs, high winds, heavy rain, and a very rough sea. As the days passed the sailors as well as the army's rank and file became extremely frustrated as they were repeatedly ordered to leave their landing boats and reboard their transports vessels. With the anticipation of a long and gruelling campaign ahead Amherst refused to risk any unnecessary loss of life during the assault landing phase.

At this point, the British senior officers were still trying to locate an appropriate landing site. Brigadier Wolfe and a small group of seamen volunteered to carry out a reconnaissance mission and sound the bay in the vicinity of Cormandière Cove where the swell was not as high. Meanwhile, on 7 June 1758, Boscawen ordered Captain John Vaughan of the *Juno* (32 guns) and a few transports vessels to feign a landing in the vicinity of Laurembecto divert the enemy's attention.[81] Despite the continuing inclement weather, the defenders were closely monitoring all British naval activities along the coastline.

Boscawen's ruse worked. This latest action unnerved, once again, the French governor who immediately dispatched, to that area, troops to counter a possible landing.[82] Later in the day there was a sudden break in the weather system. Orders were quickly issued notifying that all selected grenadiers and the first detachments of the right and left wings be loaded into their assault boats. As the soldiers were lowered into their embarkations, there was a sudden rise in the swell, and the force of the surf increased significantly. Admiral Boscawen immediately advised

Amherst that for safety reasons the operation had to be cancelled. Knowing full well that his soldiers were becoming extremely frustrated, Amherst nevertheless took it upon himself to inform them personally of the reason for this latest setback. The General explained that he did not want to lose his valiant troops to an angry sea.[83]

Whereas Amherst's landing operations attempts had been repeatedly neutralized by the worsening weather conditions, the opportunistic French defenders used each day to further consolidate their positions. To the British General's great disappointment, intelligence reports confirmed that in fact, "the enemy has been reinforcing their posts, adding to their works, cannonading and throwing shells at the ships." A concerned Amherst also noted that the energetic defenders were, "making all the preparations they can to oppose our landings."[84] The General's assessment was exact. By 6 June 1758, 2,005 French regular force infantry, gunners, and seaman were on a constant state of alert along the coastline.[85] Furthermore, another 732 officers and men of the 2nd Battalion of the Régiment de Cambis arrived on the 6, 7, and 8 June to bolster the French garrison.[86] A number of these welcomed reinforcements were immediately dispatched to further strengthen selected coastal positions.

During the evening of 7 June, weather conditions finally improved. Boscawen signalled the captains of all the ships of the line to send their longboats and cutters to the assigned transport vessels by midnight.[87] The admiral then confirmed the boarding and assembly procedures and insisted that all those involved, "keep the most profound silence."[88] Major-General Amherst also directed that, "no lights are to be shewed in any of the transports except the signals above mentioned after twelve o'clock at night." Amherst also insisted, "the most profound silence throughout the whole army and above all things, the firing of a single musket must be avoided."[89] A final inspection was conducted by all unit officers to ensure that the soldiers only took with them, as previously dictated, their weapons, ammunition, powder, and rations for two days, which consisted of bread and cheese.[90]

As the ground troops prepared to board their respective assault boats, under the cover of darkness, Boscawen sent naval officers to the transport ships. They were to ensure the efficient staging and loading of the infantry from the large transport ships to the smaller vessels that would take the assault troops to shore. The admiral also dispatched several junior naval officers who were to be placed on these vessels. Their roles were to oversee the naval portion of the command and control phases during the actual assault landing.[91] Simultaneously, Boscawen ordered all selected frigates and ships of the line to sail to their pre-determined positions along the coastline.

As these vessels glided silently towards their objectives, their gun crews stood, at the ready, by their guns.[92] Some frigates, such as the *Gramount*, ventured so close to the shoreline that they immediately came under heavy volleys of enemy small arms fire.[93] With the element of surprise now compromised, the captains ordered their crews to return fire. The British naval bombardment commenced shortly after 4 o'clock in the morning.

As the first rays of sunlight appeared in the distant horizon, the various components of the impressive assault landing flotilla were now forming up rapidly behind the frigates. Arriving at their predetermined assembly points, the sailors were instructed to maintain their positions about one-and-a-half to two miles from the coast and await further orders. The small vessels were then divided into three separate divisions each having its specific objective.[94] When all the landing craft were in position they were then ordered to spread out and form a "considerable length of line," and await the signal to begin the assault.[95] Amherst ordered the assault groups to adopt this formation to conceal their projected landing areas.

Braving the cool damp sea air, the anxious members of the amphibious assault force grew restless. Placed under Brigadier Wolfe's command were elements of the light infantry, Rangers, grenadiers and Highlanders. This specially selected force was tasked to be the first to storm ashore in the area of Cormorandière Cove. They were positioned on the left side of the invasion flotilla.[96] Wolfe was directed to carefully examine the coastline during his final approach and select the best landing site. As soon as this location was determined, Wolfe was to order his special force to land as quickly as possible, confirm the locations of the enemy's defensive positions in the area, and immediately conduct a flank attack.[97]

Meanwhile, Brigadiers Lawrence and Whitmore and their respective groups were to initiate a series of manoeuvres along the coast intended to compel the French troops to remain and hold their positions rather than reinforce Cormorandière Cove. Brigadier Lawrence's force was ordered to row in the general vicinity of Flat Point and feign a landing at Fresh Water Cove.[98] Simultaneously, Brigadier Whitmore's group was to proceed towards the left side of White Point and pretend to land in that area.[99] Before reaching his objective Whitmore sent a number of his assault vessels around the right side of White Point, thus placing additional pressure on the French defenders to maintain all their positions in that area. Shortly after four o'clock in the morning, 8 June 1758, the signal was given to begin this operation. As the British frigates continued their sustained covering fire, the three assault groups rowed vigorously towards their respective objectives.

Alerted by this new development Governor Drucour sent orders to all his senior officers to remain vigilant and be ready to attack the enemy as they landed. Observing the large numbers of assault boats heading towards various areas along the shoreline, François-Claude-Victor Grillot de Poilly suddenly had a terrible premonition. "This was a fatal day for France," lamented the worried engineer.[100] Nevertheless, most of the eager French gunners, held their fire and waited until the assault vessels were well within their range.[101] "The enemy acted very wisely," observed Major-General Amherst. They "did not throw away a shot till the boats were near in shore, and then directed the whole of their canon and musketry upon them."[102]

The invaders knew that the French had many guns and mortars of various calibre positioned along the coast, however, not all their locations had been confirmed. This was because the French troops had taken great care in camouflaging their emplacements. While rowing towards the shoreline one anonymous invader admitted the difficulty they experienced in discerning the French batteries:

> The place [coastline] had the appearance of a continued green of little scattered branches of fir and but very few of the guns on their lines were to be distinguished out of the reach of their metal; the rest was artfully concealed from our view with spruce branches until the

boats advanced towards the shore with the resolution of forcing the works. The latest destruction was then unmasked by the removal of the spruce branches.[103]

The assault boats now absorbed a deadly hail of fire. Moreover, as they began their final approach the surf became progressively more violent. Manoeuvring the fully loaded small vessels while attempting to avoid the incoming shells became increasingly difficult for the sailors. During his earlier briefings Amherst had repeatedly advised all the officers of the assault groups to ensure that a safe distance between each vessel be maintained at all times. "They must avoid huddling together," instructed the general, "and running in a lump in such a situation, they are fair mark for the adversaries and not able to employ their arms to purpose."[104] However, this sound directive was difficult to enforce as the many vessels were forced to manoeuvre towards a limited number of good landing sites. As Whitmore and Lawrence approached their respective shorelines, the frustrated brigadiers were not satisfied with their imposed landing areas. They immediately ordered their groups to pull back and find alternate sites. Struggling against an unforgiving fierce surf, the exhausted sailors summoned what energy they had left to row harder, while simultaneously attempting to stabilize their boats and change directions.

At the same time, Wolfe's assault group proceeded quickly to Cormorandière Cove. Mercifully this area was not as heavily defended. Nevertheless, Wolfe's men drew sustained enemy fire. Regrettably, this restless group of enemy gunners had opened fire too soon. Seeing this, the brigadier ordered his seamen to change course, and pull out of the enemy's range. Shortly after a few of Wolfe's assault vessels inadvertently made their way into a small secluded area identified as Anse-aux-Sables located within Cormorandière Cove. Chevalier de Johnstone, one of the French defenders who had been posted in this very location during the summer of 1757 was familiar with this area. He described it as:

> a small creek where two boats could enter at the same
> time. The creek was upon the left of the regiment of

Artois, and, through negligence, was left without a guard, although it was so surely comprehended in the general plan of the defence the year before, that in the summer of 1757, I was posted there with a detachment. Within the creek the land was at least twenty feet high ...[105]

In hindsight the invaders considered themselves to have been lucky that no French soldiers had been posted to defend this secluded area. "If only forty men had been posted at the place where we the Light Infantry went ashore," explained Lieutenant Caldwell, "the consequences would have been dreadful."[106]

Wolfe watched intently as a small group of light infantry led by Lieutenants Hopkins, Brown, and Ensign Grant of the 35th Regiment quietly scaled the rocky shoreline.[107] As soon as they reached the top they took up defensive positions and observed the adjacent terrain. An elated Wolfe signalled energetically to the other vessels in his immediate vicinity to follow him to this landing site. The impetuous brigadier knew that time was of the essence and that caution now had to be thrown to the wind. "But all of these obstacles were not so great," observed Lieutenant Henry Caldwell of the final approach, "as that offered by the surf breaking on the rocks, where the waves ran so high that we were obliged to jump overboard in the water up to our middles." He added, "Many of the boats were stove in and some men drowned."[108] Another anonymous participant later described the complexity and danger of this daring operation. "The difficulty of landing at this place was such that they thought the devil himself would not have attempted it."[109]

Amid the chaos, confusion, and desperate cries of drowning soldiers, a determined Wolfe focused solely on reaching the shoreline regardless of the cost.[110] Jumping waist high into the water the energetic brigadier urged his soldiers to follow him. The sailors attempted to position and steady their vessels to allow the anxious soldiers to disembark. Without hesitation the impatient infantry jumped into the cold dark waters to rally to their leader. Struggling through the chilly surf they desperately attempted to keep their footing. Their arduous advance was further complicated by the fact that they had to maintain their muskets and

Library and Archives Canada C-073711.

Brigadier Wolfe leading the Grenadiers ashore at Anse aux Sables, Louisbourg, 8 June 1758.

powder horns, at arms length, high above their heads, to keep them dry. Some soldiers were so eager to leave their cramped embarkations, that their enthusiastic leaps caused a few vessels to tip over.[111] Regardless, adrenaline quickly overcame fear and regard for personal safety. These soaked and shivering men were soon joined by many others who quickly scaled the jagged rocks.

Seeing that Wolfe had successfully landed, the other two assault groups rowed in earnest towards Cormorandière Cove. Upon their arrival the few French defenders posted in this area had already begun to abandon their positions. Whitmore and Lawrence scanned the shoreline and identified other possible landing sites. Now, hundreds of unopposed British infantry waded through the high waves. As they came ashore the soldiers loaded their weapons, formed up and were quickly marched off to assist Brigadier Wolfe's group.

Despite the incredible difficulties that had to be surmounted in a very short time, the soldiers had performed well. "The men behaved with great spirit," noted a very pleased Lieutenant William Amherst, and "in this affair shew'd a remarkable instance of coolness in keeping their fire. Not a shot had been fired from the boats, nor till it could do execution on the shore."[112]

With additional troops finally arriving at his location, an impatient Wolfe immediately ordered his men to begin the advance. Leaving the safety of their defensive positions the invaders quickly drew furious volleys of enemy small arms fire. "We received a warm fire for about ten minutes," confirmed Lieutenant Caldwell, "but soon charged the enemy who fled rapidly in fear of being cut off from Louisbourg."[113] As the Rangers, light infantry, and Highlanders pressed forward they could

Photographer: Heidi Moses, Parks Canada, Fortress of Louisbourg, 5081E.

Panoramic view of Kennington Cove, site of Wolfe's initial amphibious landing attempt.

now, for the first time, assess the extent and effectiveness of the enemy's coastal defensive perimeters. "The obstacles the troops had to surmount in landing," explained Gordon, "was an enemy posted to the greatest advantage, their intrenchments being 15 feet above high water mark, the approaches to which was rendered impracticable by large trees being laid very thick together upon the beach, all round the cove, their branches laying towards the sea, the distance of 20 yards in some places and 30 in other between their lines, and the waters edge."[114]

As the first French coastal positions fell to Wolfe's troops, Colonel Mascle de St-Julhien raced towards the landing site accompanied by additional companies of grenadiers taken from the Artois and Bourgogne battalions. The concerned officer hoped that it was not too late to contain enemy's advance. However, upon their arrival, the French reinforcements were greeted, "by very brisk fire," reported Governor Drucour later.[115] The situation became increasingly critical. As French casualties mounted, the defenders became even more concerned that the quick actions of the tenacious British light infantry and Rangers would cut off their withdrawal route to the fortress.

Meanwhile, Wolfe's troops continued to perform admirably. His soldiers had been specially selected to ensure the success of this demanding landing, and more important, to conduct and maintain a rapid pursuit of

the enemy's retreating coastal forces. Their aggressive spirit, marksmanship, fieldcraft, and honed abilities to fight and operate efficiently within
the rugged North American wilderness made them both a formidable and
intimidating force. One participant observed:

> Our light infantry, Highlanders and Rangers they [French
> forces] termed the English Savages, perhaps in contra-
> distinction to their own native Indians, Canadians, etc,
> the true French savages. These light infantry were a corps
> of 550 volunteers chosen as marksmen out of the most
> active resolute men from all the Battalions of regulars,
> dressed some in blue, some in green jackets and drawers,
> for the easier brushing thorough the woods; with Ruffs
> of black bear's skin round their necks, the beard of the
> upper lips, some grown into wiskers, other not so, but
> all well smutted on that part; with little round hats like
> several of our seamen — The arms were fusil, cartouch-
> box of balls and flints, and powder horns slung over their
> shoulders. The Rangers are a body who have more cut-
> throat, savage appearance. The appearance of the Light
> Infantry has in it more of artificial savage.[116]

The relentless pursuit coupled with the failure of the French high
command to plan and incorporate coordinated counterattacks during
training sessions prior to the invasion now hampered the efficiency and
chances of success of the French forces. This oversight and the lack of
operational forethought to select concealed rallying points and construct
fall back positions from which St-Julhien's troops could engage the
invaders further added to the growing state of confusion and disarray. A
discouraged Grillot de Poilly sheds some light on the defenders' lack of
proper strategic defensive planning. He revealed:

> We had all the required time to prepare but regrettably we
> did not have did not have a specialist to deal with these
> issues. We never had a coastal defense plan to cover the

intricacies of our coastline. This coastline was only super-
ficially known by our senior officers. They thought that
one only had to be a grenadier to counter a landing. However, experience revealed that a well-thought out plan and
proper maneuvers would have helped us greatly. I pointed
this out repeatedly to M. Franquet and stated that we were
loosing precious time in unbearable idleness.[117]

These deficiencies now severely impeded the chances of the French
reinforcements to slow down Wolfe's initial deployment.[118]

The reliance on a single counterattack plan devised by Governor
Drucour now came back to haunt him. It consisted simply of dispatching
troops to the landing site. In his defence, the French Governor explained
that he relied on the experience St-Julhien had "in the art of war, and
hope's that this will provide him with the most efficient means to do the
best he can for the task he was sent to carry out." Drucour added that
once on site St-Julhien had to assess the latest developments and if all
was lost then he had to, "plan his retreat towards the town if the costal
positions could no longer be defended."[119]

Seeing that it was impossible to contain or repulse this very mobile
and fast moving initial enemy contingent a disheartened Colonel St-
Julhien ordered his troops to fall back. Not versed in the art of *la petite
guerre* the French regular force infantry was unable to take the appropriate
measures to use the terrain to their advantage and hinder the advance of
the enemy's irregulars and Rangers.[120] St-Julhien's disorganized troops
offered only sporadic and ineffective resistance. Conversely, the French
gunners and personnel tasked to man and defend the coastal positions
were immediately ordered to spike their guns, abandon their stations and
return with all haste to the fortress. However, the enemy's quick pursuit
hampered the gunners' abilities to sabotage all their cannons.[121] During
the entire course of the French retreat, Wolfe's troops skilfully used
the high ground and wooded areas to their advantage while pursuing
and continually engaging the flighty French rearguards. Moreover, this
unyielding chase conducted by a well-disciplined British enemy force
further escalated the atmosphere of panic.

Not impressed by the French forces delaying tactics or willingness to fight, the invaders were nevertheless amazed by the enemy's elaborate coastal field works and defensive positions. Wolfe's troops considered themselves fortunate to have been able to flank these positions rather than being forced to conduct perilous frontal assaults. One participant noted, "Besides all their approaches to the front lines were rendered so extremely difficult by the trees they had laid very thick together upon the shore round the Cove, with the branches lying towards the sea, for the distance of 20 in some, and of 30 yards in other places between the lines and the water's edge." He added, "passing their lines would have been like that of travelling towards them through a wild forest, from interwoven branches of one tree to those of another with incredible fatigue and endless labour."[122]

Additionally, the rugged countryside behind these coastal positions was very difficult to operate in. Major-General Amherst described the terrain along the coastline as, "the roughest and worst ground I ever saw."[123] One participant added that the terrain he was forced to manoeuvre in consisted of "rocky hills and boggy morasses."[124] Lieutenant Caldwell who was part of the advance group pursuing the French soldiers also added, "the road leading up to these entrenchments was made difficult by trees laid across it with holes underneath."[125]

Regardless, the frenzied invaders bypassed these obstacles and continued to press hard. Observing his troops upbeat pursuit, a very pleased Major-General Amherst qualified his adversaries' withdrawal as now being more of a "flight."[126] The British troops' moral increased with the capture of each new French costal position. However, the officers had to continually enforce strict discipline to keep their eager soldiers under control. The forward elements were repeatedly ordered to slow down and cautioned not to over pursue. Furthermore, these orders had to be enforced because there were still not enough troops on the ground to consolidate and secure their flanks and rear positions. As British troops advanced further inland, their officers recalled Major-General Amherst's cautionary advice. He had repeatedly insisted that all lead elements of the assault groups remain extremely vigilant for possible surprise counterattacks. The senior British commander had received intelligence reports informing him of the probability of a French guerrilla force operating in the area.[127] Although these precautionary orders to slow down the advance were sound, they nevertheless frustrated Lieutenant Caldwell and his eager soldiers. The young officer deplored the fact that these directives negated a rare opportunity to cut off enemy troops. "I got forward far enough to see that five hundred of the enemy troops might have been cut off by prompt action," Caldwell explained, "but no reinforcements reached me until it was too late, and the enemy was almost in the covered way, when we did renew our advance." He added, "We marched so near the town that the French began to cannonade us, and we were ordered to fall back."[128]

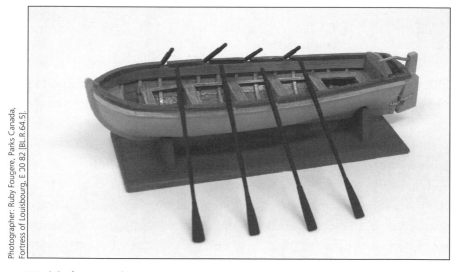

Model of a type of Royal Navy cutter used to transport British troops during the amphibious assault landing operation.

Even though their advance had been temporarily halted, the leading British officers now had the opportunity to observe the effective range of the fortress's artillery. As French gunners fired salvo after salvo, unbeknownst to them the dissimulated invaders carefully noted where the shells hit the ground. This very useful information was promptly forwarded to Major-General Amherst and his engineer officers. Amherst commented that this helpful data pointed out, "how near I could encamp to invest it [the fortress]."[129]

By noon of 8 June 1758, the final phase of the British assault landing was coming to an end. It had taken the invaders less than eight hours to prepare and assemble their amphibious assault groups, row towards the coastline, land, reorganize, begin their coordinated advance, capture, and occupy all the enemy's costal positions, while consolidating the beachheads.[130] Once the French forces pushed back, the invaders then rapidly occupied the adjacent high grounds, and monitored all roadways and paths leading from the fortress to the various coastal positions. Additionally, a series of temporary forward defensive positions were quickly set up between the fortress and the landing sites to oppose possible enemy counterattacks. Now that the situation had been temporarily stabilized, the grim task of organizing and dispatching special details to scour the shoreline to locate the dead and tend to the injured, had been started.

Simultaneously, demoralized French prisoners were rounded up, and quickly escorted to the beach head. Captured officers were transported to a specially designated vessel for interrogation, while wounded enemy personnel were sent to hospital ships for treatment.[131] The disgruntled prisoners confirmed to their captors that "the greatest part of our business was done, in the landing of our troops."[132] Meanwhile, all empty and seaworthy assault vessels were ordered to return in all haste to their transport ships to ferry the next contingent of troops.[133] As soon as the reinforcements landed, they were immediately dispatched to secure strategic locations along the coast and inland. Concurrently, naval personnel initiated the complex and challenging logistical operations of landing vast quantities of camp supplies, engineer material and tools, artillery guns, and ammunition. Regrettably the winds increased during the course of the day and this critical phase was suspended for 24 hours, leaving the assault landing groups to fend for themselves and sleep under improvised shelters.[134]

As the British troops settled in the best they could, the disheartened defenders could now only helplessly observe from the safety of their bastions the unopposed and ever increasing activities of their adversaries. As a precautionary measure, Governor Drucour sent troops and work parties to burn all the buildings located in the vicinity of the fortress's outer walls, as well as all embarkations found along the harbour's shores. Moreover, Drucour ordered Commodore Desgouttes to send 50 sailors, supplied with tar, gun powder, and sulphur, to set fire to the Royal Battery's gun platforms and wooden structures.[135]

As dark columns of billowing smoke rose towards the sky, an irate Grillot de Poilly vehemently criticized Governor Drucour's and Colonel St-Julhien's inaction during the British assault landing. The furious engineer stated that Drucour was not in his element when it came to defending the fortress, adding that as he was a career naval officer, he lacked the expertise required to plan and conduct such a military operation. Moreover, Grillot de Poilly estimated that Colonel St-Julhien had also reacted poorly and indecisively at Cormorandière Cove. The engineer deplored the fact that this senior officer had opened fire too early on Wolfe's assault vessels, and should have let all the embarkations enter and create a dangerous gridlock within the waters of this constricted cove. Grillot de Poilly also bemoaned the fact that St-Julhien failed to maintain a sustained heavy fire on these heavily loaded crafts. Additionally, he found it inconceivable that St-Julhien chose not to man a small watchtower that had been constructed in the vicinity of Wolfe's landing, during the previous year.

Lastly, the frustrated Poilly lamented the fact that when St-Julhien did lead the reinforcements to counter the landing, he didn't use a portion of these troops in a flanking manoeuvre to cut off the enemy at their landing point. The very bitter engineer concluded his assessment by stating, "This is how our coastal positions that we regarded, with reason, as being the key to the defence of the fortress were rendered useless. A novice's mistake led to its demise."[136]

On the British side, however, the naval and ground forces had trained rigorously for this demanding and dangerous landing. The repeated drills enabled all assault group participants to know exactly what was expected of them during each phase of this vital operation. The campaign's overall success depended entirely on a well-executed assault landing. Thus, efficient amphibious training coupled with disciplined leadership, individual initiative, and no small measure of luck, enabled Amherst's troops to land quickly with little loss of life and later capture the fortress of Louisbourg.

British light infantrymen who served under the command of Brigadier Wolfe during the 8 June 1758 amphibious assault landing operations. (LtoR) Private, 35th Regiment of Foot; Private 58th Regiment of Foot; and Private, 15th Regiment of Foot.

However, in hindsight, Brigadier James Wolfe downplayed the fanfare that followed the amphibious assault landing. The young brigadier offered a private critical assessment of the landing. "Amongst ourselves," confessed Wolfe, "be it said, that our attempt to land where we did was rash and injudicious, our success unexpected (by me) and undeserved; there was no prodigious extension of courage in the affair — an officer and 30 men would have made it impossible to get ashore where we did."[137]

Regardless, the successful and rapid landing enabled Major-General Amherst and his army and naval elements to conduct a triumphant campaign. After 48 days of intense siege warfare vast sections of the French fortress had been reduced to rubble. Moreover, the French squadron anchored within Louisbourg's harbour had been isolated and annihilated.[138] The spirit of the battered French defenders had been finally broken following the capture of its last two ships of the line during the early hours of 26 July. A well-executed night raid conducted by two daring groups of British sailors ended the French naval presence in Louisbourg harbour. The gravity of this latest setback forced Governor Drucour to consider, and then accept, the harsh terms of capitulation drafted by Major-General Jeffery Amherst and Admiral Edward Boscawen. The French forces capitulated on 26 July 1758. Thus, the capture of the largest French fortification in New France was made possible by the bravery and initiative of the members of the amphibious assault landing group commanded by Brigadier Wolfe. More significant, the fall of Louisbourg signalled the beginning of the end of the French military and naval presence in North America.

NOTES

1. For additional information regarding the British military situation in North America leading up to and during the Seven Years' War, (in North America this conflict was referred to as the "French and Indian Wars"), please consult Fred Anderson, *Crucible of War* (New York: Vintage Books, 2001); Robert Leckie, *A Few Acres of Snow — The Saga of the French and Indian Wars* (Toronto: John Wiley & Sons, 1999); and C.P. Stacey, "The British forces in North America during the Seven Years' War," *Dictionary of Canadian Biography, Vol. 3, 1741 to 1770* (Toronto: University of Toronto Press, 1974), xxv–xxx.

2.   For an overview of British military and naval operations against Louisbourg conducted between 1745 and 1758, please consult G.A Rawlyk, *Yankees at Louisbourg* (Orono, Maine: University of Maine Studies, Second Series, 1967); J.S. Corbett, *England in the Seven Years' War* (London: Longmans, Green and Co., 1907), Vols. 1 and 2; Julian Gwyn, ed. *The Royal Navy and North America: The Warren Papers, 1736–1752* (London: Printed for the Navy Records Society, 1975); and Michel Wyczynski, "A Particular Gallant Action: The Raid on the French Ships of the Line *Le Bienfaisant* and *Le Prudent* during the Second Siege of Louisbourg, 1758," in Colonel Bernd Horn, ed. *Show No Fear: Daring Actions in Canadian Military History* (Toronto: Dundurn Press, 2008); A.J.B. Johnston, *Endgame 1758: The Promise, the Glory and the Despair of Louisbourg's Last Decade* (Lincoln: University of Nebraska Press and Sydney: Cape Breton University Press, 2207); René Chartrand, *Louisbourg 1758, Wolfe's First Siege* (London: Osprey, Prager Illustrated Military History Series, 2000); J. MacKay Hitsman and C.C.J. Bond, " The Assault Landing at Louisbourg, 1758," *The Canadian Historical Review*, Vol. 35, No. 4, 314–330; and Captain John F. Shafroth, U.S. Navy, "The Capture of Louisbourg in 1758: A Joint Military and Naval Operation ," *U.S. Naval Institute Proceedings*, No. 64, January 1938, 78–96.

3.   To gain, ensure, and maintain total control of the North American waters, the Royal Navy officials approved the outfitting of two large squadrons during the last months of 1757, and January and February 1758. The first was commanded by Admiral Edward Boscawen. This veteran naval officer was ordered to sail to Halifax and oversee the preparations for the upcoming Louisbourg campaign. Admiral Henry Osborn commanded the other squadron and was ordered to sail to the Mediterranean. Osborn's mission was to intercept Admiral La Clue's squadron. Intelligence reports confirmed that this enemy squadron was preparing to sail from Toulon to North America. Osborn was successful in confining La Clue's vessels to the Mediterranean. Concurrently, Sir Edward Hawke sailed with seven ships of the line and intercepted a French squadron which transported much needed supplies and reinforcements from the port of Rochefort to North America. These successful naval actions enabled Boscawen to operate unhindered during the entire course of the Louisbourg campaign. Francis Parkman, *Montcalm and Wolfe* (Markham, ON:Viking, Penguin

Books Canada, Ltd., 1984), 332–333. For information on French naval activities, during the Seven Years' War, along the French Atlantic coast and in the Mediterranean, consult G. Lacour-Gayet, *La marine militaire de la France sous le règne de Louis XV* (Paris: Librairie ancienne Honoré Champion, 1910), 270–341.

4.   The first siege of Louisbourg took place from 11 May 1745 to 28 June 1745. Sir Admiral Peter Warren was conferred with the task of commanding a squadron of the Royal Navy totalling 12 war ships. His squadron consisted of three vessels that arrived from Antigua. Soon after they were joined by the *Eltham* (44 guns) and the *Bien Aimé* (24 guns) from New England; a captured French warship *Vigilant* (64 guns); and five vessels from England, the *Princess Mary* (60 guns), *Hector* (44 guns), *Chester* (50 guns), *Sunderland* (60 guns), and the *Canterbury* (60 guns). Last to arrive, and join up with Warren's squadron was the *Lark* (44 guns), which sailed from its station in Newfoundland. Canadian naval historian Julian Gwyn states that Warren's squadron, "was the greatest display of British sea power in North America since 1711, when Rear-Admiral Hovendon Walker's expeditionary forces had gathered off Cape Breton to sail up the St-Lawrence and attack Quebec." Gwyn, xxi; and *Dictionary of Canadian Biography Online, http://www.biographi.ca/EN/ShowBio. asp?Biod=41073&query [DCB Online]*, Julian Gwyn, "Sir Peter Warren." During the course of the siege, Warren protected the invasion force's supply and transport vessels, and manned a blockade off Louisbourg. Warren also provided continuous administrative and logistical support to Sir William Pepperell, commander of the land forces composed of 3,000 New Englanders. Gwyn, xviii; and *DCB Online*, Gwyn, "Sir Peter Warren;" *Ibid.*, Byron Fairchild, "Sir William Pepperrell;" and Rawlyk, 41–65 and 66–76. After seven weeks of siege work and artillery bombardments, Louis Du Pont Duchambon, commanding officer of the fortress capitulated on 28 June 1745. Three years later, in 1748, the fortress was returned to the French, in accordance with the agreed conditions of the Treaty of Aix-la-Chapelle. The second attempt to capture Louisbourg took place in late summer and early fall of 1757. The British secretary of state, William Pitt, Earl of Chatham, ordered that this expedition be conducted by Lord James Campbell, Earl Loudoun, the commander-in-chief in America, supported by Vice–Admiral Francis Holburne. The British planning and preparations

became a long and drawn out affair. During this time the French sent an impressive naval relief force of 24 warships totalling 1,380 guns. LAC Canada, Manuscript Group [henceforth MG] 2, Archives de la marine, Série B4, Campagnes, Vol. 76, Disposition que M. Le Comte Du Bois de Lamotte, et M. Le Chev. De Drucour Governeur de l'île royale y ont faites en 1757 pour s'opposer à la descente Des Anglais, folios 20r-23v, microfilm F-757. Additionally, the French governor, Augustin de Boschenry de Drucour had ample time to consolidate the fortress's structures and further strengthen the surrounding coastal defensive positions and gun emplacements built to counter beach assault landings along the Gabarus Bay coastline. Moreover, the French monarch authorized that the second battalions of the Régiment D'Artois and the Régiment de Bourgogne be sent to Louisbourg. The King ordered that these troops, totalling 1,050 soldiers, be used to defend the fortress, and that they could also be used by Louis Franquet, the fortress's head engineer as labourers for his numerous construction projects and repair works. LAC, MG 1, Archives de colonies, Série B, Lettres envoyées, Vol. 101, Order from the King to Drucour, 17 March 1755, folio 22, microfilm C-15660; and *Ibid.*, Order from the King to Drucour and Prévost, 10 April 1755, folio 30, microfilm C-15660. The second British campaign to conquer Louisbourg had been doomed from the start. Holburne left Halifax in August 1757, and patrolled the coast off Louisbourg. During the night of 25 September 1757, a hurricane ravaged the coast off Louisbourg and violently dispersed Holburne's squadron. Of his 21 vessels, 13, sustained various degrees of damage and one ship of the line had been smashed against the rocky coastline near St. Esprit. The second attempt to capture Louisbourg, thus came to an abrupt end. The *Windsor, Kingston, Northumberland, Newark, Orford, Terrible,* and *Somerset* sustained minor damages. The *Invincible, Captain, Sunderland, Grafton, Nassau, Devonshire, Eagle, Prince Frederick, Centurion* sustained various levels of damage to masts, sails, and riggings. The *Bedford* and *Defiance* were not damaged. Only one vessel was lost. It was the ship of the line the *Tilbury* (60 guns). Public Records Office, Admiral's Despatches, Vol. 481, State of the Squadron under the command of Vice-Admiral Holburne, 28 September 1757; and Admiral's List Book, Vol. 32, quoted in J. S. McLennan, *Louisbourg from Its Foundation to Its Fall, 1713–1758* (London: Macmillan and Co. Limited, 1910), 210.

5. Guy Frégault, *La Guerre de la conquête* (Montréal: Fides, 1955), 281–294; C.P. Stacey, "The British forces in North America during the Seven Years' War," in Francess G. Halpenny, General editor, *Dictionary of Canadian Biography, Vol. 3* (Toronto: University of Toronto Press, 1974), xxiv–xxx; and W.J. Eccles, "The French forces in North America during the Seven Years' War," in Francess G. Halpenny, General editor, *Dictionary of Canadian Biography, Vol. 3* (Toronto: University of Toronto Press, 1974), xv–xxiii.

6. Letter, Pitt to Abercromby, 30 December 1757, see Gertrude Selwyn Kimball, *Correspondence of William Pitt when Secretary of State with Colonial Governors and Military and Naval Commissioners in America* (London: MacMillan & Co., Limited, 1906), 134. *DCB Online*, Richard Middleton, "James Abercromby."

7. *Ibid.*; and Letter, Pitt to Abercromby, 30 December 1757, Kimball, 143–151.

8. *DCB Online*, I.K. Steele, "James Forbes."

9. Colonel Jeffery Amherst was informed of his transfer to North America, on 14 January 1758 while he was serving in Germany. LAC, MG 18, L4, Amherst, Sir Jeffery and family, Vol. 3, Packet 19, No. 8, Entry of 14 January 1758 [henceforth Journal of Jeffery Amherst]. Over the course of the past two years, while in Germany, Amherst acted as a commissary overseeing the administration of 8,000 Hessian troops serving under British command. Because of the great operational importance of the upcoming Louisbourg campaign, Amherst's appointment was qualified as "remarkable" by a skeptical Canadian military historian C.P. Stacey. Amherst was still very junior in the army, had no operational experience, and had never commanded troops in action. Nevertheless, the young colonel had the support of his former commanding officer, Sir John Ligonier, who was commander-in-chief of the forces in Britain and personal military advisor to William Pitt. Amherst also had Pitt's support. To ensure Amherst's nomination to the rank of Major-General in America, Pitt requested the assistance of Lady Yarmouth, to secure the King's final approval. *DCB Online*, C.P. Stacey, "Jeffery Amherst, 1st Baron Amherst."

10. Letter, Pitt to Abercromby, 30 December 1757, see Kimball, 143.

11. Brigadier Charles Lawrence had been in North America, since 1749. Brigadier Edward Whitemore returned to North America in 1757, where he commanded the 22nd Regiment in Lord Charles Hay's brigade, in Halifax, Nova Scotia. Brigadier James Wolfe had just returned from an unsuccessful 1757 expedition against the French port city of Rochefort located on the Biscay coast. *DCB Online*, Julian Gwyn, "Edward Whitmore," (63 years old); *Ibid.*, Dominick Graham, "Charles Lawrence," (48 years old); and *Ibid.*, C.P. Stacey, "James Wolfe," (31 years old).

12. Letter, Pitt to Abercromby, 30 December 1757, see Kimball, 148; *DCB Online*, R. Arthur Bowler, "John Montresor, (Montrésor);" *Ibid.*, Peter E. Russell, "George Williamson."

13. *Ibid.*, W.A.B. Douglas, "Edward Boscawen;" Edward Boscawen, Peter Kemp, ed. *The Oxford Companion to Ships & The Sea* (London: Oxford University Press, 1976), 97–98.

14. *DCB Online*, Julian Gwyn, "Charles Hardy."

15. Letter, Pitt to Abercromby, 30 December 1757, see Kimball, 143.

16. Letter, Boscawen to Pitt, 19 February 1758, see Kimball, 197. The vessels were: Ships of the line, *Namur*, *Royal William*, *Princess Amelia*, *Invincible*, *Lancaster*; frigates, *Shannon*, *Trent*; and fire ships, *Aetna*, and *Lightning*. To avoid any delay Pitt had written Boscawen: "His Majesty, considering how highly necessary your timely presence in North America is to the success of the important operations, which are directed to be undertaken so early in the year; I am to signify to you the King's pleasure, that you do, as soon as may be, repair to Portsmouth, and proceed from thence, with all diligence, to N. America, with such ship, or ships of the squadron under your command, as shall be actually ready for the sea, without waiting for the rest of the said ships, which you will direct to be got ready with the utmost despatch, and to follow you, as soon as possible, to such rendezvous as shall appoint them." Letter, Pitt to Boscawen, Whitehall, 2 February 1758, see Kimball, 176.

17. LAC, MG 12, Admiralty 50, Admirals' Journals, Vol. 3, *A Journal of Proceedings of his Majesty's Squadron Under the Command of the Hon. Edward Boscawen Admiral of the Blue to North America Between the 8th day of February 1758 and the Day of November Following* [henceforth *Admiral Boscawen's Log*], folio 59, microfilm C-12891. Wolf arrived two days earlier, on 8 May 1758, on board the *Princess Amelia*. Letter, Wolfe to his father, *Princess Amelia*, St. Helens, 18 February 1758, see Beckles Willson, *The Life and Letters of James Wolfe* (London: William Heinemann, 1909), 361–362; and LAC, MG 12, Captains' Logs, ADM 51, Vol. 736, microfilm B-3477.

18. Letter, Wolfe to Lord George Sackville, Halifax, 12 May 1758, see Willson, 387.

19. Major-General Amherst arrived in London, from Germany, on 25 February 1758. He then boarded the *Dublin* (74 guns), on 16 March 1758. *Journal of Jeffery Amherst*, 56.

20. These vessels were under the command of Commodore Alexander Colville. Hardy informed Pitt that they were in good condition. He sent a 50-gun ship to patrol off the port of Louisbourg. During the course of the following days he sent the frigate *Boreas* to join up with the 50-gun ship. As well, the *Hawk*, a provincial schooner manned by Colville, was patrolling the coast to protect and escort the supplies ships arriving from England. Letter, Hardy to Pitt, Halifax Harbour, 22 March 1758, see Kimball, 212.

21. *Ibid.*, 212.

22. To enforce and maintain the blockade, Sir Charles Hardy had under his command the following eight ships of the line. As of 5 April, Hardy left Halifax with the *Northumberland* (74 guns), *Summerset* (70 guns), *Terrible* (74 guns), *Orford* (70 guns), *Deffence* (60 guns), *Captain* (64 guns), *Kingston* (60 guns), *Southerland* (50 guns), and one frigate. On 2 May, Boscawen dispatched the *Juno* to join up with Hardy's squadron. On 20 May, the *Royal William* (84 guns) and the *Prince Frederick* (64 guns) joined Sir Charles Hardy's squadron for blockade duty. Despite the earlier mentioned problems the blockade was maintained and had proved

effective. During this period a total of seven supply ships, and the French frigate, *La Diane* (22 guns) were captured, and sent to Halifax. Letter, James Cunningham, on Abercromby's staff to Lord Sackville, on board the *Ludlow Castle* at sea, 30 May 1758, quoted in J.S. McLennan, 237–241. Boscawen also dispatched on 16 May the *Squirrel* (20 guns), and the *Scarborough* (20 guns) to further bolster the blockade. *Admiral Boscawen's Log*, 16 and 19 May 1758, folios 84r, 85r. Hardy's blockade forced the Count Du Chaffault de Besné's Rochefort squadron, which transported supplies, and the 2nd Battalion of the Régiment de Cambis, to change course and set sail for Port Dauphin (Englishtown) where he dropped on 29 May 1758. LAC, MG 2, Archives de la Marine, Série B4, Campagnes, Vol. 80, Escadre de Du Chauffault de Besné, folio 207, microfilm F-757.

23.   Letter, James Wolfe to Lord George Sackville, Halifax, 12 May 1758, see Willson, 363.

24.   *Ibid.*, 364.

25.   *Ibid.*, 364.

26.   Letter, James Cunningham, on Abercromby's staff to Lord Sackville, on board the *Ludlow Castle* at sea, 30 May 1758, quoted in J.S. McLennan, 237–241. As of 9 May 1758 the following infantry units were in Halifax: Amherst, Otway, Webb, Lawrence, Monckton, and Fraser's. Moreover, an artillery unit arrived from England, and a company of 80 carpenters under the direction of Mr. Meserve, and 500 Rangers were also in Halifax. Letter, Pitt to Abercromby, 20 December 1757, see Kimball, 143–151; Letter from Pitt to Abercromby, 30 December 1757, *Ibid.*, 151; and Letter, Lawrence to Pitt, 9 May 1758, *Ibid.*, 241. A diagram describing the organization of the British invasion force's line of battle is available in the Jeffery Amherst papers. Serving under Brigadier Wolfe were Colonel Murray who commanded the 15th, 35th, 40th, and 63rd Regiments; and Colonel Wilmott who commanded the 3rd Battalion of Royal Americans, and the 22nd and 45th Regiments. Serving under Brigadier Charles Lawrence were Colonel Burton who commanded the 17th, 48th, and 55th Regiments, and Colonel Robert Monckton commanding the 1st Battalion of Royal Americans and the 28th Regiment. Colonel Williamson commanded the artillery personnel. LAC,

MG 18, L4, Vol. 3, Amherst, Sir Jeffery and Family, Vol. 2, Packet 8, Letters from General Wolfe during the siege and shortly after the surrender of Louisbourg [henceforth Correspondence Wolfe to Amherst]; and Letter, Lawrence to Pitt, On Board His Majesty's Ship *Namur*, in Halifax Harbour, 23 May 1758, see Kimball, 256–257.

27.   Letter, Pitt to Abercromby, 20 December 1757, see Kimball, 143–151.

28.   Entries of 3–28 May 1758. "Journal of Capitan John Montresor, Part 3, Siege of Louisbourg, 1758," *Collections of the New-York Historical Society for the Year 1881* (New York: Printed for the Society, 1882), 153–156; and *DCB Online*, R. Arthur Bowler, "John Montresor."

29.   *Admiral Boscawen's Log*, Monday, 22 May 1758, folio 87.

30.   *Ibid.*

31.   Letter, James Wolfe to his father, Halifax, 20 May 1758, see Willson, 365.

32.   During the course of the first exercise only the embarkations of the transport vessels were used. For the second exercise Boscawen ordered that the embarkations of all the ships of the line — boats, ordnance store ships, hospital ships, fascine, and wood ships — be used to transport the soldiers. *Admiral's Boscawen's Log*, Thursday, 25 May 1758, folio 86.

33.   *Ibid.;* James Cunningham, a British officer at Halifax, provided additional information as to the second landing exercise. "We found it possible to land 3,500 Men in Boats belonging to Transports," explained the officer, "and when the Boats of the Men of War assisted, 5,000 could be landed. Letter, James Cunningham to Lord George Sackville, On board the *Ludlow Castle*, at sea, 30 May 1758, quoted in, J.S. McLennan, 239.

34.   *Ibid.*, 239.

35.   Abercromby's assault landing orders and directives were noted in *Gordon's Journal*. "The initial troops to land would be the Grenadiers and the two or three eldest Regiments, unless Boscawen sees otherwise. The boats

used to transport the first body of men for this assault will be provided by the Ordnance ships. The boats provided by the hospital ships will only be used to evacuate the wounded. A rendezvous holding point for these hospital boats must be determined once the landing takes place. The seamen rowing the transport and hospital boats will not be armed. Officers must be loaded onto each of the transport boats. Light boats must accompany the transport boats in case these capsize. The first group of soldiers that will land in Gabarus Bay must only carry their arms, ammunition and bread and cheese in their pockets for two days. Officers in each boat must ensure that no soldier fires his arm while in the boat. Additionally, bayonets must no be fixed while in the boats. These are to be fixed to the muskets after having landed on the beach. Upon approaching the shore, the men must disembark as quickly as possible, form up march directly forward and charge towards any enemy position. Furthermore, their blankets must be transported as soon as possible after the bridgehead is secured. Then, three days of rations must be transported and unloaded on the secured beachhead to support the assault force. Commander of the Grenadier and all Field Officers employed in the first landing must be aboard the boats so that they may lead their respective units and deliver follow-up orders readily." "Journal Kept by [Robert] Gordon, One of the Officers engaged in the Siege of Louisbourg under Boscawen and Amherst, in 1758," *Collections of The Nova Scotia Historical Society For the Year 1887–1888*, Vol. 6 [henceforth *Gordon's Journal*] (Halifax, Nova Scotia: Nova Scotia Printing Company, 1888), 104–05.

36. Drucour was appointed governor of Île Royale on 1 February 1754. During his short tenure he had a annual encounters with elements of the Royal Navy. In June 1755, Admiral Edward Boscawen blockaded the Port of Louisbourg and his actions disrupted commercial ventures in the town and surrounding area. The following year, 1756, the British captured several ships carrying supplies. The *Arc-en-Ciel*, which transported much awaited recruits for the Louisbourg garrison was also captured. In 1757, the British planned to invade Louisbourg. However, poor planning and a sudden hurricane which dispersed Admiral Francis Holburne's fleet, gave Drucour a brief respite. *DCB Online*, John Fortier, "Augustin De Boschenry De Drucour."

37. Drucour's war council included Louis Franquet, chief engineer; Jacques Prévost de LaCroix, colonial administrator; Mathieu-Henri Marchant de La Houlière, commander of all the ground troops; Jean Mascle de Saint-Julhien, commanding officer of the 2nd Battalion of the Régiment d'Artois; Michel Marin du Bourzt, commanding officer of the 2nd Battalion of the Régiment de Bourgogne; Henri-Valentin-Jacques d'Anthonay, commanding officer of the 2nd Battalion of the Régiment des Volontaires Étrangers; Claude-Élizabeth Denys De Laronde de Bonnaventure, the King's lieutenant. During the course of the siege these officers were convened, on a regular basis, by the governor to deliberate all important operational decisions. LAC, MG 1, Archives des colonies, Série C11B, Correspondance générale, Île Royale, Letter, Drucour to the Minister, Louisbourg, 10 June 1758, four o'clock in the afternoon, Vol. 38, folio 23v, microfilm, F-518.

38. *DCB Online*, Étienne Taillemite, "Louis-Joseph Beaussier de Lisle." The vessels under the command of Beassier de Lisle, were: Ships of the line, *L'Entreprenant* (74 guns), Louis-Joseph Beaussier de Lisle; *Le Célèbre* (64 guns), Chevalier de Marolles; *Le Capricieux* (64 guns), Chevalier de Tourville; *Le Bienfaisant* (64 guns), Chevalier de Courserac; and the frigate, *La Comète*, Chevalier de Lorgeril. These vessels were loaded with great quantities of supplies, and men. Thus, most of the guns were removed and stored in order to provide extra storage space. Once the vessels emptied, all guns were remounted by 10 May. Desgouttes' ships of the line were now ready for operational duty. Their captains received their orders and were assigned for the moment to protect the harbour's entrance. LAC, MG 1, Archives des colonies, Série C11B, Correspondence générale, Île Royale, 1758, *Journal du siège de Louisbourg* [henceforth *Journal anonyme I*], 16 April–27 July 1758, folio 2r, microfilm F-507. *L'Entreprenant* was a 74-gun ship of the line. The identity of the naval yard that built the vessel and its date of construction could not be confirmed. The vessel measured 175 feet in length. *Le Célèbre*, a 64-gun ship of the line, was built in naval yards in Brest, France, in 1755. The vessel measured 150 feet in length. *Le Capricieux*, a 64-gun ship of the line, was built in the naval yards, in Rochefort, France. The date of construction could not be confirmed. The vessel measured 150 feet in length. E. Willis Stevens, *Louisbourg Submerged Cultural Resources Survey* (Marine Archaeological Section,

National Historic Parks and Site Branches, 1994), 5 and 46. Permission was obtained to consult this restricted report.

39.   LAC, MG 2, Archives de la marine, Campagne, Série B4, 1758, Vol. 80, Letter, Desgouttes to Drucour, aboard *Le Prudent*, in Louisbourg harbour, 6 May 1758, folio 66r, microfilm F-757.

40.   LAC, MG 2, Archives de la marine, Série B4, Campagnes, Vol. 80, Relation de la descente des anglais à Louisbourg, 29 June 1758, folios 21r–21v, microfilm F-757.

41.   LAC, MG1, Archives des colonies, Série C11C, Amérique du Nord. Île Royale, Vol. 10, Prise de Louisbourg, 1758, Etat General des Trouppes tant de terre, Colones, Volontaires Bourgeois, Accadiens et Sauvages a la deffence de la Place de Louisbourg, microfilm F-518.

42.   The totals of the French defenders differ slightly depending on the primary or secondary sources consulted. J.S. McLennan, a specialist on Louisbourg history broke down the French Garrison before the British landing as follows: Artois, 520; Bourgogne, 520, Cambis, 680; Volontaires Étrangers, 680; Compagnies détachées, 1,000; and gunners, 120: total 3,520. J. S. McLennan, 263.

43.   During the British occupation following the 1745 siege, Commodore Charles Knowles provided Thomas Pelham-Holles, Duke of Newcastle with a very thorough insight as to the fortress's dilapidated state. "The fortifications are badly designed and worse executed I have already informed your grace. It may be said these are things that may be remedied. To which I answer not! For unless the climate could be changed it is impossible to make works durable. The frosts begin to cease towards the middles of May and are succeeded by fogs. These last till the end of July or beginning of August, with the intermission perhaps of one or two days in a fortnight. Towards the close of September or very early October the frosts set in again, and they continue with frequent snow till May or often the beginning June. So that allowing the fortifications to be repaired with the best materials and in the most workmanlike manner, your grace will observe, they have scarce two months in the year for the cement to dry

in. This is impossible to do. Therefore it is certain, after the nation has been at the expense of perhaps more that one millions pounds, we should have to go on again with repairing where we had begun at first. As it will take upwards of twenty years to do it in, consequently the works will be rotten and tumbling down before that time, as they are now." Letter No. 249, Commodore Charles Knowles to Thomas Pelham-Holles, Duke of Newcastle, Louisbourg, 9 July 1746, see Gwyn, 290–291.

44.   LAC, MG 4, Archives de la Guerre, Bibliothèque de la Guerre A2C, mémoire 236, 283, *Memoirs of a French Officer, an Impartial History of the Siege of Louisbourg and the Hostilities Committed in Acadia and at Cape Breton Before the Declaration of War* [henceforth *Journal of Chevalier de Johnstone*], microfilm F-734.

45.   In 1719, French colonial administrators had selected Louisbourg as a best location to establish a fishing colony with an accessible natural harbour. To protect their fishing industry and commercial ventures in this part of the Atlantic region it was decided to construct a basic fortification system. Over the course of the next 44 years Louisbourg underwent several major expansion projects. By 1758, the fortress comprised the following structures: The King's Bastion; The Dauphin Half-Bastion; The Princess Bastion, and the Queen's Bastion. All these bastions contained escarps, ramparts, parapets, embrasures, gun platforms, and cavaliers. They were joined by curtain walls, and protected by large ditches. The harbour was protected by the Royal, Island, and Rochefort Point batteries. LAC, MG 1, Ministère de la France d'outre-mer, Dépôt des fortifications des colonies, Amérique septentrional, numéro d'ordre 236, *Journal du siege de Louis-bourg avec un précis de la situation de la Place, Le Jour que Les anglais ont fais la desente, et une Relation de ce qui s'y est passé, precèdée du Caracthere des principaux officiers de Cette Place*, 1–5, [henceforth *Journal de Louis-bourg*], microfilm F-557. Although unsigned and non-paginated, comparative studies confirm that this manuscript is another and more complete version of François-Claude-Victor Grillot de Poilly's journal.

46.   Johnstone further describes in great detail the fortress's vulnerability should the enemy land and occupy the hills around Louisbourg. "About

two hundred paces from the curtain between the west gate and the King's bastion, a height (Hauteur de la Potence) overlooks a great part of the town, the parade, the wharves; enfilades the battery of the Grave which defends the harbour, where the cannoniers of this battery, whose platforms and canons are entirely discovered from that eminence, may be marked out and killed from it with muskets. Opposite to the south gate, Porte de la Reine, there is another eminence, Cape Noir, which is still much higher that the Hauteur de la Potence, discovers all across the town down to the wharves, and is only betwixt two and three hundred paces distant from the curtain. La Batterie Royale, a fort which faces and defends the entry of the harbour, is also dominated by a very high eminence, about three hundred fathoms from it, where is a sentry-box for a vidette. Such was the natural and insurmountable defects of the position chosen for a town of such importance." *Journal of Chevalier de Johnstone*, 282.

47. LAC, MG 1, Ministère de la France d'outre-mer, Dépôt des fortifications des colonies, Amérique septentrional, numéro d'ordre 240, Extrait du Siège de Louisbourg à commencer du premier juin, jour ou j'ai apercu la flotte des Anglais, faite par M. Le Marquis Desgouttes [Journal of Desgouttes], 21 July 1758, folio 13v, microfilm F-557.

48. Louis Franquet was plagued by a series of serious health issues. "Ma santé dérangée par l'escorbut," explained Franquet , "et une menace d'hydropsie accompagne de fiévre tierce,de puis deux mois." His condition severely hindered his mobility, eventually deteriorating to such a point that later Franquet conferred most the siege work operations to his senior engineer, François-Claude-Victor Grillot de Poilly. LAC, MG 1, Archives des colonies, Série C11C, Amérique du Nord, Île Royale, Vol. 10, Prise de Louisbourg, 1758, Letter, Franquet to the Minister, 22 June 1758, microfilm F-518. Grillot de Poilly noted in his journal that, "regrettably this illness, had so greatly weaken his [Franquet's] intellect, that he was no longer himself, and only had certain moments [of lucidity.]" *Journal de Louis-bourg*, 8.

49. In his memoirs, Franquet provides detailed explanations of his repairs and new construction from when he arrived in Louisbourg in 1754 to the days before the British landing in June 1758. Among these projects was

the construction of many traverses built in various locations throughout the bastions and walls to protect troops from enfilade fire from enemy batteries located on hills surrounding the fortress. LAC, MG 4, Archives de la guerre, C1, Vol. 7,Comité Technique du Génie, Place Étrangère, Louisbourg, Île Royale, article 14, pièce 7, Mémoire sur Louisbourg en l'ilse Royale; sur l'État de ses fortifications au 15 aoust 1754, que le gouvereur Et l'ingénieur principal y arriverent, sur les ouvrages nouveaux qu'on y commença relativement à un projet arrêté par M. Rouillé le 25 Mars de la dite année; sur d'autres faits en reforcement des anciens, conséquemnt aux vues offensives des anglais sur cette place, et dont on ait informé par la cour, et enfin sur tous autres ouvrages faits par M. Franquet pendant le siége. Tant pour se garantir du feu de l'artillerie de l'Ennemie, que pour courir à la deffense du chemin couvert [henceforth *Journal of Louis Franquet*], 143–144.

50. To Drucour's credit, the governor showed more initiative and foresight regarding the strategic value of costal defences than his predecessor Louis Du Pont Duchambon who was the French governor during the first siege of Louisbourg in 1745. Duchambon did not see the value of building and manning a series of costal fortifications. However, when in became apparent that the New Englanders were going to land, Duchambon dispatched a small force to intercept the invaders. This last minute action did foil the invaders' plans. Nevertheless, the New Englanders, transported in whaleboats, feigned an initial landing attempt against Flat Point Cove. Seeing the French force taking up positions in their projected landing area the invaders opted to halt the operation and returned to the transport ships. There additional troops were loaded on other whaleboats. The augmented invasion force now rowed in all haste towards its new objective, Commandière Cove. This new attempt now developed into a hotly contested race between the two forces to see who would reach the cove first. The New Englanders easily reached their mark and stormed ashore. The disheartened French force retreated into the woods, and quickly returned to the fortress. Rawlyk, 77–88; *DCB Online*, Louis Du Pont Duchambon.

51. LAC, MG 4, C2, Comité du Génie, Archives de l'inspection générale du génie, Vol. 1, manuscrit in 4, No. 66, 3–137, Entries of 29–30 April 1758. Mémoire de evenemens qui interesseront cette colonie pendant l'année

1758 par François-Claude-Victor Grillot de Poilly [henceforth *Journal of Grillot de Poilly*], microfilm F-760. This version compared to the one cited in footnote 46 only documents the defenders' activities from 1 January to 31 May 1758.

52. *Ibid.*, 1 May 1758, 59.

53. Whereas the French colonial administrators were confident that Louisbourg's geographical location provided more than adequate protection Étienne Verrier Louisbourg's first chief engineer did not share their simplistic views. "I was assured that an assault landing on the beach at Louisbourg was impossible at any time," reported the chief engineer, "and there would be no need to fortify it." Verrier conducted his own assessment of the coastline. The outcome of his reconnaissance exercise was alarming. "We came ashore at five places in a single morning," revealed Verrier. "It is wise to examine closely what one is told in America." Quoted in Bruce W. Fry, *"An Appearance of Strength" The Fortifications of Louisbourg, Vol. 1* (Ottawa: National Historic Parks and Sites Branch, Environment Canada, 1984), 54; *DCB Online*, Étienne Verrier. However, in 1757, Drucour, to his credit, was pro-active in defending the surrounding coastlines. The following coastal locations were operated and fortified: Cove near the Lighthouse Battery; Small cove on Gabarus Bay; Large Gauthier Cove; Two coves in the vicinity of the Grand Lorembec; Grand Lorembec itself; Three locations in Flat Point; and Black Point. Furthermore, the fortress's harbour defences were augmented: Lighthouse Battery; Island Battery; Royal Battery; and the Rochefort Point Battery. A total of 2,468 men, 68 canons and 2 mortars were committed to the defence of these positions. LAC, MG 1, Archives des Colonies, Séries C11C, Amérique du Nord, Île Royale, Vol. 10, Prise de Louisbourg, 1758, Manuscript C-67–11–24, microfilm F-518.

54. LAC, MG 2, Archives de la marine, Série B4, Campagnes, Vol. 80, Registre contenant tous les ordres que M. Le Marquis DesGouttes a donnés pendant le temps qu'il a comandé la division de Rochefort pour Louisbourg et ainsy que ceux qu'il a donnés après son arrivée à cette même division et à celle de Brest [henceforth Desgouttes' Orders Register], 31 May–8 June 1758, folios 108r-124r, microfilm F-757.

55. *Journal of Grillot de Poilly*, Entries of 1–23 May, 1758.

56. Orders dated 1 April and 14 May 1758. LAC, MG1, Archives des colonies, Série C11B, Correspondence générale, Île Royale, Copie des ordres données par M. le Chevalier de Drucour à Messieurs de la Tour Commandant à l'isle de l'entrée, de St-Julien au camp de la Cormornadière, Marin à celuy de la pointe platte, D'Anthonay à la pointe Blanche, in Journal ou Relation sur ce qui se passera des mouvemens pour l'attaque et la défense de la place de Louisbourg pendant la présente année 1758 [henceforth *Journal of Drucour*], folios 58r-58v, microfilm F-167. As of May 1758, two of these three battalion commanders were familiar with these costal positions and surrounding terrain outside the fortress. Lieutenant — Colonel Henri Valentine-Jacques d'Anthonay arrived in Louisbourg with his Battalion on the 24 April 1758. *Journal anonyme I*, Entry of 28 April 1758, folios 24r-24v.

57. *Journal of Drucour*, Entry of 14 May 1758, folios 58r-58v.

58. The troops were stationed in several positions in La Cormorandière, 970; Flat Point, 710; White Point, 200; Devil's Mountain, 192. *Journal of Grillot de Poilly*, Entry of 6 June 1758.

59. Letter, Brigadier James Wolfe to Lord George Sackville, Halifax, 24 May 1758, see Willson, 366.

60. *Admiral Boscawen's Log*, Entry of 28 May 1758, folio 87. There seems to be some confusion as to this officer's identity. In his entry of 1 June 1758, Major-General Amherst refers to this officer as Major Robertson. *Journal of Jeffery Amherst*, Entry of 1 June 1758, folio 20v.

61. Letter, Brigadier James Wolfe to Lord George Sackville, Halifax, 24 May 1758, see Willson, 367.

62. James Cunningham provides interesting details pertaining to the Rangers. "A Body of Rangers were forming consisting of 1,100 from Detachments of the several Corps and 500 were sent from New England, all under the Command of Captain Scott of the 70th Regiment, who was accustomed

to that service. Their clothes are cut short, & they have exchanged their heavy Arms, for the light fusils of the Additional Companies of Frasers that are left in Halifax. This body of troops will be of excellent service in protecting There Camp from Insults of the Indians." Letter, James Cunningham to Lord George Sackville, on board the *Ludlow Castle*, at sea, 30 May 1758, quoted in J. S. McLennan, 239–240. In Wolfe's 24 May 1758, letter to Lord George Sackville, the brigadier provided the following additional information regarding the assault landing. A small body of men were to land at the bottom of Gabarus Bay and entrench themselves. Additionally, as the assault landing would be taking place, Boscawen and his ships of the line would sail towards the harbour's entrance as if they were going to force this position. Letter, Brigadier James Wolfe to Lord George Sackville, Halifax, 24 May 1758, see Willson, 366.

63.   In Boscawen's ship' log, the admiral reports in his daily entries date from 18 to 27 May, 1758 that it rained nearly every day. Furthermore, winds, haze, and various degrees of fog hindered ships' signals, manoeuveres, and operations to set sail within the harbour. *Admiral Boscawen's Log*, Entries of 18–27 May 1758, folios 85–87.

64.   Letter, General Lawrence to Pitt, 23 May 1758, on board his majesty's ship *Namur* in Halifax Harbour, see Kimball, 256–257. A total of 270 soldiers were left behind in the hospital in Halifax.

65.   The total of Boscawen's fleet varies depending on the source consulted. Since Boscawen was still the head of the expedition, the numbers tabulated and reported by the admiral's log entry of Sunday, 28 May, 1758 were used. It is important to note that the total augmented as Boscawen left the port of Halifax. As Boscawen set sail for Louisbourg ships hailing from various destinations joined the invasion fleet. 29 May, the *Hawke*, and eight transport vessels arriving from the Bay of Fundy; the *Dublin* arriving from England with Major-General Amherst on board; the *Kennington* and the *Essex* transport arriving from Madeira. *Admiral Boscawen's Log*, Entry of May, 28, 1758, folio 87.

66.   *Ibid.*, 29 May 1758, folio 87.

67.   *Journal of Jeffery Amherst*, Entry of 31 May 1758, folios 20v-21r.

68.   *Journal of Desgouttes*, Entry of 7 June 1758, folio 2v. From 1 June to 8 June 1758, Desgouttes and his captains worked hard to locate and transport guns, ammunition, and supplies to the coastal positions. They also complied with orders to send additional personnel to man these positions. On 3 June, Desgouttes dispatched his *troupes de la marine* to reinforce the troops guarding Gauthier Cove. Furthermore, work parties were organized to haul guns. From 4–6 June the gun hauling tasks continued. On 7 June, the commodore was requested to provide additional gun crews to Rochefort Point, as well as 80 sailors and rations to be dispatched to Grand Lorembec. *Ibid.*, Entries of 4–6 June 1758, folios 2r-2v.

69.   *Admiral Boscawen's Log*, Entry of 2 June 1758, folio 90.

70.   *Ibid.*, Entries of 22–23 June 1758, folio 90. Amherst confirmed his participation in this naval reconnaissance, saying, "I went along the shoar in a Boat" *Journal of Jeffery Amherst*, Entry of 2 June 1758, folio 21r.

71.   Letter, Major-General Amherst to Pitt, Camp before Louisbourg, 11 June 1758, see Kimball, 271.

72.   *Admiral Boscawen's Log*, Entry of 3 June 1758, folio 90.

73.   Letter, Amherst to Pitt, Camp before Louisbourg, 11 June 1758, see Kimball, 272.

74.   The vessels tasked to bombard the French costal positions were: The *Sutherland* and the *Squirrel* in the vicinity of White Point; the *Kennington* (20 guns) and the *Halifax Snow* near Kennington Cove; and the *Gramont* (18 guns), the *Diana* (32 guns), and the *Shannon* (28 guns) were ordered to find suitable locations and position themselves between the two first groups. *An Authentic Account of the Reduction of Louisbourg, in June and July 1758 by a Spectator* [henceforth *Journal of a Spectator*] (London: Printed for W. Owen, 1758,) 8, Entry 8 June 1758.

75.   *Admiral Boscawen's Log*, Entry 3 June 1758, folio 90.

76.   Among the casualties was the bailiff of town council. *Journal of Drucour*, Entry of 3 June 1758, folio 88v; Grillot de Poilly also reports that Captain Chevalier de Chassi was wounded. *Journal de Grillot de Poilly*, 3 June 1758. Major-General Amherst confirmed that the *Kennington* had lost three sailors that day. *Journal of Jeffery Amherst*, Entry of 3 June 1758, folio 21r.

77.   *Gordon's Journal*, Entry of 3 June 1758, 106.

78.   Even though every precaution and security measures were taken to ensure that the selected vessels could operate safely during the pre-assault bombardments and covering fire during the landing phases, the rough sea conditions did cause some vessels to experience difficulties. On 4 June, a hard gale caused the *Trent* (28 guns) to strike a rock unhinging the vessel's rudder. After many rescue attempts other vessels were able to come to its assistance and tow the disabled frigate to safety. Other vessels reported that they had lost anchors. *Journal of a Spectator*, 10, Entry of 4 June 1758.

79.   To exert additional pressure on the French coastal positions, on the days preceding the landing Boscawen initiated the following actions. On 4 June the *Halifax Snow* was sent to join up with the *Kennington* and the *Halifax* and participated in the bombardment of the French costal entrenchments. During the course of the day, Boscawen sent orders that the frigates change positions. On 5 June the *Kennington* suspended its bombardment. On June 6, the frigates provided covering fire for an unsuccessful assault landing attempt. *Admiral Boscawen's Log*, Entries of 4–6 June 1758, folios 90–93.

80.   The invaders organized multiple reconnaissance missions from June 2–7, 1758. Each mission brought forth new pertinent information that enabled Major-General Amherst to amend and fine tune his assault landing plan. *Journal of a Spectator*, Entries of 2, 3, and 6June 8–9.

81.   *Admiral Boscawen's Log*, Entry of 7 June 1758, folio 93.

82.   Two small contingents were immediately dispatched to the Laurembec and Gauthier coves. *Journal of Drucour*, Entry of 6 June 1758, folio 91v.

83. Letter, Amherst to Pitt, Camp before Louisbourg, 11 June 1758, see Kimball, 272.

84. *Ibid.*

85. *Journal of Drucour*, Entry of 6 June 1758, folio 90v.

86. This battalion was ordered to report to the Port of Rochefort, France in February 1758 for overseas deployment to Louisbourg, Île Royale. There, the unit was to liaise with Comte Du Chauffault de Besné. This naval officer had been selected to transport the battalion and its equipment to Louisbourg aboard a squadron consisting of 11 vessels. The squadron left Rochefort on 21 March. However, as the vessels approached Louisbourg the French sailors noted the presence of a British blockade maintained by vessels under the command of Sir Charles Hardy. Du Chauffault de Besné immediately set course for Ste. Anne's Bay, and dropped anchor on 29 May 1758. Shortly after Du Chauffault de Besné moved his vessels to Port Dauphin (Englishtown). Du Chauffault de Besné then received orders from governor Drucour, requesting that he quickly disembark all Cambis personnel and the unit's equipment. The infantry verified their personal gear and were divided into a several smaller groups. They were then ordered to march to Louisbourg. All elements of the Battalion reached Louisbourg on 6, 7, and 8 June. LAC, MG 2, Archives de la marine, Série B4, Campagnes, Campagne d'Amérique, Vol. 80, Escadre de Du Chauffault de Besné, 1758, folio 207; *Ibid., Journal du vaisseau du roi Le Dragon*, 1758, folio 233v. For a detailed account of the activities and operations conducted by the 2nd Battalion of the Régiment de Cambis during the second siege of Louisbourg, please consult, Michel Wyczynski, "The Expedition of the Second Battalion of the Cambis Regiment at Louisbourg, 1758," in *Nova Scotia Historical Review*, Vol. 10, No. 2 (1990), 95–110.

87. The small vessels sent from the ships of the line were operated by the sailors of these ships under the command of either a lieutenant, a mate, or a midshipman. Those provided by the transports were controlled by an army officer. *Journal of a Spectator*, Entry of 8 June 1758, 9. The exact identification as to the type of vessels used for the transporting

and landing the troops during the amphibious assault phase was difficult to confirm. It is possible that a few different types may have been used during this operation. This depended on if they were supplied by ships of the line, frigates, or transports. In the days before the landing, Boscawen simply refers to these small vessels, in his log, as "boats." In his June 4 and 5 entries, the admiral also mentioned that longboats were being used for various preparatory task. *Admiral Boscawen's Log*, Entries of 4–5 June 1758, folio 91. John Bray, captain of the ship of the line, *Princess Amelia* (80 guns), reports that he sent boats to assist in the landing of Colonel Frazer' grenadiers. He also mentioned that a cutter commanded by a mate would land the Rangers. John Bray, *Princess Amelia*, Captain's Log, Number 736, see McLennan, 258. A cutter is described as a "clinker-built ship's boat, length 24–34 feet, pulling eight to fourteen oars and rigged originally with two masts with a dipping lug foresail and a standing lug mainsail." A longboat is described as being, "the largest boat carried on board a full-rigged ship, particularly in warships of the 18th century. It was a carvel built with a full bow and high sides, and furnished with a mast and sails for short cruises where required. A ship's gun could be mounted in the bows. Its principle uses on board were to transport heavy stores to and from the ship and to take empty water casks ashore to be refilled whenever fresh drinking water was required. It was also kept fully provisioned for use in any case of emergency." Peter Kemp, ed. *The Oxford Companion to Ships and The Sea* (London: Oxford University Press, 1976), 222, 496. Even though both these vessels were equipped with sails and rigging, this equipment was removed for the assault landing operation. Artwork and lithographs of that time period, as well as those created later depicting this event do not show these vessels with rigging or sails.

88. *Admiral Boscawen's Log*, Entry of 7 June 1758, folio 93. The small vessels to be used for the landing were cutters and barges. LAC, MG 12, Admiralty 51, Captains Logs, Vol. 246, Log of the *Diana*, 7 June 1758, Captain Alex Shonberg, microfilm B-3474. See also note 36, which provides detailed information as to the various embarkation preparations and assault landing drills that were devised, tested and refined by Boscawen while in Halifax. Once the troops loaded, the assault vessels would assemble in the following manner. The vessels who were part of the right wing would assemble at the *Violet* transport. As a visual reference point, this

vessel had three lights hung upon its off side near the water. The vessels of the left wing would congregate at the *St-George* transport, which had two signal lights. The grenadiers of Wolfe's group would form up at the *Neptune* transport, which had one signal light. *Gordon's Journal*, General order for evening of 7 June 1758, 112–113.

89.   *Ibid.*

90.   The assault groups' dress, personal equipment, and supplies directives were established on 20 May 1758 during the assault landing training exercises. Provisions were also made to ensure that the assault groups blankets were carefully bundled up and ready to be transported ashore after the bridgehead had been secured. Once the bridgehead stabilized three days worth of provisions would be transported to the members of the amphibious assault teams. *Ibid.*, Entry of 20 May 1758, 104.

91.   *Admiral Boscawen's Log*, Entry of 7 June 1758, folio 93.

92.   Positioned on the left side of the assault landing armada were the *Kennington* (20 guns) and the *Halifax Snow* (number of guns not confirmed). The centre group was protected by the covering fire of the frigates, the *Gramount* (18 guns), the *Diana* (32 guns), and the *Shannon* (28 guns). The ship of the line *Sutherland* (50 guns), and the frigate *Squirrel* (20 guns) would protect the advance and landing of the right group. Letter, Amherst to Pitt, Camp before Louisbourg, 11 June 1758, see Kimball, 273; and *Admiral Boscawen's Log*, Entry of 7 June 1758, folio 93.

93.   LAC, MG 12, Admiralty 51, Captains Logs, Vol. 413, Entry of 8 June 1758. Log of the *Gramount*, Captain John Stott, microfilm B-3474.

94.   Within each division a vessel was selected to fly a specific coloured flag. This identification system was used to facilitate the forming up phase. Later during the assault phase they were used as visual rallying signals to ensure that the vessels remained with their proper divisions. Wolfe's division was identified by a red flag. Brigadier Whitmore's division being the right wing of the invasion force and was identified by a white flag. The last division was the left wing of this invasion force. It was Brigadier

Lawrence's division and was identified by a blue flag. *Gordon's Journal*, Entry of 4 June 1758, 112.

95. These deployment and formation orders were the same as those issued on June 3, 1758. *Gordon's Journal*, Entry of 3 June 1758. General Orders, 110–111.

96. The troops selected to serve under Brigadier Wolf for the assault landing were: Four veteran companies of grenadiers, and light infantry, composed of a corps of 550 men selected from several regiments because of their marksmanship abilities. They were to serve as irregulars under the command of Major Scott. Also, part of Wolfe's force consisted of companies of Rangers supported the Highland Regiment and eight additional companies of grenadiers. Letter, Amherst to Pitt, Camp before Louisbourg, 11 June 1758, see Kimball, 273.

97. These hand picked soldiers had received special training for their assault landing mission and their operations in the 24 hours following the landing. This body of light troops were trained to engage, "Indians, Canadian and other painted savages of the Island." In Major-General Amherst's orders of the day (3 June 1758), the general provides additional directives as to what he expects of Wolfe's troop during this campaign: "As the air of Cape Breton is moist and foggy there must be a particular attention to the fire arms upon duty that they may be kept dry and always fit for use and the Light Infantry should fall upon some method to secure their arms from the dews and the dropping of the trees when they are in search of the enemy. The Commander of the light troops must teach his corps to attack and defend themselves judiciously, always endeavoring to get upon the enemy's flank and equally watchfully to prevent their surrounding them. They must be instructed to choose good spots and to lay themselves in ambuscade to advantage, to be alert, silent, vigilant and obedient, ready at all times to turn out without the least noise or least confusion. They must always march in files and generally fight in a single rank pushing at the enemy when they see them in confusion and that the ground favors their efforts never pursue with too much eagerness nor to give way expecting a very great unequality of numbers." *Gordon's Journal*, Entry of 3 June 1758, 108–109.

98. Lawrence's assault group consisted of elements from the Amherst, Hopson, Otway, Whitmore, Lawrence, and Warburton Regiments. *Ibid.*; Letter, Amherst to Pitt, Camp before Louisbourg, 11 June 1758, see Kimball, 273.

99. Whitmore's group consisted of elements of the Royal, Lascelles, Monckton, Forbes, Anstruther, and Webb Regiments. *Gordon's Journal*, Entry of 3 June 1758, 108–109; and Letter, Amherst to Pitt, Camp before Louisbourg, 11 June 1758, see Kimball, 273.

100. *Journal of Grillot de Poilly*, Entry of 8 June 1758.

101. Governor Drucour listed in his post campaign report the number of guns and mortars that had been installed in the various coastal emplacements. White Pointe: six, 6-pounders; two, 18-pounders; and eight mortars. Flat Point: one cast iron mortar and one iron mortar; Kennington Cove, (l'anse à Cormorandière) one, 24-pounder; four, 6-pounders; and two, 4-pounders. *Journal of Drucour*, "Artillerie mise et laissé aux retranchements cy après nommées," folio 109r. The number of guns, mortars, and calibres described by the governor varies from those listed in the *Gordon's Journal*. See note 131 for Gordon's list.

102. Letter, Amherst to Pitt, Camp before Louisbourg, 11 June 1758, see Kimball, 273.

103. *Journal of a Spectator*, Entry of 8 June 1758, 12.

104. *Gordon's Journal*, Entry of 3 June 1758, General Orders, 111.

105. *Journal of Chevalier de Johnstone*, 296.

106. Letter, Lieutenant Henry Caldwell to his brother, Louisbourg, 28 July 1758, cited in Louis des Cognets, Jr., *Amherst and Canada* (Princeton, New Jersey: Shelf-published, 1962), 88.

107. In his general orders, Amherst insisted that all his officers ensure that their troops refrain from making any unnecessary noises during the landing phase. "The General is sufficiently convinced," wrote Gordon, " of the good

disposition of the troops by what he has already seen, he desires they will not hollow nor cry out at the landing, but be attentive to the commands of their officers by which they can never be put in any confusion or fail of success. Their officers will lead them directly to the enemy." *Gordon's Journal*, Entry of 7 June 1758, General Orders, 113.

108. Letter, Lieutenant Henry Caldwell to his brother, Louisbourg, 28 July 1758, cited in Louis des Cognets, Jr., 88.

109. LAC, MG 21, British Library, Sloane and Additional Manuscript 11,813, transcript, Captain William Parry, *Journal of the Siege of Louisbourg* [henceforth *Journal of Captain William Parry*], 28 May–26 July 1758, folios 82–88.

110. Admiral Boscawen knew that the surf and swell in Gabarus Bay could be unpredictable and dangerous. Thus, during the training phase he made provision to send with each assault groups a number of empty light boats tasked to rescue soldiers who fell into the sea by accident. *Gordon's Journal*, Entry of 20 May 1758, 104.

111. Entry of 11 June 1758, *The Diary of Nathaniel Knap of Newbury, In the Province of Massachusetts Bay in New England, Written at the Second Siege of Louisbourg in 1758* (Boston: Society of Colonial Wars in the Commonwealth of Massachusetts, 1895), 8.

112. LAC, MG 18, L4, The Earl of Amherst Papers, Vol. 4, Packet 20, Part 1, Entry of 8 June 1758, *Lieutenant-General William Amherst's Journal* [in four books], from 16 March 1758, the day he embarked for America to 5 September 1760 the Day Montreal surrendered [henceforth *Journal of William Amherst*], Book 2, Entry of 8 June 1758, 8.

113. Letter, Lieutenant Henry Caldwell to his brother, Louisbourg, 28 July 1758, cited in Louis des Cognets, Jr., 88.

114. *Gordon's Journal*, Entry of 8 June 1758, 116.

115. *Journal of Drucour*, Entry of 8 June 1758, folio 92v.

116. *Journal of a Spectator*, Entry of 8 June 1758, 18.

117. *Journal de Louis-bourg*. Détail de ce qui s'est passée la journée du 8 juin a la descente des anglais.

118. In his post campaign assessment, Grillot de Poilly reveals that he repeatedly advised Governor Drucour and the chief engineer, Louis Franquet, to carefully examine the coastline and identify areas that could be used by the enemy as landing sites. He also told them that a series of pathways between Flat Pointe and Cormorandière Cove should be cleared thus facilitating troops movements along the coastline. Moreover, the military engineer strongly recommended to the senior officers that a series of field works be built to protect the troops and enable them to organize themselves for counterattacks. Lastly, Grillot de Poilly also suggested that reserve forces occupy the high ground and prepare defensive positions from which they could engage the enemy. Regrettably, his recommendations were not implemented. *Ibid.*

119. *Ibid.*, Entry of 14 May 1758, folio 84v.

120. Colonel Bernd Horn provides the following definition of *la petite guerre.* "*La petite guerre* was, in essence, small-scale irregular warfare. Key to its success was the selection of limited objectives that could be easily overcome. Stealth and surprise were of the utmost importance, ambushes and raids were preferred method of attack, and lightning-quick strikes were always succeeded by immediate withdrawals. There were no follow-on attacks or campaigns, and rarely were any of the tactical operations capable of achieving a larger strategic value other than pre-empting, delaying, or disrupting possible enemy offensive action." Bernd Horn, "*La Petite Guerre*: A Strategy of Survival," in Colonel Bernd Horn, ed., *The Canadian Way of War: Serving the National Interest* (Dundurn Press Limited: Toronto, 2006), 21–56.

121. Grillot de Poilly reports that later that evening a force of 50 men from the Volontaires Étrangers had been sent out to escort a gunner who had been tasked to spike a cannon at White Pointe. This operation was unsuccessful because British troops were occupying the position. *Journal*

of Grillot de Poilly, Entry of 8 June 1758. This position had been under the command of Lieutenant — Colonel Henri-Valentin-Jacques d'Anthonay, commanding officer of the Volontaires Étrangers. Although the guns had not been sabotaged, D'Anthonay nevertheless had the time to remove all the smaller weapons and set fire to the ammunition dump. However, the other main battery emplacements at Cormorandière Cove and Flat Point had simply been abandoned. LAC, MG 1, Archives des colonies, Série C11C, Amérique du Nord, Vol. 10 Île Royale, Prise de Louisbourg, 1758, Entry of 8 June 1758. *Journal du Siège*, Louisbourg, mars-août, folio 38r.

122. *Journal of a Spectator*, Entry of 8 June 1758, 12.

123. *Journal of Jeffery Amherst*, Entry of 8 June 1758, folio 24.

124. *Journal of a Spectator*, Entry of 8 June 1758, 17.

125. Letter, Lieutenant Henry Caldwell to his brother, Louisbourg, 28 July 1758, cited in Louis des Cognets, Jr., 88.

126. Letter, Amherst to Pitt, Camp before Louisbourg, 11 June 1758, see Kimball, 274.

127. Drucour had in his service a small force of irregulars consisting of the 60 men of the Compagnie de Joubert and another 90 men of the Acadian militia of M. de Villejoint, fils. These irregular troops did fight during the assault landing and their operational efficiency was limited during the siege. *Journal of Drucour*, Entry of 6 June 1758, folio 90v. Another larger irregular force commanded by M. de Boishébert reached Miré a few miles from Louisbourg on 1 July 1758. There he joined forces with a group commanded by Villejoint, fils. After being brief on the current situation Boishébert was not optimistic as to their role in this campaign. "Journal de ma Campagne de Louisbourg," *Le Bulletin des Recherches Historiques*, Vol. 27, No. 2, February 1921, 49.

128. Letter, Lieutenant Henry Caldwell to his brother, Louisbourg, 28 July 1758, cited in Louis des Cognets, Jr., 88.

129. Letter, Amherst to Pitt, Camp before Louisbourg, 11 June 1758, see Kimball, 274.

130. The French armament found in the abandoned coastal positions were the following: Three 24-pounders, seven 9-pounders, seven 6-pounders, 14 swivels, and two mortars as well as ammunition tools and stores. Entry of 8 June 1758. *Gordon's Journal*, 116. Also, uncovered by British troops in one location was a furnace used by the French gun crews to heat up their canons balls. This type of ordnance was intended to ignite fires aboard the frigates and incoming assault vessels. *Journal of a Spectator*, Entry of 8 June 1758, 17.

131. In the days following the landing, Governor Drucour became increasingly concerned by the lack of available information regarding the status and welfare of personnel that were confirmed missing since the landing. On 14 June, Drucour sent a letter to Major-General Amherst requesting information pertaining to the M. de Blesta, M. Langlade, Sieur Savary et Romainville. For the moment Amherst could only confirm that one grenadier officer had a serious head wound, a lieutenant of the grenadiers had a broken leg, and was also wounded in the arm. *Journal of Drucour*, Entry of 14 June 1758, folios 64r-64v. Later that day, the governor was contacted by Admiral Boscawen who provided the following additional information. The admiral confirmed that Langlade suffered a neck wound, Savary was wounded in the right leg and the left arm, and Belesta was wounded in the backside. All these officers were aboard a hospital ship. As for Romainville, the admiral stated that he had no information regarding this officer and thus presumed him to be dead. Another French officer Jean Jorge Hirsh had been transported aboard the *Princess Ameila*. *Journal of Jeffery Amherst*, Packet 4, Letters from Admiral Boscawen, 1758, Letter, Boscawen to Amherst, 14 June 1758, 24. Following the capitulation of the fortress of Louisbourg, Governor Drucour drafted a comprehensive casualty report entitled, État Général des officiers et soldats tuées et blesses depuis et compris le 1er juin jusqu'au 26 julliet 1758. Among those killed and injured on the day of the landing are the following: 2nd Battalion, Artois Regiment — Captain Belesta, captain of grenadiers, injured; Lieutenant Savary, injured and died from his wounds 5 July 1758; Lieutenant Masele. 2nd Battalion. Bourgogne Regiment

— Captain Langlade, captain of grenadiers injured; Second Lieutenant Romainville, injured; Captain Chevalier de Brouzede, injured. Second Battalion, Volontaires Étrangers — Lieutenant Hirsch and Lieutenant D'Étrangers, injured. Troupes des colonies — Ensigne Sabattier, injured. Milice Bourgoise — René Rosse. The following personnel were killed or wounded during the British frigate bombardment phase June 3–6, 1758. Milice Bourgeoise — One unidentified individual killed on 3 June; François le Moine, 4 June 1758. The summary did not included the non-commissioned officers (NCOs) or soldiers killed during this operation. *Journal of Drucour,* folios 104r-106r. Major-General Amherst reports the French prisoners and casualties as follows: "Two Captains of Grenadiers and two Lieutenant are prisoners. One officer killed, and Indian Chief killed, and several soldiers killed. 70 soldiers taken prisoners." Letter, Amherst to Pitt, Camp before Louisbourg, 11 June 1758, see Kimball, 274. A few days after the landing.

132.   *Journal of a Spectator,* Entry of 8 June 1758, 18.

133.   The British casualties of 8 June 1758 assault landing listed in the various sources differ from one to another. Gordon provides the most detailed account: "Killed; Of Amhersts. Lieutenant Nicholson, 1 Sergeant, 1 Corporal and 38 of the whole, 21 with the above mentioned officer of the 15th were drowned, a shot of the enemy had sunk their boat. Wounded: five lieutenants, 2 sergeants, 1 corporal and 51 privates. The officers names were; of the Royals, Lieutenant Fiztymonds, Bailey and Fenton. Of Whitemore's Lieutenant Butler; Of the Highland Regiment Lieutenant Frazer, who with Fenton, afterwards died of their wounds." *Gordon's Journal,* 115–116. Admiral Boscawen reports that Army troops lost during the landing totalled 49 killed, 59 wounded, three officers killed, and five wounded. Naval person lost during this operation totalled 11 men killed, 29 wounded, and 19 sailors from transport vessels wounded. *Admiral Boscawen's Log,* Entry of 8 June 1758, folio 94. General Jeffery Amherst reported the following casualties: "Captain Baillie and Lieutenant Cuthbert of the Highland Regiment, Lieutenant Nicholson of mine (Amhersts), 4 sergeants, 1 corporal , 38 men killed. Twenty one were of my Regiments (the Grenadiers) of which 8 were shot, and the rest drowned in trying to get to shore. Five lieutenants, 2 sergeants, 1 corporal

and 53 men wounded, and of five companies of Rangers, 1 ensign and 3 privates were killed, 1 wounded and 1 missing." Letter, Amherst to Pitt, Camp before Louisbourg, 11 June 1758, see Kimball, 274.

134. *Ibid.* By noon the winds and the swell increased dramatically. Boscawen reported that it took him over three hours to row back to the *Namur* from the beachhead. LAC, MG 18, L4, Amherst, Sir Jeffery and family, Vol. 1, Packet 4, Letters from Admiral Boscawen to Major-General Amherst, Letter, Boscawen to Amherst, *Namur*, 8 June 1758, 9.

135. LAC, MG 2, Archives de la marine, Série B4, Campagne, Vol. 80, Note from Drucour to Desgouttes, 8 June 1758. Registre contenant tous les ordres que monsieur le marquis Desgouttes a données pendant le temps qu'il a commandé la division de Rochefort pour Louisbourg et ainsi que ceux qu'il a données après son arrive à cette même division et à celle de Brest, folio 125r. The Royal Battery was part of a three battery defence system built to protect the various parts of the harbour as well as its entrance. The other two batteries were the Island Battery and the Rochefort Point Battery. Work on the Royal Battery began in 1724. Over the years, modifications, improvements, and never ending repairs had been made to this large structure. This battery could hold up to 30 cannons. Fry, Vol. 1, 141–144; and Fry, Vol. 2, Plate numbers 228 and 229, Royal Battery, 185–186.

136. *Journal de Louis-bourg.*

137. LAC, MG 18, L5, Wolfe, James, Vol. 5, MS 2207, (Antiquaries' Papers), Letter, James Wolfe to Captain William Rickson, Salisbury, 1 December 1758, folios 64r-66r, microfilm A-1780.

138. The following 14 French vessels were in the harbour during the siege. Ships of the line: *Le Prudent* (74 guns), Charry Desgouttes, and *Le Bienfaisant* (64 guns), Chevalier de Courserac, which were captured by a British naval raiding party during the early hours of 26 July 1758. *Le Célèbre* (64 guns), Chevalier de Marolles, burst into flames and was destroyed on 21 July 1758 during a British artillery bombardment. *L'Entreprenant* (74 guns), Louis-Joseph Beaussier de Lisle, was caught in the raging fire that started

aboard *Le Célèbre* and destroyed the same day, along with *Le Capricieux* (64 guns), chevalier de Tourville. Frigates: *L'Aréthuse* (36 guns), Captain Jean Vauquelin, set sail for France on 15 July 1758; *La Comète*, Chevalier de Lorgeril, set sail for France on 11 June 1758. Vessels scuttled in the harbour's entrance on 29 June 1758: *La Fidèlle* (36 guns), *La Chèvre*, *L'Apollon*, and the merchant ship *La Ville de Saint-Malo Le Bizare* set sail for Quebec on 11 June 1758 and *L'Écho* set sail for Quebec on 14 June 1758. *L'Écho* was captured shortly after by the *Juno. Journal of Drucour. Journal of Desgouttes; Journal of Grillot de Poilly*. For a detailed account of this raid please consult, Wyczynski, "A Particular Gallant Action."

3

"PRESENT MOMENT IS HIGHLY FAVOURABLE FOR AN ATTACK": THE BRITISH CAPTURE OF FORT NIAGARA, 19 DECEMBER 1813

John Grodzinski

Since 1796 one key fort has guarded the mouth of the Niagara River. Situated on a peninsula, Fort Niagara has the river on two sides, with Lake Ontario to the North. Originally built by the French, it was transferred to Britain in 1763 and, following the American War of Independence, was to have been given to the United States in 1783. However, Britain was reluctant to surrender it and other forts in the Great Lakes region to the Americans as that would mean the end to their control of several waterways and terminate their access to several Native allies. When they finally agreed to give the fort up in 1796, Fort George was constructed on the Canadians shore just south of Newark (modern Niagara-on-the-Lake, Ontario), the largest village on the frontier. Due to their respective locations, Fort Niagara dominated the mouth of the Niagara River, while Fort George dominated Fort Niagara.

It is difficult, however, to fully appreciate the importance and boldness of the capture of Fort Niagara on 19 December 1813, without putting it into the context of the overall campaign on the Niagara frontier during the War of 1812. At a time when inland waterways were the highways for commerce and movement of military forces throughout the interior of North America, fortifications were constructed to guard key points controlling river mouths or sources, portage routes, or the confluence of two rivers. The Europeans relied on this extensive network of rivers and lakes that made their penetration of the continent possible. The Niagara River was an important part of this system. Consequently by 1812, the 30-mile length of the Niagara River shoreline was dotted with forts or fortified points. The two major British forts, Fort George in the north and Fort Erie in the south stood as sentinels guarding access to the Niagara Peninsula. If the Americans penetrated that line and advanced inland, the British would be forced to withdraw to Burlington Bay or York (present day Toronto) and, as a result, might lose much of Upper Canada.

Library and Archives Canada C-26.

View of Fort George from Fort Niagara.

By 1812, this became a real concern. Incensed by British impressment of American seamen, violation of American neutral trading rights and territorial waters, and the refusal to end the Orders in Council and other lesser issues, American President James Madison believed a diplomatic resolution was impossible and following a vote in Congress, the United States declared war on Great Britain in a formal proclamation on 19 June 1812.[2]

Although Britain had a respectable naval presence at Halifax, it had few soldiers in North America. Most of its forces were engaged in the protracted struggle against Napoleon, campaigning in the Iberian Peninsula and elsewhere, or manning garrisons around the world. While the conflict in Europe raged, the war in North America remained a secondary struggle and received minimal reinforcements and resources. Some help came come from the Canadian militia, whose role was to augment the British regulars, but as the militiamen lacked training and equipment, the defence was borne by a handful of British regulars. This situation was further worsened by the fact that the loyalty of many American immigrants, recently new to Upper Canada, was in doubt. The United States also had 10 times the population of British North America, which gave them the ability to recruit and concentrate forces far quicker than the British. In the face of these odds, many in the British camp believed the province would quickly fall.[3]

Given its limitations, Britain adopted a defensive strategy in North America, seeking to hold the line and avoid expansion of the conflict until the end of the war in Europe. Large-scale reinforcements could then be sent to Canada, allowing the commencement of offensive operations against the Americans. These were the instructions the Prince Regent gave to Lieutenant-General Sir George Prevost, the governor general and captain general of British North America in 1811.[4] And, they were faithfully followed until June 1814, when new orders signalled a switch to the offensive.[5]

Despite their advantages, the first six months of the war went poorly for the Americans. They suffered from many difficulties including inexperience in formulating and executing strategy, a lack of adequate field leadership, and the problems that come from rapid wartime expansion, including provision of dress, equipment, and proper training. This resulted in a number of spectacular defeats during 1812, including Fort Mackinac in July, Fort Detroit in August and Queenston Heights in October.

Not everything, however, went wrong. Commodore Isaac Chauncey, the American commander on the Great Lakes, assembled a naval squadron at his base at Sackets Harbor, New York, and chased the British Provincial Marine off Lake Ontario, which gave him control of the lake at the close of 1812. The Americans then sought to exploit this success in the following year.[6]

During the winter of 1812–13, Commodore Chauncey and Major-General Henry Dearborn, commander of the northern frontier, planned for the coming campaign season from their base at Sackets Harbor. Their instructions came from Secretary of War John Armstrong, who envisaged several amphibious operations against three objectives around Lake Ontario. To do this, 4,000 regular troops were sent at Sackets Harbor, where as many as possible would board Chauncey's ships and cross the lake to destroy the fortifications and shipping at Kingston, before seizing supplies from the provincial capital of York and destroying two ships they believed to be under construction. The final operation would be directed against Fort George and Fort Erie, destroying the British military presence in the Niagara Peninsula. By the termination of operations, the Americans believed the British would be ready to participate in talks that the Americans would easily dominate.[7]

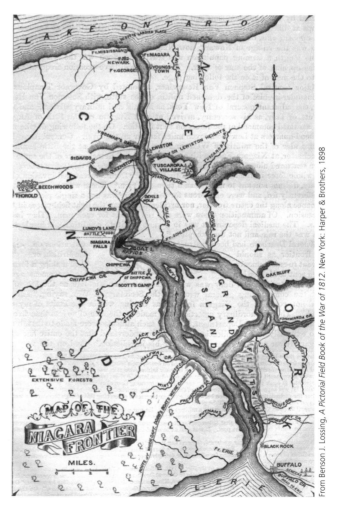

The Niagara Peninsula formed the cockpit of the northern theatre and scene of continual fighting during the War of 1812. During 1813, this became particularly bitter and included the destruction of Newark, Queenston, and Fort Erie, while the American frontier became a wasteland.

From Benson J. Lossing, *A Pictorial Field Book of the War of 1812*. New York: Harper & Brothers, 1898

As soon as this plan was approved, it began to unravel. In February 1813, the British swept the last American regulars away from the Upper St. Lawrence theatre, following an attack on Ogdensburg, New York. The Americans feared Sackets Harbor might be attacked next by forces being collected at Kingston. American commanders believed wild reports that 4,000 British regulars were forming up in Kingston and they cancelled their plans to attack it. As a result, the Americans decided that York would be the first objective, then Fort George and, once that was completed, Kingston would be attacked.[8]

American operations around Lake Ontario commenced in the spring of 1813 and proved successful, at least initially. In the early morning of 27 April, the first elements of 1,700 regular troops, carried in 13 warships and smaller craft began landing to the west of York. The Americans quickly gained a beachhead, forcing the meagre garrison under Major-General Roger Sheaffe, the victor of Queenston Heights, to withdraw towards the fort. Around noon, Sheaffe determined he could not hold the fort or the town and decided to retreat with the surviving regulars to Kingston. Before departing, he ordered the fort's main magazine to be blown up and the storehouses destroyed. The charges went off just as the Americans approached, bringing debris down on the Americans, killing 38 men outright and wounding 222. Among the dead was Brigadier-General Zebulon Pike, commander of the land forces. The outcome may have not been completely as desired, but the Americans had achieved their first major victory of the war, while demonstrating significant improvements in the quality of their forces by mounting their largest joint operation to date.[9]

Battle losses and sickness forced the Americans to return temporarily to Sackets Harbor, but within a few weeks they were ready again, and on 27 May 1813 Chauncey's squadron appeared off the northern end of the Niagara Peninsula to support the landing of 4,000 men carried in 140 smaller craft. Opposing them were just over 1,000 British regulars supported by 350 Canadian militia and 50 Native warriors. Overwhelming naval firepower allowed the Americans to rapidly establish a beachhead and then press inland towards Fort George. The British commander, Brigadier-General John Vincent, like Sheaffe a month earlier, realized the situation was hopeless, but unlike Sheaffe had developed a plan for just such a contingency. He ordered his entire command to evacuate the frontier and rendezvous at Beaver Dam before retiring to Burlington Heights, which afforded an excellent defendable position. Fortunately for Vincent, the Americans did not pursue him, choosing instead to consolidate their position around Fort George. Vincent briefly contemplated moving to York, but as this would threaten communications with Major-General Proctor's forces near Detroit and bring the complete evacuation of the Niagara Peninsula, he decided to remain where he was. The Americans may have taken Fort George, but Vincent's army was still intact.[10]

By early June, two American brigades moved off for Burlington Heights and by 5 June were encamped in a field at Stoney Creek. They had 3,000 men and were supported by Chauncey's squadron. On Burlington Heights, Vincent approved Lieutenant-Colonel John Harvey's proposal to stage a bold night attack against the Americans. Harvey took 700 men, about half the troops available, and reached the American camp in the early hours of 6 June 1813. There followed a frantic, quick action, creating considerable havoc. The British captured three guns and took two general officers prisoner, and then withdrew back to the heights.[11]

Earlier, while the Americans advanced towards Burlington Heights, even more dramatic events were unfolding on the eastern end of Lake Ontario. Lieutenant-General Sir George Prevost arrived in Kingston on 15 May 1813, in order to get a better feel of the situation. When he learned that the American squadron was at the western end of the lake, Prevost decided to attack the American naval base. Eight hundred men from the Kingston garrison boarded the vessels of the naval squadron, now led by Commodore James Lucas Yeo and manned by sailors from Royal Navy, and set of for Sackets Harbor on 27 May. The troops landed west of the harbour in the early morning of 29 May. Lacking artillery and with limited naval gunfire support, the assault force advanced a mile through obstacles and enemy fire to a point just short of the dockyard. A difficult fight ensued in the vicinity of several buildings. Prevost, who had accompanied the attack, became unsure the dockyard could be reached. Fearing Chauncey might arrive off the harbour unexpectedly, Prevost ordered a withdrawal, just as his senior officers believed victory was at hand.

Chauncey was indeed en route, having learned earlier that the British were off Sackets Harbor. He arrived at his base on 1 June and was relieved to find the hull of his new ship was intact, but was shaken enough to remain at his base until that ship was completed, thus handing control of Lake Ontario to the British for two months.[12]

At Kingston, Prevost then ordered Commodore Yeo to load his vessels with ammunition, supplies and reinforcements and sail to Vincent's aid. Yeo left Kingston on 3 June and after stopping at York, continued to Niagara. Four days later, he captured 16 boatloads of supplies bound for the Americans. Yeo also spotted an American camp at Forty Mile Creek, east of their former position at Stoney Creek. Yeo closed in, and his ships bombarded the Americans. Yeo then went ashore and met Vincent who described the action at Stoney Creek. He explained that although the British had been repulsed, the Americans were in such disorder in the attack's aftermath that their new commander, Colonel James Burn, decided they should withdraw to Forty Mile Creek.[13] Vincent and Yeo planned to strike them, only to discover that they had disappeared. General Dearborn had decided to consolidate his forces and ordered them back to Fort George. The last American troops from Forty Mile Creek arrived at Fort George on 10 June.[14]

Other detachments in the Niagara were also ordered to Fort George. At the southern end of the peninsula, Fort Erie was burned on 9 June, while Chippawa was also abandoned. The southern end of the Niagara Peninsula became a no man's land as troops moved into Fort George, where preparations commenced for a siege. Meanwhile, Vincent advanced cautiously from Burlington Heights to Forty Mile Creek and sent a detachment to reoccupy a forward depot at Beaver Dam. Reinforcements also arrived from Kingston, while Yeo intercepted supply-laden bateaux and schooners destined for American occupied Fort George.

Prevost took advantage of the lull in the fighting to make some changes and replaced Major-General Sheaffe with Major-General Francis de Rottenburg as commander of Upper Canada on 19 June. He also reorganized the province into three geographic divisions, with the area from York to the Niagara River becoming known as the Centre Division under General Vincent.[15]

The American difficulties continued. An attack on Beaver Dams on 24 June failed, bringing to an end Major-General Dearborn's command of the northern theatre that July. Brigadier-General John Boyd temporarily held the post until a new commander could be appointed. Boyd was also instructed to "engage in no affair with the enemy that can be avoided." He had little choice. From having gained control of almost the entire Niagara Peninsula, the American's were reduced to holding a small corner of it centred on Fort George and Newark. Their forward picquets went no further than Two Mile Creek. The Americans had 6,600 men around Forts George and Niagara. They were opposed by 4,400 British regulars and militia, while Commodore Yeo was intercepting their supplies.

There were continual skirmishes and raids all along the frontier, including a failed amphibious raid on Burlington Heights and another raid on York in late July. A large attack planned against de Rottenburg was stopped by the arrival of Yeo. The raiding took on a viciousness that not only witnessed the usual destruction and seizure of public property, but grew to include private property as well.[16]

Sir George Prevost arrived in the Niagara frontier on 21 August. At that time there were 2,883 British troops blockading Fort George. Prevost issued instructions for a large "close reconnaissance" to determine the enemy's strength. The British attacked on 24 August and pushed through five out of the six American piquets (also "pickets"), coming within artillery fire of Fort George but not close enough for musket fire, and entering the town of Newark, before being ordered back. In a situation similar to the attack on Sackets Harbor, Prevost, called off the attack, believing, in this case, it would require siege artillery and simultaneous attacks on both Fort George and Fort Niagara to succeed.

Many of the officers and men thought differently and questioned his tactical skill. Prevost hastened back to Kingston while de Rottenburg considered besieging Fort George, but the position was too strong and naval support could not be guaranteed. On 4 September, Major-General James Wilkinson finally arrived at Fort George, directing his attention not to the situation there, but to reinforcing Sackets Harbor and preparing for a new major offensive aimed at taking Montreal. In October, he left for Sackets Harbor with 4,000 regulars, leaving 1,800 men, many of them sick, at Fort George. De Rottenburg responded by withdrawing from Fort George and sending reinforcements to Kingston.

Then on 9 October, he learned of the British defeat at Moraviantown in southwestern Upper Canada. Fearing the Americans cut him off from the head of the lake, he terminated the blockade of Fort George and withdrew to Burlington Heights. Once again there were very few British troops between Fort George and Burlington Heights and the initiative went back to the Americans.[17]

When Wilkinson had left for Sackets Harbor in October, he left Colonel Winfield Scott in command at Fort George, while Brigadier-General George McClure was appointed overall commander. The forces present now included Scott's U.S. 2nd Artillery Regiment, some Natives, and 1,500 New York militiamen. McClure had immigrated to the United States from Ireland and after working in several trades, commenced a successful career in local politics that brought appointments as a judge of the Surrogate Court and brigadier-general commanding a brigade of New York State militia.[18]

What McClure lacked in experience was made up for in zeal, bravado, and arrogance. Aided by similarly minded subordinates, he obtained permission from the Secretary of War to enlist up to 1,200 men, who pledged their lives to capture, destroy, or expel the whole of the enemy's force from the peninsula before the season was over. On 11 October, 1,110 men left Fort George to execute this plan. Movement was difficult as many of the bridges had been destroyed and many roads obstructed by felled trees. McClure was unable to maintain discipline and his troops plundered the local populace. Getting no further west than Twenty Mile Creek, McClure headed east, eventually arriving at Chippawa, before returning to Fort George carrying property and plunder of every description.[19]

On 13 October, Colonel Scott was ordered to take most of the remaining regulars to Sackets Harbor, leaving McClure in command of 60 regular artillerymen and infantry, plus 1,500 unreliable New York militiamen. Aside from two companies of the 1st Artillery at Fort Niagara, there were no other regular troops between the Detroit River and Sackets Harbor. The defences were now left to volunteer militia whose term of service would expire at the end of the year.[20]

At the end of October, Major-General Harrison arrived at Fort George from Detroit with 1,000 regulars. They had recently fought at Moraviantown and after being diverted from their next objective on Lake Huron by bad weather, were sent to the Niagara frontier. Harrison agreed to join McClure's attack on Burlington Heights. Commodore Chauncey then arrived and met with Harrison at Newark on 15 November to discuss the situation. The British were withdrawing from Burlington Heights to Kingston and nothing would be gained by attacking an abandoned outpost. On the other hand, Chauncey continued, it was imperative to reinforce Sackets Harbor, which had been undefended since Wilkinson's army had gone down the St. Lawrence for Montreal. Chauncey's base was now threatened from Kingston. Harrison agreed and on 16 November, he embarked 1,100 men onto the ships and headed for Sackets Harbor. Once again, the militia were left holding the frontier.[21]

During this time, McClure sought to determine British intentions and was aided by a unit that would prove valuable. In July 1813 General Dearborn authorised the formation of the Canadian Volunteers, a mounted unit made up of Canadians sympathetic to the American cause. Leading them was Major Joseph Willcocks a former member of the Legislative Assembly of Upper Canada. Within a few days of receiving approval to raise the unit, Willcocks recruited 52 men and went about scouting throughout the Niagara, providing the Americans with fairly accurate information on British troop movements and plans. The Canadian Volunteers continued to grow in strength, as did the hatred directed at them by loyal Canadians and the concern by military and civilian authorities in Upper Canada over their activities.[22]

Harrison was sufficiently impressed by Willcocks to urge McClure to employ him, particularly in dealing with civilian matters in the American occupied area around Newark. McClure readily accepted this recommendation and appointed Willcocks as "police officer" for Fort George and Newark, giving him control over the movement of all local citizenry. Willcocks readily accepted the appointment and "seems to have unleashed a miniature reign of terror" on the Niagara Frontier. He arrested and imprisoned many people for spying. Patrols were also continually mounted to look for any signs of movement by the British.[23]

The general belief that the British were abandoning Burlington Heights and withdrawing eastward to York, or even Kingston, was a consequence of the Battle of Moraviantown. On 10 September, the Americans defeated the British naval squadron on Lake Erie, throwing open the flank of Major-General Proctor's Right Division at Amherstburg and forcing him to withdraw to the northeast, along the Thames River. Major-General William Harrison's 3,000 strong Army of the North West followed in hot pursuit. On 5 October, after a poorly managed retreat, Proctor made a stand at Moraviantown and lost most of his 800 men. The first reports received by Vincent, de Rottenburg, and Prevost, were twisted by the outrageous claims of Lieutenant John Reiffenstein, a former regular officer now serving with the Lower Canada militia. John Richardson, a 15 year old volunteer with the 41st Foot, described him as a "little red faced, yellow haired, obese German." As Reiffenstein rushed eastwards, he made "false reports and speculations upon the extent and consequence of Major-General Proctor's defeat ... and have created the greatest alarm." By 17 October, Reiffenstein was in Montreal and told Prevost that 10,000 to 12,000 American troops were advancing on Burlington. This led to a series of decisions that almost had the British abandon Burlington Heights and with that the Niagara Peninsula.[24]

Vincent faced the prospect of being encircled by Harrison and McClure. The Americans controlled Lake Erie and could land anywhere along the southern shore of Upper Canada, while further to the east, it was uncertain whether Wilkinson's army at Sackets Harbor was going to strike at Kingston or elsewhere in Upper Canada. Reiffenstein's "erroneous intelligence" led to conflicting orders from Prevost and de Rottenburg. Vincent was ordered to remove "all stores, provisions and other incumbrances [sic] to York, preparatory to falling back with the troops to that place" and "continuing your retreat towards" Kingston. A large quantity of "public property," including all varieties of stores, clothing, and blankets were destroyed as there were too few bateaux and wagons to move stores and the sick. At Twelve Mile Creek several cases of muskets were left behind. More accurate reports received by the end of October revealed that Reiffenstein's claims were completely false. Burlington was not threatened, while Wilkinson had now moved towards

Montreal, ending the threat to Kingston. Vincent was instructed to retain "possession not only of York but of Burlington." Eight hundred troops would be posted at Burlington. Vincent was to ensure the enemy did not "establish himself at any point betwixt Burlington and Fort George" and was to send "detachments of troops towards the Niagara frontier as a preparatory step to the re-occupation of that territory and the expulsion of the enemy therefrom." The military balance was about to shift once more, this time in favour of the British.[25]

Before leaving Fort George, Harrison confirmed McClure's appointment as commander at the fort and reinforcing the instructions given to him earlier. McClure was reminded to "keep a vigilant eye over the disaffected part of the inhabitants," and to employ Colonel Willcocks and his men to gain intelligence. He also gave a warning to ensure Willcocks did not oppress friends the Americans had gained among the population. The British were withdrawing to York and Kingston, but they might retain some presence on Burlington Heights. Harrison told McClure, it would be "desirable to have any supplies they may have collected in the neighbourhood destroyed."[26]

It was now McClure who suffered from faulty information regarding his opponent. He dismissed claims made by a British deserter that 1,500 men were at Burlington Heights, calling them "magnified." He was concerned that the British were now "reinforcing, fortifying, and building barracks, whereas "at one time" they "appear[ed] to be sending down their stores and detachments of troops to York." McClure immediately sent 200 militiamen "to penetrate the enemy's lines as far as practicable" and planned to send a second, larger party out. He also hoped to recruit locals into the ranks and gain the sympathy of the remainder by distributing broadsheets calling for their support.[27]

Reports from the patrols and the Canadian Volunteers told a chilling tale. Mounted patrols under Colonel Willcocks had gone as far of the head of the lake, within sight of the British piquets at Stoney Creek. They confirmed the British had "twelve to fifteen hundred regulars and nine hundred Indian warriors" and were not destroying their stores and moving towards York; they were in fact preparing to winter on Burlington Heights and Stoney Creek. McClure was eager to act against them and attack, however his "force was insufficient for that object," while the weather was making large-scale movement difficult. McClure had other problems as well. The term of service for the drafted would expire in three weeks and their discipline was eroding. The volunteers also had to be kept active; otherwise they would go home, leaving no one to defend the frontier at a time when it faced the "imminent danger of invasion."[28]

Given the seriousness of the situation, McClure was authorised to use whatever measures necessary to "insure the protection of Fort George and the Niagara Frontier until other means of defence can be provided." McClure was authorized to offer additional bounties, which he believed would secure another "one or two months" service. Governor Tompkins called for "officers, non-commissioned officers, and musicians" to march to Fort Niagara. McClure also tried to convince some of Britain's Native allies to join him. None of these efforts achieved the desired results.[29]

To his credit, McClure continued sending expeditions towards Burlington. These were nowhere near as grand as previous ones, but they did secure some 400 barrels of desperately needed flour.[30]

Then, late in the afternoon of 29 November, British piquets reported one of Willcocks' patrols near Stoney Creek. Colonel John Murray, a British regular officer who had been posted to Canada in 1811 and appointed an inspecting field officer of militia, was sent out with an advance guard hoping to encounter that "enterprising and obnoxious partisan" near Forty Mile Creek. Murray led 379 men, one 5 1/2-inch howitzer and a 6-pounder gun from the Royal Artillery, a troop of the 19th Light Dragoons, 340 men from the 100th Foot, 20 volunteers, and 70 Natives. He also had 14 soldiers from the Provincial Dragoons, a Canadian unit led by Captain William Hamilton Merritt and comprised of locals who volunteered to serve on a more permanent basis than the militia. These men were intimately familiar with the area and held a grudge with the Canadian Volunteers. Willcocks avoided any engagement and McClure abandoned his latest expedition, retiring to the safety of Fort George.[31]

McClure's command was getting smaller with each day. By 6 December he had no more than 200 regular troops, many of them sick, and about 100 Natives, but their total fluctuated daily. Three days later the militia draft ended and they "re-crossed the river almost to a man returning to the United States," leaving McClure with 60 effective regulars of the 24th Infantry and 40 volunteers. To make matters worse, Murray was closing in. Commodore Chauncey could not help, as his vessels had been hauled into winter moorings on 9 December, and the harbour was already frozen over. As a result, on the morning of 10 December McClure called a council with his principal regular and militia officers at Fort George. They all agreed "the fort was not tenable with the remnant of force left in it" and McClure gave orders "for evacuating the fort."[32]

Immediately, work began to move stores, light artillery and anything else to Fort Niagara. This was a Herculean task, worsened by there being only three boats. Heavy ordnance was thrown into the ditches around the fort and the magazines destroyed. Before leaving, McClure wanted to ensure the "enemy were completely shut out from any hopes of wintering in the vicinity of Fort George." In accordance with orders received from the secretary of war, McClure ordered the town of Newark to be burned to the ground.[33]

McClure based this decision on a letter from the secretary of war addressed to the "Commanding Officer at Fort George," dated 4 October 1813, which provided provisional instructions for the defence of Fort George:

> Understanding that the defence of the post committed to your charge may render it proper to destroy the town of Newark, you are hereby authorised to apprise its inhabitants of this circumstance and invite them to remove themselves and their effects to some place of greater safety.[34]

McClure had consulted with his council of war. They had agreed that to deprive the British of winter quarters and to force them to withdraw to Stoney Creek or Burlington Heights such drastic action would be necessary. As a result, McClure ordered the town to be burned, but only after his men ensured the houses were unoccupied, believing most "were generally vacant long before."[35]

Newark lay about three-quarters of a mile northwest of Fort George. It was established in 1791 and was the provincial capital until 1796. On the eve of the War of 1812, it had 80 homes, a courthouse, churches, and shops, and a population of about 500 people.[36] On 10 December 1813 as the evacuation of Fort George was underway the inhabitants of Newark were given 12 hours to remove themselves and any property from their residences. After that, the town would be torched. That duty was given to Willcocks' Volunteers, "who only seemed too glad to obey" and take vengeance on their opponents. Efforts to stop Willcocks' men were in vain and Newark was set aflame. The flames attracted Murray's scouts, who rushed into the village and managed to kill two of Willcocks' men and capture several others before the remainder escaped across the river. Word of the disaster was sent to Murray at Twelve Mile Creek who immediately ordered a "rapid and forced march" to relieve the villagers from a "merciless enemy." He was "determined to attack … that night." A violent snowstorm reduced visibility and hampered their movement, but Murray urged his men to move as quickly as possible on their sleighs. Their unexpected movement may have caused McClure to hasten his men and "evacuate Fort George by precipitately crossing the river and abandoning the whole of the Niagara frontier."[37]

Murray was impressed by the "indefatigable exertions of this handful of men" as they raced on. His light troops reached the burning village around 9:00 p.m. and found several women and children by the roadside, "suffering from terror and dismay." Newark was in ashes, "a ruin, nothing to be seen but brick chimney standing." Altogether, 80 structures were destroyed and 400 people were homeless, but the fortifications of Fort George were intact, "evidently so strengthened … as might have enabled General McClure to have maintained a regular siege."[38] The arsenal "had been burnt to the ground" and the principal magazine blown up, several temporary magazines were intact and the fortifications had not been damaged.

The speed of the American departure was evident as "the whole of his tents were left standing." The snow and darkness made it impossible to see the heavy ordnance in the ditch and on the following day, one long 18-pounder, four 12-pounders, two 9-pounders, "an immense quantity of shot," and camp equipage for 1,500 men was collected. The guns were immediately employed "on a more important purpose," while patrols were sent out, with Captain Kerby and his men moving south to reconnoitre as far as Fort Erie.[39]

Once back on the American shore, McClure expected the British would soon attack and requisitioned another draft of 1,000 men from the state militia, while Captain Nathaniel Leonard, the senior gunner present, was given command of Fort Niagara. The garrison in the fort included two companies of artillery and two companies of the 24th Infantry. McClure also sent a detachment of the 7th New York Artillery to Lewiston to destroy the buildings at Queenston, depriving the British of their shelter. The gunners used "hot shot," solid spherical metal rounds that were heated until they glowed and quickly loaded into the guns before being fired. The red-hot rounds hit several buildings, which immediately caught fire and a large part of Queenston was lost.[40]

Official reaction to the destruction of Newark was immediate. On the American side, Governor Tompkins regretted the destruction and feared swift retaliation from the British, which would be directed against his state. McClure insisted his orders authorized him to destroy the town, but Armstrong disagreed. The secretary of war called it a "great error" and was angered by McClure, since his orders "were to burn it if necessary to the defence of Fort George but not otherwise." It had been agreed that Fort George would be razed if it were to be abandoned; instead McClure left the fort intact and burned the town. General James Wilkinson was ordered to write Sir George Prevost and publicly disavow McClure's conduct.[41]

For the British and Canadians, there was elation with the re-occupation of Fort George and outrage over the burning of Newark, an act that Lieutenant-General Drummond, the newly appointed commander of Upper Canada, called "barbarous and unjustifiable." He wrote Brigadier-General McClure asking if "this atrocious act had been committed by the authority of the American Government ... or an individual." McClure chose not to reply. Drummond could not let this pass; "retributive justice demanded of me," he wrote, "a speedy retaliation on the opposite shore of America."[42]

Drummond's appointment to Upper Canada resulted from Prevost's dissatisfaction with de Rottenburg's performance. Drummond arrived in the Niagara on 16 December and he brought new energy and an offensive spirit to his command. He also believed conditions favoured an immediate attack on Fort Niagara. He would do more than that and within two-weeks, Drummond not only got his vengeance, but also achieved what Major-General Isaac Brock had desired in the first weeks of the war: the destruction of American forces and fortifications along the Niagara frontier.[43]

The day after taking command, Drummond decided to storm Fort Niagara by direct attack — a daring and dangerous endeavour. Fort Niagara had several formidable stone structures within its walls that could prove difficult to take. If Fort Niagara were to be secured, these structures would have to be taken quickly, because losses and worsening weather conditions might not allow another attempt. The assault had to be carefully planned and made in consultation with Royal Engineer officers, who held the technical expertise on fortifications. There were few of these officers available and the best were with Wellington in the Iberian Peninsula. Those engineers deemed unfit for service in Europe "considered as quite good enough for the Canadian market." The only one available to the Right Division was Lieutenant Freidrich de Gaugreben, of the King's German Legion Engineers, who was deemed an officer of questionable ability. Nonetheless, Colonel John Murray, the officer appointed to lead the attack, sought de Gaugreben's views "in suggesting arrangements previous to the attack and securing the fort."[44]

Fort Niagara was situated on an elevated triangular piece of land, forming a peninsula that had Lake Ontario on its northern side and the Niagara River to the west. The main defences were placed on the landward approach along the southeastern face of the fort. By 1813 these included a pair of half bastions connected by a thick earthen "curtain" or straight wall, fronted by a dry ditch. Opposite the ditch was a triangular earthen outer work known as a "ravelin," that gave added protection to the main wall. A two-storey redoubt constructed of limestone was placed within each half-bastion. These strong self-contained "forts within a fort" were Fort Niagara's main defences with roof level serving as an elevated gun platform, while the interior had space for a guard of 20 men. Access to the North Redoubt was through a small door on its western side, while the South Redoubt was pierced by the gateway, which the French named

A view of Fort Niagara looking east from the Niagara River, 1814. The South Redoubt is on the extreme right, while the gate Murray's forlorn hope entered on 19 December 1813 is on the centre right.

"Gate of Five Nations." This gate was sealed up before the War of 1812 and replaced by a less elaborate gate placed in the middle of riverside wall of the fort.[45]

The remaining walls ran atop the bluffs of the riverbank and the lakeshore, considered far less likely as an avenue of approach. They were constructed of earth and wood that eroded continuously from the elements, the lake and the river. There was at least one battery along the river wall, facing towards Fort George. With the creation of the international boundary along the Niagara River and the construction of Fort George, the British fortification threatened the weakest side of Fort Niagara. Fort Niagara had a small peacetime garrison before the war, making it difficult both to maintain and improve the fortifications. In 1812 the river walls were bolstered as they faced the main threat, from Fort George. After that, maintenance was haphazard. The interior of the fort had been cleared of many buildings and those remaining were constructed mainly of masonry and included the French Castle, the Red Barracks, which was used as a hospital, a magazine, storehouses, Mess House, and other buildings. All these structures were placed along the walls, leaving the centre of the fort open.[46]

It is uncertain how the 27 pieces of ordnance were distributed along the walls and redoubts during 1813. In report submitted later that year, Winfield Scott reported the number of guns mounted at Fort George, but said nothing of Fort Niagara, a peculiar oversight for an artillery officer. It is likely that each bastion had at least one brass 6-pounder gun each, easily capable of hurling a spherical round weighing six pounds at Fort George, 1,200 yards away. There was also one gun atop the Mess House.[47]

The plan presented to Colonel Murray was a risky one. It would be an all or nothing assault — for if it failed, the resulting casualties would make an immediate second attempt impossible. The troops would gain additional cover by going at night, which meant artillery support was impossible. Silence was the absolute key to success, which demanded the strictest discipline from the troops. Several bateaux recently brought from Burlington Heights by James Kerby contribute to the surprise as the crossing of the Niagara River was to be made in "two embarkations." Mounting a "silent" assault also meant the muskets "must on no account be suffered to load without the orders of their officers." Silence, speed, and reliance "chiefly on the bayonet" were to be the key elements of the attack, and the fort was to be taken by "escalade," that is by using scaling ladders to get the men up and over the walls and into the fort. Drummond instructed Murray to ensure his men brought axes for bashing in doors along with 18- and 20-foot scaling ladders that would be divided among the attacking forces to scale the walls of Fort Niagara.

To split the defences, Murray was told to strike at two points, one on lake face of the fort and the other along the riverbank. The troops allocated to Murray included 350 men from the 100th Regiment of Foot, 100 grenadiers from the 1st Foot, 100 men from the flank companies of the 41st Regiment and 12 men from the Royal

Lieutenant-General Gordon Drummond (1772–1854) took command of Upper Canada in December 1813 and quickly ordered the capture of Fort Niagara and the destructive raids along the American frontier. In the spring of 1815, he replaced Prevost as governor of British North America and returned to Britain in 1816.

Author's Collection.

Artillery, giving a total of 562 men, just slightly more than the garrison of Fort Niagara.[48]

The evacuation of Fort George put Fort Niagara back into the American front line. After crossing the Niagara, General McClure scurried off for Buffalo, leaving command of the fort to Captain Nathaniel Leonard, of the 1st Artillery. Almost every regular along the frontier had been left to defend it — 324 personnel present with another 45 absent for various reasons. This amounted to one company of artillery and three of infantry. Before leaving, McClure warned Leonard that the British might attack and expressed confidence in his "long experience and knowledge of duty." He added that Leonard would be "well supported by ... the artillery ... and the officers of infantry."[49]

Existing garrison orders specifying the positions troops would occupy in an emergency were dusted off and updated on 13 December. If the walls and redoubts became untenable, the defenders were to fall back on the stone buildings within the fort, namely the two redoubts and the Mess House. A drum beating "retreat" would signal the move. Most of the troops would move into the Mess House, while 20 men under Captain Frank Hampton of the 24th Infantry would occupy the South Redoubt. If required, the guard detachment at the guardhouse would join them; otherwise they would remain at their post. Fifty men under Lieutenant Adam Peck, also of the 24th, would hold the North Redoubt. The gunners initially manned two positions, one in the south bastion and a "Marine Battery" on the northern side of the fort. Once ordered to retire, they would disable their ordnance and "instantly man the guns" in the redoubts.[50]

Leonard believed that although the British might make it past the walls, they would be unable to take the three buildings. Loopholes in the redoubts offered excellent fields of fire that would pin down any potential assault. If the British did reach the walls, grenades would be hurled down upon them. It was a reasonable plan, based upon an expectation that infantry unsupported by artillery would conduct the assault. Leonard had his men rehearse the plan several times. During one such practice, a squabble over seniority erupted and Lieutenant Carey Trimble replaced Peck as commander of the North Redoubt, but otherwise all the preparations seemed complete. Vigilance was established initially, but appeared to wane because of the cold.[51]

Across the river, it was impossible to conceal preparations for the assault and the Americans continued to receive reports of the British activity around Fort George. McClure, before his departure, used the threat of invasion to stir the local populace, telling the inhabitants of Niagara, Genesee, and Chatauqua that the enemy were "preparing to invade" and "let their savages loose upon your families and property." He then asked that every able man take up arms to stop them. He warned that those who chose not to would be "inhumanly butchered, their property plundered and their buildings destroyed," by the enemy, "who are now laying waste to their own country." The results were mixed and some men came forward, while others took their families away from the frontier.[52]

Murray assembled his men at St. David's and at 10:00 p.m. on 18 December, began marching silently through the woods and descended a bank to a narrow beach where two or three boats awaited them. General Drummond and his staff were there, bidding the men luck as they filed by. Once the boats were loaded, militia volunteers navigated them across the river, which was accomplished without incident.

Captain James Kerby was apparently the first man to land at Five Mile Meadows, about three miles above the fort. The first elements ashore then found shelter around a farmhouse and waited for the remainder to be ferried across the river. Once everyone was across, the scaling ladders and stores were loaded onto a confiscated wagon and they marched off quietly, with arms shouldered, down the "dirty, muddy ... half frozen" River Road towards Fort Niagara[53]

About three quarters of a mile from the fort, the advance party arrived at the hamlet of Youngstown and came across a cluster of houses occupied by a detachment from the fort, supported by an artillery piece. The sentries were nowhere to be seen as they had moved indoors to stay warm. Several British soldiers crept forward to one of the buildings. Looking through an open window, they saw a group of officers playing cards. When one of the officers asked, "what's trump?" a soldier cried out "bayonets are trump!" as he smashed in the

Courtesy Bernd Horn.

The "French Castle" was the original sole structure of Fort Niagara. It is the oldest building in North America's Great Lakes area and is seen here restored to its 1727 appearance.

window. Several men rushed in through the door, while the remainder surrounded the building. Within a few minutes the assailants cleared all the buildings, conducting their "work of human destruction in grim silence" as everyone was put to the bayonet; an act one British officer later described as, "a lamentable but necessary act." Not a shot had been fired, as "there was no time for resistance."[54]

The silent march towards Fort Niagara then continued. As they approached the fort, Murray divided his men into three columns for the assault. The main attack would be led by Colonel Murray and directed against the main gate and adjacent works. A second column was to "storm the eastern demi-bastion" (the North Redoubt), while the third column would escalade the salient angle, that is the wall forming the centre of the land defences.[55]

Getting into a fort was the most difficult part of any assault and Murray relied upon the traditional "forlorn hope" to get the initial foothold. The forlorn hope was made up of experienced soldiers led by a junior officer who volunteered, as a result of a promise of promotion or money should they succeed and survive, for the dangerous duty. The 20 volunteers were led by Lieutenant Irwin Dawson of the 100th Foot, who was no stranger to bold or unusual actions, having participated in the capture of the American sloops *Eagle* and *Growler* on Richelieu River the previous June. Captain John Norton, a Native chief and officer of the Indian Department also accompanied the forlorn hope.[56]

Behind Dawson came the grenadier company of the 100th Foot under Captain Richard Fawcett and the 12 men of the Royal Artillery, under Lieutenant George Charleton. Each of the gunners carried grenades. Behind them were the remaining five companies of the 100th under Lieutenant-Colonel Christopher Hamilton, a firebrand of an officer who had lost a leg many years earlier in Holland. Unable to accompany his men on foot, he insisted on having a horse ferried across the Niagara, which was achieved "with great difficulty. The flank companies of the 41st Foot under Lieutenant Richard Bullock were posted along the flanks of the column. Bullock was an experienced officer, having participated in several battles during 1812 and 1813.[57]

The North Bastion was to be taken by three line companies of the 100th under Captain John Martin, while the grenadiers of the 1st Foot led by Captain Charles Bailey were to assault the salient angle. Each of the detachments had guides from the Lincoln Militia, including Captain James Kerby and Lieutenants John Ball, Daniel Servos, and Hamilton.[58]

It was still dark when Irwin Dawson's party moved up the hill towards the main gate. They found the wicket was open, apparently to allow an American soldier in. Sergeant Andrew Spearman, a large and powerful man, immediately stepped into the darkness and was approached by the sentry. Mimicking an American "twang," Spearman responded to the challenge "Who comes there?" with "I guess Mister, I come from Youngstown." The sentry hesitated and Spearman used the delayed reaction to his advantage, slipped his upper body into the wicket and bayoneted the man before he could cry out a warning. The remainder of the forlorn hope surged through and onto the parade square. They were in. It was approximately 6:30 a.m.,[59] an hour before dawn, 19 December 1813.[60]

The two other columns reached the walls at about the same time. Martin's group quickly entered the northern end of the fort, and secured the North Redoubt before Lieutenant Trimble and his men could react. At the main wall between the two redoubts, Captain Bailey and his 100 grenadiers faced no resistance.[61]

The main British column followed the forlorn hope into the fort, either by moving through the gate, or by scaling the walls. Once inside, they wheeled left towards the Mess House, which lay along the wall just past another building known as the Red Barracks. As they moved along, fire suddenly erupted from the Red Barracks, as the wounded and sick patients from within engaged the attackers. The British soldiers rushed into the building and again made work with their bayonets, "despite the cries for quarter." Within moments they were gone, leaving those within "nearly all slaughtered" as one civilian described, and continued onto the Mess House, which fell without a fight. Colonel Murray moved through the gate at this time and was immediately hit with musket fire, giving him a severe wound to the arm and forcing him to transfer command of the assault to Lieutenant-Colonel Hamilton.[62]

When the main column had begun its attack on the Mess House, a "heavy and galling fire" erupted from the South Redoubt. The 6-pounder gun atop the redoubt hurled solid shot at the men in the open, while musket fire issued form the loopholes in the wall. It is unknown whether Captain Hampton reached the redoubt before the door was bolted shut, but there were enough men inside to lay down "an incessant tho' random fire." Captain David Davies, commanding No. 4 Company of the 100th Foot turned to Lieutenant-Colonel Hamilton and volunteered to lead what Hamilton would later call "one of the most dashing attacks of the morning" against the redoubt. Davies led his 37 men company towards the redoubt, using the north wall of a storehouse beside the redoubt for cover. Once they reached the end of the building, they paused momentarily to catch their breath and then rushed towards the redoubt, only to be repulsed. Five men were killed and two wounded. Davis retired his men to the shelter of the storehouse and turned to a prisoner that had been dragged along, threatening the man with death if refused to guide them to the tower's entrance. The man quickly agreed to help.[63]

Davies waited until the firing ceased. Judging the Americans were reloading their weapons; he turned to his men and shouted, "Follow me, my boys," and sprinted across the 40-foot space from the storehouse to the base of the redoubt. They door was located and within minutes, it was battered down by soldiers using sledges and large billets of wood brought along for the job. As they plunged into the darkness inside the redoubt, they were met by a group of Americans who had been firing through the loopholes. A clash of steel and musket fire followed and the defenders were forced to flee up to the next level. As Davies' men pursued them, they had to move their way through the dead and wounded on the ground and stairway. Among them was Lieutenant Maurice Nowlan, "a very promising officer" and one of the first to enter the redoubt. He now lay at the bottom of the stairs, his body pierced by a deep bayonet wound, as well as the effects of one musket ball and three buckshot wounds.[64] At his feet lay an American, "killed by a pistol shot, while the cloven skulls of two others attested his strength of arm and desperate valour." The men rushed up the stairs, some of them carrying large firebrands, "from which they blew sparks and flashes," illuminating the way "up the intricate stairs." Some men called to those outside to scale the walls with the ladders they had brought. Facing a difficult fight in the tight space on the second floor, Davies ordered his men to "bayonet the whole," which had the desired effect. Cornered, the defenders feared they would be killed outright, and all 64 men surrendered.[65]

Outside there was chaos as the fort was secured. Some Americans attempted to flee. Near the Red Barracks, one American subaltern and 20 men escaped by scaling the pickets. Another group tried escaping by way of the covered sally port in the South Redoubt, but were stopped by Lieutenant Edward Murray of the 100th Foot, who had them lay down, while he and his men protected them from any further harm. By now all remaining resistance within the fort had ceased. The British had taken Fort Niagara in a short and sharp action taking no longer than 30 minutes to complete.[66]

In all 65 Americans had been killed and 14 wounded. Including losses from the encounter near Youngstown, the total number of Americans killed was approximately 80. Fourteen officers and 330 men were also taken prisoner and escorted back to York. British losses included Lieutenant Nowlan and five privates of the 100th killed, while Colonel

Murray, Assistant Surgeon Alexander Ogilvie of the Ordnance Medical Department, two men of the 100th, and one of the 41st wounded.

In the aftermath, eight Canadians and several Natives taken prisoner earlier in campaign by the Americans were released. They told their liberators the Americans were expecting an attack and had been on alert for several nights, however, on this night, they believed the alarm was over and let their guard down as the "whole garrison had indulged themselves in retiring to rest." Captain Leonard had left the fort to visit friends two miles away. When he heard the firing, he hurried back and arrived after it was all over, only to be taken prisoner by the British sentry who now guarded the entrance to Fort Niagara.[67]

The British also captured a vast quantity of stores, supplies, and ordnance: 29 pieces of artillery; 7,000 muskets; rifles; and other ordnance stores "so immense" that it took time to compile a complete account. They also found 7,000 pairs of shoes and clothing belonging to the 8th and 49th Regiments, captured on their transports on Lake Ontario in June 1813. According to reports compiled afterwards, over $1 million in property was taken.[68]

The seizure of so much American public property was good news to the troops. All those present were entitled to rewards or prize money once the legality of the seizure was confirmed. By regulation, each soldier was entitled to a certain number of "shares," based upon rank, ranging from a single share for a private soldier, five for sergeants, 20 for lieutenants, and 150 for colonels. As an incentive, those who actually participated could receive more. A private would then have five shares, a corporal eight, a sergeant 12, and officers up to lieutenant-colonel paid by the next higher rank level. Variations also existed based on local regulations and militia troops were not always granted higher-level share privileges. So much public property had been taken that three separate payments were issued for the capture of Fort George and other actions along the frontier. The first dividend totalled £7,287 and was paid out to 3,324 shares, allowing roughly £2 per share. James Kerby of the Lincoln Militia, who escorted one of the columns, received £36; Colonel Murray, who led the attack and was wounded, received £240, and Lieutenant-General Drummond was paid £160. The largest payments went to the 1st, 41st, and 100th

Foot, with £1,449 being paid out to the latter regiment. A second dividend paid out £7,097, while a third of £2,651 was sent to the Royal Hospital Chelsea, a type of retirement home for soldiers. It is difficult to express the value of this money in modern currency, but for everyone involved, whether private, corporal, sergeant, or officer, this represented a handsome sum.[69]

Shortly after Fort Niagara fell, General Drummond rode through the gate and found soldiers from the 100th Foot dancing on the barrack rooftops. He immediately called for the forlorn hope to be formed up on the square and thanked them all warmly for what they had achieved. Drummond was also presented with the large, 24-foot by 28-foot, 15-star American flag that had flown over Fort Niagara. He had it sent to England where it was presented to the Prince Regent. Drummond was allowed to keep the flag and the Drummond family retained it in Scotland until 1994, when it was returned to Fort Niagara and is now on display at the Old Fort Niagara Visitor Centre.[70]

Taking Fort Niagara was only the beginning to Drummond's campaign. Earlier that night, Major-General Riall crossed the Niagara with 1,000 regulars and 500 western Natives in order to ravage the village of Lewiston. After crossing the river, they awaited a signal to proceed. A single shot fired by an artillery piece confirmed Fort Niagara had fallen and Riall ordered his men towards Lewiston. The 300 men defending the town withdrew without firing a shot, and the village was then sacked and burned. Riall's men also took two guns, some small arms, nine barrels of powder, and 200 barrels of provisions. Several villagers were killed and at least two scalped by the Natives. Drummond's appeal to the Native chiefs to avoid scalping had little effect. The British force then moved northwards and the villages of Youngstown, Manchester, Tuscarora, and Schlosser suffered the same fate. At Schlosser, the Canadian Volunteers attempted to check Riall but were unable to save the depot. Riall then returned to Lewiston and crossed the river over to Queenston.[71]

Alarm and fear now spread throughout the western part of the state. Governor Tompkins ordered Major-General Amos Hall of the New York State militia to replace McClure and within a few days, he had concentrated 2,000 men around Buffalo and Black Rock. Drummond

Library and Archives Canada C-121163.

Period artwork depicting *A Soldier's Wife at Fort Niagara* during an artillery exchange with Fort George.

intended to disperse them, so they could not recover Fort Niagara or continue "his atrocious system of laying waste our peaceful frontier." He ordered the destruction of the "villages of Buffalo and Black Rock in order to deprive the enemy of the cover which" they afforded.

As a result, on 29 December the British landed 1,400 men[72] above and below Black Rock. The militia below the town fled at first contact, while Hall tried to stop the others. The militia broke and fled, while the Canadian Volunteers charged Riall's men several times, but to no avail. Hall ordered the remaining defenders to withdraw. When the British moved forward, they found two 24-pounder cannon, three 12–pounders, and one 9-pounder. With the defenders dispersed, Buffalo was then sacked and put to flame.[73] The schooners *Ariel, Little Belt, Chippawa,* and *Trippe* were also destroyed along with a large quantity of stores. The British troops marched back to Black Rock, and returned to Canada. They brought 53 prisoners and several horses, needed by the Royal Artillery to haul guns. British losses totalled 112 killed and wounded. Fort Erie was also reoccupied and Lieutenant de Gaugraben commenced work on improving the fortifications. Satisfied with the results, Drummond then ordered his troops into winter quarters, although aggressive patrols continued to penetrate western New York until January 1814. Altogether, these attacks turned 25 miles of frontier into a wasteland.[74]

The American attempt to destroy the British presence in the Niagara had failed. Despite a good start the capture of Fort George proved their last success of the year. Their plan failed for a variety of reasons. Although considerable effort had gone into preparing the attack on Fort George, subsequent arrangements were made haphazardly. Once the Americans withdrew back into Fort George in June, the British established a blockade, while the American regular forces were bled off, largely in response to illusory threats to Sackets Harbor. This left the Niagara Frontier to be guarded by the New York State militia, which, led by an inexperienced general officer, was a task beyond their training and experience. Most of the senior leadership — Armstrong, Wilkinson, Harrison, and Scott — were drawn elsewhere, while McClure and Hall were far from competent. McClure's destruction of Newark and Queenston could not be defended, while Captain Leonard was criminally negligent for failing to carry out his responsibilities professionally. It is somewhat ironic that the most capable defenders the Americans had positioned in this theatre were a group of renegade Canadians.[75]

The British committed errors as well, but boldness favoured them. The raid on Sackets Harbor and the attack at Stoney Creek were risky but paid excellent dividends. Moraviantown created a difficult situation that almost led to the loss of the Niagara peninsula. Once that was corrected, Vincent was back on the offensive, sending Colonel Murray to probe the American defences. Drummond acted decisively and re-established control of the Niagara Peninsula. Prevost praised the "brilliant manner" by which his plans were executed. Riall performed will too, but his experience resulted in his misjudging American soldiers the following July.

Civilians also found themselves thrust into a new reality. The people of Lewiston, Black Rock, and Buffalo paid dearly for the army's mistakes, while McClure's burning of Newark forced President Madison and Secretary of War Armstrong to go out of their way to ensure the British understood that act resulted from the "misapprehension of one officer & not an order from the government." Prevost blamed the Americans as "the enemy set an example ... by firing the town of Newark ... that has produced calamitous consequences to himself." While confessing his disgust in a letter Lord Bathurst, the secretary for war and the colonies wrote, "Painful is such retribution ... I have felt the authority most repugnant and I sincerely hope it may not again be excited." Unfortunately, whatever sentiments the commanders on either side shared, they were not realized and the destruction of villages continued as the war entered its third and bloodiest year.[76]

As 1813 ended, the Americans held Amherstburg and the Detroit frontier; they controlled Lake Erie, but the Union Jack still waved over every location of the "extended frontier." The Niagara peninsula was reclaimed, Fort Niagara taken, Kingston and Montreal no longer threatened, while the entire 50-mile length of the Niagara Frontier from Youngstown to Buffalo was devastated "for the miseries inflicted upon the inhabitants of Newark."[77]

NOTES

1. Lieutenant-Colonel Harvey to Colonel John Murray, 17 December 1813. E. Cruikshank, ed. *The Documentary History of the Campaigns Upon the Niagara Frontier, in 1812–1814, Vol. 9* [henceforth DH] (Welland: Lundy's Lane Historical Society, 1908), 3.

2. The literature on the causes of the war is vast. One of the best sources for the American perspective is J.C.A. Stagg. *Mr. Madison's War: Politics, Diplomacy, and Warfare in the Early American Republic, 1783–1830* (Princeton: Princeton University Press, 1983), while Reginald Horsman's "The Causes of the War of 1812" (Philadelphia: nd, 1962) offers a good, brief examination of the main causes. The literature from the British perspective is not as extensive, with Robin Reilly's *The British at the Gates: The New Orleans Campaign in the War of 1812* (Toronto: Robin Brass Studio, 2002) being the best, and J. Mackay Hitsman's *The Incredible War of 1812: A Military History* (Toronto: Robin Brass Studio, 1999), offers a good general overview of the key points.

3. John R. Grodzinski. "The Vigilant Superintendence of the Whole District: The War of 1812 on the Upper St. Lawrence," Royal Military College of Canada, MA Thesis, 2002, 34–39.

4. British North America included the Provinces of Upper and Lower Canada, New Brunswick, Nova Scotia, the Island of Prince Edward, Cape Breton, Newfoundland, and the Bermudas.

5. Hitsman, 41. The 1814 instructions appear at 289–290.

6. Hitsman, 68–103. For naval aspects, see Robert Malcomson, *Lords of the Lake: The War of 1812 on Lake Ontario* (Toronto: Robin Brass Studio, 1998).

7. Malcomson, 83–85.

8. In May 1813, the British garrison at Kingston totalled 541 regulars and anywhere from 267–400 militia. Grodzinski,147–48; and Malcomson, 88.

9. Malcomson, 106–108.

10. Malcomson, 125–26; and Hitsman, 144.

11. Malcomson, 147; and Hitsman, 150.

12. Malcomson, 129, 135, 138, 141, 146.

13. The shoreline of Lake Ontario was pierced with a series of creeks, named after their distance from the Niagara River. Several of these, such as Twelve Mile or Twenty Mile Creeks, offered suitable defensive positions. John N. Jackson. *Names Across Niagara* (St. Catharines: Vanwell Publishing, 1989), 13–16.

14. Hitsman, 151; and Malcomson, 148–49.

15. DH, Vol. 6, General Orders, Kingston, 19 June 1813, 97. *Ibid.*, General Order, Kingston, 15 June 1813, 87. Hitsman, 151.

16. DH, Vol. 6, Secretary of War to General Boyd, 7 July 1813, 201; Hitsman, 178.

17. DH, Vol. 7, Memo by Lieutenant-Colonel Glegg, 24 August 1813, 58; *Ibid.*, General Order, 23 August 1813, 52–54; DH, Vol. 6, The Secretary of War to General Dearborn, 6 July 1813, 187; Jon Latimer, *1812: War with America* (Cambridge: Belknap Press, 2007), 194; Lieutenant-Colonel E. Cruikshank, *Drummond's Winter Campaign, 1813*, 2nd ed. (Welland ON: Lundy's Lane Historical Society, 1900), 3; Wesley B. Turner. *British Generals in the War of 1812: High Command in the Canadas* (Montreal and Kingston: McGill-Queen's University Press, 1999), 39.

18. Cruikshank, *Drummond's Winter Campaign*, 9. Major-General de Rottenburg to Sir George Prevost, 11 November 1813.

19. John Armstrong. *Notices of the War of 1812, Vol. 2* (New York: Wiley and Putnam, 1840), 39; Cruikshank, *Drummond's Winter Campaign*, 10.

20. Colonel Winfield to the Secretary of War, 31 December 1813. *American State Papers, Military Affairs, Vol. 1* (Buffalo: William S. Hein & Co. Inc., 1989), 483; Hitsman, 193.

21. DH, Vol. 8, Major-General de Rottenburg to Sir George Prevost, 11 November 1813, 151; Cruikshank, *Drummond's Winter Campaign*, 11; *Ibid.*, , General McClure to General Harrison, 15 November 1813, 181; *Ibid.*, General Harrison to General McClure, 15 November 1813, 191; *Ibid.*, General Harrison to the Secretary of War, 16 November 1813, 204; *Ibid.*, Commodore Chauncey to the Secretary of the Navy, 21 November 1813, 224.

22. Donald E. Graves. "Joseph Willcocks and the Canadian Volunteers: An Account of Political Disaffection in the Upper Canada During the War of 1812." (MA Thesis, Department of History, Carleton University, 1982), 41–42, 45, 47, and 54.

23. Graves, 54.

24. DH, Vol. 8, Major-General de Rottenburg to Sir George Prevost, 16 October

1813, 68–69; *Ibid.*, General Order, Montreal, 18 October 1813, 82–83. Sandy Antal; and *A Wampum Denied: Proctor's War of 1812* (Ottawa: Carleton University Press, 1997), 358.

25. DH, Vol. 8, Major-General de Rottenburg to Major-General Vincent, 23 October 1813, 88; *Ibid.*, Major-General de Rottenburg to Major-General Vincent, 1 November 1813, 117; *Ibid.*, Major-General de Rottenburg to Colonel Baynes, 26 November 1813, 237.

26. "General Harrison's Orders to General McClure, 15 November 1813, *American State Papers*, 484.

27. General McClure to Secretary of War, 17 November 1813. *American State Papers*, 484.

28. Brigadier-General McClure to the Secretary of War, 21 November 1813, *American State Papers*, 485; DH, Vol. 8, Governor Tompkins to Major-General Hall, 28 November 1813. 240–241.

29. Secretary of War to General McClure, 25 November 1813, *American State Papers*, 485; Mr. Parker, Chief Clerk War Department to General McClure, 27 November 1813, *American State Papers*, 486; and DH, Vol. 8, General McClure to Governor Tompkins, 6 December 1813, 253.

30. General McClure to the Secretary of War, 21 November 1813, *American State Papers*, 485; DH, Vol. 8, General Order, Headquarters, Newark, 30 November 1813, 244.

31. DH, Vol. 8, Return of the Troops Comprising the Advance of the Right Division of the Army under Colonel Murray, 273; Stuart Sutherland, *A Desire of Serving and Defending my Country: The War of 1812 Journals of William Hamilton Merritt* (Toronto: Iser Publications, 2001), iii.

32. DH, Vol. 8, General McClure to Governor Tompkins, 6 December 1813, 253; General McClure to the Secretary of War, 10 December 1813, *American State Papers*, 486.

33. General McClure to Secretary of War, 10 December 1813, *American State Papers*, 486.

34. United States National Archives, RG 107, Micro 6, Reel 7, Vol. 7, Armstrong to Commanding Officer at Fort George, 4 October 1813, 98.

35. Graves, 62; DH, Vol. 8, General McClure to the Secretary of War, 10 December 1813, 263.

36. At this time, the population of York was 684 and Kingston 1,000.

37. Graves, 63; Cruikshank, *Drummond's Winter Campaign*, 15; DH, Vol. 8, Colonel John Murray to Major-General Vincent, 12 December 1813, 270; *Ibid.*, Lieutenant-General Sir Gordon Drummond to Sir George Prevost, 6 December 1813, 259; *Ibid.*, General McClure to the Secretary of War, 10 December 1813, 262; *Ibid.*, Colonel John Murray to Major-General Vincent, 12 December 1813, 270; and Sutherland, 15.

38. Graves, 63; and Cruikshank, *Drummond's Winter Campaign*, 15.

39. DH, Vol. 8, Colonel John Murray to Major-General Vincent, 12 December 1813, 270; *Ibid.*, Colonel John Murray to Major-General Vincent, 13 December 1813, 275; E.A. Cruikshank. *A Memoir of Colonel the Honourable James Kerby, His Life in Letters* (Welland: Welland County Historical Society, 1931), 28; Cruikshank, *Drummond's Winter Campaign*, 16.

40. Robert S. Quimby. *The U.S. Army in the War of 1812: An Operational and Command Study* (East Lansing: Michigan State University, 1997), 356; and Cruikshank, *Drummond's Winter Campaign*, 16.

41. DH, Vol. 9, General McClure to Governor Tompkins, 20 December 1813, 25. Graves, 64–65, 67.

42. DH, Vol. 8, General Order, Headquarters, York, Upper Canada, 14 December 1814, 277; and *Ibid.*, Lieutenant-Colonel Harvey to Brigadier General McClure, Commanding the American Forces in Fort Niagara, 14 December 1814, 278.

43. DH, Vol. 8, Proclamation, Upper Canada, 13 December 1813, 276; Malcomson, 234. Lieutenant-General Gordon Drummond was born in 1772 and joined the army in 1789. By 1794 he was commanding the 8th Foot and saw active service in the ill-fated Netherlands expedition of 1794–95. In 1799 he took his regiment to the Mediterranean and participated in the Egyptian campaign in 1801. In 1804, he was promoted brigadier-general and was a major-general in the following year. During 1805–07, he was second-in-command in Jamaica, followed by a posting as second-in-command of Canada for three years. In 1811 he was promoted lieutenant-general and given a district command in Ireland. Two years later, he was selected to command Upper Canada. Biographical data from John Philippart. *The Royal Military Calendar, Vol. 2* (London: T. Egerton, 1815); Stuart Sutherland, *His Majesty's Gentlemen: A Directory of British Army Regular Officers of the War of 1812* (Toronto: Iser Publications, 2000), 129.

44. DH, Vol. 9, Colonel John Murray to Lieutenant-General Drummond, 19 December 1813, 12. Grodzinski, 205.

45. Brian Leigh Dunnigan and Patricia Kay Scott, *Old Fort Niagara in Four Centuries: A History of its Development* (Youngstown: Old Fort Niagara Association, 1991), 38–43; and Brian Leigh Dunnigan, *Forts Within a Fort: Niagara's Redoubts* (Youngstown: Old Fort Niagara Historical Association Inc., 1989), 15.

46. Dunnigan and Scott, *Old Fort Niagara in Four Centuries*, 40, 42.

47. Dunnigan, *Forts Within a Fort* 87; and DH, Vol. 9, Colonel Winfield Scott to the Secretary of War, 31 December 1813, 68.

48. *Ibid.*, Lieutenant-Colonel Harvey to Colonel John Murray, 17 December 1813, 3–4; Cruikshank, *Drummond's Winter Campaign*, 18; and Cruikshank, *James Kerby*, 28.

49. Dunnigan, *Forts Within a Fort*, 44.

50. *Ibid.*, 45.

51. Dunnigan. *Forts Within a Fort*, 45; and Walter Lowrie, ed. *American State Papers*, 394, 407, 487.

52. DH, Vol. 9, General McClure's Address to the Inhabitants of Niagara, Genessee and Chautaugua, 8.

53. Cruikshank, *James Kerby*, 29; and Carl F. Klinck and James J. Talman, *The Journal of Major John Norton, 1816* (Toronto: The Champlain Society, 1970), 345.

54. DH, Vol. 9, "The Capture of Fort Niagara, By One Who Served in 1814," Lieutenant Driscoll, 100th Regiment, 19; and Cruikshank, *Drummond's Winter Campaign*, 19.

55. *Ibid.*, 19.

56. Dunnigan. *Forts Within a Fort*, 45–46. Robert Malcomson, *Historical Dictionary of the War of 1812* (Lanham: The Scarecrow Press, Inc., 2006), 158; Klinck and Talman, 346; and Sutherland, *His Majesty's Gentlemen*, 119.

57. Cruikshank. *Drummond's Winter Campaign*, 19.

58. *Ibid.*, 18–19; Sutherland, *His Majesty's Gentlemen*, 53, 81, 96, 141, 178, and 257; William Gray, *Soldiers of the King: The Upper Canadian Militia, 1812–1815* (Toronto: Boston Mills Press, 1995), 134–36, 160.

59. Sunrise time based upon calculation provided by the Astronomical Applications Department of the U.S. Naval Observatory, accessed at *http://aa.usno.navy.mil/index.php*.

60. Dunnigan. *Forts Within a Fort*, 45–46; DH, Vol. 9, "The Capture of Fort Niagara, By One Who Served in 1814," Lieutenant Driscoll, 100th Regiment, 19; Sutherland, *His Majesty's Gentlemen*, 119; and Malcomson, *Historical Dictionary*, 158.

61. Dunnigan. *Forts Within a Fort*, 46.

62. *Ibid.*, 46; and DH, Vol. 9, "Deposition of Robert Lee," 17; and *Ibid.*, "Return of Killed and Wounded in an Assault on Fort Niagara," 13.

63. Cruikshank, *Drummond's Winter Campaign*, 19–20; and Dunnigan. *Forts Within a Fort*, 47–48.

64. The British musket fired a one-ounce ball, whereas the American weapons fired a slightly smaller round, to which was added three small buckshot balls to increase the hitting power, hence the term "buck and ball," to denote the typical volley fired by an American infantryman.

65. DH, Vol. 9, Colonel John Murray to Colonel Baynes, 17 April 1814, 298–300; Cruikshank. *Drummond's Winter Campaign*, 19–20; Dunnigan, *Forts Within a Fort*, 47–48; DH, Vol. 9, "The Capture of Fort Niagara, By One Who Served in 1814," Lieutenant Driscoll, 100th Regiment, 20; and *Ibid.*, Lieutenant-General Drummond to Sir George Prevost, 20 December 1813, 22.

66. DH, Vol. 9, "The Capture of Fort Niagara, By One Who Served in 1814," Lieutenant Driscoll, 100th Regiment, 20.

67. Cruikshank. *Drummond's Winter Campaign*, 20–21; Klinck and Talman, 346; Dunnigan. *Forts Within a Fort*, 49; and DH, Vol. 9, "Deposition of Robert Lee," 17.

68. Cruikshank, *Drummond's Winter Campaign*, 20–21; Cruikshank, *James Kerby*, 29; and DH, Vol. 9, Colonel Murray to Lieutenant-General Drummond, 19 December 1813, 12–13.

69. National Archives, Kew, London, "Regulations and Orders for the Army to 1st January 1816," 147–48; and *Ibid.*, "Niagara, Black Rock and Buffalo," WO/64/555, 1, 90, 109, 208.

70. Cruikshank. *Drummond's Winter Campaign*, 21. Details regarding the Fort Niagara Flag provided by the Old Fort Niagara Visitor Centre, Youngstown, New York.

71. Robert S. Quimby, *The U.S. Army in the War of 1812: An Operational and Command Study* (East Lansing: Michigan State University, 1997), 358. Cruikshank, *Drummond's Winter Campaign*, 28; and Graves, 67–68.

72. They were provided by the 1st Foot, 8th, 41st, 89th, 100th (grenadiers), 50 militia, and 400 Natives. See DH, Vol. 9, Major-General Riall to Lieutenant-General Drummond, 1 January 1814, 70.

73. It was later reported that the buildings destroyed included 66 wooden houses, two brick, one stone; 16 stores; and 15 shops. At Black Rock, 16 frame houses, 11 log homes, and eight barns were destroyed, while another 20 frame houses, 67 log homes, 29 barns, and 30 shops were destroyed elsewhere. See Cruikshank. *Drummond's Winter Campaign*, 29. DH, Vol. 9, Return of the Killed, Wounded and Missing ... 30 December 1813, 73.

74. Cruikshank, *Drummond's Winter Campaign*, 28; DH, Vol. 9, District General Order, 28 December 1813, 61; *Ibid.*, Lieutenant-Colonel Harvey to Major General Riall, 29 December 1813, 61–62; and D.A.N. Lomax. *A History of the Services of the 41st (The Welch) Regiment, from Its Formation in 1719 to 1897* (Davenport: Hiorns & Miller, 1899), 96n1.

75. Graves, 70.

76. DH, Vol. 9, Sir George Prevost to Earl Bathurst, 6 January 1814, 98–99.

77. Hitsman, 196.

4

"UNDER THE COVER OF DARKNESS": THE CANADIAN TRENCH RAID OF 8–9 JUNE 1917

Ken Reynolds

La Chaudière Military Cemetery is but one of a dozen or so military cemeteries lying within the shadows of Vimy Ridge. Located on the edge of the small, northern French village of the same name, most of the soldiers buried there are Canadian, some of them killed during the April 1917 fighting at Vimy, many of them victims of battles near the village in June of that year. A visitor to the Vimy Memorial on Hill 145 — just two kilometres away, up the ridge — can look down upon La Chaudière and out across the Douai Plain as a whole, north towards the cities of Avion and Lens, which lie in the distance. The landscape is dotted by coal slag heaps, some there during the 1917 offensive.

PLANNING THE RAID

It appeared that all the land below the ridge was abandoned by the Germans as they hurriedly retreated in the face of the Vimy onslaught in April. It is perhaps difficult, then, to believe that two months after the victory at Vimy Ridge Canadians would still be meeting their deaths in clear view of Hill 145. Yet they were, and for some fairly practical reasons. Eastward movement by the Canadian Corps slowed down immensely in the weeks after Vimy. The soldiers were exhausted; they were facing another line of German defences anchored south of Avion and Lens;

Author's Collection.

A view over the Douai Plain looking out towards Avion.

and much of the Corps' supporting artillery was withdrawn to support British operations in Flanders.

Originally, 1 Corps (British) had planned to attack the northern outskirts of Lens in May 1917, but this attack was postponed. Instead, I Corps and the Canadian Corps were ordered to push forward through the area surrounding the Souchez River — the British to the north, the Canadians to the south — in an attempt to break the enemy's defensive line between Avion and Lens.[2]

In mid-May, Canadian Corps' headquarters tasked its subordinate formations with pushing towards Avion. 4th Canadian Division, on the left front, was ordered to capture the village of La Coulotte and the area southwest of Avion. This resulted in attacks in late May and early June, the enemy responding with repeated counterattacks that were broken up by Canadian artillery and small arms fire.[3] Divisional headquarters described it as a period of "continuous aggression."[4]

Without more supporting artillery, however, it was becoming increasingly costly for the Canadians to hold these newly-captured positions. Lieutenant-General Julian Byng, commanding the Canadian Corps, met with Major-Generals Louis Lipsett, commanding 3rd Canadian Division, and David Watson, commanding 4th Canadian Division, 4 June to discuss options. Byng "pointed out that in view of the Artillery situation it was difficult to prevent the enemy from concentrating overwhelming artillery fire on any new trenches captured by us in that Area, and suggested that the object might be obtained equally well by carrying out the operations in the form of a big raid, i.e., the attack to be carried out exactly as planned in full strength to ensure getting in to the German trenches, and that after killing and capturing all the German garrison, destroying dugouts, machine-gun emplacements, etc. the troops should be withdrawn under cover of a Rear Guard. The whole operation to take place under the cover of darkness."[5]

Lipsett and Watson agreed. General Sir Henry Horne, commander of the First Army (the Canadian Corps higher formation), visited the

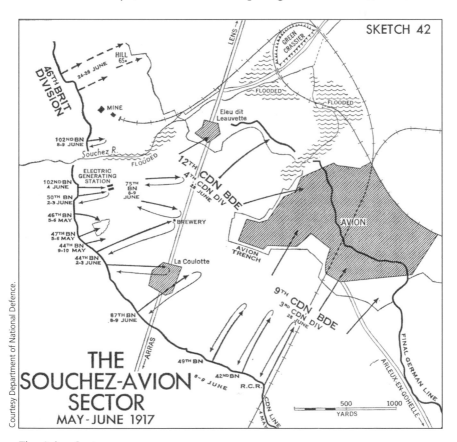

The Avion Sector.

Canadian Corps headquarters within an hour. He approved of Byng's idea. The "big raid" was on.[6]

First Army headquarters issued new orders for the two corps the following day. These noted the change in methodology. The orders already issued for the Canadian attacks south and west of Avion were now changed. The new direction clarified the attacks were to "be carried out as a raid on a large scale."[7]

Canadian Corps headquarters followed suit the same day: "The same objectives and boundaries between Divisions will hold good and the attack will be carried out as already planned, but after killing or capturing the German garrison, and thoroughly destroying dugouts, machine-gun emplacements, and all defences, the troops will withdraw to our Lines covered by Rear Guards." The 3rd and 4th Canadian Divisions were instructed to submit revised operation orders and to alter their practice schedule to incorporate the need for a "retirement, at night."[8]

Both participating Canadian divisions soon revised their plans.[9] The 11th Canadian Infantry Brigade, 4th Division, would conduct the raid on the left of the Corps' front using the 102nd, 75th, and 87th Battalions. On the right, the 7th Canadian Infantry Brigade, 3rd Division, would provide The Royal Canadian Regiment, the 42nd, and 49th Battalions. All six of these battalions had originally been tasked with carrying out the upcoming attack on the enemy's Avion defences. As a result, preparation for what was now a large-scale trench raid was already underway.

The 7th Brigade battalions had been in the rear area at Villers-au-Bois, a few miles west of Vimy Ridge, since 21 May, training for the upcoming attack. Just as at Vimy, taped trenches were set up "on the exact scale of the trenches to be attacked and various coloured flags were used to represent the [enemy] railway embankment, dugouts, machine-gun and trench-mortar emplacements."[10] Other soldiers slowly carried flags forward, mimicking the timings of the supporting barrage, allowing the practicing troops to get a better sense of the pace they would need to keep to maintain contact with their protective cover.[11]

Officers and men trained day and night, launching mock attacks over the taped course. New ideas were incorporated and, after the attack became a trench raid, the battalions modified the structure of their attacking sub-units, mainly into raiding parties. The regimental historian of The Royal Canadian Regiment later wrote: "No pains were spared to familiarize all ranks with the duties they would be called upon to perform."[12]

11th Brigade's participating battalions trained similarly. They, too, had recently pulled back, in their case to Chateau-de-la-Haie and Berthonval Wood, to train on another set of taped trenches.[13] Building on the Vimy Ridge experience, the 102nd Battalion also used a large map of the enemy position to explain the plan of the upcoming attack to the entire battalion.[14]

Although the six infantry battalions would supply all the raiding parties, they were not going in alone. The plan for the trench raid incorporated as much heavy weapons support as the Canadian Corps could provide, beg, or borrow. Artillery support for the raid included many field and heavy artillery batteries.[15] The artillery support for the 11th Brigade battalions, as an example, incorporated four brigades of Canadian, British,

Library and Archives Canada PA-648.

"Over the top" Canadians rehearse offensive operations in preparation of returning to the front.

and Australian field artillery, three 6-inch heavy batteries, and one 9.2-inch heavy battery.[16]

Initially, the field artillery barrage was to focus on the German front and support lines, before pushing ahead on timings to the reserve line and beyond. The plan called for continuous fire that would last for three hours after the launch of the raid. Part of this support was to include counter battery fire groups responding to enemy batteries with high explosive and gas shells.[17] The heavy artillery was to work on destroying the enemy's barbed wire the afternoon before the raid, while providing active support during when it was underway.[18]

Trench mortar batteries, including the 3rd Canadian Divisional Trench Mortar Group and the 11th Canadian Trench Mortar Battery, were also to form part of the supporting barrage with their 3-inch Stokes mortars,[19] as were the machine gunners of the 7th, 11th, 12th, and 15th Canadian Machine Gun Companies, their Vickers machine guns being deployed strategically to provide direct and indirect fire.[20]

THE ROYAL CANADIAN REGIMENT

The Royal Canadian Regiment, Canada's only regular infantry unit at the start of the war, held the right of the line during the raid. The battalion's orders tasked its raiders with attacking northward along both sides of the Lens-Arras railway line. On the western side of the railway, the objectives were the German front and support lines then, another 400 yards or so ahead, their reserve trench line. This third line also contained a strong point constructed among some ruined houses. Two raiding parties from "D" Company (Coy) were assigned these objectives, their combined strength numbering two officers, two platoons of riflemen, eight to 10 grenade-wielding bombers, two Lewis machine-guns crews, two ammunition carriers, and six stretcher-bearers.[21]

"C" Coy, on the railway's eastern side, was to supply another three raiding parties with orders to form a defensive flank in the enemy lines through the creation of trench "blocks" so as to prevent any German counterattacks. The three parties totalled three officers and about 90

Courtesy The RCR Museum and Archives.

A soldier from the RCR prepares to fire a trench mortar.

soldiers. The first party was the largest, and included one officer, nine bombers, four rifle grenadiers, 20 "moppers up" (troops responsible for clearing trenches and destroying dugouts), one Lewis gun and crew, two carriers, and three stretcher-bearers. It was not a glamorous role for the troops on the eastern side, but it was essential.[22]

The Royal Canadian Regiment marched into the front line on the evening of 7 June led by their temporary commanding officer, Major Charles Willets. Twenty-four hours later the battalion noted the beginning of the "show up north" (the 102nd Battalion's raid at 8:30 p.m.) and the "considerable retaliation by the enemy." The Germans also began firing on the battalion's trenches, enemy shells wounding nine "A" Coy troops. Finally, the barrage let up and the raiders moved forward into their jumping-off positions.[23]

Soldiers went into the line wearing "battle order," but left their haversacks in a pile behind the lines. The rifle grenadiers each carried 15 rifle grenades as well as two smoke bombs. Each of the bombers carried

15 grenades, while each carrier toted an additional two smoke bombs. Each "mopper up" carried five grenades and two smoke bombs, while, collectively, they were to carry up to 60 Stokes mortar bombs.[24]

Captain Charles Thompson, the senior officer participating, reported five minutes before the start of the raid: "all happy and Company in jumping off trench." For the next five minutes, the night reportedly turned "strangely quiet. A drizzle of cold rain was falling and the wind blew cheerlessly." Then the supporting barrage opened up, muzzle flashes lighting up the sky as shells roared towards the German trenches. The enemy responded immediately with red, orange, and green flares, all bursting into gold or silver stars, a frantic attempt to get their own artillery to respond.[25]

By this time the Canadians were already 10 minutes and dozens of yards into the raid. "D" Coy followed the barrage closely, reaching the first objective "safely and without resistance." Captain Thompson

A period illustration, *Leaving the Trench for a Raid*, by Lieutenant A. Sherriff Scott.

Author's Collection.

led the first raiding party into the front and support trenches, then the second party moved up and moved through towards the final objective. Thompson later reported that "everything was successful. Casualties light and mostly walking cases."[26]

Everything went according to plan for the battalion. The raiders occupied the trenches, then blew up enemy dugouts with Stokes bombs and grenades. Hand-to-hand fighting, described as "bayonet and bomb," formed most of the individual combat. The rifle grenadiers, meanwhile, targeted enemy snipers lurking in shell holes beyond the final objective. The battalion was quick to praise the supporting barrage, calling it "perfect," and noting the enemy wire was nearly non-existent, their trenches practically destroyed.[27]

"C" Coy, meanwhile, had already rapidly moved forward on the right of the railway line, taking each successive trench line and setting up its blocks. Early on, an enemy machine gun hidden underneath the railway embankment threatened the entire advance. Lieutenant Milton Gregg took charge, leading a flank attack with some bombers, and eliminating the obstacle. Sergeant William Deo led the company's bombers on a determined campaign to destroy every dugout in sight, his "great gallantry" earning him a Military Medal. Otherwise, the raiders had a largely uneventful evening, Captain John Woods later noted: "everything went splendidly. No prisoners and not many casualties."[28]

At 1:15 a.m. battalion headquarters launched a series of flares, signalling the end of the raid. The main body of raiders withdrew, followed by the covering parties half an hour later. "C" Coy suffered most of its casualties when German trench mortar shells landed as it withdrew down the communications trench to Canadian lines. At one point, Lieutenant Edward Davis fell, mortally wounded. Lieutenant Gregg, although wounded himself, picked Davis up and carried him back, completing an individual performance described by his commanding officer as "magnificent." Across the battalion's front, unit medical personnel treated the wounded and evacuated all but three fatalities. Casualties for The Royal Canadian Regiment would later be listed as 13 officers and men killed, two missing and presumed dead, and 54 wounded.[29]

42ND BATTALION (ROYAL HIGHLANDERS OF CANADA)

Lieutenant-Colonel Bartlett McLennan's 42nd Battalion was located in the middle of the 7th Brigade front, spread out along the line beginning seventy-five yards west of the railway and stretching about 500 yards to the north-west. As elsewhere, the 42nd's first objectives were the German front and support lines and the final objective the enemy's third defensive line, which was about 500 yards further ahead. Lieutenant-Colonel McLennan committed nine officers and 420 other ranks to the raid. "D" Coy and one platoon from "B" Coy were tasked with the first objective. "A" Coy and "C" Coy were then to leapfrog through and take the final objective.[30]

The Montrealers saw the evening of 8 June become "unusually dark with the sky heavily overcast and a drizzle of rain falling." They also remarked on the quiet that fell over the front after the attack to the north ended. The relatively few artillery exchanges, rifle cracks, and bursts of machine-gun fire "only served to intensify the stillness." By 11:30 p.m. all the raiders were in place in the jumping-off trenches, just 150 yards short of the enemy's front line.[31]

Fifteen minutes later the supporting barrage opened up, shattering the quiet. The German artillery response was aimed at Canadian trench lines the raiders had already vacated, well behind the jumping-off positions. Later praising the supporting barrage for destroying the enemy's wire, the 42nd also noted that the entrances to many dugouts in the first two enemy trenches were mostly destroyed, many of them containing a "considerable number of Germans who were reluctant to come up." Stokes bombs were dropped inside the entrances of the remaining dugouts, presumably sealing the fate of any enemy still inside. The supporting barrage was also so evenly paced that it shielded the 42nd's soldiers so well that they could drop down onto several enemy machine-gun nests before the Germans "could come fully into position."[32] Unfortunately, this tactic had a downside. Any shells falling short, or soldiers pushing too hard into the barrage, were bound to result in casualties, and the battalion later reported that the Canadian barrage caused seventy percent of its casualties that night. Yet, the 42nd was still happy with the supporting fire, realizing that anything else would have allowed the enemy positions to be "brought more fully into action and [would have] caused heavier casualties."[33]

The advance of "A" and "C" Companies to the final objective ran into stronger opposition than that encountered early on.[34] Sergeant Edward Greaves was tasked with taking out two machine guns on the left flank. Jumping into the enemy trench, he led four riflemen and bombers down the line, attacked both machine-gun nests, and killed all but three of their crews. Sergeant Greaves was severely wounded, but continued to help clear the enemy out of this portion of the trench. The small group bombed twelve dugouts in the process. Greaves was rewarded for his leadership and heroism with a Distinguished Conduct Medal.[35]

Elsewhere along the final objective, Sergeant William Bestwetherwick and Private Donald Macdonald were also earning honours. Sergeant Bestwetherwick single-handedly attacked three Germans, killing one and capturing the others, before assuming command of his platoon after his platoon commander was struck down. He was awarded a Bar to his Military Medal. Private Macdonald, a stretcher-bearer, gathered together a group of men separated from their sections and led them in clearing a section of the trench still held by the enemy. He was awarded a Military Medal for his actions.[36]

Overall, though, the enemy put up a "feeble defence" on the 42nd's front and both objectives were taken quickly and with light casualties. Most of the enemy — except their machine gunners — "either fled or surrendered easily." Battalion outposts were, nonetheless, pushed out beyond the final objective, watching for a possible German counterattack.[37]

Flares were launched at 1:45 a.m. marking the end of the raid. All the battalion's dead and wounded were retrieved and the raiders returned to battalion lines within forty-five minutes. The withdrawal as a whole was also helped by "two lines of white tape" strung from the final objective back to the jumping-off trench. There, another route was taped out, leading back to the nearest medical stations. Private Will Bird later commented that in the "dark they looked like pathways for ghosts." The battalion later commented that they "proved invaluable, not only for stretcher carrying parties but in enabling the raiding parties to get quickly back to their places in [the Canadian] support and second line trenches.[38]

The 42nd considered the raid the "most thoroughly organized and brilliantly carried out minor operation" it ever took part in. Decorations awarded to members of the battalion appear to reinforce this sense of satisfaction, perhaps including (without citations to some awards it is impossible to be entirely certain), one Bar to the Military Cross (for Major Samuel Mathewson), two Military Crosses, one Distinguished Conduct Medal, two Bars to the Military Medal, and eight Military Medals. An estimated 26 German prisoners and three machine guns were also captured.[39] Obviously, this came at a cost. By early morning on 9 June, the battalion was reporting an estimated 50 casualties suffered. These numbers were later revised to reflect six soldiers killed and 73 wounded.[40]

49TH BATTALION (EDMONTON REGIMENT)

The 49th Battalion's commanding officer, Lieutenant-Colonel Robert Palmer, lined up his raiding parties in a jumping-off trench about 150 yards ahead of the battalion's front line. The German front line trench meandered only 200 to 250 yards ahead of them, with the enemy's support line just another 50 yards farther in depth. These two positions formed the 49th's first objective. The final objective encompassed the enemy's third and fourth defensive lines, the latter being approximately 700 to 800 yards from the jumping-off position.[41]

The Edmonton unit took over its "battle front" during the night of 7–8 June and quickly began making last minute preparations for the raid. Each raider was issued special equipment and two days of rations. All four rifle companies were ordered to participate in the raid, three out of four platoons in each company getting the task. In total, 14 officers and 514 other ranks were to go over the top.[42]

German artillery fire harassed the soldiers in their final preparations for the raid, "considerable" enemy shelling causing a handful of casualties to "A" Coy as it began to move forward. However, by 10:30 p.m. "A" and "B" Companies were in the front line, where they would begin the raid.

"C" and "D" Companies then moved through, arriving in the jumping-off trench a little over an hour later. Meanwhile, the already hazy sky began to produce a light rain, as a light wind blew and visibility worsened.[43]

When the barrage began at 11:45 p.m. "the men went over the top like clockwork." Four minutes into the raid the first German artillery shells landed along the battalion's front. Unfortunately, so did some of the supporting artillery barrage. The 49th found the supporting barrage very difficult to follow, noting a "considerable number of shells" were consistently falling short and causing many casualties. The advance continued, nonetheless, the battalion maintaining contact with the 42nd's raiders on the right, while attempting to do likewise with those from the 87th Battalion on its left.[44]

Despite the apparent problems with parts of the supporting barrage, the gunners were doing a masterful job on the enemy positions. The German front line was badly damaged, the entrances to the dugouts "being nearly earthed up." Little German opposition was encountered and a few prisoners were taken. For good measure, two Stokes bombs were thrown into each open dugout entrance "causing no doubt a good deal of trouble to any of the enemy who were a little slow in leaving their dug-outs." The German support line was "practically demolished and in places unrecognizable as a trench."[45]

The first objective in hand, "A" and "B" Companies leapfrogged forward to the final objective. Again, little opposition was met with, the trenches "practically destroyed" and a few more prisoners were taken before the final objective was consolidated just 21 minutes after the launch of the raid. However, the Edmonton battalion suffered at least one setback when an enemy machine gun "which apparently had escaped the moppers-up of the 87th" began firing on "D" Coy's left flank back at the first objective. Lieutenant John Downton led the charge against the machine gun and "succeeded in stopping its fire," but was killed in the process.[46]

At the final objective, Canadian soldiers stood in what had been the enemy's reserve trench and observed as "fairly large numbers" of Germans ran ahead of the pursuing barrage. Soon after, evacuation of the 49th's wounded began, the few German prisoners being used as stretcher-bearers. At 1:15 a.m. "A" and "B" Companies, minus the covering parties, began to withdraw. The enemy barrage now increased in strength, unfortunately, and the 49th suffered more casualties as it pulled back. Lieutenant George Kinnaird, severely wounded at this point, noted the "moppers-up were mopped up." Half an hour later the covering parties pulled out, "cleaning up casualties as they did so." "C" and "D" Companies began to withdraw around 2:00 a.m., "searching the ground for any casualties that had been missed."[47]

The night sky, the conditions of the ground, fatigue, and the "fog of war" likely all played a part in the fact that not all of the battalion's dead and wounded were recovered. The battalion concluded that most of the missing men had been in trenches and "must have been buried by shell fire." When the final, postwar numbers were tallied, 16 members of the 49th Battalion remained on the battlefield.[48]

In total, the battalion reported 25 officers and men killed, 15 missing, and 132 wounded. The 49th also reported an estimated 200 German troops killed and 35 taken prisoner, their trenches destroyed, their wire demolished, and 20 dugouts blown up by Stokes bombs.[49]

87TH "OVERSEAS" BATTALION (CANADIAN GRENADIER GUARDS)

On 7 June Lieutenant-Colonel James O'Donahoe issued orders to his 87th Battalion for the upcoming operation. The purpose of the trench raid was straightforward and was meant "to inflict casualties, obtain identifications, destroy strong points, dugouts and trenches."[50]

Like the 49th to its right, the Montreal battalion's plan called for three platoons from each of its companies to carry out the raid. "B," "C," and "D" Companies were each tasked with advancing on a frontage half a platoon wide, three waves of two lines each deep. "A" Coy would provide a platoon to each of the three lead companies as a fourth wave to mop up.[51]

The 87th's raiders had two main objectives. The first wave was to capture the German front and support trenches south of La Coulotte and immediately south of Fosse 7 (a local pit and coal works). The second objective belonged to the second wave and consisted of the enemy's third defensive line running east of La Coulotte. The third wave of raiders were then to push up the western part of this line towards the northeastern outskirts of the village and enemy positions at some farm buildings north of Fosse 7. The "C" Coy soldiers assigned the latter target were to use their Lewis guns, rifles, and flares to make the "enemy think this line is being held and consolidated." The fourth wave was ordered to mop up in the territory between the enemy's support trench, the third defensive line, and Fosse 7.[52]

Orders governing the raid noted the raiders would not wear their webbing, but would wear their box respirators, and that bayonets would be fixed on their Lee-Enfield rifles. Details were also given as to what each "type" of raider would carry besides the basic requirement, 50 rounds of small arms ammunition and a full water bottle. Each rifleman was to carry an additional 10 grenades, every other rifleman, a smoke grenade, and every third rifleman a mobile charge. The bombers were equipped in a similar manner, with each carrying two extra grenades and one smoke grenade. Each rifle grenadier was to carry two grenades, 12 rifle grenades, and two rifle smoke grenades. Finally, although each Lewis gunner needed only to bring two grenades, he and his crew were also burdened with 20 magazines for each gun.[53]

The 87th launched its raid on schedule, battalion headquarters noting: "Our men got away in fine style." Almost immediately, the supporting barrage was answered by a German barrage from their 77-millimetre (mm) field guns. Throughout the raid the Montrealers reported seeing various colours of enemy flares being launched to relay information about the Canadian raid and coordinate the artillery response to it.[54]

The first wave reached the enemy front line 16 minutes into the raid. Here, the soldiers of "D" and "B" Companies saw the "very considerable damage" done to the enemy trenches by their supporting barrage. Numerous dugouts were laid waste, their entrances collapsed. The surviving enemy garrison was then either killed or captured. Meanwhile, members of the battalion's scout section moved around, gathering documents and unit identifications to aid the overall intelligence situation.[55]

The enemy support line was "fairly heavily held," but resistance there also collapsed under the weight of the 87th's attack. German trench mortar and machine-gun fire was gaining strength but the latter appears to have been aimed too high and "caused little damage." The difficulty of facing enemy machine-gun fire in the dark of night cannot be easily dismissed. The raiders even encountered a machine gunner wearing not only his steel helmet, but also a "steel jacket." Canadian machine-gun fire also seems to have been aimed too high and, on the right flank, the troops reported seeing bullets ricocheting off the buildings in Fosse 7. The 200 drums of burning oil projected into that area as part of the supporting barrage had, according to the 11th Brigade, "a marked moral effect, but the physical effect was not material, the oil burning up too instantaneously."[56]

The darkness, the battalion later reported, combined with the "difficult nature of the ground and buildings" made it difficult for the raiding parties "to maintain formations and cohesion." Yet, the 87th's moppers-up reportedly "showed great initiative and courage in entering enemy works and dugouts, and in close fighting."[57] Lieutenant George Morris's name was highlighted by brigade headquarters as having "engaged an enemy machine-gun crew putting all, excepting one man, out of action, the latter being captured and sent back, together with the gun, for the purpose of identification."[58]

By 12:30 a.m. the second and third waves had covered the next 500 yards and reached the final objective. Here, some troops continued to push forward, others cleaned up the position, and yet others protected the flanks. The battalion history later recorded that "coolness and persistence of individuals was a feature of the exploit. One of ours on entering a dugout faced a German officer about to drink a cup of tea. He held the German up at revolver point, drank the tea, frisked the prisoner of papers containing useful information, and brought them away."[59]

During the raid the 87th estimated it had inflicted 300 enemy casualties and captured about 100 more, along with four machine guns and two "Granatenwerfers" (grenade launchers). The battalion also reported destroying 10 dugouts, including one concrete installation.[60]

The battalion considered its part in the raid a "complete success: a classic example of perfection in planning and execution," and was especially delighted with the "spirit of resourcefulness shown by the individual soldier" during the operation. Naturally, this spirit came at a cost and the battalion lost 26 soldiers killed, nine missing, and 104 officers and men wounded.[61]

75TH (MISSISSAUGA) BATTALION

Orders for the 75th Battalion were issued by Lieutenant-Colonel Colin Harbottle on 7 June, revising those previously issued for an all-out attack. The Mississauga unit was also tasked with skirting La Coulotte to the west, northwest, and north. The battalion's first objective included the enemy front and support lines, trenches surrounding the Central Electric Generating Station northwest of La Coulotte, and a sunken road running northwest towards the Souchez River.[62] The battalion's second, and final, objective called for it to move around La Coulotte to a German trench line north of the village, pushing forward to link up with the 87th's raiders northeast of the village. This goal also included the Brewery compound on the Lens-Arras Road and its surrounding area.[63]

Nine platoons drawn from "A," "C," and "D" Companies were to carry out the raid, each company pushing forward three waves. It is not clear what specific equipment the raiders were carrying, but the short duration of the operation was emphasized through instructions to leave mess tins behind, rolled up in their greatcoats during the raid. In addition, the raiders were ordered to take "great care" while assembling so "that no movement is observed from the enemy lines. This is of the most serious importance, as discovery of assembly will undoubtedly result in disaster."[64]

This sense of foreboding was well-founded and it was a deadly wait for some soldiers as the clock ticked down to the raid. Between 8:00 and 9:30 p.m. on 8 June the 75th lost 38 soldiers killed and wounded as the enemy laid down a barrage on the front and support lines.[65] Private John Becker, "D" Coy, was in the front line when the enemy shells began to land. He later wrote: "Shrapnel flew in all directions. Powder smoke became nauseating and dirt flew for yards from the explosions." A shell landed in front of his trench, striking him with dirt and knocking him into the trench with its concussion. As Private Becker climbed back up a second shell struck, burying him in the trench, only his head and one arm clear until his platoon mates could dig him out.[66]

In the final moments before the start of the raid Becker, Lieutenant Howard Langford (his platoon commander), and three or four other soldiers waited, all but the officer carrying heavy bags filled with grenades. He noted "all [were] very silent and the only word spoken was an occasional one from Langford looking at his luminous-dial wrist watch" counting down the time left to go. Then "three minutes — get ready boys." Finally, the "oppressive" silence was broken and the "earth and heavens seemed to open at the same time."[67]

Battalion headquarters reported all of its troops "got away in good shape being well clear of our own Front Line before [the] enemy S.O.S. Barrage came down." The 11th Brigade was obviously impressed with the 75th's ability to shrug off the pre-raid artillery casualties, noting it "attacked with vigour and carried out a difficult task." "A" Coy, on the left, captured and cleared its objectives, returning at the end of the night with an enemy machine gun and a prisoner.[68]

"C" Coy, in the centre of the advance, had a tougher time. An enemy machine gun blanketed the advance of Captain James Falkner's men during the early going, causing "severe casualties." The company eventually achieved all of its objectives, destroyed dugouts in the trenches and along the nearby railway embankment, and returned with two prisoners.[69]

On the right flank, "D" Coy also met strong resistance. Private Becker, part of the first wave, later wrote he was initially "dazed by the shaking earth, the smoke, the flying dirt, the whine of bullets and the succession of clashes." Recovering, he and two other soldiers cleared out part of an enemy trench, even throwing Stokes bombs down the entrances to two dugouts, causing "terrific explosions." Becker came out of the raid intact, a close encounter with a German potato-masher grenade singeing the back of his hand.[70] Ultimately, "D" Coy was unable to take its final objective in the face of "very stiff opposition." The company did, however, destroy 10 dugouts and capture one prisoner. The 75th suffered 28 soldiers killed, 11 missing, and 118 officers and men wounded.[71]

102ND "OVERSEAS" BATTALION (NORTH BRITISH COLUMBIANS)

On the far left flank of the Canadian Corps, Lieutenant-Colonel John Warden's 102nd Battalion occupied one of the nastiest locations on the entire front. Stretching northward from the Central Electric Generating Station to the edge of the Souchez River, the 102nd's front also bordered, across the river, a series of interconnected German trenches known as "The Triangle."[72]

The British Columbia troops had moved back into this area on 3 June — before the planned attack was turned into a raid. At this point the battalion's objectives were to: capture and mop up The Triangle in cooperation with troops of I Corps north of the river; capture a concrete machine-gun nest in a railway embankment near the river; and, establish a new front line east of the generating station.[73]

Two days later Major Howard Scharschmidt's "B" Coy moved forward, machine guns and rifle grenades in support, and captured the generating station. The 20 soldiers in the enemy garrison either fled or were killed. Major Scharschmidt then led his men further east, pushing out towards the Brewery compound. However, he and 10 others were badly gassed by an enemy barrage the next evening, and the Canadians fell back to the generating station.[74]

Also early on 5 June Lieutenant Henry Dimsdale and six soldiers set off to capture the concrete machine-gun nest near the railway line. The attack failed after the party was spotted moving forward. Three hours later Lieutenant Dimsdale tried again with four other soldiers, but was again discovered, and further casualties were suffered. Lieutenant George Lowrie led another attempt to take the nest that evening, but it, too, was unsuccessful.[75]

Not surprisingly, the Corps' decision to substitute trench raid for attack did little to change the 102nd's objectives. Battalion headquarters issued new orders on 8 June governing the raid but noted there would be no pulling back at the end of the raid from any positions gained east of the generating station or across the river in The Triangle.[76]

The 102nd's focus on its two separate targets, The Triangle and the generating station, were to be pursued by two separate operations on the evening of 8 June. Lieutenant Lowrie was ordered to lead one platoon from "B" Coy northward to attack and capture the concrete machine-gun nest before crossing the river and establishing an outpost on the northern side in The Triangle, linking up with the British in the process. To help avoid "friendly fire" casualties, the Canadians would carry red and green flags, while the two platoons of the 5th Leicesters coming down from the north would carry yellow artillery discs painted with a black cross. Once captured, all of The Triangle would be handed over to the Leicesters and the Canadian platoon would pull back across the river.[77]

"B" Coy's attack began at 8:30 p.m. and immediately resulted in a German artillery response heard and felt all along the Canadian front. Lowrie was killed by a rifle bullet just three minutes into the assault. Lieutenant John Knight moved forward, took command of the platoon, and "under a hail of machine-gun bullets and high explosive shells the men cut through the wire and bombed their way to the enemy positions." As the supporting barrage lifted, the Canadians descended on the garrison before the enemy could take up defensive positions. Bayonets thrust, rifles fired, and grenades exploded while Canadian bombers slipped grenades inside the concrete emplacement, overpowering the troops inside. The British Columbians then moved on, capturing their part of The Triangle within 40 minutes, killing 30 Germans, and capturing 12 more before handing the position over to the British.[78]

Two members of the 102nd were killed and another five wounded in what Corps' headquarters described as a "most successful" attack. Brigadier-General Victor Odlum, commanding 11th Brigade, asked that Lieutenant Knight be told of his "sincere appreciation of the work he did [....] The operation in 'The Triangle' was as brilliant as anything I have seen in France." Knight would later be decorated with the Military Cross.[79]

The battalion's second raid that evening — the 11:45 p.m. operation — involved pushing the battalion's positions around the generating station further east and capturing the next enemy trench line and nearby positions. "A" Coy and one platoon each from "B" and "C" Companies were tasked with the raid but it is clear that the 102nd's participation in the Corps' trench raid was much smaller than that of the five other battalions. Led by Major Richard Burde, some of the raiders carried mobile charges to destroy dugouts and each soldier was ordered to carry two extra hand grenades and full water bottles. Lieutenant-Colonel Warden was particularly concerned about two aspects of this raid: that the jumping-off positions east of the generating station were "most exposed" and, given recent operations, that "there was no possibility of a surprise."[80] If the other battalions in the late evening operation considered it a raid — get in, destroy, and get out — that opinion was not shared by the officers and men of the 102nd. To them, the raid was clearly just the latest in a series of attacks south of Avion.

When the supporting barrage opened up the 102nd dutifully "advanced to the attack." At 12:55 a.m. battalion headquarters received a message from Major Burde, sent an unknown time earlier, reporting "C" Coy was "going in good order, meeting some wire, but getting round it, finding shells but no enemy." Fifteen minutes later "A" Coy reported it had encountered wire "too thick to pass through." The advance stalled. An officer was sent forward "with orders that the men must make further endeavours to reach their objective."[81] Brigade headquarters later concluded the 102nd suffered from the Canadian and German trenches in the area being so close together that "fear of hitting our own men probably led the artillery to shoot over, consequently the barrage did not come down on the enemy."[82]

Sergeant Zebulon Kirby, "A" Coy, "rallied the men in a desperate endeavour to penetrate the enemy's position" and frantically tried to cut the obstructing wire. Although later awarded the Distinguished Conduct Medal for his efforts, his attempt was unsuccessful and he retreated to his company's jumping-off position.[83]

Nothing worked. The battalion's war diarist wrote, "all efforts having proved futile," the raiders were ordered to hold their current positions. Artillery fire was called in to drench the enemy positions and two machine guns were sent forward to reinforce the Canadian position.[84]

At the end of the night, battalion headquarters reported: "The main objects of the operation had not been realized, but the enemy dug-outs [...] were successfully raided, & Casualties amongst the enemy were very heavy. Relative positions were as formerly." Despite the involvement of just six platoons, the 102nd's casualty figures give weight to the difficulties faced with eight officers and men killed and 70 wounded.[85]

To add insult to injury, the 5th Leicesters were expelled from The Triangle across the river before the second raid was launched, the Germans recapturing the position. The 102nd did not receive word of this in time to prevent one of their platoons from moving near the south shore to clear up the area. As a result, it suffered 30 casualties from enemy machine-gun and rifle fire from a "position which a short time before was in our hands."[86]

CONCLUSION

In the hours and days after the end of the 8–9 June 1917 trench raid the response of the military chain of command was overwhelmingly positive. The 7th Brigade described the work of its battalions as entirely successful: "At all points our troops successfully penetrated [the] enemy's defences and the final objective was reached by all concerned, on time." Enemy trenches were demolished, dugouts destroyed, prisoners and machine guns captured. Initially, casualty figures were described as extremely low.[87] The 11th Brigade said much the same. It estimated German casualties at about 1,000, although admitting these were "chiefly inflicted by our barrage," and noted the numbers of prisoners and machine guns captured, before admitting a higher cost of about 350 officers and men killed, missing, or wounded during the raid.[88]

Canadian Corps' headquarters ultimately echoed the positive analysis of the brigades, describing the operation as "a successful and extensive raid."[89] Nearly 50 years later, the official history was more muted, noting: "the entire raid went as planned." In the final tally, the Canadians inflicted approximately 1,300 casualties on the Germans and captured more than 130 more. Canadian losses were described as "relatively light," including 100 killed and missing and another 609 wounded.[90]

Participants such as Private Becker of the 75th Battalion would later reject such views of success,[91] but the differences between the view from the top, necessarily calculating and seemingly heartless, and the trenches, where the men bled and died, are only to be expected. What can be seen for certain, as a visitor stands at the Vimy Memorial, is that the battle for the Douai Plain took place, not only atop the ridge, but also down there, in the daily — and nightly — grind of "minor operations."

NOTES

1. My thanks to Dr. Steve Harris, Major Paul Lansey, and Corporal Loni Robertson from the Directorate of History and Heritage, Department of National Defence, and my wife, Ms. Barbara Dundas, for their assistance with this chapter.

2. Colonel G.W.L. Nicholson, *Canadian Expeditionary Force 1914–1919: Official History of the Canadian Army in the First World War* (Ottawa: Queen's Printer, 1964), 279.

3. Nicholson, 279–281.

4. LAC, RG 9, III D 3, Vol. 4859, War Diary, 4th Canadian Division — General Staff, July 1917, Appendix 6, Operations of the 4th Canadian Division, April 25th–July 2nd, 1917.

5. *Ibid.*, Vol. 4815, War Diary, Canadian Corps — General Staff, 4 June 1917. Nicholson, in his official history of the Canadian Expeditionary Force, states the idea of the raid was Lieutenant-General Arthur Currie's "suggestion." Nicholson, 281. However, the document he cites makes no mention of Currie being the originator of the idea. Currie succeeded Byng as commander of the Canadian Corps on 9 June 1917. I could find no proof of Currie being present at the 4 June conference between the commander of the Canadian Corps and Major-Generals Lipsett and Watson. LAC, RG 9, III D 3, Vol. 4815, War Diary, Canadian Corps, General Staff, 10 June 1917; and *Ibid.*, Vol. 4832, War Diary, 1st Canadian Division, General Staff, 9 June 1917.

6. *Ibid.*, Vol. 4815, War Diary, Canadian Corps — General Staff, 4 June 1917; and Nicholson, 281.

7. LAC, RG 9, III D 3, Vol. 4815, War Diary, Canadian Corps — General Staff, June 1917, Appendix I, First Army Order, No. 125, 5 June 1917.

8. *Ibid.*, Vol. 4815, War Diary, Canadian Corps — General Staff, June 1917, Appendix II, Canadian Corps Operation Order No. 123, 5 June 1917.

9. *Ibid.*, Vol. 4853, War Diary, 3rd Canadian Division — General Staff, June 1917, Appendix 721, 3rd Canadian Division Operation Order No. 104, 6 June 1917; and *Ibid.*, Vol. 4859, War Diary, 4th Canadian Division — General Staff, June 1917, Appendix 4, 4th Canadian Division Operation Order No. 38, 6 June 1917.

10. *Ibid.*, Vol. 4893, War Diary, 7th Canadian Infantry Brigade, June 1917, Appendix A, Report on Minor Operation Carried out by the 7th Canadian Infantry Brigade on night 8th/9th June 1917.

11. R.C. Fetherstonhaugh, *The Royal Canadian Regiment, 1883–1933* (Montreal: Gazette Printing Company, 1936), 287.

12. LAC, RG 9, III D 3, Vol. 4893, War Diary, 7th Canadian Infantry Brigade, June 1917, Appendix A, Report on Minor Operation Carried out by the 7th Canadian Infantry Brigade on night 8th/9th June 1917; *Ibid.*, Vol. 4940, War Diary, 49th Canadian Infantry Battalion, June 1917, Appendix, 49th Canadian Battalion (Edmonton Regiment), Narrative Report on Raid; Fetherstonhaugh, 287; and G.R. Stevens, *A City Goes to War* (n.p., 1964), 89.

13. LAC, RG 9, III D 3, Vol. 4904, War Diary, 11th Canadian Infantry Brigade, June 1917, Appendix D, 11th Canadian Infantry Brigade, Operation Order No. 57, 25 May 1917; and Colonel A. Fortescue Duguid, *History of The Canadian Grenadier Guards, 1760–1965* (Montreal: Gazette Printing Company, 1965), 147–148.

14. L. McLeod Gould, *From B.C. to Baisieux, Being the Narrative History of the 102nd Canadian Infantry Battalion* (Victoria, BC: Thos. R. Cusack Presses, 1919), 54–55.

15. LAC, RG 9, III D 3, Vol. 4973, War Diary, Canadian Corps, Heavy Artillery,

8 June 1917; and *Ibid.*, Vol. 4859, War Diary, 4th Canadian Division — General Staff, 8 June 1917.

16. *Ibid.*, Vol. 4904, War Diary, 11th Canadian Infantry Brigade, June 1917, Appendix X, 11th Canadian Infantry Brigade Report on Minor Operations from June 5th to June 12th, 1917.

17. *Ibid.*, Vol. 4957, War Diary, General Officer Commanding, Royal Artillery, Canadian Corps, June 1917, appendix, Artillery Order No. 34, by G.O.C., R.A., Canadian Corps, 7 June 1917; *Ibid.*, Vol. 4973, War Diary, Canadian Corps, Heavy Artillery, 8 June 1917; and *Ibid.*, Vol. 4853, War Diary, 3rd Canadian Division — General Staff, June 1917, Appendix 726, 3rd Canadian Division Summary of Intelligence No. 260, from 5:00 a.m. 8th to 5:00 a.m. 9th June, 1917.

18. *Ibid.*, Vol. 4973, War Diary, Canadian Corps, Heavy Artillery, May 1917, appendix, Artillery Order No. 28 by G.O.C., R.A., Canadian Corps, 27 May 1917; *Ibid.*, Vol. 4957, War Diary, General Officer Commanding, Royal Artillery, Canadian Corps, June 1917, appendix, Artillery Order No. 34, by G.O.C., R.A., Canadian Corps, 7 June 1917; and *Ibid.*, Vol. 4853, War Diary, 3rd Canadian Division — General Staff, June 1917, Appendix 726, 3rd Canadian Division Summary of Intelligence No. 260, from 5:00 a.m. 8th to 5:00 a.m. 9th June, 1917.

19. *Ibid.*, Vol. 4980, War Diary, 3rd Canadian Divisional Trench Mortar Group, 8 June 1917; *Ibid.*, Vol. 4904, War Diary, 11th Canadian Infantry Brigade, June 1917, Appendix X, 11th Canadian Infantry Brigade Report on Minor Operations from June 5th to June 12th, 1917; and *Ibid.*, Vol. 4904, War Diary, 11th Canadian Infantry Brigade, June 1917, Appendix E, 11th Canadian Infantry Brigade, Operation Order No. 61, 6 June 1917.

20. *Ibid.*, Vol. 4983, War Diary, 7th Canadian Machine Gun Company, 8 June 1917; *Ibid.*, Vol. 4984, War Diary, 12th Canadian Machine Gun Company, 8 June 1917; *Ibid.*, Vol. 4984, War Diary, 15th Canadian Machine Gun Company, 9 June 1917; and *Ibid.*, Vol. 4904, War Diary, 11th Canadian Infantry Brigade, June 1917, Appendix X, 11th Canadian Infantry Brigade Report on Minor Operations from June 5th to June 12th, 1917.

21. *Ibid.*, Vol. 4911, War Diary, Royal Canadian Regiment, June 1917, Appendix 1, The Royal Canadian Regiment, Preliminary Scheme for Raid to be Carried out on "Z" Day, 5 June 1917; *Ibid.*, Appendix 2, The Royal Canadian Regiment, Scheme for Raid, 7 June 1917; and Fetherstonhaugh, 288.

22. LAC, RG 9, III D 3, Vol. 4911, War Diary, Royal Canadian Regiment, June 1917, Appendix 2, The Royal Canadian Regiment, Scheme for Raid, 7 June 1917; and Fetherstonhaugh, 288.

23. LAC, RG 9, III D 3, Vol. 4911, War Diary, Royal Canadian Regiment, 8 June 1917; *Ibid.*, War Diary, Royal Canadian Regiment, June 1917, Appendix 4, Summary of Operations of The Royal Canadian Regiment; and Fetherstonhaugh, 288–289.

24. LAC, RG 9, III D 3, Vol. 4911, War Diary, Royal Canadian Regiment, June 1917, Appendix 4, Summary of Operations of The Royal Canadian Regiment.

25. *Ibid.*; and Fetherstonhaugh, 289.

26. *Ibid.*

27. *Ibid.*

28. *Ibid.*; and Fetherstonhaugh, 289–290 and 445.

29. *Ibid.*; and Fetherstonhaugh, 290–291.

30. LAC, RG 9, III D 3, Vol. 4938, War Diary, 42nd Canadian Infantry Battalion, 8 June 1917; and C. Beresford Topp, *The 42nd Battalion, C.E.F., Royal Highlanders of Canada in the Great War* (Montreal: Gazette Printing Company, 1931), 138–139.

31. LAC, RG 9, III D 3, Vol. 4938, War Diary, 42nd Canadian Infantry Battalion, 8 June 1917; and Topp, 139.

32. LAC, RG 9, III D 3, Vol. 4938, War Diary, 42nd Canadian Infantry Battalion, 8 June 1917; and Topp, 139–140.

33. LAC, RG 9, III C 3, Vol. 4154, folder 8, file 3, Operations Minor (R.C.R.), 7th Cdn. Inf. Bde., 3rd Cdn. Division, S.C. Norsworthy, Major, for OC 42nd Can Bn., to Hqrs, 7th Can Inf Bde, 14 June 1917.

34. *Ibid.*, Vol. 4938, War Diary, 42nd Canadian Infantry Battalion, 8–9 June 1917; and Topp, 140–141.

35. *Ibid.*, 141; and David K. Riddle and Donald G. Mitchell (Comps.), *The Distinguished Conduct Medal awarded to Members of the Canadian Expeditionary Force 1914–1920* (Winnipeg: The Kirkby-Marlton Press, 1999), 99.

36. Topp, 141–142.

37. LAC, RG 9, III D 3, Vol. 4938, War Diary, 42nd Canadian Infantry Battalion, 8–9 June 1917; and Topp, 140.

38. LAC, RG 9, III D 3, Vol. 4938, War Diary, 42nd Canadian Infantry Battalion, 8–9 June 1917; Topp, 140–141; and Will R. Bird, *Ghosts Have Warm Hands: A Memoir of the Great War, 1916–1919* (Nepean, ON: CEF Books, 1997), 35.

39. LAC, RG 9, III D 3, Vol. 4938, War Diary, 42nd Canadian Infantry Battalion, 8–9 June 1917; Topp, 137 and 368–376; and David K. Riddle and Donald G. Mitchell (Comps.), *The Military Cross Awarded to Members of the Canadian Expeditionary Force, 1915–1921* (Winnipeg: The Kirkby-Marlton Press, 1999), 211.

40. LAC, RG 9, III D 3, Vol. 4938, War Diary, 42nd Canadian Infantry Battalion, 8–9 June 1917; and Topp, 142.

41. LAC, RG 9, III D 3, Vol. 4940, War Diary, 49th Canadian Infantry Battalion, June 1917, Appendix, 49th Canadian Battalion (Edmonton Regiment), Narrative Report on Raid.

42. *Ibid.*; and *Ibid.*, Vol. 4154, folder 8, file 4, Operations Minor (R.C.R.), 7th Cdn. Inf. Bde., 3rd Cdn. Division, report, 49th Canadian Battalion (Edmonton Regiment) to 7th Canadian Infantry Brigade, 13 June 1917.

43. LAC, RG 9, III D 3, Vol. 4940, War Diary, 49th Canadian Infantry Battalion, June 1917, Appendix, 49th Canadian Battalion (Edmonton Regiment), Narrative Report on Raid.

44. *Ibid.*

45. *Ibid.*

46. *Ibid.*; and Stevens, 90.

47. *Ibid.*

48. *Ibid.*, Vol. 4154, folder 8, file 4, Operations Minor (R.C.R.), 7th Cdn. Inf. Bde., 3rd Cdn. Division, report, 49th Canadian Battalion (Edmonton Regiment) to 7th Canadian Infantry Brigade, 13 June 1917. The remains of one of the missing soldiers, Private Herbert Peterson, were discovered in 2003 and reinterred at La Chaudière Military Cemetery in April 2007.

49. *Ibid.*, Vol. 4940, War Diary, 49th Canadian Infantry Battalion, 8 June 1917; and *Ibid.*, War Diary, 49th Canadian Infantry Battalion, June 1917, Appendix, 49th Canadian Battalion (Edmonton Regiment), Narrative Report on Raid.

50. *Ibid.*, Vol. 4944, War Diary, 87th Canadian Infantry Battalion, June 1917, Appendix B, 87th Battalion Canadian Infantry (Canadian Grenadier Guards), Operation Order No. 39, 7 June 1917; and Duguid, 147.

51. *Ibid.*, Vol. 4944, War Diary, 87th Canadian Infantry Battalion, June 1917, Appendix B, 87th Battalion Canadian Infantry (Canadian Grenadier Guards), Operation Order No. 39, 7 June 1917.

52. *Ibid.*

53. *Ibid.*, War Diary, 87th Canadian Infantry Battalion, June 1917, Appendix B, 87th Battalion Canadian Infantry (Canadian Grenadier Guards), Operation Order No. 39, 7 June 1917, Appendix "A."

54. *Ibid.*, Vol. 4944, War Diary, 87th Canadian Infantry Battalion, 8 June 1917.

55. *Ibid.*

56. *Ibid.; Ibid.*, Vol. 4815, War Diary, Canadian Corps — General Staff, 1 June–31 July 1917; *Ibid.*, Vol. 4904, War Diary, 11th Canadian Infantry Brigade, June 1917, Appendix X, 11th Canadian Infantry Brigade Report on Operations from June 5th to June 12th, 1917; *Ibid.*, Vol. 4904, War Diary, 11th Canadian Infantry Brigade, June 1917, Appendix E, 11th Canadian Infantry Brigade, Operation Order No. 61, 6 June 1917; and *Ibid.*, Vol. 4944, War Diary, 87th Canadian Infantry Battalion, June 1917, Appendix B, 87th Battalion Canadian Infantry (Canadian Grenadier Guards), Operation Order No. 39, 7 June 1917.

57. *Ibid.*, Vol. 4944, War Diary, 87th Canadian Infantry Battalion, 8 June 1917.

58. *Ibid.*, Vol. 4904, War Diary, 11th Canadian Infantry Brigade, June 1917, Appendix X, 11th Canadian Infantry Brigade Report on Operations from June 5th to June 12th, 1917.

59. *Ibid.*, Vol. 4944, War Diary, 87th Canadian Infantry Battalion, 8 June 1917; and Duguid, 149.

60. *Ibid.*

61. *Ibid.*, Vol. 4944, War Diary, 87th Canadian Infantry Battalion, 8 June 1917; and Duguid, 149–150.

62. *Ibid.*, Vol. 4943, War Diary, 75th Canadian Infantry Battalion, June 1917, Appendix, Operation Order No. 50 by Lieutenant-Colonel C.C. HARBOTTLE, Commanding 75th Canadian Infantry Battalion, 7 June 1917.

63. *Ibid.*

64. *Ibid.*

65. *Ibid.*, Vol. 4943, War Diary, 75th Canadian Infantry Battalion, June 1917, Appendix I, Account of Raid Night June 8/9th 1917.

66. John Harold Becker, *Silhouettes of the Great War: The Memoirs of John Harold Becker* (Ottawa: CEF Books, 2001), 74–76.

67. Becker, 76–77.

68. LAC, RG 9, III D 3, Vol. 4943, War Diary, 75th Canadian Infantry Battalion, June 1917, Appendix I, Account of Raid Night June 8/9th 1917; and *Ibid.*, Vol. 4904, War Diary, 11th Canadian Infantry Brigade, June 1917, Appendix X, 11th Canadian Infantry Brigade Report on Operations from June 5th to June 12th, 1917.

69. *Ibid.*, Vol. 4943, War Diary, 75th Canadian Infantry Battalion, June 1917, Appendix I, Account of Raid Night June 8/9th 1917.

70. *Ibid.*; and Becker, 76–78.

71. LAC, RG 9, III D 3, Vol. 4943, War Diary, 75th Canadian Infantry Battalion, June 1917, Appendix I, Account of Raid Night June 8/9th 1917; and Becker, 79.

72. Gould, 54.

73. *Ibid.*, 54–55.

74. LAC, RG 9, III D 3, Vol.4815, War Diary, Canadian Corps, General Staff, 5 June 1917, "Summary from 6:00 a.m. June 4th to 6:00 a.m. June 5th"; and *Ibid.*, Vol. 4904, War Diary, 11th Canadian Infantry Brigade, June 1917, Appendix X, 11th Canadian Infantry Brigade Report on Minor Operations from June 5th to June 12th, 1917; and Gould, 55.

75. *Ibid.*

76. LAC, RG 9, III D 3, Vol. 4904, War Diary, 11th Canadian Infantry Brigade, June 1917, Appendix F, 102nd Canadian Infantry Battalion, Operation Order No. 52, 8 June 1917.

77. *Ibid.*; *Ibid.*, Vol. 4815, War Diary, Canadian Corps — General Staff, 9 June

1917; *Ibid.*, Vol. 4815, War Diary, Canadian Corps — General Staff, June 1917, Appendix I, First Army Order No. 125, 5 June 1917; *Ibid.*, Vol. 4815, War Diary, Canadian Corps — General Staff, June 1917, Appendix III, Canadian Corps Summary of Operations, June 7th to June 14th, 1917; and Gould, 55.

78. *Ibid.*, Vol. 4815, War Diary, Canadian Corps — General Staff, June 1917, Appendix III, Canadian Corps Summary of Operations, June 7th to June 14th, 1917; *Ibid.*, Vol. 4904, War Diary, 11th Canadian Infantry Brigade, June 1917, Appendix X, 11th Canadian Infantry Brigade Report on Minor Operations from June 5th to June 12th, 1917; and Gould, 55.

79. *Ibid.*; and Riddle and Mitchell, *Military Cross*, 174.

80. LAC, RG 9, III D 3, Vol. 4944, War Diary, 102nd Canadian Infantry Battalion, 8 June 1917; *Ibid.*, Vol. 4904, War Diary, 11th Canadian Infantry Brigade, June 1917, Appendix F, 102nd Canadian Infantry Battalion, Operation Order No. 52, 8 June 1917; and Gould, 55.

81. LAC, RG 9, III D 3, Vol. 4944, War Diary, 102nd Canadian Infantry Battalion, 8–9 June 1917.

82. *Ibid.*, Vol. 4904, War Diary, 11th Canadian Infantry Brigade, June 1917, Appendix X, 11th Canadian Infantry Brigade Report on Minor Operations from June 5th to June 12th, 1917.

83. *Ibid.*, Vol. 4944, War Diary, 102nd Canadian Infantry Battalion, 9 June 1917; Gould, 55; and Riddle and Mitchell, *Distinguished Conduct Medal*, 141.

84. LAC, RG 9, III D 3, Vol. 4944, War Diary, 102nd Canadian Infantry Battalion, 9 June 1917.

85. *Ibid.; Ibid.*, Vol. 4904, War Diary, 11th Canadian Infantry Brigade, June 1917, Appendix X, 11th Canadian Infantry Brigade Report on Minor Operations from June 5th to June 12th, 1917; and Gould, 55.

86. *Ibid.*

87. *Ibid.*, Vol. 4893, War Diary, 7th Canadian Infantry Brigade, June 1917, Appendix A, Report on Minor Operation Carried out by the 7th Canadian Infantry Brigade on night 8th/9th June 1917; and *Ibid.*, Vol. 4853, War Diary, 3rd Canadian Division — General Staff, June 1917, Appendix 726, 3rd Canadian Division Summary of Intelligence No. 260, from 5:00 a.m. 8th to 5:00 a.m. 9th June, 1917.

88. *Ibid.*, Vol. 4859, War Diary, 4th Canadian Division — General Staff, 8 June 1917; and *Ibid.*, Vol. 4904, War Diary, 11th Canadian Infantry Brigade, 9 June 1917.

89. *Ibid.*, Vol. 4815, War Diary, Canadian Corps, General Staff, June 1917, Appendix VII, Canadian Corps Communique, 10 June 1917.

90. Nicholson, 281.

91. Becker, 82.

5

A CLASH OF WILLS:
THE CANADIAN STRUGGLE FOR MOUNT SORREL, 2 JUNE 1916

Andrew Godefroy

As dawn broke over the Canadian front lines southeast of Ypres on 2 June 1916, two elderly gentlemen conversed in quiet voices as they cautiously made their way forward to the heights of Tor Top and Mount Sorrel. The weather that morning was looking favourable, but neither found any comfort in the good visibility it offered. Major-General Malcolm Mercer, the venerable commander of the 3rd Canadian Division was being taken by Brigadier-General Victor Williams, the commander of the 8th Canadian Infantry Brigade, to observe and discuss the growing threat to his increasingly exposed position. Over the past several weeks the enemy had made great effort, despite constant harassment by Canadian artillery and machine-gun fire, to push his own front line trenches forward and to the flanks of the salient held by Brigadier-General Williams's troops. During the last few days, Canadian fighting and reconnaissance patrols out past the wire had confirmed that it appeared an attack was imminent. With so many ominous indicators, Major-General Mercer needed to see and assess the situation for himself.[1]

Upon reaching the reaching the front line trenches of the 4th Canadian Mounted Rifles (4 CMR) located on the 8th Brigade's right, the two senior officers were greeted by the unit's commanding officer, Lieutenant-Colonel John Ussher. A handsome gentleman from York Mills, Ontario, he had forfeited his civilian employment as a broker in Toronto to serve overseas with the Canadian Expeditionary Force (CEF).[2] Now commanding a front line unit east of Ypres, he too was concerned about the possibility of a German attack in force against his position. The three senior officers and their small staff conducted a quick tour of the 4 CMR trenches to examine the state of the defences, and were just returning to the battalion headquarters dugout 25 yards behind the front line when they heard the massive "whump" of a nearby exploding shell. A second later a hundred more explosions followed, unleashing a fury of hell all along the Canadian front line the likes of which they had never before seen. Though few would live to later describe it, what they had witnessed was the opening move of a bitter contest for control of the Ypres salient. It was a battle where fortune favoured the brave.

THE CANADIAN CORPS ON THE WESTERN FRONT

At the outbreak of the First World War, Canada responded to the call to arms with great speed and dedication. Within weeks of the 4 August 1914 declaration of war, the country had dispatched its first contingent overseas to England, a complete division and its supporting elements numbering some 30,000 men. Upon arrival the formation immediately began training hard for war and soon after two thirds of the combat ready contingent crossed the channel over to France. The 1st Canadian Division landed at Le Havre in mid-February 1915, and barely eight weeks later the Canadians fought their first major battle against the Imperial German Army in late April, successfully spoiling a neutralizing attack by its Fourth Army and refusing to let the enemy fix them in place while preparing for other operations.

The defence of the area east of Ypres was, however, very costly and after two weeks of hard fighting the 1st Canadian Division had suffered 5,975 casualties. It was a terrible introduction to battle, but it was indicative of the human cost of modern and industrialized warfare. It was also not the last time that the Canadians would suffer tremendous losses fighting on the Western Front.

A year after the Second Battle of Ypres, the CEF had grown as an organization and had learned a considerable amount about the environment

Library and Archives Canada PA-004485.

Observatory Ridge and the corner of Armagh Wood, taken from Mount Sorrel.

in which they fought. Yet despite these ameliorations, the environment continued to test them. By 1916, though some tactical flexibility remained, the opposing armies on the Western Front were strategically deadlocked. The Germans dug in defensively and sought to destroy the French and Anglo-allied armies through attrition, while British, Canadian, French, Australian, and other armies of the Entente constantly sought innovative ways to unhinge them.[3] It became largely a problem of innovation, tactics, and industry, and the Battle of Mont Sorrel in the summer of 1916 would offer the first opportunity for the recently created Canadian Corps to put new tactical ideas to the test. Yet, like so many other battles before it, so much still depended on the courage and skill of individual soldiers.

The Entente alliance agreed that the Somme region of France would be the central focus of the British war effort on the Western Front in 1916. It was here that Commander-in-Chief of the British Expeditionary Force (BEF), Field Marshal Douglas Haig, prepared to launch his "big push" through the German lines on 1 July, break into their rear, and force their armies into defeat. The preparations for the British offensive were monstrous, and demanded almost all the BEF's available resources.[4] What little could be spared was less than adequate to defend other areas of the British front, including the Ypres sector where the Canadians were still fighting during the first half of 1916. It was a dangerous situation at best but one that simply could not be avoided. Field Marshal Haig had chosen to concentrate his forces for attack elsewhere. Meanwhile the approach to Ypres had to be held against any German attack. What remained was not much, but it would have to do.

The Entente armies had controlled most of the wooded highlands east of Ypres since the battles of the previous summer.[5] In May 1916, the Canadian Corps' three divisions were responsible for an area of the front line extending roughly from the Menin Road and the village of Hooge in the north to the Ypres-Menin Railway line in the south. The area along the ridge itself was largely wooded — or had been largely wooded — until a year of constant shelling had splintered and destroyed a great deal of the trees. As well, the grassy knolls and rolling slopes leading gently down towards Ypres were largely without their usual flora and fauna. A wet winter combined with the constant churning of the soil by men and shell had turned the farmland into mud, sludge, and constantly seeping water. One soldier described the consistency of the ground at this time as being similar to cream cheese. It was not a promising situation for tired and overburdened soldiers trying to move quickly under constant enemy shelling.

DEFENDING MOUNT SORREL

With much of the focus on General Rawlinson's Fourth Army preparations for the coming British offensive at the Somme, the British Second Army was forced to make do with what it had for the moment despite the dangers it continued to face on the Ypres front. As part of Second Army's force, the Canadian Corps was still situated east of the city of Ypres and north of St. Eloi in late May 1916, with the 2nd Canadian Division still in front of St. Eloi itself, while the 1st and 3rd Canadian Divisions held the roughly north-south line along the Ypres Salient. Its soldiers were also just getting accustomed to the news of the appointment of Lieutenant-General Sir Julian Byng as their new commander, though the arrival of this new senior British officer appeared to have little immediate effect on improving the overall situation for the troops stuck out defending the ridge.

The Ypres salient was considered one of the most important yet deadly sectors of the British front line, and defending it against constant

German attack proved to be a daily nightmare for the soldiers burdened with the task. The area was scarred from repeated battles going back over a year where it was the scene of some of the fiercest fighting between British, Canadian, and German forces during the summer of 1915. Most of the structures in the area were long ago reduced to smashed and burnt out rubble, while most of the green fields and woods had been churned into brown splinters and muck. As one historian later commented, "despite being midsummer — June 1916 — the landscape had a wintry feel with only the distant trees being in full leaf, the others being shell-swept and struggling to sprout greenery following the devastating barrages ..."[6]

Yet, the front lines had shifted little from the previous year. To the north the British still held the ground just in front of a small wood named "Y Wood" because of its distinctive shape. From there, the front line snaked south between the village of Hooge and its chateau. Turning south across the Menin Road the Canadian front line took over and followed roughly the eastern edges of Sanctuary and Armagh woods along the high ground. Opposite to them the Germans held tenaciously onto a north-south route known as Green Jacket Ride as well as a large feature known as Stirling Castle. The 3rd Canadian Division line continued south here along a series of high features identified as Tor Top (Hill 62), Hill 61, and Mount Sorrel.[7] Just past this feature was the divisional boundary, with the 1st Canadian Division defending the front line from this point southwest towards Hill 60 and the Ypres-Menin railway embankment.

As much as the dominating terrain of Mount Sorrel and its surroundings favoured the Canadians, other areas of this front favoured their enemy. Upon reoccupying familiar stomping grounds at the north end of Sanctuary Wood and around Hooge, soldiers of the Princess Patricia's Canadian Light Infantry noted that much of their front line was commanded by the German position. It was also situated dangerously close to the enemy, and the commanding officer of the PPCLI, Lieutenant-Colonel Herbert Buller, felt that if the Germans made a determined attack, they would likely wipe out his front line trenches. A particularly annoying enemy strong point was located just behind the enemy front

Courtesy Department of National Defence.

Sanctuary Wood, 2 June 1916.

lines on the grounds of Stirling Castle. Nicknamed the "Bird Cage" by the Canadians, the Germans could observe most of the PPCLI front line as well as enfilade considerable parts of it from this position.[8]

The precarious situation in front of the Patricias' defences was repeated nearly all down the Canadian front line. Rocky terrain intersected with tree roots and high water tables along the salient through the woods made digging extremely challenging. In some areas soldiers watched helplessly as trenches filled with water and their sandbag breastworks spread and sank into the slime. The construction of a completely interlocked line of defence was impossible here. To compensate for these breaches in the defence, the Canadians built revetted breastworks with parados where they could as well as a number of strong points, but often these positions could only be reached by overland route, thus, exposing soldiers and pickets to enemy fire as they moved between them.[9]

Though such field works offered some form of defence, soldiers often remained susceptible to shrapnel fragments and exploding tree splinters. Wire entanglements were also reinforced to offer additional protection, but again the available supplies were limited. Simply put, the ground conditions were grim for the Canadian defenders and they knew it, but worse, their adversary knew it as well. Had the dominating terrain not commanded such a good view of the German rear areas while protecting the road to Ypres, one wonders if the Canadian commanders would have chosen to hold the line elsewhere.

To add even more complexity, defences had to be considered not only above ground but below it as well. During the First World War it was common practice for armies to attack their adversaries by tunnelling underneath their positions as well as over the top. The British had blown mines dug under the German front line on the southern edge of the Ypres Salient near Hill 60 in April 1915, and had packed and blown another mine laced with 1,600 kilograms of explosives near Hooge on 19 July 1915. The latter explosion killed hundreds of German soldiers and created a massive crater that was fought over constantly, and still exists today. For their part, the German Army also sought to mine under the British front line causing no end of angst for those defending Hooge and salient to its south.

At least the Canadians had an advantage in manpower. With 19,772 soldiers of all ranks, the Canadian division dwarfed its German competitor. Whereas Canadian divisions consisted of three infantry brigades, German divisions contained only a single infantry brigade along with a pioneer battalion and a field artillery regiment. Apart from the lone pioneer battalion, the German infantry brigade contained three regiments consisting of 2,789 officers and men (including headquarters), formed into three battalions of approximately 910 soldiers, which were in turn divided into four infantry companies and one machine-gun company.[10] By comparison Canadian infantry brigades (including headquarters) consisted of approximately 5,200 officers and men, with each of the four infantry battalions totalling approximately 1,240 all ranks.[11] At every tactical level, the Germans were decisively outmanned; however, they were on the offensive and well supported with additional firepower to compensate for the lack of personnel.

Thus, on the eve of battle at the end of May, the Canadian defensive disposition north to south along the Ypres Salient was as follows. Next to the "V" (British) Corps boundary was 7th Canadian Infantry Brigade (7 CIB) with companies of The Royal Canadian Regiment (RCR) holding Hooge and companies of the PPCLI forward holding a defensive line

Library and Archives Canada PA-004486.

Mount Sorrel with Armagh House in foreground.

through the north end of Sanctuary Wood. The 42nd and 49th Battalions belonging to 7 CIB remained in reserve. The 8th Canadian Infantry Brigade was situated to the south of 7 CIB, with the 1st Canadian Mounted Rifles (1 CMR) holding a defensive position through the south end of Sanctuary Wood and along Observatory Ridge to Tor Top. To their right was 4 CMR. Here the mounted riflemen held the ridge from Tor Top to Mount Sorrel, and they would soon find themselves at the very centre of the coming battle. "C" Company was situated on the left, with "D" Coy in the centre, and "A" Coy on the right. "B" Coy was held in reserve at Ypres near the Lille Gate. The 3rd Canadian Division boundary touched the 1st Canadian Division boundary just past Mount Sorrel and ran back through Square Wood. To the right of 4 CMR was the 1st Canadian Division's 5th (Western Cavalry) Canadian Infantry Battalion (5 Bn).

It was hardly the ideal arrangements for defence but the Canadians did their best to maintain their positions while at the same time trying to appear threatening to the Germans opposite them. For some of the Canadian soldiers things even seemed routine. Rifleman Harry Laird of 4 CMR noted in his memoir, "May 31st was another quiet day … you are dependent entirely upon the enemy for your amusement (if one may call it that) and when they choose to sit idly without firing a shot an hour seems a long time."[12] Little did he know that the Germans were being anything but idle at that moment.

GERMAN PLANS AND PREPARATIONS

German commanders knew the tactical value of the Canadian position on Mount Sorrel. If they could capture Tor Top, the hills that straddled it, and the positions along Observatory Ridge, they would gain vital ground to the rear of the Canadian position and deny the Canadians direct observation of their own rear areas. Once consolidated, the Germans would be able to bring both indirect and direct fire to bear on the Canadian support lines, and, with enough pressure, perhaps even force the Canadians to withdraw completely out of the salient. Even if not successful in taking the position in an attack, the Germans felt confident that the tactical value of the salient to the Entente would force them to draw resources from their preparations at the Somme to commit to the defence of Mount Sorrel. It was a calculated risk, but in the eyes of the Imperial German Army, one worth taking.

The German Fourth Army held the line along the Ypres Salient opposite the Canadians. Its commander, Crown Prince Rupprecht, gave the task of seizing Mount Sorrel from the "tommies" to General der Infanterie Freiherr Theodor von Watter, commander of 13 (*Königlich Württembergisches*) Armeekorps.[13] Overall, his troops were in good fighting condition despite increasing food, material, and personnel shortages, and were prepared to undertake new offensive operations. Watter's Armeekorps consisted of two infantry divisions, 26 Division (*1. Königlich Württembergische*) under the command of General der Infanterie Duke Wilhelm von Ulrach[14], and 27 Division (*2. Königlich Württembergische*) under the command of General der Infanterie Friedrich Woldemar Franz Graf von Pfeil und Klein-Ellguth.[15] Besides his infantry, General Watter's Wurttemberg Corps included one battalion of the 13th Foot Artillery Regiment as well as a number of pioneers, combat support, aviation, and ancillary troops.[16]

Much in the same way that the Canadian Corps would evolve to see itself as a distinct entity within the much larger BEF that it was subordinate to, the Wurttemberg troops often perceived themselves, politically at least, as somewhat independent from their Prussian masters. Though its own state forces were fully integrated into the Prussian Army after the period of German unification, the Kingdom of Wurttemberg as a whole remained semi-autonomous in some military matters of command, force generation, and employment. Its soldiers saw themselves, much like the Bavarian Army, as distinct from the rest of the Prussian Army, and similar to the Canadians this sense of national pride had earned the Wurttembergers a fierce reputation on the battlefield.

A Wurttemberger division was organized into four groups — infantry, artillery, pioneers, and divisional support such as medical, transport, labour, and communications. The divisional cavalry originally assigned to the Wurtemberg, as well as other German Corps, were stripped away at the outbreak of war to form separate cavalry divisions and reconnaissance units.[17] The other support and ancillary units, however, remained with their respective divisions making it the main tactical manoeuvre element in the Imperial German Army. The divisional headquarters staff was manned by 20 to 25 officers and officials and further supported by approximately 80–90 men.[18] The commander's right hand men consisted of the infantry brigade commanders and the divisional artillery commander; this trio did most of his fighting.

In mid-1916 the German divisions were still employing the "box" model symmetrical tactical structure, with each division consisting of two infantry brigades of two regiments each, a field artillery brigade of two regiments, and a company of pioneers. The experiences of trench warfare had also resulted in the creation of various regimental specialists who were attached to these manoeuvre elements. These included light machine-gun sections, *minenwerfer* (trench-mortar) detachments, and signallers.

At the time of the Mont Sorrel battle the 1896 n/A pattern 7.7 centimetre gun (7.7 cm FK 96 n/A) remained the standard instrument of destruction of the German field artillery brigades. With a range of approximately 7,100 metres, well-trained Württemberg gunners were able

Library and Archives Canada PA-000186.

German dead by their trenches, which were demolished by artillery during the Battle of Mount Sorrel, June 1916.

to put hundreds of rounds on or near target in a matter of minutes. Yet for this operation General Watter was given even more artillery reinforcement. Besides his integrated artillery, 13 Corps was provided the support of heavy artillery from 23 Reserve Corps and 26 Reserve Corps on either flank, as well as all calibres of trench mortars.

With the task confirmed the Wurttembergers secretly made a detailed reconnaissance and survey of the Canadian front lines in early April, and then employed this information to develop a set of dummy trenches behind their own lines on which to prepare for the assault. The main objective was to seize a defensible line beyond Mount Sorrel, Tor Top, and Observatory Ridge, from which a commanding position over the British and Canadian rear areas could be retained. The total advance was about 500 yards (450 metres) and was broken into two stages. The first phase consisted of seizing the Canadian front lines, codenamed the "Iron Line." Phase two consisted of attacking to the edge of Observatory Ridge and consolidating a new defensive position codenamed the "Golden Line." A secondary objective would be the capture of Hooge. Here the Germans would make a demonstration against the town to pin down Canadian forces and deny them the ability to reinforce breaches farther south at Mount Sorrel. If the conditions were favourable, sub-unit commanders were authorized to assault and capture the town.

On this system of dummy trenches the Germans trained for their attack while artillery and supplies were inconspicuously moved forward to support the assault. Though the Royal Flying Corps (RFC) later discovered these dummy trenches, there is no evidence to suggest that the revelation led to any changes in GHQ's defensive or resource allocation priorities to the Ypres Salient. This was most likely because other obvious indicators of an attack were lacking. No additional troops were seen to arrive behind the German front, and they had made every effort to conceal the placement of additional artillery in the German forward lines at this time. Batteries were brought forward just a few nights before the offensive, and straw was bandaged to wheels and the hooves of horses to conceal the noise. Tracks were immediately ploughed over, and German aviation was employed to ensure the concealment of any noise of their own artillery and supply trains coming forward.

Finally the assaulting force moved into their jumping off positions. In the north opposite 1CMR the two battalions of the 121st and 125th Regiments were poised to strike, while to their south, in front of the 4 CMR positions, a single battalion of the 120th Regiment stood ready. The 119th Grenadier Regiment (26 Division) and the 127th Regiment (27 Division) were held in reserve. To the far north opposite Hooge, the 117th Division was ready to make its diversionary attack against Hooge.

By the end of May 1916 all was ready for the assault. Though they could never be certain, it appeared that the Wurttembergers' preparations had gone unnoticed. All General der Infanterie Freiherr Theodor von Watter could hope for now was retention of surprise and favourable weather. He got both.

THE ASSAULT

> *We believed we had as many guns as the enemy and could withstand any attack. We had been lulled into a false sense of security.*
>
> Private Morley Louis Ackerman,
> 14th (Royal Montreal Regiment) Battalion[19]

On the evening of 1 June 1916, German artillery harassment of the Canadian positions suddenly petered out. Brigade commanders immediately stood to for an attack, but after waiting intensely for hours there was no sign of it coming. Then in the early morning hours the random shelling resumed and those in the front lines stood down in their trenches and went about their daily business. Nothing appeared out of the ordinary as the dawn gave way to the day. Little did the defenders know that the reduction in shelling had been deliberate. Sending out wire cutting parties in the dark, the Wurttembergers had not wished to hit their own men as they quietly cut lanes through the barbed wire for their assaulting troops.

It was general concern about the state of the defences along the Ypres Salient that led the commander of the 3rd Canadian Division and the 8th Canadian Infantry Brigade to conduct a personal reconnaissance on the morning of 2 June. The situation was not good and something needed to be done about it. Major-General Mercer had also requested the company and input of the newly appointed Corps commander, Lieutenant-General Sir Julian Byng, a few days earlier at his headquarters. However the recently arrived GOC deferred his involvement on this occasion, suggesting, "No. You had better go yourselves tomorrow and make your own proposals. I will come around and see them on Saturday."[20] It was a decision that likely saved his life.

Generals Mercer and Williams had just finished their examination of the front line defences when suddenly and without warning German artillery began crashing into the Canadian positions. Instantly there was chaos everywhere as the defenders were surprised by both the suddenness and intensity of the bombardment. The "whump" of exploding shells and the snapping of trees splintered by explosions was deafening. Artillery and mortars smashed the flimsy trenches and sagging breastworks, tossing dirt, sandbags, wood, and bodies into the air. The two senior officers found themselves caught in the eye of a deadly hurricane with no escape, and a moment later both were knocked to the ground. Mercer and his aide-de-camp, Captain Lyman Gooderham were both punched flat out with ears ringing but still unwounded. Brigadier-General Williams, however, took shrapnel directly in the head and face and lay writhing in agony. Brave soldiers of the 4th Canadian Mounted Rifles scrambled out into the fury to pull their two senior officers into safety of the headquarters dugout, while others attempted to man their posts and find cover amid the deadly rain of shells and mortars. A barrage of this magnitude meant an attack was sure to follow and they needed to be ready. Unfortunately the poor riflemen didn't have a chance.

The initial German artillery assault fell squarely on the 3rd Canadian Division, with a particular concentration of firepower against the 8th Canadian Infantry Brigade on the division's right. As their artillery pounded selected targets all along the Canadian position and immediate rear, massed trench mortars annihilated their front lines. According to calculations made by the Second German Army, a single battery of its mortars (three guns) could destroy 100 metres of enemy trench with 325 rounds. With simple firing procedures, the average German mortar crew could deliver that many rounds in a few minutes. It did not take long to cave in the 915 metres held by 4 CMR.[21]

The German artillery and mortars pounded the Canadian positions all morning. General der Infanterie von Watter watched anxiously as his gunners went about the business of reducing the Canadian defences before the infantry assaulted. Privately he was confident the Wurttembergers would take the heights. Nothing could survive the maelstrom he was delivering upon the Canadians.

The 2nd Canadian Tunnelling Company, Canadian Engineers, had been busily dropping new shafts under the German defences from the reverse slope of Mount Sorrel since early spring, but on the morning of 2 June their "weapon" (a tunnel from which to plant explosives under the German positions) became their sanctuary. As the shelling intensified, wounded soldiers were brought into the narrow tunnel, which was just over a metre wide and less than two metres high. Brigadier-General Williams had been brought here to have his wounds dressed until he could be moved to safety. When Lieutenant-Colonel Ussher went to check on him, German shelling caved in both entrances and the CO of the 4 CMR found himself trapped underground with about 30 other men. Lieutenant-Colonel Ussher's heart sank even further when he felt a series of muffled explosions followed by concussions, the signature of the detonation of an underground mine. Up above his riflemen were being annihilated.

Outside in the trenches it was near chaos. Those still capable of acting at Mount Sorrel sent immediate requests to the Canadian Artillery for support. Emergency flares were fired and runners sent out, but the success was minimal. The riflemen even attempted to get messages through by way of carrier pigeon, but like other methods success was spotty at best. The Canadian artillery responded where it could but with the front lines smashed to pieces, artillery boards could not be seen and the signal lines were cut so no adjustments could be made to falling rounds.[22] Some found their targets but too many did not. Shells killed both friend and foe as the situation became confused.

Every conceivable form of enemy artillery and mortar shelled the mounted riflemen mercilessly for over four hours. Mount Sorrel and its surrounding woods were reduced to splintered heaps of woods, with the Canadian defensive positions completely demolished. At about 1:00 p.m. the shelling subsided, but only to signal the beginning of the ground assault. This next attack began with the temporary blotting out of the sun. Just as few surviving mounted riflemen wondered if they had survived the worst, there was a sudden muffled boom and then instantaneous groaning and heaving of the ground as mines detonated under their position.[23] This final insult hurled a large section of the Canadian front line and its defenders into the air, wiping out what remained of "A" Company 4 CMR and effectively ending any form of resistance along this portion of the front. Lieutenant J. Harvey Douglas, one of the last 4 CMR officers still alive, was nearly killed when a flying piece of trench debris smashed him to the ground badly wounded. Miraculously, however, he lived to be captured by the Germans soon after when the 120th Regiment overran his position.[24]

Desperate to get back in action Major-General Mercer and Captain Gooderham decided to make a break for it. They sprinted through the torn up ground back towards the divisional headquarters, but once out in the open they became easy targets. A random bullet snapped through the General's leg and broke it, causing him to crumple to the ground. Gooderham bandaged the wound quickly and dragged his superior into the relative safety of a ditch, but their situation had grown worse. They were trapped once again, still out of action, but now dangerously in the open under the barrage and counter barrage for the remainder of the day.[25]

Much to their own good fortune the Wurttembergers had effectively decapitated the 3rd Canadian Division's command and control in a single stroke. The divisional, brigade, and two battalion commanders were all incapacitated in the opening strike at Mount Sorrel, leaving a gaping vacuum of confusion concerning the immediate defence. Though soldiers defending the front lines didn't require orders to begin firing into the advancing groups of soldiers from the 13 Wurttemberg Corps, it was near impossible to synchronize efforts and achieve effective defence of the position without higher command. Should the Canadians hold? Where was the defensive artillery? Were reinforcements coming? Should they withdraw to better positions of defence? With most of the communication lines cut by enemy shellfire there was no way of knowing for sure, and without any orders forthcoming it was up to the surviving battalion, company, and platoon commanders to take the initiative. When these men were killed or incapacitated, sergeants and corporals led and fought on.

At about 1400 hours, the first Wurttemberg soldiers crossed their line of departure. Survivors in the Canadian line could see waves of men in grey coats carrying pickaxes, shovels, and other trench stores, obviously intended for the consolidation of their soon to be captured trenches. The audacity of the Wurttembergers was remarkable but despite the punishment they had inflicted on the Canadians they were about to discover that there was still plenty of fight left in their adversaries. The storming and bombing parties of the Wurttemberg 120th and 125th Regiments were soon into the Canadian front line, overrunning the 4 CMR and 1 CMR positions, taking prisoners and killing those who refused to surrender or still attempted to fight.

Yet, despite the stunning blow of the bombardment, riflemen, sappers, and even signallers resisted where they could. Surviving machine gunners from 1 CMR remained in action even as the Germans were storming their parapets with bombs, and when the ammunition ran out riflemen used their weapons as clubs. When the Wurttembergers could not overrun parts of the Canadian line at Sanctuary Wood with bullets and bombs they used flamethrowers to burn away any resistance. It was a bitter and brutal contest, but one that the shelled, exhausted, and injured Canadians could not win. Eventually the mounted riflemen were beaten. The commanding officer of the 1st Canadian Mounted Rifles, Lieutenant-Colonel Alfred E. Shaw, was killed making a last stand at his battalion headquarters, but after the battle his body was never recovered. Today he is commemorated on the Menin Gate Memorial to the Missing at Ypres.

As the Wurttembergers exploited their breaches along observatory ridge they ran smack into two strong points equipped with 18-pounder field artillery pieces belonging to the 5th Battery, Canadian Field Artillery. Here the Canadian gunners fired on their attackers with shrapnel at point blank range, inflicting terrible casualties among the leading German ranks. Unable to take the positions at first, the Wurttembergers either called in artillery or used flamethrowers to kill the crews, for soldiers later reported seeing one of the gun pits burning. A young aspiring poet and graduate of the Royal Military College, Lieutenant Harold Stratton Matthews, was last seen firing until his ammunition ran out. Another young officer, Lieutenant Charles Penner Cotton, fired his last round and then defended his gun with his sidearm and fists. A German regimental historian later noted that the Canadians would not surrender the guns and defended themselves with revolvers to the last man. Lieutenant Cotton was either shot down or burned alive where he stood and fought to his last breath. For a short time it was rumoured that Matthews was wounded and taken prisoner, but the Germans did not report his capture and his body was never found. The 22-year-old from Peterborough, Ontario, was added to the ever-growing list of those missing somewhere near Ypres.

Those to the left and right of 8th Canadian Infantry Brigade could hardly believe their eyes. They stared in near disbelief as Sanctuary and Armagh woods were pounded into submission. From the short distance away the artillery flashed and rolled thunder and a gentle shockwave out across the grass from the ridgeline. Soon, grey-clad soldiers were observed scrambling across Mount Sorrel, Tor Top, and Observatory Ridge. The Germans were coming. To the north Lieutenant-Colonel Herbert Buller was damned if he was going to let the Germans punch through his line. Though a couple of his forward companies had been caught in the initial onslaught he reorganized what remained of the PPCLI and conducted an orderly withdrawal under pressure. This manoeuvre allowed him to effectively control his troops and keep them alive while making the Wurttembergers pay dearly for every inch taken. Using his machine-gun section to great advantage he tore into the Wurttemberg right flank, crippling the Infanterie-Regiment Alt-Württemberg Nr.121 (3. Württembergisches) as it attempted to gain a foothold in Sanctuary Wood. A prisoner from this regiment captured during a later Canadian counterattack admitted that his unit suffered heavily from enfilade machine-gun fire and a leading company was practically wiped out.[26]

By late afternoon the German attack began to stall. The PPCLI stemmed the tide of German advance through Sanctuary Wood and the 5th (Western Cavalry) Canadian Infantry Battalion to the south of Mount Sorrel had checked the lead elements of the enemy around this point. Though General der Infanterie von Watter had achieved both surprise and success in taking the ridge, it had still cost him terribly and now he was stuck attempting to defend ground that had already been difficult to consolidate and certainly made even more untenable by the days' bombardment. His assaulting units, the 120th, 121st, and 125th, had also paid dearly for their gains despite the tremendous bombardment and mining that had proceeded them, and reinforcement or relief was not forthcoming. A few days later these attackers found themselves being served a bitter spoonful of their own medicine as Major-General Arthur Currie smashed what remained of the Wurttembergers in a crushing counterattack that firmly reasserted Canadian control over the heights east of Ypres. What remained of the 13 Wurttemberg Corps was chased back across the Green Jacket Ride.

Still, the fighting on 2 June had exacted a terrible price on the 3rd Canadian Division. Major-General Mercer, the divisional commander, was killed by friendly artillery fire when Captain Gooderham attempted to carry him back to safety. Brigadier-General Williams was captured. Lieutenant-Colonel Buller, commanding officer of the PPCLI, was killed in action leading a counterattack at Sanctuary Wood.[27] Two commanding officers of the Canadian Mounted Rifles, Lieutenant-Colonel Alfred Shaw (1 CMR) and Lieutenant-Colonel George Baker (5 CMR) were killed, and Lieutenant-Colonel John Ussher (4 CMR) was wounded and made a prisoner of war. The rank and file of the mounted riflemen and the PPCLI also suffered heavily, with their fighting strength severely sapped on the first day.

Down the slopes in front of Ypres on the evening of 2 June, however, the exhausted and dejected Canadians licked their wounds and collected together their dead where they could. Yet, their escape from battle was only temporary, as General Byng planned to send them back into the cauldron as soon as he could issue the order, and the first Canadian counterattack would launch back up Observatory Ridge the following morning. It was the first Canadian riposte in a bitter clash of wills that was ultimately decided in their favour.

CONCLUSION: DEFEAT INTO VICTORY

Popular historians are quick to pass judgment on the opening stages of the Battle of Mount Sorrel. "The inexperienced Canadians," lamented one writer, "took a curiously passive role in their defence."[28] Yet, a more thorough examination of the engagement does not support such accusations. The British preparations for the July offensive on the Somme precluded any requests for additional resources or artillery to defend the Ypres sector. The weather throughout late May 1916 favoured the attacker and concealed German preparations. It also hindered the Canadian ability to prepare detailed defensive fires or air-assisted counter-battery programs. The ground itself was notoriously difficult to defend, and by mid-1916 was a mess of blasted tree roots and high water tables, a challenge to effectively dig into and providing little natural protection against concentrated enemy artillery.

The 3rd Canadian Division had made what preparations it could to defend against an attack it knew was imminent, but predicting the exact moment of attack was a difficult if not altogether impossible task even under the best circumstances. The Canadians aggressively patrolled no man's land and learned what they could. The combat intelligence that was gained by up to the night of 1 June could not ascertain the locations of new German artillery or staging positions. No new enemy troops were observed in opposite the Canadian sector. Nothing implied an attack would take place the following morning. The Canadians had not failed to properly prepare for the defence of Mont Sorrel as some might suggest, the conditions did not favour them and they were simply beaten by a well prepared and better supported adversary who had ground, time, weather, and luck on their side.

There are other misconceptions about the first day of battle as well. For example, total casualties in some units were actually not as severe as

Canadian soldiers searching captured German prisoners.

Library and Archives Canada PA-001329.

later reported. Published in 1926, the official history of the 4 CMR notoriously announced that the unit had suffered 89 percent casualties by the morning of 4 June, and future historians subsequently quoted this figure without any further scrutiny.[29] However, when the unit strength and casualty figures were examined in detail employing nominal rolls, casualty rolls, as well as data from the Commonwealth War Graves Commission, a different picture of 4 CMR's fate is revealed. On 2 June the battalion's total strength was 1,247 not 702 as quoted in Colonel Nicholson's official history of the CEF.[30] Even if the smaller quoted figure was only meant to represent the number of soldiers up in the front line (remember that "B" Coy 4 CMR was kept in reserve near the Lille Gates), it would be exceeding small even to be considered "trench strength" for three fighting companies, the machine-gun section, and all the headquarters elements who were known to be there.[31] As well, casualty rolls show that 4 CMR suffered a total of 416 casualties (killed, wounded, missing, and made prisoner of war) between 2 and 14 June 1916. Even if one accepted that these all occurred only in the front line (very unlikely) it would still only total a 59 percent casualty rate across the entire 12 days of battle not two days. Accepting that the total battalion strength was originally 1,247, as other historians have more accurately calculated, real loss to the 4 CMR between 2 and 14 June 1916 was only about a third of its total strength, not the alarmingly high 89 percent as originally claimed. The actual loss on 2–3 June was even less than a third of the unit's total strength.

The Canadians rapidly counterattacked the Germans the following day, but the necessity of acting quickly resulted in a uncoordinated and unsupported riposte that was only partially successful. Lieutenant-General Byng could not afford to let General der Infanterie von Watter consolidate his position on Mount Sorrel and had to strike fast before the Wurttembergers could organize their defence. Unfortunately the only readily available asset in his arsenal was the infantry. He ordered the counterattack to take place at night to offset some of the disadvantage in firepower, but Byng lacked a clear picture of the battle and rushed his brigade commanders to execute their attacks. Against typical reserve, *landwehr*, or ersatz Prussian infantry the gamble might have succeeded, but against the disciplined Wurttembergers it failed miserably in several places. The Canadians did manage to recapture some of Observatory Ridge but it was not enough to force the Germans to retire. A deliberate attack was the only thing that would dislodge the enemy from the heights and time was needed to prepare such an assault.

The Germans attacked again on 6 June at Hooge and inflicted serious casualties on the 28th (Northwest) Canadian Infantry Battalion when they blew four mines under the garrison and wiped out a whole company of its soldiers.[32] The German assault was eventually stemmed by the RCR and the 31st (Alberta) Canadian Infantry Battalion, but not before Hooge and its surroundings were captured. Both sides continued to trade insults and blows for several more days while the Canadian Corps prepared a deliberate set-piece attack to retake the salient. The man tasked to plan and execute the attack was Major-General Arthur Currie. Conducting aggressive intelligence collection on the Germans and preparing extremely detailed and accurate target lists for the artillery and mortars, Currie ensured that when he sent his soldiers back into battle they would form the tip of a very coordinated spear. On the night of 12 June he launched his assault against the German positions at Mount Sorrel, and by late the next morning the Canadians had retaken all the ground lost nearly a fortnight before.

In every sense the Battle of Mount Sorrel was a gruelling contest between two peer adversaries fuelled by natural robustness and a hint of national pride. On the first day of the engagement, 2 June 1916, fortune certainly favoured the brave, but the nearly 12,000 Canadian killed, wounded, and missing that the battle would eventually claim might suggest that in war no amount of bravery or luck can absolutely ensure one's survival on the battlefield. War has and will remain a terrible business.

NOTES

1.   For the British official account of the battle see Brigadier-General Sir James E. Edmonds, *Official History of the War: Military Operations France and Belgium 1916, Vol. 1* (London: Macmillan and Co. Ltd. 1932), 227–245. The Canadian official account see Colonel G.W.L. Nicholson, *Official History of*

the Canadian Army in the First World War: Canadian Expeditionary Force, 1914–1919 (Ottawa: Queen's Printer and Controller of Stationary, 1964), 147–154.

2. LAC. RG 150, Accession 1992–93/166, Box 9882–23. Personnel Service Record of John Frederick Holmes Ussher, Canadian Expeditionary Force [CEF].

3. German strategy in the west is mostly recently examined in Robert T. Foley, *German Strategy and the Path to Verdun: Erich von Falkenhayn and the Development of Attrition, 1870–1916* (Cambridge University Press, 2005); and British generalship and strategy is assessed most recently in Simon Robbins. *British Generalship on the Western Front, 1914–1918* (London: Routledge, 2005).

4. Recent studies of the Somme battle include Martin Gilbert, *The Battle of the Somme: The Heroism and Horror of War* (Toronto: McLelland and Stewart, 2006), and Robin Prior and Trevor Wilson, *The Somme* (New Haven: Yale University Press, 2005).

5. This refers to the Triple Entente of France, Russian, and Great Britain opposed to the Triple Alliance of Germany, Austria-Hungary, and Italy.

6. Peter Barton, *The Battlefields of the First World War* (London: Constable and Robinson, Ltd., and the Imperial War Museum, 2005), 118–119. This book and its CDs offer amazing panoramic landscape shots of the Mount Sorrel and Hooge battlefields during 1915 and 1916.

7. Interestingly, the name "Mount Sorrel" is not an indigenous one, but the name given to this high feature by a British officer from the Leicestershire Regiment who before the war served as the director of the Mountsorrel Granite Company.

8. Ralph Hodder-Williams, *Princess Patricia's Canadian Light Infantry, 1914–1919, Vol. 1* (Toronto: Hoder and Stoughton, 1923), 99–103.

9. Peter Chasseaud, *Rats Alley: Trench Names of the Western Front, 1914–1918* (Gloucestershire: Spellmount, 2006), 36–37.

10. David Nash ed., *German Army Handbook April 1918* (London: Arms and Armour Press, 1977), 33–35. This publication was originally issued by the British Expeditionary Force General Staff as, *Handbook of the German Army in War, April 1918*, having been amended and updated from the March 1917 edition distributed the previous year.

11. For Canadian war establishment tables 1915–1917, see Nicholson, *Canadian Expeditionary Force*. Reproductions of original British War Establishment tables for the Division and Battalion (1915–16) are reprinted in Norm Christie, *For King and Empire: The Canadians at Ypres, 22nd, 26th April 1915* (Ottawa: CEF Books, 1996), 10–12.

12. Harry Laird. *Prisoner Five-One-Eleven* (Toronto: Ontario Press Ltd, 1919), 35.

13. Watter's career is described in Hans Möller-Witten. *Geschichte der Ritter des Ordens pour le mérite im Weltkrieg* (1935).

14. Born as Prince Wilhelm Karl Florestan Gero Crescentius of Urach, Count of Wurttemberg, he was the elder son of Wilhelm, 1st Duke of Urach, the head of a morganatic branch of the Royal House of Wurttemberg, and his second wife, Princess Florestine of Monaco, occasional acting Regent of Monaco. After the war he made a failed attempt to be anointed the King of Lithuania.

15. The young Leutnant Erwin Rommel, destined to become the most famous German general in the Second World War, originally served as an officer with No. 7 Company, Infanterie-Regiment König Wilhelm I (6. Württembergisches) Nr. 124 of the 53. Kgl. Württembergische Infanterie-Brigade (27 Div). However, he was transferred to the Wurttenberg Mountain Battalion in the fall of 1915, and was fighting on the Eastern front at the time of the battle of Mount Sorrel.

16. Günter Wegner, *Stellenbesetzung der deutschen Heere 1815–1939* (Biblio Verlag, Osnabrück, 1993), Bd. 1

17. Hermann Cron et al., *Ruhmeshalle unserer alten Armee* (Berlin, 1935); and

by the same author, *Geschichte des deutschen Heeres im Weltkriege 1914–1918* (Berlin, 1937).

18. David Nash ed. *German Army Handbook April 1918* (London: Arms and Armour Press, 1977). This publication was originally issued by the BEF General Staff as, *Handbook of the German Army in War, April 1918*, having been amended and updated from the March 1917 edition distributed the previous year.

19. Fort Frontenac Army Library [FFAL], Manuscripts Collection [MC] 3, "Only a Buck Private," Memoirs of Morley Louis Ackerman, 14th (Royal Montreal Regiment) Battalion, Canadian Expeditionary Forces [CEF], 54.

20. Brigadier-General Sir James E. Edmonds, *History of the Great War Military Operations France and Belgium, 1916* (London: Macmillan & Co., Ltd., 1932), 231, fn.1. There is no source cited for Byng's statement though it has been taken as factual in later publications discussing this event.

21. German ordnance, firing tables, and procedures are discussed in Herbert Jager, *German Artillery of World War One* (Wiltshire: The Crowood Press, 2001).

22. An artillery board was one of the references observers would employ to direct and adjust artillery fire forward of friendly positions. It usually consisted of a wooden board placed in the trench, clearly marked with trench names and/or map references, and obviously facing the rear towards friendly lines.

23. Though the timing of the detonation was recorded as 1:07 p.m. the exact number of mines blown in front of the Canadian positions has been disputed by historians. Some Canadian accounts identify only one mine, whereas the British official history cites three mines blown, while some German accounts of the battle suggest as many as five were detonated.

24. The experiences of this soldier can be further explored in J. Harvey Douglas, *Captured: Sixteen Months as a Prisoner of War* (Toronto: McLelland, Goodchild & Stewart, 1918).

25. A detailed account of this event may be found in Gordon MacKinnon, "Major General Malcolm Smith Mercer: The Highest Ranking Officer in the Great War Killed by Friendly Fire," *Canadian Military Journal*, Vol. 8, No. 1 (Spring 2007), 75–82.

26. LAC, RG 9, Series III-D-3, Vol. 4813, File 5, Canadian Corps War Diary (General Staff) 1916, 154.

27. Hodder-Williams, 123–124.

28. Tim Cook. *At The Sharp End: Canadians Fighting the Great War: 1914–1916* (Toronto: Viking Canada, 2007), 349.

29. This figure was repeated in Nicholson, *The Official History of the Canadian Expeditionary Force*, 149; and most recently in Cook, 351.

30. The figure of 1247 was compiled one name at a time by 4 CMR historian Ian Forsdike and is consistent with authorized paper strengths for CEF battalions in 1915–1916. Details of his personnel research may be found on the battalion history website, *http://www.4cmr.com.*

31. In June 1916 a CEF battalion consisted of a HQ element, signallers, attachments such as a medical officer and paymaster, pioneers, a machine-gun section, four infantry companies, and a base detail that included the first reserve and the unit band.

32. A Company, 28th Battalion, occupied trenches 70 to 72 where the mines were blown. Except for a few men who were dispersed to other tasks, the entire company was effectively annihilated in a single stroke.

6

ONE TOUGH FIGHT:
CANADIAN PARATROOPERS PENETRATE THE REICH,
24 MARCH 1945

Bernd Horn

The briefing hut was heavy with silence. The assembled British and Canadian paratroop commanders anxiously waited for the briefing on their next major operation from their brigade commander. They were not disappointed. "Gentlemen," bellowed Brigadier James Hill, the well-respected commander of the 3rd Parachute Brigade, "the artillery support is fantastic! And if you are worried about the kind of reception you'll get, just put yourself in the place of the enemy." What would you think he said, "if you saw a horde of ferocious, bloodthirsty paratroopers, bristling with weapons, cascading down upon you from the skies?"[1]

The image set all at ease. Among those assembled for the briefing on Operation Varsity, the airborne assault that would pierce the Reich itself, were a small group of Canadians who belonged to the 1st Canadian Parachute Battalion (1 Cdn Para Bn). The unit itself was a dark horse. During the early years of the war Canadian commanders and politicians dismissed the idea of airborne forces as a luxury that the Canadian Army could not afford and frankly had no use for. However, the continuing American and British development of these forces and subsequent belief that paratroopers were a defining element of a modern army led the Canadians, in July 1942, to form a similar capability, but on a much smaller scale. Unsure what to do with these forces, the Canadian Government attached its paratroopers to the British 6th Airborne Division in the summer of 1943. The unit subsequently distinguished itself during the Normandy Invasion and breakout campaign in June-August 1944. They quickly demonstrated themselves to be pre-eminent combat troops.

The Battalion had just returned to England from its emergency deployment to the Ardennes where it assisted in stemming the surprise German Christmas offensive. They now prepared for their next mission where they would once again be thrust into the forefront of battle.

Hitler's failed gamble in the Ardennes (Battle of the Bulge) in December 1944, exhausted what little reserves the Germans had been able to cobble together. Conversely, the Allies had, by mid-January 1945, beaten off the desperate German counterattack, and, despite heavy losses sustained in the battle, amassed almost four million men under arms in Northwest Europe. As a result, the Allied steamroller once again began its relentless advance. By 10 March 1945, the Germans were forced to withdraw to the East bank of the Rhine River in a last effort to defend the German frontier itself.[2]

Planning for the crossing of the Rhine River had begun as early as October 1944. At this time, Allied planners targeted the Emmerich-Wesel area as a crossing point because of its strategic location close to the vital Ruhr region, as well as the suitability of its terrain for a rapid breakout by mechanized forces once a bridgehead was achieved. In addition, the ground lent itself to the possibility of large airborne operations in support of the complex river crossing. Field Marshal Montgomery and his 21st Army Group were charged with conducting the assault into Germany, which was given the code name Operation Plunder.

"My intention," declared Montgomery, "was to secure a bridgehead prior to developing operations to isolate the Ruhr and to thrust into the Northern plains of Germany."[3] He planned to cross the Rhine on a front of two armies between Rheinberg and Rees with the Ninth U.S. Army on the right and the Second British Army on the left. He demanded that the bridgehead be large enough to cover Wesel in the south from enemy and ground action, and capable of encompassing bridge sites to the north in Emmerich. Equally important, the bridgehead had to provide enough space to form up large formations for the final drive that would culminate in the complete collapse of German resistance.[4]

Courtesy Ted Zuber.

Mass landing by Canadian paratroopers during Operation Varsity. Pencil sketch by Canadian war artist Ted Zuber.

Montgomery assigned to Lieutenant-General Sir Miles Dempsey's Second Army the task of thrusting across the Rhine and seizing Wesel. To assist Dempsey in this feat, the Army Group commander was given the support of the First Allied Airborne Army (FAAA), which was responsible for dropping the American 18th Airborne Corps, commanded by Major-General Matthew Ridgway, in direct support of the operation. The 18th Airborne Corps consisted of the U.S. 17th and British 6th Airborne Divisions. Its mission was to "disrupt the hostile defense of the Rhine in the Wesel Sector by the seizure of key terrain by airborne attack, in order to rapidly deepen the bridgehead to be seized in an assault crossing of the Rhine by British ground forces, in order to facilitate the further offensive operations of the Second Army" and its link-up with the U.S. Ninth Army.[5] The airborne part of the assault into Germany was designated Operation Varsity.

The finalized 18th Airborne Corps plan centred on dropping the two divisions abreast to seize the Diersfordter Wald and high ground three to five miles east of the Rhine River and north of Wesel up to the Issel River. Allied commanders felt that this was critical to the success of the assault river crossing because it would bottle up potential reinforcements and, more significantly, deny enemy artillery observers the ability to call down accurate and devastating fire from the ridge that dominated the Rhine River. Equally important, was the necessity to seize control of the five-by-six mile tract of woods covering the high ground that could mask camouflaged, well-entrenched enemy infantry and gun positions capable of inflicting punishing casualties and significant delay to the crossing and subsequent breakout operations. As a result, the 17th U.S. Airborne Division was ordered to seize, clear, and secure the high ground east of Diersfordt, and a number of bridges over the Issel River to protect the southern flank of the airborne corps and to establish contact with 1 Commando Brigade in Wesel to its right, 6th British Airborne Division to its left, and 12 British Corps to its rear. The 6th British Airborne Division was specifically tasked to seize the high ground east of Bergen in the northwest part of the Diersfordter Wald, the town of Hamminkeln, as well as a number of bridges over the Issel River. It was also responsible for protecting the northern flank of the airborne corps and for establishing contact with 12 British Corps moving up from its rear and the 17th U.S. Airborne Division on its right.[6]

In turn, the mission assigned to 3 Parachute Brigade, to which the Canadian paratroopers belonged, was to drop first and secure the drop zone and then clear the northern part of the Diersfordter Wald. More important, it was given the daunting mission of seizing the 150-foot high Schnappenburg feature that was defended by the well-blooded 7th German Parachute Division. It was essential that all enemy artillery positions and infantry entrenchments in the woods and surrounding farms and villages be silenced.

Within the Brigade, the 8th Battalion was assigned the task of seizing the northern part of the Brigade's allocated section of the Wald, while the 9th Battalion was given responsibility for the southern part, including the Schnappenburg feature. The Canadian paratroopers were responsible for the central part, specifically the western part of the woods, a number of buildings, and a section of the main road that ran north from Wesel to Emmerich.[7]

The overwhelming force available to smother German resistance was not the only component of the outline plan that foreshadowed success. Airborne operations had matured dramatically since the beginning of the war. As such, Allied planners and airborne commanders applied the hard lessons learned to date, with the result that some dramatic departures from established practice were exercised. Most significant was the decision to drop the airborne troops after the actual crossing of the Rhine River by ground forces. FAAA commanders and planners quickly noted that an airborne operation before the crossing would "hamstring artillery for the assault crossing." Moreover, they argued that the river crossing was not the most difficult part of the operation, the real challenge being "the subsequent expansion of the bridgehead and in particular the capture of the Diersfordter wood" to ensure that the assaulting division would not be hemmed in on the far bank.[8]

Montgomery endorsed this plan. Both he and his airborne commanders were convinced that a daylight drop would be desirable. It would avoid the problems experienced in previous airborne operations that hampered navigation to the objective and led to missed drop zones, which dispersed the paratroopers. A daylight attack would also lessen difficulties in assembling the the men in a timely fashion once they were on the ground and make it easier to provide them with adequate protective fire.

The plan called for both divisions to be dropped directly on their objectives within range of their supporting guns that were sited on the west side of the river. This available fire support would not only provide immediate assistance to the paratroopers but it would also facilitate link-up with ground forces on the first day.[9]

The hazards of a daytime drop, however, particularly into an area that was easily recognized by the enemy as ideal for an airborne assault and known by the Allies to be bristling with flak positions and machine-gun nests, was well understood by airborne commanders such as Ridgway, Gale, Bols, and Hill. Nonetheless, they felt that the risk of a daylight drop directly on the objective would be mitigated by concurrent actions of the ground force, as well as the preparation of the battlefield by the Allied Air Force. They believed that by conducting the river crossing first, the German commanders would react accordingly and be preoccupied with the hordes of Allied forces flowing across the Rhine. "Well, gentlemen, you'll be glad to know," announced Major-General Eric Bols, commander 6th Airborne Division, "that this time we're not going to be dropped down as a carrot held out for the ground forces." He explained that the "Army and the Navy are going to storm across the Rhine, and just when they've gained Jerry's attention in front — bingo! we drop down behind him."[10]

The airborne commanders also placed faith in the bombing campaign, which, supported by artillery from the friendly bank, would theoretically disorientate and destroy German infantry, artillery, and anti-aircraft positions. They also felt that by landing directly on their targets, the paratroopers would avoid a long drawn out fight to their objectives and be able to simply overwhelm any enemy force that survived the aerial and artillery bombardment.

To that end, it was decided that the airborne force be "put down in the shortest possible time" into a concentrated area.[11] In addition, the glider element of the parachute brigades was increased above the normal allocation to enable the carriage of heavy weapons, jeeps, stores, and reserve ammunition. This also allowed for a margin of safety should attrition en route to and on the objective be excessively high. Finally, of equal importance, as already noted, landing on the objective enabled the airborne force the ability to link up with ground forces on the first day, relieving the lightly armed paratroopers from the task of defending captured positions for lengthy periods, which had been the case at Arnhem, in Holland, six months earlier.

The overall plan was carefully knit together and the necessary coordination completed. On 14 March 1945, a firm decision was made to conduct both Operations Plunder and Varsity on 24 March.[12] Despite the overwhelming force that was amassed to crush German resistance, further steps were taken to guarantee unhindered success. During the three days before the operation the Allies commenced, a massive sustained bombing campaign was carried out. It was designed to suppress the German capacity to fight, hinder his defensive preparations, and disrupt his communications. In the initial phase, Allied bombers flew over 16,000 sorties and dropped nearly 50 thousand tons of bombs.[13] These strikes not only hampered the movement of vital economic traffic from the Ruhr industrial region, but also denied the enemy the ability to communicate and facilitate large scale reinforcement or redeployment of men and material to the targeted Rhine area. In addition, 14 bridges and viaducts were made impassable, enemy headquarter complexes and hutted camps were completely demolished, 160 enemy aircraft were destroyed either on the ground or in the air, and 23 known flak positions in the area of the designated parachute dropping zones (DZ) and glider landing zones (LZ) were neutralized.[14] In sum, the German defences suffered colossal damage before the first Allied soldier crossing the river.[15]

Although, initial planning for Operation Varsity had begun in October 1944, ongoing operations and the temporary crisis in the Ardennes had pushed the planning process to the back burner. When it was resurrected in February-March 1945, there was little time to mount the large preparations that were seen before Normandy. What is more, there was neither the same interest, nor the same sense of significance. Everyone was tired of the war and it was apparent that the German army was rapidly crumbling. "There was also some feeling," acknowledged veteran paratrooper Sergeant Andy Anderson, "that the success of the mission, perhaps did in fact mean a rapid end to the war."[16]

So, when the 1st Canadian Parachute Battalion returned from seven days of leave awarded after their return from the Ardennes campaign on 7 March 1945, there was little time for much worry or preparation. The Battalion was brought up to full strength. All personnel were once again tested on their weapon drills, and then conducted field firing exercises and a review of battle drill. However, the need to pre-position and prepare equipment, as well as the desire to avoid injuring soldiers before the operation meant that no large-scale exercise or practice parachute drop was conducted. This did not sit well with the Canadian paratroop commanders. Their men had not jumped since Exercise Eve in November 1944, and now, they were expected to jump onto the objective, into waiting enemy guns, without the ability to rehearse their parachuting drills.

These concerns were soon put aside so that all could deal with the realities of a complex operation. On 19 March, follow-on equipment in the form of large packs were prepared and passed on for transit overseas. The next day the Battalion was confined to Hill Hall Transit Camp in East Anglia in England. For the next three days the paratroopers were briefed on plasticine models and enlarged maps in regard to the entire operation and their part in it. Weapons were repeatedly cleaned and checked. Personal equipment was nervously prepared and, in many cases, final letters written for loved ones back home. The waiting was always the worst part. Nonetheless, the Battalion was set. "If ever a fighting unit was ready for anything," one veteran paratrooper declared, "this had to be it."[17]

At 2100 hours, on 23 March 1945, the guns suddenly lifted their bombardment. Under the cover of darkness British commandos commenced their attack on Wesel. An hour later, the first of a series of assaults that were to continue throughout the night across the Rhine River were conducted by the Second British and Ninth U.S. Armies. By first light, nine small bridgeheads had been secured across the Rhine between Emmerich and Wesel.[18]

As the Allied ground troops swarmed across the Rhine in the eerie darkness, the airborne forces were just beginning to form up in bases in England and France. The aerial armada — 1,696 troop transports and 1,050 tug aircraft towing 1,348 gliders, departing from 26 airfields — met in the crowded airspace over Belgium. In their cramped fuselages were crammed approximately 14,000 American and British airborne soldiers.[19] In support, 889 fighters escorted the air fleet to ensure it was not molested by German fighter aircraft, and another 2,153 fighter aircraft maintained an umbrella over the target area or ranged far over Germany hunting for any German plane that would dare to take off.[20]

The Canadians awoke at 0200 hours and emplaned aboard 35 C-47 Dakota aircraft. At 0730 hours they departed from Chipping Ongar airfield, in Essex, for their two hour and 10 minute flight to Germany. The aircraft were crewed by airmen of the American 9th Troop Carrier Command. "They were the scruffiest-looking guys, with baseball hats and cigars," asserted Major Richard Hilborn, "but they were awfully good."[21] Another veteran opined, "The Yanks radiated matter-of-fact confidence, well suited to the fleeting but vital relationship between parachutists and aircrews."[22] In fact, their skill was one of the primary reasons that Brigadier Hill based his plan on successfully dropping 2,200 fighting men in a comparatively restricted area, measuring approximately 800 by 1,000 yards, in six minutes.[23]

Courtesy 1 Canadian Parachute Battalion Association Archives.

Deadly ground — the Rhine DZ, 24 March 1945.

The flight across the English Channel and France was uneventful. The weather was perfect — a clear blue sky and negligible winds. "It was a gorgeous morning," recalled Dan Hartigan, "one of the most beautiful days I've ever experienced."[24] Joe King agreed. "Going across the channel," he said, "seeing all those aircraft in the beautiful morning sky was fantastic."[25] Moreover, not a single German aircraft penetrated the Allied fighter shield. "We met no opposition until we were right over the dropping zone," boasted one airborne commander, "The air cover was wonderful."[26]

The tranquility, however, was somewhat deceiving. The ground told a different story. "When dawn came pilots who flew east of the Rhine and north of the Ruhr," reported one journalist, "had never seen anything like it — whole towns and villages burning in an utter holocaust."[27] The Canadian paratroopers would soon find themselves dropping into this furnace. "Looking out the window briefly before 'Stand Up' my impression is of a very wide lake," wrote Sergeant Anderson, "I have no idea what I expected, but the river was massive, cold and uninviting … within seconds someone hollered the customary, stand up and hook up."[28] But Anderson's attention, as with that of so many others, was soon focused on their battle for survival. The transport planes, flying in nine aircraft formation, held true to their course and maintained a steady formation despite the heavy flak that now spit up from the earth. "We went out in a tight formation," confirmed Private Jan de Vries, "the pilots took no evasive action."[29] Private Zakaluk reminisced that "it was a ride to enjoy." However, as they neared their objective, "I could see puffs of smoke in the air between hundreds of planes," he recalled, "anti-aircraft shells exploding and tracers arcing their way into the sky," mixed with "balls of fire" screaming down to earth as aircraft were hit.[30] "Lying on the ground, looking up taking off my chute," remembered Lieutenant William Jenkins, "I could see these things [C-47s] blasted all over the sky." He added, "I couldn't help but admire those guys."[31] The deputy commanding officer during the jump, then Major Fraser Eadie, noted, "They came in a little higher than we wanted — we wanted 450 feet."[32] Nonetheless, "the Yank aircraft did a hell of a job for us," praised Eadie, "I have never been on a better drop, not training or operational."[33] Major Hilborn concurred. "The pilot," he remarked, "put us down approximately 100 yards from where I wanted to be within a minute of the time I had to be there."[34]

The descent was not so uneventful. Neither the aerial bombing, nor the artillery bombardment was as effective as the airborne soldiers had been praying for. Private Zakaluk was relieved to feel his parachute open and find himself floating down to earth. But his relief soon dissipated. "Buzzing all around me!" he recalled, "I can't see them, but I can hear them." Then it hit, "Hey! These guys are shooting at me!" He was not only one. "I heard bullets going by and looked up to see bullet holes in my chute," reminisced Private de Vries, "it sounds just like being in the rifle butts!" His thoughts, he admitted, "were to get down fast." Major Eadie also became the target of some well-aimed shots that cracked about his

Courtesy 1 Canadian Parachute Battalion Association Archives.

"Suicide Woods" — named so for good reason. In the foreground can be seen the cost paid to wrest control of the wood line from the German defenders.

ears. He quickly went limp in his harness feigning death hoping this would fool his tormentors. It seemed to work, although his landing left a lot to be desired.

On the ground the airborne forces met with varying resistance. In some areas opposition was negligible, but elsewhere troops dropped directly on entrenched enemy positions and dug-in artillery and air defence guns. From Eadie's vantage point "It was hot!" One paratrooper recalled that he landed "like a rock," and found himself stretched out on the ground, somewhat amazed to find nothing broken, and his kit bag still intact. Like others, he unpacked his gear and started for the rendevous point (RV) at the edge of the woods about 200 yards away. "Crouched low, running like hell," he recalled, I was "conscious of fire coming from somewhere, and several men lying motionless on the DZ." A paratroop officer later acknowledged, "It was real flat-out fighting until about noon." Another simply said it was "Two hours of real killing."

Brigadier James Hill, the imperturbable commander of 3 Parachute Brigade, had imparted to his paratroops that "speed and initiative is the order of the day," emphasizing that "risks will be taken [and] the enemy will be attacked and destroyed wherever he is found."[35] He further drilled home this point with his NCOs: "If by chance you should happen to meet one of these Huns in person," he explained, "you will treat him, gentlemen, with extreme disfavour."[36] Evidently, the enemy was given the same type of briefing by their commanders. Although the Third Reich was crumbling, its soldiers were still proving to be a formidable foe. "The Germans we were up against on this operation put up a pretty good fight," acknowledged Company Sergeant-Major (CSM) Johnny Kemp, "they were as good as us."[37] Even the 6th Airborne Division intelligence staff had to begrudgingly agree. Although they reported that the German First Parachute Army was severely mauled in the preceding month on the west side of the Rhine River, the "Estimate of the Enemy Situation" before Operation Varsity warned that the enemy's fanaticism and level of skill was still such that they would be able to provide fearsome opposition. And they did. Every farm was turned into a stronghold. "Morale was fairly high and this was especially true in the Fallschirm divisions," confirmed Lieutenant-General Gustav Hoehne, commander of the German 2nd Parachute Division in a postwar interrogation.[38] But many of the Canadian paratroopers already knew this — the contested areas of the drop zone were murderous. "They were young and full of fight," reminisced Dick Creelman. Another paratrooper remembered, "they fought like tigers."[39]

The German tenacity did not bode well for the paratroopers. As the first Allied wave of aircraft carrying paratroops appeared over the target at 0952 hours, an unexplained eight minutes early, enemy reaction began slowly but quickly gained momentum. The Canadians jumped three minutes later. Dug in on the edge of the woods, the German machine guns and light flak cannons now wreaked havoc on the DZ. It was utter chaos. "We were getting pretty badly hammered from some houses on the edge of the field we landed in," recollected CSM Kemp, "we knew we had to attack them right away."[40] Most of the Battalion faced heavy machine-gun and sniper fire, which accounted for most of the unit's casualties.[41] "We were fighting right on the dropping zone immediately as we landed," lamented Lieutenant Bob Firlotte, "It was pretty bad."[42]

But this was not totally unexpected. "Listen clear now! Pay attention!" bellowed senior NCOs in the different aircraft, "As soon as you hit the bloody deck, and you're out of your parachutes, fix bayonets and go for the goddam woods!"[43] Most followed this advice. The DZ became a hive of activity with small groups of men shedding their parachute harnesses and rushing the wood line, firing from the hip. Officers and NCOs attempted to rally men to form organized assaults wherever possible. But the initiative of the airborne soldier came to the forefront once again. Private James Quigley gathered a number of men who were milling around him on the DZ but were uncertain of the direction to the RV point. Despite the intense fire, "by his dash and contempt for the hail of bullets he inspired them to follow him" and destroy a company objective.[44]

The Battalion quickly gained the upper hand despite the variance in the quality of the enemy and the subsequent level of resistance encountered. "It was individual fighting in the first stages until we got organized," explained Major Hilborn, "and the boys did a terrific job."[45] And once organized, there was no stopping them. "C" Company, just as in Normandy, was once again the first Canadian sub-unit to jump. They raced off the DZ to their RV points from where platoons quickly assaulted their objectives — a series of road junctions, wood lines, and the Hingendahlshof farm. Within 30 minutes they had achieved all their tasks. This they accomplished without their senior leadership. The company commander, Major John Hanson, broke his shoulder on landing.

Courtesy 1 Canadian Parachute Battalion Association Archives.

Two members of the Battalion dug in on the edge of the DZ.

Furthermore, Second-in-Command (2IC), Captain John Clancy, as well as a platoon commander, Lieutenant Ken Spicer, failed to even reach the DZ. Their aircraft was hit by flak on the approach and turned into blazing torch. As the aircrew struggled to keep the airplane aloft, the paratroopers managed to bail out. However, all were dispersed and Clancy unfortunately landed in enemy territory and was captured. Nonetheless, Sergeants Miles Saunders and Bill Murray quickly organized the available troops and successfully executed the Company's mission. With their objectives secure they then dug in on the north side of the Battalion perimeter and adopted a defensive posture. But for them the pressure remained. For the next 16 hours they held off German probing attacks and exchanged direct and indirect fire with an enemy that simply would not quit.

Concurrently, "A" Company landed on the eastern end of the DZ. They had an extremely accurate drop and within 30 minutes were organized in their RV with approximately 70 percent of their men. Officer Commanding (OC), Major Peter Griffin, decided to mount an immediate attack on a group of buildings that were designated for use by Battalion headquarters. Initially, they met fierce enemy resistance and the attack seemed to falter. Without hesitation, and under heavy fire, Company Sergeant-Major George Green organized covering fire and then led a PIAT anti-tank weapon detachment up to the first house. Using the weight of fire to his benefit, he then personally led the assault into the building. After vicious close quarter combat, the structure was rid of its hostile hosts. Green then went on to clear the remainder of the houses in a similar manner. He was awarded the Distinguished Conduct Medal for his "contempt of danger" and "inspiration to the men."[46]

The sub-unit reported their objective clear by 1130 hours and subsequently, took up their company position at the southern end of the village of Bergerfürth. Later in the day the enemy attempted to recapture the lost territory but the counterattack was easily beaten off.

"B" Company's reception, much like that of "C" Company was heavily contested. The company 2IC described the DZ as a "holocaust." "Everyone running in all directions," he wrote, "but finally following NCOs and Officers to the RV." The Company formed up in the rendevous point "with the

An airborne Bren gunner and PIAT (anti-tank) team remain vigilant on the edge of the woods skirting the DZ for possible German counterattack, 24 March 1945.

usual confusion which is attached to a reorganization."[47] The OC, Captain Sam McGowan showed up late, bleeding heavily and sporting a bullet hole in his helmet that miraculously entered the front, travelled around the inside rim and then exited through the back. He immediately directed the platoons to assault their objectives. As a result, a group of farm buildings and a wooded area were quickly brought under attack. Under a heavy covering fire from their Bren guns, "B" Company quickly "overran the bunkers and buildings, driving the enemy out with grenades and gunfire." The Bren gun coverage kept the enemy's head down, explained one veteran, "we ran in right after the explosion and shot up anyone still there."[48] It was controlled chaos. "We are off and running," confided Sergeant Anderson to his diary, "firing wildly from the hip covered by Bren fire. We overrun bunkers, toss grenades into the houses and barns, generally raise hell and take a few prisoners."[49]

In less than 30 minutes they too had secured their objectives.

Once established in his defensive position, the "B" Company commander dispatched a patrol to clear the woods in the immediate vicinity of the sub-unit's perimeter. Shortly thereafter, Sergeant A. Page and his six man patrol returned with 98 prisoners. Throughout the day the Company engaged enemy soldiers who were attempting to flee from the field of battle.

By noon, the Battalion was firmly in control of its area of responsibility. In fact, this was the case for the entire formation. Within 35 minutes of the drop, 85 percent of the Brigade had reported in.[50] Shortly thereafter, the respective objectives began to fall. A pattern now began to emerge. Throughout the day, as the Battalion settled into its defensive position, stragglers continued to report in, many wounded, to their respective organizations. In addition, by 1400 hours it seemed as though direct enemy resistance in the immediate area had ceased. As a result, patrols were dispatched to ensure the DZ and surrounding woods were clear of enemy, while searching for missing paratroopers who could be wounded and in need of aid. They also attempted to bring in much needed supplies from the damaged gliders that laid strewn about the landing zone.

Throughout the night the enemy made attempts to infiltrate the position or simply to escape the Rhine bridgehead that had been established.

The alert paratroopers with the aid of their Vickers medium machine guns (MMG) and mortars ably responded to the enemy movements. However, at first light a number of self-propelled (SP) guns began to fire at the Battalion positions from 400 yards out. The SP guns specifically targeted the Vickers MMGs and the mortars because of their effectiveness. German infantry then commenced an assault but quickly withdrew as a result of the withering fire that poured into their ranks. One SP gun was destroyed and another pulled back when they were fired on by four PIAT anti-tank weapon teams, who responded to the threat, and well-directed mortar fire.[51] The defeat of this attack marked the end of the German's countermoves. Although the enemy had now largely disappeared, they still maintained harassing mortar and artillery fire that became more of a nuisance than an actual threat.

The battle was brief but exceptionally bloody. Two-and-a-half hours after the commencement of the airborne assault, all Allied paratroops had been dropped and were in possession of their designated objectives. Moreover, 109 tons of ammunition, 695 vehicles, and 113 artillery pieces had been landed by gliders.[52] But the cost was high. Within the 6th Airborne Division approximately 45 percent of the vehicles, 29 percent of the 75 mm Pack Howitzers, 50 percent of the 25-pounder artillery pieces, and 56 percent of the 17-pounder anti-tank guns delivered by gliders were damaged or destroyed.[53] The casualty count for the Division was 1,297 killed, wounded, or missing.[54] The Battalion's share of the butcher's bill was 67 of approximately 475 personnel.[55]

Included in this count was the commanding officer, Lieutenant-Colonel Jeff Nicklin. When he failed to show up at the RV, Fraser Eadie immediately took command. However, as time went on, concern began to mount. A clearance patrol found Nicklin approximately 36 hours after the attack. He was discovered hanging from a tree still in his parachute, his body riddled with bullets. He had dropped into the trees directly above German entrenchments and never had a fighting chance. The news was a bit of a shock to many. He was "one who almost seemed indestructible," remarked Sergeant Anderson, "six foot, three inches tall, football hero back home, a stern disciplinarian, physical fitness his specialty."[56] Ironically, Nicklin normally jumped in the middle of the stick so that he could have half of his headquarters on either side of him upon landing. However, for this operation he wanted to be the number one jumper so that he could lead his troops into battle.[57] That fateful decision cost him his life and the Battalion their commanding officer.

As the members of the Battalion reflected on their accomplishments and lost comrades, fatigue and quiet personal rejoicing swept over the survivors. Harrowing tales of close calls and stories of individual gallantry and heroism now surfaced. One such account revolved around Corporal Frederick Topham who earned the only Victoria Cross to be awarded in the 6th Airborne Division during the Second World War. The 27-year-old Toronto native was the eleventh Canadian to win the British Empire's highest award for bravery in the war.

During the initial battle, while treating casualties on the drop zone, Corporal Topham and several other medical orderlies heard a cry for help emanating from the fire-swept DZ. Two medics moved forward to rescue the wounded soldier, but they were shot and killed. On his own initiative and without hesitation Topham braved the intense fire to assist the wounded paratrooper even though he had seen the other two orderlies killed before his eyes. "I only did," he later modestly stated, "what every last man in my outfit would do."[58] As he treated the wounded soldier he was shot through the nose. Bleeding profusely and in great pain he completed first aid and then carried the wounded man slowly and steadily through the hail of fire to protective cover in the woods.

For the next two hours Topham refused medical attention for his own wound and continued to evacuate casualties from the drop zone with complete disregard for the heavy and accurate enemy fire. "I didn't have time to think about it," he later explained, "I was too busy."[59] It was not until all the wounded paratroopers had been evacuated that he consented to have his wound treated. By now his face had swelled up enormously and the medical officer ordered his evacuation. He interceded with such vigour that he was allowed to return to duty. On his way back to his company, he came across a Bren gun carrier that had just received a direct hit. It lay burning fiercely, amid explosions of enemy artillery shells and the mortar ammunition it had been carrying. Despite the direction of an experienced officer on the spot who warned everyone not to approach the carrier, Topham immediately went out alone and rescued the three occupants and arranged for their evacuation. Topham's valour was unrivalled. "For six hours," read his commendation, "most of the time in great pain, he performed a series of acts of outstanding bravery, and his magnificent and selfless courage inspired all those who witnessed it."[60]

Bravery and courage by all belligerents aside, it became clear early on that the airborne assault had been a success. "The sight of the massive drop," wrote one Canadian veteran, "descending in an area about ten by ten kilometers square, floored the enemy."[61] The show of force could not but impress even the Allied soldiers. "The concentrated drop," wrote a medic, "gave an impression of irresistible might."[62] A British infantry captain,

Courtesy 1 Canadian Parachute Battalion Association Archives.

A moment's pause. Members of 1 Platoon take a breather in a shell scrape on the edge of the DZ following the battle.

voicing the opinion of many, questioned "how on earth can they go on in face of this?"[63] German prisoners provided the answer. They attested to the hopelessness they felt once they witnessed the overwhelming number of paratroopers that seemed to flow from an endless stream of aircraft. Major-General Fiebig, Commander 84th Infantry Division, confessed "he had been badly surprised by the sudden advent of two complete divisions in his area" and throughout his interrogation reiterated "the shattering effect of such immensely superior forces on his already badly depleted troops."[64]

The effect on the enemy quickly translated itself to events on the ground. By 1500 hours the reconnaissance elements of the 15th Scottish Division linked-up with the 1st Canadian Parachute Battalion. By 0430 hours the next morning the first armoured columns of tanks and Bren gun carriers of the 15th Scottish Division began to pass through the unit's position. The paratroopers welcomed them warmly. They had achieved link-up with the ground force in less than 24 hours. But there was little time to celebrate. The final push was now commencing.

The following day, on 26 March, almost 48 hours exactly to the hour of the Battalion's fateful drop into Germany, they were ordered into a brigade assembly area for a hot meal and some rest. "The battalion," boasted Hill, "really put up a most tremendous performance on 'D' day and as a result of their dash and enthusiasm they overcame their objectives, which were very sticky ones, with considerable ease killing a very large number of Germans and capturing many others."[65]

Overall, Allied commanders declared that Operation Varsity was an enormous success. "The airborne drop in depth," explained Major-General Ridgway, "destroyed enemy gun and rear defensive positions in one day — positions it might have taken many days to reduce by ground attack." He added, "the impact of the airborne divisions at one blow shattered hostile defence and permitted the prompt link-up with ground troops. The increased bridgehead materially assisted the build-up essential for subsequent success." The tenacious drive eastward and "rapid seizure of key terrain," he concluded, "were decisive to subsequent developments, permitting Allied armor to debouch into the North German plain at full strength and momentum."[66]

The Canadian paratroopers played an integral part in this success. Once again they achieved all their missions, earning a Victoria Cross in the process. Despite the fatigue and the realization that casualties were once again heavy, they were buoyed by the realization that the war was coming to a rapid conclusion. All that lay ahead was to roll-up the final vestiges of Hitler's vaunted Third Reich.[67]

NOTES

1. Quoted in Brian Nolan, *Airborne* (Toronto: Lester Publishing Ltd., 1995), 146.

2. The Americans, on 7 March 1945, had by bold action and good fortune already secured a foothold on the West bank of the Rhine River by capturing the Ludendorff Bridge at Remagen. Within 24 hours a complete infantry division and a pontoon bridge had been established in the pocket Unfortunately, Remagen was in near impossible terrain to facilitate the massive armoured breakout that was required for the Allied assault into the industrial heartland of the Ruhr. See Brigadier-General Denis Whitaker and Shelagh Whitaker, *Rhineland* (New York: Stoddart, 2000), 278–282.

3. Canadian Airborne Forces Museum [henceforth CAFM], HQ British Army of the Rhine, "Operation Varsity. XVIII United States Corps (Airborne) in the Crossing of the River Rhine, 24 and 25 March 1945," November 1947, 7; and Historical Section (G.S.), Report No. 17, 12.

4. Field Marshal The Viscount Montgomery of Alamein, *Despatch Submitted to the Secretary of State for War Describing the Part Played by the 21st Army Group, and the Armies Under Command, From D Day to VE Day* (London: U.K. Information Services, 1946), 62; and Field Marshal The Viscount Montgomery of Alamein, *21 Army Group Normandy to the Baltic* (Germany: British Army of the Rhine, 1946), 247–248.

5. CAFM, Major-General James M. Gavin, *Airborne Warfare* (Washington: Infantry Journal Press, 1947), 132; HQ British Army of the Rhine, "Operation

Varsity. XVIII United States Corps (Airborne) in the Crossing of the River Rhine, 24 and 25 March 1945," November 1947, 23; and Historical Section (G.S.), Report No. 17, 13.

6. Public Records Office (PRO), War Office (WO) 205/204, War Office: 21 Army Group: Military HQ Papers, Second World War, 1942–47. Operation Varsity: Revised outline, plan and appreciation — March 1945, "HQ First Allied Airborne Army Outline Plan for Operation Varsity (Revised)," 10 February 1945; LAC, RG 24, Vol. 15299, March 1945, 1 Cdn Para Bn War Diary, 17 March 1945, Appx F, "Operation Varsity — Plunder, 1 Cdn Para Bn Operations Order No. 1;" CAFM, HQ British Army of the Rhine, "Operation Varsity. XVIII United States Corps (Airborne) in the Crossing of the River Rhine, 24 and 25 March 1945," November 1947, 23; and General Sir Richard Gale, *Call to Arms. An Autobiography* (London: Hutchinson of London, 1968), 152. The 12th British Corps was tasked with assaulting across the Rhine on a two brigade front. The 15th Scottish Division was responsible for capturing the bridges over the Issel River west of Dingden and relieving the 6th Airborne Division in the area of Hamminkeln. 1st Commando Brigade was tasked with the capture of Wesel.

7. PRO, WO 171/4306, War Office: Allied Expeditionary Force, North West Europe (British elements): War Diaries, Second World War, 1943–46, HQ, January-August 1945, "Operation Varsity — Plunder, 1 Cdn Para Bn Operations Order No. 1, 2–4; *Ibid.*, "Operation Varsity — Plunder — 3 Para Bde Operations Order, No. 20," 15 March 1945, 5; Whitaker, 320; and Willes, 125.

8. PRO, WO 205/200, Operation Varsity — Part I, "Agenda for Airborne Conference on 9 February 1945 — Role of Airborne Troops," 8 February 1945 and "Minutes of Conference Held at Main HQ 21 Army Group, on 9 February 1945 to Consider Operation Varsity," 10 February 1945. The staff also concluded that "the German Air Force will have a better opportunity to interfere with 'Varsity' if the operation is mounted at night." PRO, WO 205/204, "Operation Varsity Revised Appendix 'C' — Appreciation of GAF, Part 1 — German Air Defences," HQ First Allied Airborne Army, 2 March 1945. This is significant as it was estimated that the Luftwaffe could muster up to 570 fighters to oppose the airborne force. " PRO, WO

205/200, "Op Order No. 531 For Operation Varsity," HQ No. 38 Group RAF, 16 March 1945.

9. Montgomery, *Normandy to the Baltic*, 254. In Normandy, for instance, approximately 75 percent of the paratroopers were missing for a considerable period. During Operation Market Garden in September 1944, part of the failure to quickly capture the bridge at Arnhem was the fact that drops were made too far from the actual objective. This criticism was substantiated by the German defenders who were given time to mobilize their defence and respond to the threat. Much of the blame has been levelled at Major-General Roy Urquhart who was appointed division commander with no prior airborne experience. He made the fateful decision to go with DZ locations between five to eight miles from the objective, distances contrary to airborne doctrine. He preferred good DZs at a distance compared to bad DZs close to the objective. He later admitted this was an unnecessary and fatal error. It cost the division the advantage of surprise and forced it to divide its forces to maintain DZ security for follow-on operations. Dr. John Warren, *Airborne Operations in WWII, European Theatre* (Kansas: USAF Historical Division, Air University, 1956), 149.

10. Stanley Maxted, "I Crossed the Rhine with the Glider Troops," Maclean's *Magazine*, 15 May 1945, 54.

11. PRO, WO 205/947, War Office: 21 Army Group: Military HQ Papers, Second World War, 1942–47. Operation Varsity: 6th Airborne Division, March-May 1945, "6th Airborne Division Report on Operation Varsity — The Advance from the Rhine to the Baltic, 24 March to 2 May 1945," 1.

12. FAAA, "Narrative of Operation Varsity," 1.

13. Directorate of History and Heritage [henceforth DHH], file 181.003 (D721), "Bomber Command Intelligence Digest, No. 30 — Operation Varsity," 4 April 1945; and Montgomery, *Normandy to the Baltic*, 255.

14. DHH, file 181.003 (D721), "Bomber Command Intelligence Digest, No. 30 — Operation Varsity," 4 April 1945. The numbers (loads) given for the initial drop are: Troops — 14,865; ammunition and explosives — 109 tons;

vehicles — 695; artillery pieces — 113; and equipment and supplies — 765 pieces. During the three days before the landings 2,090 effective sorties dropped over 5,375 tons of bombs.

15. *Ibid.*, In sum, the overall air effort against Germany during by the Allied Air Forces in the week 18–25 March 1945 resulted in a total of 44,894 sorties and 38,505 tons of bombs dropped.

16. 1 Canadian Parachute Battalion Association Archives [henceforth 1 Cdn Para Bn Assn Archives], Anderson, R.F., file 11–2, R.F. Anderson, "From the Rhine to the Baltic."

17. *Ibid.*

18. FAAA HQ, "Narrative of Operation Varsity," 4–5.

19. Charles B. MacDonald, *The United States Army in World War II. The European Theater of Operations. The Last Offensive* (Washington, D.C.: Center of Military History United States Army, 1990), 309. Numbers on aircraft vary slightly. DHH, file 181.003 (D721), "Bomber Command Intelligence Digest, No. 30 — Operation Varsity," 4 April 1945 gives the numbers as 1,589 aircraft and 1,337 gliders with initial loads dropped as: Troops — 14,865; ammunition and explosives — 109 tons; vehicles — 695; artillery pieces — 113; and equipment and supplies — 765 pieces. A resupply drop by 240 Liberator bombers after the troops had landed inserted an additional 582 tons of supplies and equipment into the battle zone.

20. MacDonald, 309.

21. Whitaker, 316.

22. 1 Cdn Para Bn Assn Archives, David Owen Fond, Series 2, Memoirs, Diaries and Scrapbooks, 224 Parachute Field Ambulance, *Over the Rhine. A Parachute Field Ambulance in Germany* (London: Canopy Press, 1946), 8.

23. Jean E. Portugal, *We Were There — The Army. A Record for Canada, Vol. 2 of 7* (Toronto: The Royal Canadian Institute, 1998), 966.

24. Dan Hartigan, interview with Bernd Horn, 30 October 2000.

25. Joseph King, interview with Bernd Horn, 31 January 2002.

26. Douglas Amaron, "Paratroops Tell Story," *The Canadian Press News, London, England*, 31 March 1945.

27. CAFM, "Mightiest Airborne Army Safely Landed By 6,000 Aircraft," 26 March 1945, newspaper clipping.

28. 1 Cdn Para Bn Assn Archives, Anderson, R.F., file 11–2, R.F. Anderson, "From the Rhine to the Baltic."

29. Jan de Vries, interview with Bernd Horn, 18 January 2001. Dan Hartigan wrote, "The pilots of U.S. 9th Troop Carrier Command fly straight and level. Probably, one of the clearest examples of mass, self-sacrificing airmanship in World War II." 1 Cdn Para Bn Assn Pamphlet, 1988, 10. 1 Cdn Para Bn Assn Archives, Toseland, N., file 7–7, Dan Hartigan, "1st Canadian Parachute Battalion Assault on the Rhine. The Ride, The Drop, and the Objectives."

30. 1 Cdn Para Bn Assn Archives, Gavinski, T.E., file 8–7, Private M. Zakaluk's "Recollections of Rhine Drop — March 1945."

31. William E. Jenkins, interview with Michel Wyczynski, 19 December 2001.

32. Lieutenant-Colonel Fraser Eadie, interview with Bernd Horn, 20 November 2000. The Carrier Command policy was that "*NO* evasive action will be taken between the IP and DZ — LZ area" and "that *NO* paratrooper or gliders will be returned to friendly territory." Direction was given that "In the event that aircrews fail to locate designated DZ or LZ on first pass, paratroops and gliders will be released as near to the assault area as possible." Field Order No. 5, IX Troop Carrier Command, 16 March 1945, PRO, WO 205/203, War Office: 21st Army Group: Military HQ Papers, Second World War, Operation Varsity: Field Order No. 5, Briefing map information.

33. Lieutenant-Colonel Fraser Eadie, interview with Bernd Horn, 20 November 2000. The issue of drop altitude is an interesting one. Interview and written

accounts by veterans range from a low of 200–300 feet to a high of 1,000 plus feet. However, the most consistent and reliable accounts place the drop, for 3 Para Bde at any rate, at around 600 feet. There is also some disagreement on speed. The 1 Cdn Para Bn War Diary states that the aircraft failed to slow down and lift their tails resulting in wide dispersion. Yet, most other accounts, including most veterans, state otherwise. The fact that the Brigade assembled so quickly and achieved their objectives so early, would support a concentrated drop.

34. Dick Hilborn, interview with Bernd Horn, 5 May 2001. "You have so much to think about," noted Hilborn, " that I wasn't airsick." He added , "I had faith in the pilot — you had to have faith in someone." Dick Hilborn, interview with Bernd Horn, 27 April 2001.

35. LAC RG 24, Vol. 15299, March 1945, 1 Cdn Para Bn War Diary, 17 March 1945, Appx F, "Operation Varsity — Plunder, 1 Cdn Para Bn Operations Order No. 1."

36. Nolan, 141.

37. Harold Johnstone, *Johnny Kemp, DCM. His Story With the 1st Canadian Parachute Battalion* (Nanaimo, BC: Private Printing, 2000), 24.

38. LAC, RG 24, Vol. 15299, March 1945, "2 AB Div Intelligence Summary, No. 35, Estimate of the Enemy Situation on 17 March 1945," 1 Cdn Para Bn War Diary, 17 March 1945, Appx F, "Operation Varsity — Plunder, 1 Cdn Para Bn Operations Order No. 1."

39. Whitaker, 310. Hoehne conceded that material losses and lack of equipment hampered his Army Group. "At one time," he stated, "Army Group H had 50,000 men for whom there were no weapons." *Ibid.*

40. Johnstone, 24.

41. LAC, RG 24, Vol. 15298, 1 Cdn Para Bn War Diary, 24 March 1945.

42. Whitaker, 332.

43. 1 Cdn Para Bn Assn Pamphlet, 1988, 1 Cdn Para Bn Assn Archives, Toseland, N., file 7–1, Dan Hartigan, "1st Canadian Parachute Battalion Assault on the Rhine. The Ride, The Drop, and the Objectives."

44. 1 Cdn Para Bn Assn Archives, Green, Dwight, file 15–1, Military Medal Commendation, G7194 Pte James Oliver QUIGLEY, Canadian Parachute Bn.

45. Douglas Amaron, "Paratroops Tell Story," *The Canadian Press News, London, England*, 31 March 1945.

46. 1 Cdn Para Bn Assn Archives, Green, Dwight, file 15–1, Distinguished Conduct Medal Commendation, B62282 Sergeant (Acting Warrant Officer Class II, Company Sergeant-Major) George William Green, Canadian Infantry Corps.

47. LAC, RG 24, Vol. 15298, 1st Cdn Para Bn War Diary, 24 March 1945, Appendix J.

48. Johnstone, 25.

49. 1 Cdn Para Bn Assn Archives, Anderson, R.F., file 11–2, R.F. (Andy) Anderson, "From the Rhine to the Baltic. The Final Operation of The 1st Canadian Parachute Battalion, March 24th to May 8th, 1945, 2. Unpublished Diary.

50. Whitaker, 328.

51. LAC, RG 24, file 15300, March 1945, Battle accounts, "Vickers Platoon D and D Plus One," "PIAT Platoon," and "Mortar Platoon," 1 Cdn Para Bn War Diary, 24 March 1945. Both the Vickers platoon commander and the mortar platoon commander attribute the SP gun kill to mortars, while the PIAT platoon commander claims the kill was done by his platoon.

52. MacDonald, 313.

53. CAFM, AB 1, 1 Cdn Para Bn Assn Archives, Vol. 5, file 9, "Operation Varsity — Losses in Vehicles and Guns," 6th Airborne Division, "Report on

Operation Varsity and the Advance from the Rhine to the Baltic, March 24 to May 2 1945, Appendix F.

54. Total casualties for the airborne component of Operation Varsity was approximately 2,500 personnel. 1 Cdn Para Bn Assn Archives, Jenkins, William, file 38–1, HQ British Army of the Rhine, "Operation Varsity. XVIII United States Corps (Airborne) in the Crossing of the River Rhine, 24 and 25 March 1945," November 1947, 101; and Nolan, 167.

55. DHH, Report No. 17, Historical Section (G.S.) Army Headquarters, 27 October 1947.

56. Anderson, 3.

57. Alf Tucker, interview with Bernd Horn, 23 June 2001. Tucker, the signals officer, was normally the number one jumper.

58. 1 Cdn Para Bn Assn Archives, Firlotte, Robert, file 11–2, Jack Karr, "I'll Go Into Hiding Until this Blows Over — New V.C." Newspaper Clipping, 3 August 1945, unknown publication,

59. *Ibid.*

60. DHH, Canadian Army Headquarters, Historical Section (G.S.), Report No. 17, "The First Canadian Parachute Battalion in the Low Countries and in Germany. Final Operations (2 January–18 February and 24 March–5 May 1945)," 35; "Corporal Wins V.C." *The Maple Leaf,* 3 August 1945, Vol. 1 No. 62; and Peter Harclerode, *"Go To It!" The Illustrated History of the 6th Airborne Division* (London: Caxton Editions, 1990), 125.

61. Hartigan, "1st Canadian Parachute Battalion Assault on the Rhine," 13.

62. 224 Parachute Field Ambulance, 20.

63. Captain J.E. Thomas, "Crossing the Rhine — March 1945," *The Army Quarterly,* Vol. 1, No. 2, July 1945, 226.

64. CAFM, AB 1, 1 Cdn Para Bn Assn Archives, Vol. 5, file 9, "Interrogation Report on Maj Gen Fiebig, Commanding 84 Infantry Division captured near WISMAR 2 May 1945," 6th Airborne Division, "Report on Operation Varsity and the Advance from the Rhine to the Baltic, March 24 to May 2 1945, Appendix D.

65. Otway, 154. "D" day often used in populist literature to describe the Normandy invasion in a definitive manner, is actually the military designation for the day a specific operation is to commence. For example, 6 June is D-Day for Operation Jubilee and 24 March is D-Day for Operation Varsity.

66. G. G. Norton, *The Red Devils* (Hampshire: Leo Cooper/Secker & Warburg, 1971), 124.

67. After the very short, but bloody battle, the Battalion, as part of 6 AB Div embarked on six-week, 300 mile race across Germany to Wismar, on the Baltic Sea. As a precursor to the Cold War, British Prime Minister Winston Churchill had personally ordered the 6 AB Div to beat the Russians to that port city. On 2 May 1945, the Canadians led the Division into Wismar, mere hours before the arrival of the first Russian troops. The War in Europe was declared over on 8 May 1945. The Battalion was returned to England later that month. On 31 May, it was repatriated to Canada — the first complete unit to return home after the war. On arrival in Halifax, it received a hero's welcome. The paratroopers then took some well-deserved leave and returned to Niagara-on-the-Lake where the unit was disbanded in September 1945.

7

THE BATTLE OF KAP'YONG, 23–26 APRIL 1951

William Johnston

While the Korean War is often remembered for the deadlocked front-line and seemingly interminable peace negotiations that characterized its final two years, the dramatic cut and thrust of the conflict's opening stages are sometimes overlooked. During the war's first 10 months, a series of stunning battlefield reversals moved the fighting up and down the Far East peninsula. Perhaps not surprisingly, it was a battle fought during this opening phase of the war that caught the nation's attention and became on of the best-known Canadian actions of the entire campaign.

Canada's contribution of ground forces early in the war was limited to a single infantry battalion, the 2nd Battalion, Princess Patricia's Canadian Light Infantry, which arrived in the theatre in December 1950 just as the intervention forces from communist China turned the tide once again in their war against the United Nations. Although the Chinese onslaught was eventually halted and the UN was able to push the invaders back to the 38th parallel, an advance in which 2 PPCLI engaged in several tough battles against the enemy rearguard, the Canadian battalion fought a particularly distinguished action in April 1951, when it was ordered to hold a key feature along the Kap'yong River during another Chinese offensive. For standing firm in their hilltop entrenchments against waves of attacking infantry and halting the drive of the Chinese 118th Division, 2 PPCLI was awarded a United States Presidential Unit Citation, the only Canadian unit ever to be so recognized.[1]

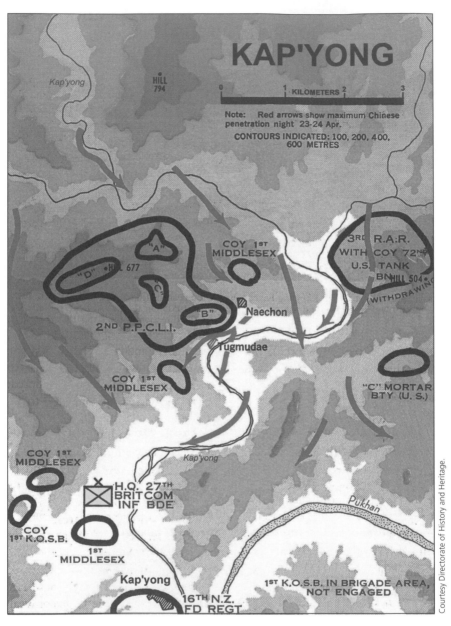

The Action at Kap'yong.

In large measure, it was the wildly changing tides of the Korean War's first year that found a lone Canadian battalion serving in a Commonwealth brigade of British, Australian and New Zealand units in the spring of 1951. Following the success of communist North Korea's invasion of the country's southern half on 25 June 1950, the United States had called on member countries of the United Nations to provide assistance to the Washington-backed government of the Republic of Korea (ROK). Although the Americans quickly despatched troops to the peninsula from the four divisions on occupation duty in Japan, as well as air and naval forces in the region, the intervention U.S. forces initially did little to stem the communist onslaught and by early August the ROK and American divisions of the U.S. Eighth Army were left defending a 140-mile perimeter around the southeastern port city of Pusan.

Although other United Nations' member countries — most notably Britain, Turkey, and Australia — had committed to send troops to Korea while the situation had deteriorated throughout July, the Canadian government was initially reluctant to send ground forces to the Far East. It was not until the evening of 7 August 1950 that Prime Minister Louis St. Laurent announced that the country would recruit an infantry brigade for service in Korea. Recruiting for the "Special Force" brigade quickly exceeded expectations and three new infantry battalions, created as 2nd Battalions of the regular army's existing infantry units, were filled by month's end. Army headquarters also planned to reduce the amount of time needed to train the new brigade by enlisting experienced veterans from the large number of those who had returned to civilian life after the Second World War.

While the Special Force units were still engaged in their initial training at various bases across Canada, the actual need to send a brigade to Korea appeared to have been overtaken by events on the ground. In mid-September, the UN commander in the Far East, U.S. General Douglas MacArthur, launched a daring amphibious assault by two American divisions on the port city of Inch'on, only 40 kilometres from the South Korean capital of Seoul. Combined with a simultaneous breakout by Eighth Army from the Pusan Perimeter, the thoroughly routed North Korean forces were driven back across the 38th parallel by month's end.

With a triumphant MacArthur in Seoul and UN forces preparing to cross the parallel to mop up the defeated communists, it appeared the war would end before any Canadian troops were sufficiently trained to take part.

When it was suggested that Canada might at least send one infantry battalion to "show the flag" as part of a UN occupation force, Ottawa agreed to send 2 PPCLI from Calgary. Commanded by a decorated Second World War battalion commander, Lieutenant-Colonel J.R. Stone, the battalion was chosen because of the proximity of its training base to Canada's west coast. Since 2 PPCLI was not expected to see any combat, the fact that the Patricias had not conducted any meaningful unit training before embarking for the Far East on 25 November 1950 did not appear to be a serious handicap.[2]

By the time the Canadian battalion arrived at Pusan on 18 December, however, yet another of the conflict's shifts in fortune had altered the unit's mission from occupation duties to warfighting. After the UN forces crossed the 38th parallel in October to pursue the defeated communists, the government of neighbouring China decided to intervene in the conflict. By 15 November, Peking had covertly dispatched over 300,000 of its soldiers across the Yalu River to take up positions in the mountains of North Korea. Ignoring growing evidence of a substantial Chinese military presence in the north, a confident MacArthur launched a new offensive to reunite the two halves of Korea on 24 November with a promise to have the UN troops home by Christmas. Two days later, however, his forces were ambushed by masses of Chinese infantry descending on them from the mountains of North Korea.

Moving along ridgelines to surround UN units in the valleys below, the Chinese counteroffensive struck Eighth Army's right flank and over-ran one ROK corps and a U.S. infantry division. Further to the east, two U.S. divisions were surrounded in the mountains around the Chosin reservoir and had to make a costly fighting withdrawal back to the coast in bitter winter weather before being evacuated. With several of his divisions virtually ceasing to exist as fighting formations in the rout that followed, MacArthur hastily pulled his forces back below the 38th parallel, abandoning Seoul to the communists for a second time on 4 January before finally forming an effective defence line some 80 kilometres south of the capital by mid-month.[3]

Having been sent to the Far East before the battalion had undergone any unit-level training, 2 PPCLI was far from being a cohesive, operational battalion when it arrived. Despite several attempts by Eighth Army headquarters to commit the Patricias to action soon after their arrival in theatre, Lieutenant-Colonel Stone convinced his American superiors that his men needed to spend their first two months engaging in intensive company and unit training before being sent to the battlefront. It was not until 18 February, therefore, that the battalion joined the 27th Commonwealth Brigade — composed of an Australian and two British infantry battalions and a New Zealand artillery regiment — to begin operations just as the latest enemy offensive, the Chinese Fourth Phase Offensive, had been brought to a halt. As a result, the Canadians joined the 27th Brigade just as Eighth Army began its own counteroffensive to drive the communists back to the 38th parallel.

For the next several weeks, the Eighth Army counteroffensive drove the communists back to the 38th parallel with 2 PPCLI fighting a series of actions against Chinese holding hilltop positions in central Korea. The costliest of these battles was a joint attack by the Patricias and the 3rd Battalion, Royal Australian Regiment (3 RAR) on 7 March against a stubborn rearguard holding Hill 532. The day's fighting killed seven Canadians and wounded 37 others while the 3 RAR suffered 12 killed and 24 wounded in an unsuccessful assault. It was not until the following morning, after the enemy had withdrawn during the night, that the two battalions were able to occupy the feature. In all, 2 PPCLI's first three weeks fighting in the push north cost the battalion 14 killed and 43 wounded.[4]

Assessing the initial performance of his battalion, Stone endorsed the army's decision to recruit a large proportion of Second World War veterans for the Special Force. As he informed Army headquarters in Ottawa on 9 March, the Patricias were "fit, morale high, show lots of guts in close contact…. Troops are very well led and the aggressiveness they display in attack under difficult circumstances is a very great credit to the officers."[5] Although Stone may have rued the altered circumstances of the war that had suddenly changed his battalion's role from occupation to combat, his comments reflect his satisfaction with the way combat-experienced senior officers and NCOs had been able to take a raw battalion — though many of the soldiers had previous Canadian Army experience — and whip it into shape in a relatively short space of time. That level of experience was enhanced, as he later explained, by the fact that the battalion was composed primarily of "adventurers: those who joined the army because there was a war to fight and they wanted to be there." The result was "a first-class, high-spirited group of soldiers."[6]

Continuing to pursue the retreating Chinese throughout the last days of March, the 27th Brigade finally pushed across the 38th parallel on 8 April as they moved up the valley of the Kap'yong River. The ruggedness of the valley's hills, rising some 750 to 1,000 metres above the river, allowed the enemy to use a smaller force to delay the Commonwealth troops in that particular sector of central Korea than in the wider valleys to the east and west of Kap'yong. Just how difficult it was to capture a high hilltop position from even a relatively small group of infantry was demonstrated once again on 14 April when "D" Company attacked the battalion's final two ridgeline objectives. According to the Patricia war diarist:

> At 1655 hours the company attack went in with artillery support on [Hill 826] and MMG [medium machine-gun] and 81-mm mortar fire on [Hill 795]. This attack was successful in reaching [Hill 795] but the position was untenable due to the proximity of the dominating hill on the same ridgeline and the vulnerable position of the company on a ridge having easy flank approaches. Lieutenant M.G. Levy [the 10 Platoon commander] led the attack with great spirit and succeeded in reaching the well-held Chinese bunker on [Hill 795] with his platoon. However the company withdrew on the CO's orders.[7]

Although the company suffered only five wounded in the attack, a second attempt to take the more northerly Hill 826 the next day only managed to reach the feature's lower slopes before darkness ended the assault.

It was not until the morning of 16 April, after the Chinese rearguard had withdrawn, that the final objective was secured.

After turning over their frontline positions to the 6th ROK Division on 18 April, the 27th Brigade, less the New Zealand artillery regiment that remained in place to support the South Koreans, moved into corps reserve for some rest just north of Kap'yong, a village on the Route 17 highway that connected Seoul with the city of Ch'unch'on. The stiffening resistance the Patricias had encountered during the final stages of their push north was an indication of a communist build-up for a spring offensive. The arrival of three fresh armies from China in February and the reinforcement of depleted formations gave the communist command 630,000 soldiers, most of whom were massed above Seoul for a drive to capture the capital. Although the total UN forces counted only 418,000 troops, including rear echelon personnel, it was believed that Eighth Army, with its greater air and artillery assets, could defeat the anticipated enemy offensive. The UN forces consisted of 245,000 Americans, 152,000 South Koreans, 11,500 Commonwealth troops divided between the 27th and 29th Brigades, and 10,000 troops from other UN countries. Although the Americans were not particularly confident of the fighting abilities of the ROK divisions, the U.S. formations were expected to stem a Chinese onslaught as the entire Eighth Army braced for an attack.[8]

The communists opened their Fifth Phase Offensive at 2000 hours on 22 April with an assault on the 6th ROK Division in the mountains north of the Kap'yong Valley. Despite attacking with little artillery support, the troops of the Chinese 60th Division easily infiltrated around the individual ROK battalions and routed them. By 2300 hours, the 6th Division commander admitted that he had lost all communication with his units as the South Koreans abandoned their weapons and vehicles and streamed south. It was only the inability of the attackers to exploit the South Korean collapse during the night that eventually allowed the ROK divisional commander to organize 2,500 of his men in a blocking position at the head of the Kap'yong Valley by the morning of the 23rd. With the 27th Brigade's New Zealand artillery and a detachment of the 1st Battalion, The Middlesex Regiment acting in support of the ROK rearguard, the 9th Corps commander, Major-General William Hoge, hoped to be able to organize a new defence line across his front with the 24th U.S. Infantry Division to the west of the South Koreans and the 1st U.S. Marine Division to its east. As a precaution against the Chinese breaking through to Route 17 — the main highway between Seoul and Ch'unch'on — Hoge also ordered the 27th Brigade to set up a blocking position along the hills north of the village of Kap'yong.[9]

Although 9th Corps had been forced to retreat all across its front, the main thrust of the communist attack fell on the 1st Corps formations north of Seoul, one of the principal objectives of the offensive. Directly in the path of the Chinese drive on the capital was the 29th British Brigade holding a line of hills on the south bank of the Imjin River across the Route 11 highway to the city. Led by three divisions of the 63rd Army, a total of 30,000 troops, the Chinese penetrated around and between the individual battalions of the British formation during intense fighting on 23 April, virtually surrounding the isolated battalions on the hills south of the river. The most hard-pressed of the surrounded British units, the 1st Battalion, The Gloucestershire Regiment holding the brigade's western flank, was granted permission to withdraw at 0900 hours on 24 April but promises that a relief column would attempt to break through to their position convinced its commander to wait rather than leave his wounded behind.

Unfortunately, the 29th Brigade's commander failed to inform the 3rd U.S. Division, under whose orders he was operating, about the dire situation and the American commander did not provide the British with sufficient reinforcements to relieve the beleaguered units. By the time the British battalions were told to attempt a breakout back to the 1st Corps lines on the morning of 25 April, only two of the three surrounded units managed to do so with the aid of British tanks. The Gloucestershire Regiment, meanwhile, was virtually wiped out with only 40 of its men escaping capture. In all, the 29th Brigade's defence of Route 11 cost it 1,091 casualties with the Gloucesters losing 622 of the 699 men it took into the battle, 530 of whom were captured. The British formation's fate provided a graphic example of the perils that could befall a force facing masses of attacking infantry and the sort of unnecessary losses that could occur when a national commander failed to exercise his own discretion in preserving his force.[10]

Directorate of History and Heritage 681.019 [D2].

The view looking north from the village of Kap'yong towards Hill 677 as photographed by a Canadian Army historical officer in September 1953.

Fifty kilometres to the east of the British disaster, the 27th Brigade set about establishing a blocking position on the morning of the 23rd. The position chosen by Brigadier B.A. Burke lay on a curve of the Kap'yong River some four miles north of the village along a prominent line of hills straddling the river. With a portion of The Middlesex Regiment still to the north guarding the New Zealand gunners, Burke had only 2 PPCLI and 3 RAR available to occupy the eight-kilometre wide line that extended over the two hills selected for defence, Hill 504 east of the river and Hill 677 three kilometres to the west.

The Patricias were assigned the higher of the two hills, while the Australians took up the defensive position to the east. That same afternoon, the brigade was reinforced by the assignment of two companies of the 2nd U.S. Chemical Heavy Mortar Battalion and a company of tanks from the 72nd U.S. Tank Battalion. Informed in mid-morning on the 23rd that his battalion was to defend Hill 677, Lieutenant-Colonel

Stone (who had only returned to the battalion the previous day after a month's absence recovering from a mild case of smallpox) organized a reconnaissance of the position to decide on the best locations for his companies. As he later recalled:

> I took forward a large reconnaissance party of company commanders, gunner rep[representative], mortar rep, and the battalion MMG and mortar platoon commanders. We were able to look at the feature from the enemy side, which gave us a good idea of probable attack approaches. Therefore, I was able to select the vital ground which had to be defended to deny the approaches to the enemy.
>
> Hill 677 is about a mile and a half across, gullied, wooded and impossible to defend in the classic manner of deploying companies to support each other. Each company had to develop its own individual defended locality, the platoons being mutually supporting. The gaps between the companies would have to be covered, to some extent, by defensive fire tasks of the MMGs, the battalion 81-mm mortars, the US mortar company and the New Zealand 25-pounder regiment [which returned to the brigade later that night amongst the routed South Koreans].
>
> I issued orders in the late afternoon of April 23 and we commenced moving into position that afternoon. The defensive plan followed the lines of my appreciation in that companies were in individual defended localities, deployed so that the platoons were mutually supporting. Our six Vickers MMGs were deployed by sections, giving depth to the defence and covering the gaps between the companies. The battalion mortars supported the defensive fire tasks. A company of US 120-mm mortars were supporting the total brigade effort, but when the battle got hot on the Australian front, the FOO from the US mortars on my front walked out and never a pop did we get from his company.[11]

Across the river, the four rifle companies of 3 RAR took up their positions on Hill 504 supported by the 15 Shermans of the 72nd Tank Battalion. The Australian battalion's headquarters, however, was assigned to a position on the valley road southwest and across the river from the feature in the hope that it would act as a check on the retreating South Koreans. Burke's foresight was evident soon after dark when the rearguard position the 6th ROK Division had established to the north was attacked and routed by elements of both the Chinese 60th and 118th Divisions. While the 60th Division then veered off to the west to take part in the enemy's main drive on Seoul, the 118th Division continued down the Kap'yong Valley in pursuit of the fleeing South Koreans.

In order to seize the Route 17 crossroads in the confusion of the ROK collapse, however, the Chinese division was forced to leave its supporting artillery and most of its supplies behind. By 2000 hours, the waiting Australians and Canadians could see masses of retreating South Korean soldiers streaming down the valley road through their lines. Included in the procession were the men of the New Zealand artillery, the Middlesex battalion and a 105-mm battery from the 213th U.S. Field Artillery Battalion. While the Kiwi gunners quickly redeployed immediately north of Kap'yong in the dark, they were unable properly to survey their position and were severely limited in the amount of close fire support they could give the Australian companies on Hill 504 that night.[12]

The advance elements of the 118th Division, two battalions of its 354th Regiment, were concentrating on their pursuit of the fleeing ROK troops and would not initially have been aware of the Australian presence in their path, and certainly would not have known the exact location of its various companies. When they launched their first attack against 3 RAR's more forward "B" Company at 2130 hours, they were easily repulsed by small arms and U.S. tank fire. Undeterred, the two Chinese battalions made repeated attacks on "A" and "B" Companies for much of the night, with the heaviest attacks falling on "A" Company further up the hill. Although some of the assaults were supported by mortar fire, many were simply launched by waves of infantry. With apparently overwhelming numerical superiority, the Chinese rushed forward over heaps of their dead and wounded to close with the Australians.

Meanwhile, the third battalion of the 354th Regiment crossed the river and circled around 3 RAR headquarters before attacking it from the south. The sound of the battle was sufficient to stampede the men of Company "B," 2nd U.S. Chemical Mortar Battalion from the position 500 metres to east of the Australian headquarters (HQ). The jittery Americans promptly abandoned their weapons and vehicles without firing a shot and fled 16 kilometres to the east soon after the battle commenced.

Although the 3 RAR rifle companies held firm throughout the night, the situation on the valley road forced the Australian commander to withdraw his headquarters into the perimeter established by the Middlesex Regiment two kilometres to the south. The battalion continued to hold the Chinese at bay until the afternoon of 24 April when the problems of resupply and removing the wounded from Hill 504 convinced Brigadier Burke that the four Australian companies should be withdrawn rather than risk having them cut off and overwhelmed after dark. Ordered to withdraw at 1730 hours, the four 3 RAR companies successfully moved off the feature with the support of the U.S. tanks and close-in fire from the New Zealand gunners who had finally been able to survey their position accurately at daylight on the 24th.

The 24-hour battle cost 3 RAR 32 killed, 59 wounded, and three captured, with most of the casualties falling on "A" Company and battalion headquarters. Their stout defence had inflicted much greater casualties on the Chinese, virtually halting their advance against the brigade's right flank, and requiring them to reorganize their depleted ranks before finally turning their attention to the imposing Canadian-held hill across the river.[13]

Having spent the night of 23–24 April listening to the sounds of the Australian battle three kilometres across the valley from Hill 677, the Patricias did not notice any appreciable enemy activity on their front until the following morning. Aware that 3 RAR was being hard-pressed and might have to withdraw, in mid-morning Lieutenant-Colonel Stone ordered "B" Company to shift from its forward location north of the feature's summit to the heights overlooking the valley road to the east of battalion headquarters, a position that would cover the Patricias' eastern flank. During the course of "B" Company's shift to the right, however, a mishap occurred when one of the platoons lost direction and strayed into a girdle of No. 36 grenades that had been set with trip wires to protect battalion headquarters. According to the battalion history, "someone stumbled over a tripwire and a grenade exploded, killing one man and wounding another. A second grenade lay smoking in the midst of the platoon. Corporal S. Douglas shouted to everyone to fall flat, dashed forward and snatched up the grenade to throw it clear. It exploded, blowing off his hand but saving the others from injury."[14] Douglas' courageous act was subsequently recognized with the award of a Military Medal.

By the time the move was completed at 1100 hours on 24 April, the battalion's four rifle companies were deployed in a northward curving arc from the summit of Hill 677 in the west to the high ground nearest the Kap'yong River on the eastern flank. "D" Company held the summit of the feature on the battalion's left flank while "C" Company occupied the forward slope in the center with "A" and "B" Companies positioned across the right flank. Given the size of the feature, the Patricia companies were arranged as individual strongpoints, each some 200 to 400 metres across and capable of all-around defence. With companies spread some 300 to 500 metres apart, it was not possible to organize mutually supporting positions and the ground between the company positions and all likely avenues of approach to them had to be covered by artillery and mortar fire.

Throughout the daylight hours of the 24th, defensive fire tasks were registered and given codenames to allow for rapid response by the gunners and mortarmen to calls for urgent assistance by the infantry. The rugged nature of the feature's terrain also limited the enemy's approach routes and gave them little cover for their assaults. According to the Patricias' intelligence officer, Captain A.P.P. Mackenzie, "D" Company's "position on Hill 677 and the ridgeline leading to the west was covered by high grass" that had been crushed under the previous winter's snow so that it stood only "a foot to a foot-and-a-half in height" at the time of the battle. "The summits of all the small ring contours along the ridgeline were topped by isolated trees. Only in the bottoms of the valleys and in steep re-entrants was tree cover heavy.... A direct north-south movement was hard for the enemy because of the steepness of the slopes and the type of cover found on the lower slopes.... For the most part artillery and mortar D[efensive] F[ire] fires were concentrated on the ridgeline approaches to the positions. Invariably because of the steepness of the slope, LMGs and MMGs were [also] sited to fire along ridgelines. The steeper approaches to the company and platoon positions were covered by rifle fire and hand grenades."[15]

Following the withdrawal of 3 RAR from Hill 504, the Canadian companies dug in on the crest lines of Hill 677 were now the most northerly — and exposed — of the UN units holding the Kap'yong Valley. Nonetheless, the brigade's defence had been reinforced during the afternoon of the 24th by the arrival of two battalions of the 5th U.S. Cavalry Brigade sent earlier in the day by the 9th Corps commander to ensure that the Route 17 crossroads would be held. While one of the American units occupied Hill 425 across the river from the 1st Middlesex position, the other U.S. battalion moved onto the ridges two kilometres south of the Patricias' "D" Company on the summit of Hill 677. The brigade's artillery assets had also been increased during the afternoon when 9th Corps placed the American 213th and 61st Field Artillery Battalions and a U.S. battery of 8-inch howitzers under the control of the New Zealand (NZ) gunners. With the 16th NZ Field Regiment's gun positions accurately surveyed during the daylight hours of the 24th, they were able to provide 2 PPCLI with close-in fire support around their entrenchments — something the Australians had not enjoyed on Hill 504 until their fighting withdrawal — while the U.S. guns were available to fire on the surrounding approaches.[16] Although one of the Australian rifle companies and battalion headquarters had been hard hit in the previous night's battle, 3 RAR's remaining rifle companies had not suffered heavily and were redeployed to the immediate south of the Middlesex. The arrival of a second British battalion that same afternoon gave Burke six battalions with which to confront the two Chinese regiments of the 118th Division that were trying to reach the Route 17 highway between Seoul and Ch'unch'on. Since the Chinese had probably suffered more than 1,000 casualties in forcing the Australians off Hill 504, the American reinforcements meant that the UN defenders of Kap'yong actually outnumbered their communist opponents by last light on the 24th.[17]

The Chinese, meanwhile, were most likely unaware of the reinforcements that had added depth and firepower to the Commonwealth brigade's defence of Kap'yong. They did know that they would not be able to open the valley road to the passage of the artillery and supply vehicles they would need for any further drive south until they forced the Canadians off the dominating heights of Hill 677. Important as they were to the overall defence of the crossroads, the reinforcements were also of little immediate consolation to the Patricias as they awaited attack on the upper slopes of the feature. Although the battalion had been largely undisturbed by enemy activity during the Australians' fighting withdrawal on the eastern side of the valley, the Canadian forward companies continued to report a build-up of enemy forces throughout the daylight hours of the 24th.[18] In particular, "B" Company, newly dug in on the battalion's eastern flank, was able to observe Chinese movements along the valley floor to the north and east and reported an increasing number of enemy moving into the village of Naech'on at the foot of their position. A small number of Chinese were reported to have infiltrated south of Hill 677 by mid-day but, according to the regimental history "not in sufficient strength to be more than nuisances."[19]

By late afternoon, small groups of enemy had also infiltrated as far south as the village of Tungmudae along the river road south of the "B" Company position but were blocked from moving further south by both the 1st Middlesex and the reorganizing 3 RAR battalions covering the

Directorate of History and Heritage 681.019 [D2].

The ridge above the village of Naech'on that was held by B Company, 2 PPCLI, as seen from the valley road to the east in September 1953.

rear of the Patricias' positions. Such was the deteriorating situation in the valley as the Australians prepared to withdraw from Hill 504, that Sherman tanks of the 72nd U.S. Tank Company, engaged in evacuating 3 RAR wounded, fired on the "B" Company entrenchments above Naech'on in the belief that the Canadians were Chinese troops. Fortunately, only one Patricia was slightly wounded. As light faded from the battlefield on the 24th, "D" Company, dug in around the summit of Hill 677, also reported increased enemy movement to the north of its position.[20]

Even in the darkness of the clear, crisp night (the moon would not rise until 0100 hours), the Canadians were able to observe the enemy as they approached their entrenchments. At 2130 hours, several hundred Chinese were spotted forming up at the base of "B" Company's ridge and the company commander, Major C.V. Lilley, called for artillery and mortar support. Despite heavy defensive fire that disrupted the cohesion of the attack, the size of the enemy force allowed them to press up the slope to the Canadian entrenchments with, in Lilley's words, "the usual accompaniment of bugle calls, mortaring, and red directional tracer. The attack overran a section of 6 Platoon on the left spine but the remainder held fast and retook the position."[21] The 6 Platoon commander, Lieutenant Harold Ross, later recalled that "the Chinese fight with a fanatical determination even though their tactics of massing men and sacrificing torrents of charging troops is archaic.... A section is overrun. [Private] Don Morrow, [Private Ed] Richardson and [Private Wayne] Mitchell and their mates are forced to withdraw to another section's trenches. Mitchell, wounded about the eye, fights throughout the night.... Mitchell charges the enemy three times with his Bren [light machine gun]. He inflicts maximum casualties to the enemy, even though he suffers a second wound in the chest.... After an hour or so 6 Platoon with fixed bayonets retake their position in a bloody fight. The Chinese do not easily give up their ground, but when they see the Patricias are not to be denied they turn and run, firing wildly."[22]

One hour later, a somewhat larger number of enemy once again scrambled up the steep slopes to attack 5 and 6 Platoons as well as company headquarters. Although two sections of the more-exposed 6 Platoon were overrun, "the remainder of the company stood fast." In

Lilley's words, "confused fighting followed. No. 6 Platoon headquarters and the section that remained ran out of ammunition and were ordered to fix bayonets and stand their ground. Wireless communications with the platoon broke down and the platoon commander decided to break out."[23] As one of the Patricias in 6 Platoon later recalled, Lieutenant "Ross gave us the order to move out. Just as we jumped up Ross added that anyone with ammo left should cover the retreat of the wounded. I had three shells left so I dropped back down and fired them off. Just as I jumped up again I fell over a Chinaman who was running up the side of the hill. He let fly and got me in the neck then ran into the end of my bayonet. I was spun completely around. When I got my bearings I started back but it was quite a way to the rest of the company."[24]

Despite the confusion of 6 Platoon's fighting withdrawal, the battalion war diary recorded that by 2300 hours "the greater part of the over-run platoon had managed to return to the co[mpan]y defensive perimeter."[25] Although by daylight Private Mitchell "could hardly stand for loss of blood" and had to be evacuated by helicopter, he had continued to man his Bren light machine gun throughout the night, actions for which he was subsequently awarded the Distinguished Conduct Medal.[26]

At the same time that "B" Company was consolidating its position in the wake of 6 Platoon's withdrawal, another group of some 100 Chinese "attempted to infiltrate the battalion area by approaching up the behind Tac[tical] HQ. The machine guns of the mortar platoon engaged this enemy and succeeded in beating off this threat."[27] Observing the movement from "B" Company headquarters, Major Lilley had called Stone to warn him of the pending attack. Lilley later recalled that "the probe against battalion headquarters was a well-organized and well-executed attack in strength which I estimated at that time to be between one and two companies and which 'B' Company was powerless to stop as it came in through our back door. It was a heartening sight to see the battalion 81-mm mortars firing at their shortest range (200 yards) together with their .50-calibre machine guns which literally blew the Chinese back down the ravine."[28]

Lieutenant-Colonel Stone also remembered the devastating effect of the mortar platoon's defensive fire. "The mortar platoon in those days," he explained, "was mounted for travelling on twelve half-tracks, six of which were deployed in the vicinity of battalion headquarters." He added, "Each half-track was equipped with one .50 and one .30 Browning machine-gun. These were loaded one tracer to four ball. We held fire until the Chinamen broke through the trees about 200 yards away, and then twelve machine-guns cut loose together. What with the rattle of the guns and the mortars firing at their shortest range, the enemy never had a chance."[29]

With the rise of a bright half-moon at 0100 hours, the Patricias were able to discern enemy formations from a greater distance allowing attacks to be broken up before they could reach the Canadian entrenchments. Some time after the repulse of the Chinese sortie up the draw towards tactical headquarters, "B" Company reported a large concentration of the enemy fording the river to the south of the village Tungmudae. The enemy force was hit with both artillery and mortar fire and by the machine-gun fire of the mortar platoon's half-tracks firing down the draw at a range of 800 metres. The Patricias had a clear view of the slaughter as the Chinese broke and fled back across the river. The next morning the Canadians counted 71 enemy dead lying on the banks of the river.[30] The ability of the defenders to spot and engage enemy formations in the river valley with artillery fire after 0100 hours also brought an end to the sustained attacks being made against "B" Company. In Major Lilley's view, the successful defence of the battalion's positions was made easier by the rudimentary nature of the Chinese tactics:

> The Chinese telegraphed the direction and timing of their attacks by using MMG tracer ammunition for direction, sounding bugles as signals to form up on their start line and for their assault. This gave company and platoon commanders time to bring down accurate artillery, mortar and machine-gun fire on them.
>
> Before attacking in strength the Chinese did not accurately locate our defensive positions by patrolling nor did they give accurate artillery and mortar supporting fire to their troops.

The steep gradients to our positions forced the Chinese to use a monkey-run attitude in their final assault; although rifle fire in the darkness was not too effective at such small targets, grenades trundled down the hills had a devastating effect.

Rocket launchers were used in an anti-personnel role and proved deadly.

The Chinese appeared to be well-trained and disciplined but lacked initiative. Only on orders would their squads fire their weapons or throw grenades.

Their consistent attacks en masse on obvious approaches in an attempt to overwhelm our positions by sheer weight of numbers presented ideal targets for our artillery, mortars and machine-guns.[31]

The absence of enemy artillery fire was one of the consequences of the 118th Division's headlong rush down the Kap'yong Valley. In pursuing the fleeing 6th ROK Division out of the mountains, the enemy had left its guns and supplies well to the north, while much of the mortar ammunition the infantry carried with it was expended against the Australians in capturing Hill 504. As a result, the enemy had few mortar rounds left to fire at the Canadian positions. It also meant that "A" and "C" Companies, occupying the battalion's center, were left undisturbed as the fighting raged around them. It was understandably nerve-wracking for the soldiers to sit in their slit trenches and listen to the sounds of battle to the east, then to the south and finally to the west of their positions without knowing the outcome of the various attacks or if the battalion was being overrun but, as one "A" Company soldier recalled, "we were surrounded by battles but we never fired a shot."[32]

With the end of major attacks on the battalion's eastern perimeter next to the river, the action quickly shifted to the summit of Hill 677 where the visibility provided by the moonlight also aided "D" Company's defence. Its three platoons were dug-in from west to east with 10 Platoon on the western slope of the summit facing the ridgeline that led off towards Hill 865 to the west. No. 12 Platoon's entrenchments were northeast of the summit on the far side of a small hillock although one of its sections was dug-in 75 metres to the west covering the Vickers medium machine-gun position north of 10 Platoon.

No. 11 Platoon, meanwhile, was in position across a gully to the east of 12 Platoon while the acting company commander, Captain J.G.W. Mills, and company headquarters was situated on the reverse slope behind the feature's summit. The men of "D" Company spotted a Chinese build-up on the lower slopes to the north of their entrenchments shortly before last light but it was not until 0030 hours on the 25th that Mills reported considerable enemy movement to the west and north of 10 Platoon. At the same time, isolated groups of Chinese made several small attacks that were easily driven off by mortar and machine-gun fire, a move which the battalion's intelligence officer later surmised "were probably used to locate our DFs [defensive fire tasks] and MG and LMG positions."[33]

Having gleaned what limited information they could from their initial probes, the Chinese mounted their first serious attack on "D" Company an hour later when it became "apparent that a considerable force, later estimated at 200 men, was moving against 'D' Co[mpan]y. The axis of their attack lay along the ridge line leading to Hill 677 from the west."[34] According to Mills's subsequent report on the action, his three platoons had remained largely undisturbed while the fighting raged around "B" Company, out of sight to the east. Sitting in their slit trenches, they had listened anxiously to the:

> amazingly large volume of small arms fire from the direc-
> tion of Tac[tical] HQ and B [Company] positions. This fire
> finally subsided until we could hear only the occasional
> burst. At approximately 0110 hours we [at company head-
> quarters, located on the reverse slope 100 metres south
> of his platoon positions] received word, via the wireless,
> from Lieutenant Levy, 10 platoon commander [holding
> the western-most position], that Corporal Clouthier had
> reported the enemy were assembled in the saddle [that
> led off towards Hill 865] known [by the artillery fire task
> code-word] as FOX III. Immediately we received this

word, we heard a Bren gun from 10 Platoon open fire. I called for first task FOX III. Levy asked the MMG in 12 Platoon positions to open fire on the enemy.

The machine gunners immediately fired on the enemy with such deadly accuracy that the enemy stopped his main attack on 10 Platoon. The enemy then directed his main assault against the MMG thus relieving the pressure on 10 Platoon. The enemy in their attack against the 10 Platoon feature used machine-guns and mortars to cover their assault. The enemy attacked across the small saddle overrunning one section of 12 Platoon and the MMG. This was accomplished by sheer weight of numbers. The machine-gun continued firing until the crew was completely overrun. Four men from the 12 Platoon section, which were protecting the MMG post, were able to disengage and make their way over to 10 Platoon positions where they carried on the fire fight. They reported that the two machine gunners had been killed at their post. Also two Koreans, who comprised part of the MMG section, were able to make their way to 10 Platoon positions. The enemy having gained possession of our MMG endeavoured to use it but 10 Platoon covered the gun and the position with LMG fire by Private Baxter and rendered the MMG useless. Sergeant Holligan [the 12 platoon commander who remained dug-in with his remaining two sections on a low hillock seventy-five metres east of the Vickers machine-gun position] reported that the enemy were building up in the area known as fire task ABLE I. We asked for fire on FOX III and ABLE I, as this seemed to be the main line of approach.[35]

Before they were overwhelmed and killed, however, the two Vickers machine gunners, Privates Maurice Carr and Bruce MacDonald, had provided an effective enfilade fire on the Chinese attacking 10 Platoon from the saddle that led to Hill 865 to the west. According to 10 Platoon's commander, Lieutenant Mike Levy, the Vickers crew inflicted heavy casualties on the attackers and forced them to hesitate in their assaults. Levy had been raised in China and interned by the Japanese in 1942 but later escaped and joined the British Army in India where he was commissioned a second-lieutenant. Assigned to the British Special Operations Executive (SOE) Force 136, Levy had parachuted behind enemy lines in Malaya in 1945 and led a band of guerrillas against the Japanese.[36] Fluent in the Shanghai dialect, the 10 Platoon commander easily understood the shouted commands being directed at the wavering Chinese as they assaulted his position. During a lull in the action resulting from the Vickers' devastating fire, Levy, speaking in Chinese, exchanged insults and demands to surrender with the enemy commander. He recounted, "This infuriates the Chinese officer, who orders his troops to 'Press harder! Press harder! Kill! Kill! Kill the Imperialist Pigs!' I reply: 'We are Canadian soldiers. Come to us, we have lots of food and medicine, and you will be well treated.' The Chinese officer screams: "Don't listen to that Son of a Turtle!' … a terrible insult in Chinese." As Levy later recalled, after one of his "exchanges with the Chinese commander, one of my men shouts 'Tell the bloody platoon commander to Shut Up!' Each time our verbal exchange takes place the Chinese intensify their attacks."[37]

Despite their officer urging them to press their attacks against the Canadian platoon position, however, the Chinese were held at bay by the effectiveness of the artillery, mortar, and machine-gun fire of the defenders. Another of the men in 10 Platoon recalled that one of the Chinese soldiers hit during one of the attacks "had a phosphorous grenade on him, which exploded in a ball of fire. He lay out there, alive for most of the night, smoldering and screaming. I wanted to go out there and put him out of his misery, but it wasn't beyond the Chinese to have an ambush party waiting to catch anyone who might do that. We let him holler."[38]

The prearranged defensive fire tasks in front of "D" Company, from both the 16th New Zealand Field Regiment and the Patricia's own mortar platoon, also helped to break up the Chinese assaults as they were attempting to reorganize. The battalion's 81-mm mortars — a weapon that was new to the Canadian Army, having replaced the 3-inch mortars used during the Second World War — would prove particularly useful in Korea with their ability to lay down accurate defensive fire close in to the forward defended localities. (Six months later, for instance, the 1 PPCLI war diarist recorded after one Chinese attack that "the accuracy of the 81-mm mortar astounds us; such close support would be unheard of with a 3-inch mortar. Tonight completely sells us on the 81mm."[39])

Altogether during the Kap'yong battle, the battalion's 81-mm mortar platoon fired some 1,400 rounds of mixed heavy and light bombs in support of the forward companies. As the battalion's intelligence officer later explained, the 60-mm mortars were "brigaded at [each] company headquarters in order to provide the weight of fire on any one point that would be delivered, under normal circumstances, by a section or one 81-mm mortar." The company mortars covered the ridge lines leading to the platoon positions and "could be fired at a high rate for some time without getting too far off their target. Their ability to hit the narrow ridge lines consistently was of great assistance at Kap'yong."[40] The New Zealand gunners, meanwhile, were firing at the "slow" rate of two rounds per gun per minute so that 24 rounds landed every 30 seconds in the target areas that were only some 200 yards wide. The rate of fire was subsequently halved to the " slow" rate to conserve ammunition, but the weight of the Chinese assaults on 10 Platoon prompted the Canadians to request that it be increased back to the "slow rate."[41]

Unable to make progress against 10 Platoon as long as it was being covered by the enfilading fire of the Vickers, at 0230 hours the Chinese eased the pressure on Levy's men in order to mount a more determined attack against the medium machine-gun position and its covering section from 12 Platoon. Through weight of numbers the enemy was able to over-whelm and kill MacDonald and Carr at their weapon. By 0300 hours the rest of the 12 Platoon section supporting the Vickers had made their escape as best they could, some back to 12 Platoon's main position over the hillock to the east, some back to company headquarters in the rear and a handful scrambling up the slope to the 10 Platoon entrenchments.[42]

No longer having to contend with the devastating fire of the medium machine gun, the Chinese were free to make another push against Levy's men. As the platoon commander later remembered, with the enemy pressing towards his position from the direction of the Vickers, he asked

Mills to have the New Zealanders fire on the captured position and then directed their fire "to impact within 10–15 metres of our position." With the American batteries adding to the supporting fire at the request of the New Zealand commander, Levy was able to "direct the artillery up or down, left or right, depending on where I see the Chinese massing, and again upon their charging our position." Despite the supporting fire, the Chinese attackers were able to press their attacks against the 10 Platoon entrenchments, twice coming to within seven metres of the Canadian slit trenches, sufficiently close to effectively cut the platoon off from the rest of the company.[43] As the battalion diarist recorded, "Lt. M.G. Levy asked for close in mortar and arty support. The acting coy commander, Captain J.G.W. Mills, realising that his outnumbered coy must have some relief, called for the support request by Lt. Levy bringing fire to bear very close to his own coy positions. Most of this fire was concentrated on the most heavily engaged platoon of the coy [i.e., 10 Platoon]."[44]

At tactical headquarters, Lieutenant-Colonel Stone recalled Mills's call "over the telephone (the line was miraculously intact) that his position was over-run and that the enemy had infiltrated everywhere. After some conversation, in which he assured me that the company was well dug in, he asked for an artillery concentration right on top of his position. I obliged."[45] The decision of the combat-experienced Mike Levy — described by his Second World War superiors as being "full of guts"[46] — to ask Mills to shift the supporting fire on top of his own entrenchments finally had the desired effect. The battalion diarist recorded that "the Chinese continued to attempt an infiltration of the battalion area through 'D' Coy despite the art[iller]y and mortar fire. Each time arty engaged them they were forced to withdraw, but continued to engage 'D' Coy with accurately sighted MMG and mortar fire. With the approach of daylight, the Chinese withdrew."[47] One of the 10 Platoon soldiers remembered hugging the bottom of his slit trench during each of the defensive bombardments: "Our slit trenches were within hollering distance, when we got the word, we all crouched down in the trench. The artillery dropped a ten minute barrage on top of us. It stopped that attack, but the Chinese came at us again. They were about to over run us, when another ten minute barrage came in. Later, we were hard pressed and called in a third ten minute barrage. We were convinced the artillery would kill us all, but there were no direct hits on any of the slit trenches. The Chinese, caught out in the open, were stopped cold."[48] Although the enemy continued to probe "D" Company's entrenchments for the rest of the night, by 0600 hours they had largely broken off close contact.

Department of National Defence SF-1338.

Men of 2 PPCLI and their Korean porters carry supplies up a typically steep slope at the head of the Kap'yong Valley on 16 April 1951.

Even as "D" Company was heavily engaged atop Hill 677, Lieutenant-Colonel Stone had become concerned for the battalion's resupply situation after enemy infiltration along the Kap'yong Valley south of the Patricias' positions cut road communication with the rest of the brigade. At 0430 hours the commanding officer (CO) "requested an airdrop of ammunition, food and water. Six hours later, four C119s dropped, by parachute, everything requested, including 81-mm mortar ammunition."[49] Stone's request had to travel up the chain of command to Japan where the required mix of British and American supplies were organized onto the aircraft. Only four of the parachutes landed outside the battalion area on Hill 677. As an appreciative Stone later remembered, "When it comes to supply, you cannot beat the U.S. forces."[50]

By first light, the enemy had largely pulled back from the battalion perimeter, allowing "B" Company to reoccupy the forward platoon position it had lost during the night. Although harassing fire, both machine-gun and sniper, was being maintained on "D" Company's entrenchments from the high ground to the west, a shortage of ammunition in 10 Platoon prompted Lieutenant Levy to call for a volunteer to return to the Vickers machine-gun position and recover bandoleers of .303 ammunition. Private Ken Barwise, one of the men driven from the MMG position during the night, bravely offered to make the attempt. With the men of 10 Platoon looking on from the high ground above, Barwise dodged sniper fire to cross the gully separating the two positions and retrieve 10 bandoliers at 0630 hours. The private then made a second dash over the 50 metres of ground to recover a box of No. 36 grenades lying near the lost machine gun, only to find upon return that they lacked their primers. Watching Barwise's bravery in the face of the Chinese snipers, Levy decided to recommend him for a Military Medal.[51]

Barwise, however, was not yet finished for the day. Elated by his successful retrieval of the ammunition bandoliers and anxious to recover the abandoned Vickers, Barwise tried to convince some of the soldiers of 10 Platoon to help him haul the machine gun back up to their entrenchments. After the strain of an intense, night-long action and with no Chinese in sight to threaten recapture of the Vickers, Levy's men were simply too exhausted to bother trekking down to the machine gun and risk enemy sniper fire. Not satisfied with the response of his comrades, Barwise walked over to "C" Company at 0900 hours and convinced its commander, Major Del Harrison, of the need to retake the machine gun. With his company not having seen any action during the previous night's fighting, Harrison agreed to send Lieutenant R.D. Whittaker and two sections from 9 Platoon to accompany Barwise back to the abandoned machine-gun position. With the young lieutenant urging them on and Barwise assuring them of the enemy's presence even though the Chinese had retreated from the area four hours earlier, the two sections of 9 Platoon men were anticipating opposition as they approached the position from the reverse slope. Without apparently peering over the crest to see if anyone was at the emplacement, friend or foe, the Patricias tossed several grenades, at least two of which failed to clear the slope and rolled back on the would-be attackers. With two of the 9 Platoon men slightly wounded by their efforts, it was left to Barwise to proceed over the hillock and down to the where the Vickers lay, as well as to carry the heavy weapon back to the 12 Platoon entrenchments to the east.[52]

Other than occasional bursts of long-distance harassing fire on "D" Company from the west, the Chinese remained relatively passive and out of sight throughout the daylight hours on the 25th. The main concern for the Canadians at daybreak were the Chinese that had infiltrated south of Hill 677 during the night. Having set up blocking positions on the roads leading down the valley, 2 PPCLI was effectively cut off from resupply. Stone's foresight in calling for an air drop at 0430 hours relieved the immediate problem following the arrival of the C-117s from Japan in mid-morning.

As the "C" rations and ammunition were distributed among the men, "the companies continued to improve their positions in case of a delay of the battalion's relief and in anticipation of continued Chinese attack" later that night. The Middlesex battalion, meanwhile, sent out patrols to clear the enemy from south of the Canadian-held hill but it was not until 1400 hours that patrols from the Patricias' "B" Company "reported the road at the base of the battalion position clear of the enemy and Lieutenant-Colonel Stone requested further supplies and reinforcements be brought up by vehicle as rapidly as possible."[53]

During the afternoon the Patricias were assisted in clearing pockets of the enemy from the forward slopes of Hill 677 by the Sherman tanks of the 72nd U.S. Tank battalion moving up the valley road to the north of the Canadian positions. In addition, any concentrations of Chinese that were observed were also engaged by "frequent artillery shoots" and by an air strike that "was put in with good effect."[54] At the same time, the Middlesex battalion relieved the American battalion on the high ground southwest of 2 PPCLI so that the 5th U.S. Cavalry Regiment could mount an attack to recapture Hill 504. The enemy resisted the American regiment's assault until 1600 hours when the 118th Division withdrew north, back up the Kap'yong Valley. Another 5th Cavalry tank-infantry force patrolled to the east of the village along Route 17 without making contact with any enemy while American patrols to the north of Hill 504 were also not engaged by the retreating Chinese. As the 27th Brigade's war diarist noted, by last light on the 25th "the situation on the brigade front was quiet and reports of enemy had ceased. It appears that the enemy has failed completely to dislodge the brigade and 5th Cavalry Regiment from these positions guarding Kap'yong and so has failed to cut the important Seoul/Ch'unch'on road in the Kap'yong area."[55]

The Canadian battalion continued to hold their positions throughout the next day when they were relieved by one of the battalions from the 5th Cavalry Regiment and the Commonwealth brigade was withdrawn into 9th Corps reserve. The movement was part of Eighth Army's general withdrawal south of some 20 to 30 miles, made to gain some breathing space in light of intelligence indications that the communists were planning to renew their Fifth Phase Offensive. By the end of April, however, it was evident that the initial Chinese offensive had lost momentum. During its first week, the Chinese had lost 13,349 known dead, while Eighth Army headquarters estimated that a total of 24,000 enemy had been killed, with total communist casualties in the 75,000 to 80,000 range. Eighth Army casualties over the same period amounted to 547 killed, 2,024 wounded and 2,170 captured, a disparity that reflected the devastating effect of the UN's enormous firepower when directed against massed Chinese infantry.

The communists finally renewed their offensive on the evening of 16 May, this time by concentrating the bulk of their forces on the eastern side of the peninsula to attack the two ROK corps on the flank of the U.S. 10th Corps. Badly mauled once again by UN firepower, the enemy high command called off the offensive five days later, thus allowing Eighth Army to begin yet another — this time final — push back across the 38th parallel.[56]

Department of National Defence SF-836.

The Patricias cross a stream during their initial push north to the 38th parallel in March 1951.

The abandonment of the Kap'yong position only a few days after the Commonwealth brigade's successful battle irked Lieutenant-Colonel Stone who considered the strategic withdrawal to have "been unnecessary." He explained, "After breaking contact and falling back twenty miles, it was found there were no Chinese within eighteen miles."[57] Despite his disappointment, the Patricia CO was undoubtedly proud of what his men had accomplished on Hill 677. At a cost of 10 killed and 23 wounded, the battalion had successfully held the point position of the UN's defence of the Kap'yong Valley and prevented the Chinese from reaching the important Route 17 supply line. Together with 3 RAR, the two battalions had had been attacked by the equivalent of two regiments of the 118th Division totalling some 6,000 men. As the battalion's intelligence officer during the battle has explained:

> Although the 6th ROK Div[ision] units ahead of the 27th B[ritish] I[nfantry] B[rigade] disintegrated, even in disintegrating they imposed a certain delay upon the 118th Division. For this reason it is considered that the Chinese force which attacked the 3 RAR positions and flowed over on to the 2 PPCLI position the following night did not consist of more than two brigades. These two brigades were committed piece-meal. If a concerted attack had been made upon the 3 RAR positions by the enemy it is considered that the 3 RAR would have been over-run in a very brief time. However, because of the piece-meal commitment of their forces, occasioned by their delay in moving over the extremely rough country to the north, the Chinese were never able to concentrate sufficient force at any one time against any one point on the brigade perimeter. In fact, by the time the leading elements of the Chinese units came up against the 27 BIB positions, it was estimated that they had lost 60% of their momentum. In addition, they were rapidly running out of supplies and ammunition. Their mortar fire although concentrated did not last for any great length of time and once the attack on the 3 RAR had been repulsed the amount of mortar fire brought to bear on 2 PPCLI rapidly dwindled until few bombs came in, at any one time....
>
> It is considered that only sub-units, rapidly collected together from the three regiments composing the 118th Infantry Division, were deployed against the PPCLI or the 3 RAR at any one time. The attack on Baker Coy

of the PPCLI could not have been closely co-ordinated with the attack on Dog Coy of the PPCLI because the interval between the subsidence of the attack on Baker Coy and the commencement of the attack on Dog Coy permitted the switching of mortar and artillery DFs from one company area to the other without in any way reducing the defensive capabilities of either company at a critical period.[58]

Although the Australians had been forced to withdraw from Hill 504, 2 PPLCI did have some distinct advantages over their Commonwealth allies in making their stand to the west. The 16th New Zealand Field Regiment did not reach their gun positions until 2100 hours on 23 April after returning from the north in the chaos of the South Korean retreat. In the darkness, the gunners did not have the opportunity to survey their gun positions accurately before the Chinese attacked Hill 504, which limited the fire support they could provide to the Australians, because they were unwilling to fire close to the 3 RAR companies for fear of hitting them by accident. By the following evening the New Zealanders had achieved pinpoint registration of their guns, enabling them to bring down defensive fire tasks immediately in front of the Canadian positions, which helped to drive the attackers away from their entrenchments. The Canadians were the beneficiaries of another development on the afternoon of the 24th, when the additional firepower of two American field artillery battalions and a U.S. battery of 8-inch howitzers were placed under the control of the New Zealanders.

The Australian battalion had also been hampered in its defence by the retreating South Koreans pouring down the valley road, allowing Chinese soldiers to infiltrate close to the 3 RAR positions before they could be identified as enemy.[59] In addition, as the Patricia's intelligence officer observed, the limited amount of mortar ammunition the 118th Division had carried with it during its pursuit of the South Koreans was largely expended in the fight to capture Hill 504.

For his part, the combat-experienced Lieutenant-Colonel Stone was able to place the battle in some perspective:

Kap'yong was not a great battle, as battles go. It was a good battle, well-planned and well-fought. Personally, I believe that Kap'yong was the limit of the planned offensive of the Chinese at that time. Had that limit been five miles further south we should have been annihilated, as were the Glosters [sic]. The numbers that the Chinese were prepared to sacrifice against a position meant that eventually any unsupported battalion in defence must be over-run. The Chinese soldier is tough and brave. All that he lacked at the time of Kap'yong were communications and supply. Perhaps death was preferable to the life he was compelled to lead, for he certainly was not afraid to die. Therefore, I say that we were lucky that he did not persist with his attacks.[60]

Contrary to Stone's view, however, it was the relatively small size of the attacking force at Kap'yong that prevented 2 PPCLI from meeting the same fate that the 1st Gloucesters suffered in their battle on the Imjin River. The Commonwealth brigade only had to face a single, disrupted Chinese division, one that was trying to take advantage of the 6th ROK Division collapse to seize the Seoul — Ch'unch'on crossroads in a *coup de main*. The 29th British Brigade, on the other hand, was holding a position on the direct route to Seoul and had to fight three fresh divisions of the Chinese 63rd Army that were making their initial assaults in a drive that was intended to take them to the South Korean capital. As a result, the Chinese divisions had supporting artillery and mortar fire available to them in their attack across the Imjin. The 63rd Army was able to infiltrate large masses of infantry around the British battalions, isolating them and making retreat costly.

Although two of the 29th Brigade battalions were able to cut their way to safety with the aid of British armour, the 1st Corps commander, inadequately informed by the British commander of the dire situation facing his brigade, did not provide sufficient reinforcements to extricate the surrounded Gloucester battalion. In the Kap'yong sector, the 9th Corps commander sent an entire regimental combat team to assist the

Department of National Defence 681.019 [D2].

The summit of Hill 677 held by "D" Company as seen from the northern slope of the feature in September 1953.

27th Brigade as well as placing the additional artillery assets at their disposal. Although the 5th U.S. Cavalry did not take an active role in the fighting until they recaptured Hill 504 on the afternoon of 25 April, they were in position behind the Patricias and available to assist them by the evening of the 24th.

Nonetheless, the entire 27th Brigade, and particularly the Canadian and Australian battalions, had ample reason to be proud of their achievement in stopping the 118th Division's drive to Route 17. At a cost of 127 casualties to the two battalions, 3 RAR and 2 PPCLI held off repeated assaults by some 6,000 enemy troops while likely inflicting, with the help of the New Zealand-led artillery, some 1,500 to 2,000 casualties on the attackers. The Patricias themselves estimated that they had killed some 300 Chinese during their night action (the Chinese government still has not released casualty figures for the Korean War).[61]

The Commonwealth brigade's steadiness under fire was emphasized by the failure of other UN units and formations to hold their ground when facing the Chinese offensive. During the opening stages of the battle, for instance, the men of Company B, 2nd U.S. Chemical Mortar Battalion had abruptly abandoned their weapons and equipment in position south of Hill 504 and fled without ever being fired upon. The fear of being overrun by hordes of advancing Chinese was noticeably absent from the ranks of the Canadians and Australians. As the American official history has pointed out, "that two battalions and a tank company had withstood attacks no weaker, and perhaps stronger, than those that twice had routed the ROK 6th Division underscored how completely control had broken down in the [South Korean] division. The huge tally of equipment lost as a result of the division's successive debacles emphasized the breakdown further."[62]

The determined stand at Kap'yong also did not go unnoticed by the American high command as 2 PPCLI, 3 RAR and Company "A," 72nd U.S. Tank Battalion were each subsequently awarded a U.S. Presidential Unit Citation.

The Canadian battalion's impressive stand was also aided by the battle experience of its commanding officer. Although the extent of the ground to be covered meant that the companies were too far apart to provide supporting fire to each other, Lieutenant-Colonel Stone had positioned them on terrain "that was vital to the defence of the area." His timely shift of "B" Company to cover 2 PPCLI's right flank in anticipation of the Australian withdrawal from Hill 504, for instance, had prevented the enemy from turning the battalion position at the outset of the contest. The battalion's strong leavening of Second World War veterans among its officers and NCOs also helped to steady the men under fire and provide them with battle-proven leadership as Stone readily acknowledged. "The success of Kap'yong," he insisted, "was due mainly to high morale and to good company, platoon and section commanders. In their isolated defence areas they kept their heads down, the morale of their troops up, and their weapons firing. Whatever support I could give, I gave, but the battle was theirs." The CO recognized that once the companies had been placed on the most advantageous ground possible, it was the men themselves who determined the battle's outcome. The Patricias had "trained and fought together for some eight months; we believed in one another, and the morale of the battalion was high. No one panicked, even when we knew we were surrounded and that there was some infiltration of the position by the enemy ... We could have run, panicked in some way, or surrendered. We stayed, fought and withdrew on orders in a soldierly fashion. This, in itself, was unique in Korea where 'bug-outs' were the normal manner of withdrawing. In the circumstances, I say that the award [of the U.S. Presidential Citation] was well earned and the battalion deserved the public recognition of its actions of April 24/25, 1951."[63]

Although the Korean War continued for another 27 months after Kap'yong, with 2 PPCLI being joined by the rest of the 25th Canadian Infantry Brigade in the Far East a few weeks after the battle, the battalion's stand on Hill 677 in April 1951 has often been the subject of what little attention the war has received. Certainly the nature of the action — Canadian soldiers seemingly alone in their hilltop entrenchments and badly outnumbered by waves of advancing Chinese — has all the romantic elements of other last-ditch battles such as the Spartans' defence of the pass at Thermopylae or the U.S. 7th Cavalry's miscalculation at the Little Big Horn, though with a decidedly more favourable result for the defenders. Although other Canadian battles over the course of the next two years would result in greater casualties than Kap'yong — the Chinese raid on "B" Company, of the 1st Battalion, The Royal Canadian Regiment (1 RCR) holding the forward position on Hill 355 in October 1952, and a similar raid in early May 1953 on Hill 97 defended by "C" Company, 3 RCR being two such examples — they did not capture the public imagination. The stout defence of the shoulder of Hill 355 by "D" Company, 2nd Battalion, The Royal 22nd Regiment in October 1951, meanwhile, was an equally creditable feat of arms by hard-pressed Canadians holding on while others retreated around them, but came in the midst of what was generally perceived to be an interminable deadlock across the Korean peninsula. For most Canadians, Kap'yong is likely to remain the most memorable battle of a largely forgotten war.

NOTES

1. Joint Task Force 2 was awarded a Naval Presidential Unit Citation for its service in Afghanistan in 2001–02 as part of Task Force K-Bar in Operation Enduring Freedom.

2. For a more detailed discussion of the circumstances surrounding the recruiting and training of the Special Force, see William Johnston, *A War of Patrols: Canadian Army Operations in Korea* (Vancouver: UBC Press, 2003), 11–54.

3. *Ibid.*, 37, 44.

4. *Ibid.*, 69–76.

5. Department of National Defence, DHH, 112.009 (D87), Stone to Chief of General Staff, 9 March 1951.

6. Colonel J.R. Stone, "Memoir: Kapyong," *Infantry Journal* (Autumn 1992), 12.

7. LAC, RG 24, Vol. 18, 2 PPCLI War Diary, 14 April 1951, 318.

8. Johnston, 85–87.

9. *Ibid.*, 91–92.

10. *Ibid.*, 88–90.

11. Stone, 13–14.

12. Johnston, 96.

13. *Ibid.*, 96–97.

14. G.R. Stevens, *Princess Patricia's Canadian Light Infantry, 1919–1957* (Griesbach, AB: The Historical Committee of the Regiment, 1957), Vol. 3, 300.

15. DHH, 145.2P7.013 (D5), Captain A.P.P. Mckenzie, "2 PPCLI Action Kapyong Area — 23 to 26 April 51," 26 November 1954, 10–11.

16. Robert O'Neill, *Australia in the Korean War, 1950–53*, Vol. 2, *Combat Operations* (Canberra: Australian Government Publishing Service, 1985), 140–41; and Anthony Farrar-Hockley, *The British Part in the Korean War*, Vol. 2, *An Honourable Discharge* (London: Her Majesty's Stationery Office, 1995), 156–57.

17. Johnston, 99.

18. LAC, RG 24, Vol. 18, 2 PPCLI war diary, 24 April 1951, 318.

19. Stevens, 300.

20. DHH, 145.2P7.013 (D5), Lieutenant-Colonel Herbert Fairlie Wood, *Strange Battleground: The Operations in Korea and Their Effects on the Defence Policy of Canada* (Ottawa: Queen's Printer, 1966), 76; and Captain A.P.P. Mckenzie, '2 PPCLI Action Kapyong Area — 23–26 April 51,' 26 November 1954, 10–11.

21. Lilley report on action quoted in Stevens, 301; and DHH, 145.2P7.013 (D5), Mckenzie, "2 PPCLI Action Kapyong," 26 November 1954, 11.

22. Lieutenant H. Ross quoted in Hub Gray, *Beyond the Danger Close: The Korean Experience Revealed, 2nd Battalion Princess Patricia's Canadian Light Infantry* (Calgary: Bunker to Bunker Publishing, 2003), 89.

23. Lilley report on action quoted in Stevens, 301.

24. Unnamed Patricia quoted in Captain Michael G. McKeown, *Kapyong Remembered: Anecdotes From Korea, Second Battalion Princess Patricia's Canadian Light Infantry, Korea 1950–1951* (np: privately published, 1976), 24.

25. LAC, RG 24, Vol. 18, 2 PPCLI war diary, 24 April 1951, 318.

26. Wood, 77.

27. LAC, RG 24, Vol. 18, 2 PPCLI war diary, 24 April 1951, 318.

28. Major C.V. Lilley quoted in Wood, 77.

29. Stone, 14.

30. LAC, RG 24, Vol. 18, 2 PPCLI war diary, 25 April 1951, 318; and Wood, 77.

31. Lilley quoted in Wood, 79.

32. Private Dan Johnson quoted in Robert Hepenstall, *Find the Dragon: The Canadian Army in Korea, 1950–1953* (Edmonton: Four Winds Publishing, 1995), 93.

33. DHH, 145.2P7.013 (D5), Mackenzie, "2 PPCLI Action Kapyong Area — 23 to 26 April 51," 26 November 1954, 11–12.

34. LAC, RG 24, Vol. 18, 2 PPCLI war diary, 25 April 1951, 318.

35. Mills's report quoted in Johnston, 102–03.

36. Gray, *Beyond the Danger Close*, 4–5.

37. *Ibid.*, 101.

38. Corporal Ken Campbell quoted in Hepenstall, 96.

39. LAC, RG 24, Vol. 18, 1 PPCLI war diary, 6 November 1951, 312.

40. DHH145.2P7.013 (D5), Mackenzie, "2 PPCLI Action Kapyong Area — 23 to 26 April 51," 26 November 1954, 19–20.

41. Johnston, 103.

42. Gray, 102.

43. *Ibid.*, 110, 114.

44. LAC, RG 24, Vol. 18, 2 PPCLI war diary, 25 April 1951, 318.

45. Stone, 14.

46. Gray, 5.

47. LAC, RG 24, Vol. 18, 2 PPCLI war diary, 25 April 1951, 318.

48. Campbell quoted in Hepenstall, 96.

49. Stone, 14.

50. *Ibid.*, 14; and Wood, 78.

51. Gray, 114. The only other Patricia to be awarded a medal for the Kap'yong battle was the "D" Company acting commander even though Mills's main role had been to pass Levy's artillery requests back to tactical headquarters. Gray, a 2 PPCLI officer at Kap'yong, does point out that Stone was a good friend of Mills's older brother, Captain Andrew Mills. *Ibid.*, 8.

52. *Ibid.*, 131–35.

53. LAC, RG 24, Vol. 18, 2 PPCLI war diary, 25 April 1951, 318.

54. DHH, 681.018 (D1), Extracts from 27 Brigade war diary, 25 April 1951.

55. *Ibid.*; and Johnston, 104.

56. Johnston, 108, 112–14.

57. DHH, 681.011 (D3), "'Notes on talk given by Lt-Col J.R. Stone at AHQ, 0900 hours 5 June 51," nd.

58. DHH, 145.2P7.013 (D5), Mackenzie, "2 PPCLI Action Kapyong Area — 23 to 26 April 51," 26 November 1954, 27–8.

59. O'Neill, *Australia in the Korean War*, Vol. 2, 140–41.

60. Stone, 14–15.

61. DHH, 681.011 (D3), "'Notes on talk given by Lt-Col J.R. Stone at AHQ, 0900 hours 5 June 51," nd.

62. Billy C. Mossman, *Ebb and Flow, November 1950-July 1951* (Washington, DC: U.S. Government Printing Office, 1990), 407.

63. Stone, 15.

8

DEADLY STRUGGLE ON "LITTLE GIBRALTAR," 23 OCTOBER 1952

Bernd Horn

The ground heaved and trembled as the Chinese bombardment climaxed in ferocity. The Canadian soldiers hunkered in their bunkers and weapon pits were literally bounced out of their sanctuary. Concussed and fighting for oxygen as the air became thick with dust and smoke, they tried to make out the enemy who they knew would soon engage them in close combat. They could already hear the whistles, trumpets, and orders, as well as the hollow booms of Bangalore torpedoes as the Chinese infantry breached the wire. Private Charlie Morrison gripped his Bren gun and braced himself. At last, the bombardment would end and battle would be joined. Finally, he could lash back at his antagonists who had been tormenting him and his comrades for almost a month. He could barely see as the smoke and debris in the air acted as a shroud. And then, paradoxically, almost unexpectedly the Chinese infantry with their burp guns and grenades were upon them. Charlie began to hammer away with his Bren gun, changing magazines as quickly as he could, careful not to touch the barrel of his gun that now overheated because of the rate of fire. As Charlie slammed in another magazine he wondered how he found himself in this position.

The Korean War was already into its second year of bitter, and at times savage fighting. For the 1st Battalion, The Royal Canadian Regiment, the war started about five months prior when it replaced its sister battalion, 2 RCR. After only nine days in Korea and two in the line, 1 RCR found itself manning the front lines and dispatching patrols into no man's land. Out of necessity, the Battalion quickly focused on learning the ropes. In the first few weeks patrol schedules ensured everyone was able to gain confidence and experience in operating in the new combat environment. By late May, activity on both sides increased dramatically. Each night the Battalion had approximately 40–60 all ranks engaged in a standing, fighting, and reconnaissance (recce) patrols. The "Royals" also introduced the "jitters" patrol that was intended to keep the enemy in a state of anxiety. To achieve this, equipment such as bugles, whistles, tin-cans, and any other noise making instrument was employed.[1]

Patrols ranged from 20 men to entire companies and were supported by heavy supporting fire from tanks and artillery. Patrols passed through their own wire and defensive minefields through existing gaps and crossed the floor of the valley and worked their way to the hills opposite them.

The war had in many ways evolved into a war of patrols, with deadly raids and attacks designed more to inflict casualties and dominate ground than actually seize terrain. The conflict seemed to teeter between overwhelming boredom and sheer terror. And as the fall of 1952 progressed, tensions along the front lines increased once again. The Royals continued with their active patrolling and the constant struggle to dominate no man's land.

On the night of 24 September one particular daring snatch patrol was conducted to obtain a prisoner and deliver the enemy a psychological blow. Lieutenant H.R. Gardner and Corporal E.D. Fowler, stealthily infiltrated deep into a Chinese defensive position to their field kitchen area behind Hill 227. Once in position, they cut a signals wire and waited for a Chinese technician to come repair the line. They did not have long to wait. As the unsuspecting Private Wang Teh Shen began to fix the break, Gardner struck him with a blackjack, while Fowler attempted to pin his arms. A furious struggle commenced with Shen shouting for help. It took several minutes, but Shen finally submitted when he was threatened with a gun. However, just as the prisoner was being lifted to his feet, the first of the armed enemy response arrived. A hot pursuit was now undertaken as the Royals withdrew with their prisoner. Fortunately,

Gardner had planned well, and a series of firm bases through which he could pass assisted his party, with prisoner in tow, in breaking clean of the enemy pursuit.[2] The 1 RCR War Diary graphically captured the safe arrival of the group: "the snatch patrol came in about 0730 hrs complete with a Chink prisoner — Cpl Fowler brought him in by the scruff of the neck."[3] The daring nature and success of the patrol was seen as "a feather in the cap of the Regiment."[4]

The brave feat, however, came at a price. Within a week, the Royals noted that "the front is continually being probed by small numbers of enemy with no damage being done."[5] At the time not much was thought of the activity. But, as events began to unfold, a chilling foreboding struck the Royals. By end March 1952, 1 Commonwealth Division intelligence staff had developed a fairly comprehensive picture of Chinese tactics. Large scale attacks and battalion size raids were generally preceded by a series of nightly probing attacks increasing in size each night. In addition, the actual attack was always preceded by

Library and Archives Canada PA-151744.

Lieutenant H.R. Gardner and Corporal Karl E. Fowler after the daring prisoner snatch raid.

artillery fire. The bombardments generally started hours before the actual assault working up to intense fire at H-Hour. The Chinese Army was known to attack through their own supporting fire. Large scale attacks were always accompanied by at least a battalion size diversionary attack to a flank. Often tanks and self-propelled guns were used to support the attack by providing direct fire on bunkers and entrenchments. Directional tracer, flares, bugles, and whistles were all methods used to control and guide attacking enemy elements.

An attack on a given objective was always made by a direct assault on the feature itself with an effort at a simultaneous envelopment from two sides. The enemy was adept at leaving troops to contain and attack defended localities while passing other troops between these strong points to attack positions in depth such as command posts and gun areas. The assaulting troops were invariably armed only with submachine guns and grenades. Bangalore torpedoes and home made devices were normally utilized by assaulting elements to remove defensive wire that was not destroyed by the artillery bombardment. The Chinese had stopped using mass attacks on a large front because of initial failures, preferring, at this stage of the war, to concentrate on obtaining complete superiority at a given point, so they could concentrate destructive power of their support weapons.[6]

The Royals would soon experience this first hand, because a tempest was brewing. The War Diary captured the harsh reality:

> Patrol activity continued … 6 Royals had accomplished what the remainder of the Div[ision] had been trying to do in capturing a prisoner. All ranks are very proud of Lt Gardner and his gallant men. Other patrols were of a less spectacular nature. There were short, sharp, bitter clashes by night where the courage and common sense of the patrol members triumphed over the enemy and the darkness. Each day … has been a testing of one or several members of this Battalion. Tests have been met.[7]

Courtesy Captain [Retired] Robert H. Maha.

Corporal E.D. Fowler escorts Private Wang Teh Shen, a prisoner snatched on a daring patrol behind Chinese lines.

And so, 1 RCR continued its vigilance on Hill 355, labeled "Little Gibraltar" by the Americans because it bore a striking resemblance to the real thing in the Mediterranean from the rear. To the north and west, however, its features were more gradual. It was the highest feature of the surrounding area. Five company positions secured Hill 355, also known as Kowang-San on Korean maps. Area 1, which was on the South East portion of the position was garrisoned by "E" Coy and faced the enemy positions on Hill 227. Area 2 was secured by "D" Coy. This critical piece of ground lay on the immediate opposite side of the saddle that ran between Hill 227 and Hill 355. In many ways, it was the doorway to "Little Gibraltar." Areas 3 and 4, manned by "A" and "C" Coy respectively, anchored the northern front of Hill 355, and Area V, was a reserve position manned by "B" Coy. The Battalion felt secure on Kowang-San. In fact, one "Royal" wrote, "D Coy is settled in and ready for whatever happens. We on 355 feel secure in the knowledge that no Chinks can sneak up on us."[8]

October literally began with a bang. Much with the keeping of the Chinese offensive doctrine they began a systematic hammering of the Hill

355. On 1 October 1952, the Chinese fired nearly 1,000 rounds, primarily into Area II. The next day, the enemy dropped in another 600 rounds and succeeded in destroying the defences in the Vancouver Outpost, which was subsequently abandoned, as well as knocking out the tank in the southern platoon area. A similar intense bombardment occurred on the third day, after which firing slackened somewhat until 17 October when the intensity of fire picked up once again. On 21 August, 1,600 rounds thundered into 1 RCR. The next day, "1 RCR received 2,426 rounds from the 'friendly' Chinamen … 18 tons of assorted misery," captured the War Diary.[9] In the interim, "B" Coy relieved "D" Coy in Area 2, the hardest hit, after last light on 22 October.

The effect of the prolonged bombardment was clearly evident. Major Bob Richards, the officer commanding "D" Coy, spent 21 days under shell fire in crowded dug-outs. "Its bunkeritis, that's what gets you," Richards observed. "Its knowing that you can't walk around or you'll get hit," he explained, "It gets so that even when there's almost no shelling at all you still get nervous." He added, "and, when they pour in 1,275 a day you've got a problem." Richards acknowledged, "The odd man breaks, and then you risk getting a run of it." He proudly noted, however, "They all were getting a bit starey-eyed toward the end, but they all came out with their weapons."[10] Lieutenant M.F. Goldie stated, "Life there is very primitive indeed. You can't move an eyebrow without being hit." He lamented, "You just lie all day with your face in the dirt."[11]

Others were buried by the dirt. Privates Wilfred Main and Wilfred Mangeon had to make themselves air holes to prevent smothering and then dig themselves out with their bare hands. Main lost his boots and manned an observation post for 48 hours in his stocking feet.[12]

"Casualties weren't so heavy though," reported Major Richards, "That was due to the discipline." He explained, "The only casualties were from direct hits on bunkers and trenches and you can't control that." He conceded, "But reactions got slower all the time. At the beginning you'd give an order and they'd jump to it. Later they got to looking for shelter on the way. They'd get there all right, but it would take longer."[13]

When "B" Coy arrived into the position they found the field defences badly damaged and the greater part of the reserve ammunition, which was

Courtesy Captain [Retired] Robert H. Mahar.

RCR hilltop positions. This picture captures the steep terrain with its heavy foliage and covered approaches.

stored in the weapons pits, buried. In addition, the bunkers were caved in and the telephone lines cut. The fire continued throughout the day on the 23rd and into the night. "B" Coy stayed on alert after dark. Throughout, they could hear the detonation of heavy explosions, distinctly different from the incoming artillery and mortar shells. The soldiers knew the Chinese were blowing gaps in the wire, however, the intensity of the fire, prevented them from providing any form of response.

Throughout the day the bombardment had continued to wreak havoc on the company position. Bunkers, command posts, and trenches collapsed. Ominously, during the day, the enemy moved several self-propelled guns and infantry guns forward. Around 1700 hours, the scale of the destruction led Lieutenant Gardner and Sergeant G.E.P. Enright to attempt to reorganize the platoons, which now had approximately 30 men each.

At 1730 hours the firing almost completely ceased. "The silence was eerie," recalled Lieutenant Scotty Martin, "and somewhat unsettling after so many days of harassment."[14] The reprieve was not to last long. Approximately 45 minutes later the enemy hurled its most intense concentration of shells to date, focusing particularly on the leftmost platoon of "B" Coy and the rightmost platoon of "E" Coy. The Chinese had chosen the seam between the two sub-units for their break-in. As the bombardment reached its climax, the Chinese poured in shells and mortar rounds at a rate of 6,000 shells an hour for 30 minutes.[15] This effectively destroyed any remaining field defences. "At 1815 hours," Martin recalled, "Baker and Easy companies disappeared in clouds of smoke and dust."[16] Private Ted Zuber, who would go on to become a famous war artist, remembered, "the smoke was so thick you couldn't see anything, it burnt your lungs."[17] Lieutenant D.G. Loomis later wrote:

> Its effect can hardly be described. It was shattering. I stopped counting the rounds about halfway through this bombardment — at 700 — and I only counted the orange flashes which I could see. Before it was over visibility was less than an arm's length due to the heavy pall of black fumes which caused everyone's eyes to water.[18]

The fire then lifted and shifted to the positions next to "B" Coy. The sub-unit was now effectively cut off from the other positions as the enemy fire pummelled "A" and "E" Coys on the flanks for 45 minutes. The Chinese then launched an attack to take the 460 metre peak.

As the bombardment continued on the flanks an enemy battalion swarmed over "B" Coy's shattered position. "At 1815 hrs," recorded the War Diary, "the tense words came to the CO, 'B' Coy was being overrun." It noted, "Heavy mortaring and shelling was followed by the enemy charging into "B" Coy position in the gathering dusk."[19] Private Arthur Alexander chillingly remembered, "The Chinese came in almost on top of the barrage screaming and firing their burp guns and throwing grenades."[20] The OC and his HQ, reported, "the sound of 'burp-guns,' horns bugles and whistles were heard even before the bombardment lifted."[21] Lieutenant Martin recalled, "Loud Chinese voices, whistles and bugles could be heard in Baker Company position only 50 yards away."[22]

The Chinese attack was expected, so a defensive fire plan had been organized. It was now executed. Artillery and 4.2-inch mortars

Courtesy The RCR Archives and Museum.

An RCR soldier enjoys a private meal in the trenches.

thundered in support, hammering likely form-up points (FUPs) and approach routes. In addition, all possible Battalion heavy machine guns (HMGs), MMGs, and 81-mm and 60-mm mortars were called in for defensive fire (DF) tasks. As a result, a curtain of fire now rained down in front of "B" Coy and on to the approaches to the North of Hill 355. The "A" Coy War Diary recorded, "The enemy attacked 'B' Coy in estimated 2 Bn [battalion] strength, quickly overran 'B' Coy position and part of left hand Platoon 'A' Coy before being brought to a standstill."[23]

The battle for Area 2 had dissolved to desperate, savage close quarter, hand-to-hand combat. During the barrage Private Johnny Johnston crawled from foxhole to foxhole to repair weapons. He cleaned each part with gasoline and ensured they were ready when called upon. Later he calmly stripped two jammed Bren guns in the heat of the action and put them back in service. "He's the calmest man I've ever seen," praised his platoon commander, Lieutenant Edward Mastronardi, after the battle.[24]

But he was not alone. Private Charles Morrison was rooted in his fighting trench when the Chinese hordes swarmed their position. He remained in place and fought desperately to enable his comrades to withdraw. "When last seen he was engaged in close combat with enemy."[25]

Sergeant Gerald Enright of 5 Platoon also displayed selflessness and courage. Ordered by his platoon commander to report their situation after all radio communications broke down, Enright fought his way through to "A" Coy's position under heavy fire. He reported the desperate plight of "B" Coy and then grabbed a radio and as much ammunition as he could carry and made his way back into the anvil of fire to assist his comrades beat back the seemingly endless tide of Chinese attackers.

Similarly, Lieutenant John Clark set a stirring example as he tenaciously held his position. Throughout he remained in the thick of the fighting. "He personally took an active part in the close fighting, throwing grenades and manning in turn a rifle, Bren, and Sten until each weapon's ammunition was expended."[26] When he realized that the remaining options were either annihilation or surrender, he reorganized the remainder of his platoon and successfully withdrew, carrying one of his wounded soldiers on his back, from their position to "A" Coy's entrenchments where they continued the fight.

"B" Coy by now was completely cut-off. Its neighbouring sub-unit, "E" Coy was the source of information for the Battalion HQ. Bingham was on leave, so the fight was now in the hands of the acting CO, Major Francis Klenavic. Observation was obscured by the smoke and dust of the raging fire-fight.

The first clear information occurred at 1836 hours, when the 4 Platoon commander arrived to Battalion HQ and reported that his platoon had been overrun. At this time it was impossible to contact the leftmost platoon of "A" Coy and it was presumed that they too had been overwhelmed. "D" Coy, in the unit's depth position, was warned off at 1850 hours to put in a counterattack at 1900 hours. At 1910 hours, OC "A" Coy called in a close-in DF. To this point the extent of the enemy attack or penetration had not been determined. It was not until later, that

Courtesy Captain [Retired] Robert H. Mahar.

Chinese positions being hammered. This photograph shows the varied terrain that the "Royals" had to deal with.

it became clear the Chinese had merely conducted a diversionary attack against "A" Coy's position.

At 1916 hours, OC "E" Coy deployed a small patrol to investigate the status of "B" Coy. They determined that the Chinese now possessed Area 2. "A" and "C" Coys continued to report movement directly to the front of their positions and continued to call in "danger close" artillery shoots. At 1943 hours, OC "B" Coy reported that he, 5 Platoon commander, and 12 men had reached the left platoon of "A" Coy. He grimly reported that no friendly troops remained in action in the former "B" Coy area. As a result, Area 2 was now swathed with fire.

Plans were now consolidated for the counterattack to regain the lost position. By 2045 hours, all was set. A relieving force from "A" Coy, took over "D" Coy's position and all supporting tank and air assets were coordinated. The plan entailed a complex pincer movement with one platoon attacking from behind "E" Coy's position, while another platoon (a diversion) would attack through "A" Coy.

As the final preparations were made for the counterattack, Battalion HQ could still not determine the intent of the enemy. The weight of the attack, and the enemy's continuing activity to the west and north of Hill 355 reinforced the belief that this was just Phase 1 of a larger attack. At 2110 hours, a sudden increase in enemy artillery and mortar fire on "E" Coy seemed to indicate an impending assault.

In response, all available artillery and mortar assets fired an impressive response. Area 2 and all approaches to Hill 355 were now covered in a blanket of fire. It appeared that the speed and weight of the response fire took the steam out of the enemy's advance. Chinese supporting fire faltered, slackened, and then tapered off to harassing fire for the remainder of the engagement.

By 0105 hours, 24 October, "D" Coy was poised to launch the counterattack. Seven minutes of artillery fire preceded the assault. 10 Platoon assaulted from the left and into the extreme most position of Area 2. They encountered no opposition. At the same time 12 Platoon attacked from "A" Coy's position on the right and occupied the centre position in Area 2. Once again, they too met no opposition. The enemy had melted away. By 0331 both assaulting platoons linked up and the situation was restored.[27]

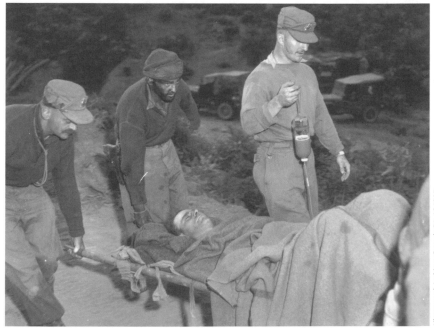

A wounded "Royal" is evacuated for further medical attention.

Library and Archives Canada PA-184805.

"D" Coy then cleared out the rubble and made the position "fightable." The grim task of evacuating the dead and the wounded then commenced.

In the end, the battle cost the Battalion 18 killed, 35 wounded, and 14 taken prisoner. Interestingly, RCR prisoners released at the end of the war reported that the Canadian attack that triggered the Royal's desperate struggle was the daring snatch patrol on Little Gibraltar the month earlier. In fact, they insisted that the Chinese were looking for Lieutenant Gardiner and Corporal Fowler. Nonetheless, 1 RCR fought valiantly and inflicted a heavy price for the damage the Chinese had caused. The Regimental Banner," captured the War Diary proudly, "atop 355 is shot and shelled — but it still flys."[28]

NOTES

1. "Battalion Notes," *The Connecting File* (Spring-Summer 1952), 31.

2. DHH, File 410B25.013 (D17), "1 RCR Fighting Patrol, 1 Offr and 5 OR, 24 Sep 52 — Debriefing."

3. RCR Museum Archives, War Diary entry, 24 September 1952; and *Ibid.*, War Diary of "C" Coy [1 RCR], 1 September 52 to 30 September 52.

4. RCR Museum Archives, War Diary entry, 24 September 1952; and *Ibid.*, War Diary, 1 RCR, 1 September 52 to 30 September 52.

5. RCR Museum Archives, War Diary entry, 30 September 1952; and *Ibid.*, War Diary, 1 RCR, 1 September 52 to 30 September 52.

6. "Intelligence Brief (based on info available up to 25 March 52) Prepared by: General Staff (Intelligence) HQ 1 Commonwealth Division), 7; and RCR Museum Archives, War Diary, 2 RCR 1 March 52- 31 March 52.

7. RCR Museum Archives, War Diary entry, 30 September 1952; and *Ibid.*, War Diary, 1 RCR, 1 September 52 to 30 September 52.

8. RCR Museum Archives, War Diary entry, 12 August 1952; and *Ibid.*, War Diary of "D" Coy [1 RCR], 1 August 52 to 31 August 52.

9. RCR Museum Archives, War Diary entry, 22 October 1952; and *Ibid.*, War Diary, 1 RCR, 1 October 52 to 30 October 52.

10. RCR Museum, Album Miscellaneous RCR Clippings, Bill Boss, "Reactions of Men Under Fire for 21 Days are Described [Reactions]" Unidentified newspaper clipping.

11. *Ibid.*

12. RCR Museum, Album Miscellaneous RCR Clippings, Bill Boss, "Canadians Get Buried, Shelled, but they carry on," Unidentified newspaper clipping.

13. Boss, "Reactions"

14. J.W. Martin, "The Short, Valiant Life of Easy Company," *Remembering the Forgotten War, Korea 1950–1953* (Kemptville, ON: Veterans Publications, May 1997), 35.

15. RCR Museum, Album Miscellaneous RCR Clippings, Bill Boss, "Colonel Says Sound Basic Training Essential Requirement of Troops," Unidentified newspaper clipping.

16. Martin, 35.

17. Interview with author, 30 July 2007.

18. Quoted in Lieutenant-Colonel Herbert Fairlie Wood, *Strange Battle-Ground. Official History of the Canadian Army in Korea* (Ottawa: Queen's Printer, 1966), 208.

19. RCR Museum, Album Miscellaneous RCR Clippings, War Diary entry, 23 October 1952; and *Ibid.*, War Diary, 1 RCR, 1 October 52 to 30 October 52.

20. RCR Museum, Album Miscellaneous RCR Clippings, William Drylie, "RCR's Princess Pats Beat Back 1,000 Reds in Hand-to-Hand Fight," Unidentified newspaper clipping.

21. RCR Museum Archives, Series 9, Korean War, 1950–1953, Vol. 13, File 25, "Report B Coy's Part in Action Night 23/24 Oct," Appendix A, to "Report on 1 RCR Action Night 23/24 October 52," 25 November 1952.

22. Martin, 36.

23. RCR Museum Archives, War Diary entry, 23 October 1952. War Diary of "A" Coy, (1 RCR), 1 October 52 to 30 October 52.

24. RCR Museum, Album Miscellaneous RCR Clippings, "Shelled Four Days 100 RCR's Cut 1,000 Chinese to Ribbons," newspaper clipping.

25. RCR Museum Archives, RCR Korea Awards & Citations, "Award of Mention-In-Dispatches (Posthumous) to SB 10793 Private Charles Joseph Morrison, 1st Battalion.

26. RCR Museum Archives, RCR Korea Awards & Citations, "Award of Military Cross to ZB 4331 Lieutenant John Clark, 1st Battalion, The Royal Canadian Regiment."

27. RCR Museum Archives, Series 9, Korean War, 1950–1953, Vol. 13, File 25, "Report on 1 RCR Action Night 23–24 October 52," 25 November 1952; and DHH, File 410B25.013 (D24), "The Attack on 'Little Gibraltar' (Part 355), 23 October 52." As a result of much of the reserve ammunition being buried during the preparatory bombardment, a new ammo scale was implemented. Bren gunners now carried a minimum of six magazines; Riflemen carried four Bren magazines and 50 rounds of .303 ammo; Sten gunners carried no fewer than six Sten and two Bren magazines; and all ranks carried two grenades.

28. RCR Museum Archives, War Diary entry, 22 October 1952. War Diary, 1RCR, 1 October 52 to 30 October 52.

9

"DOIN' THE BIZ":
CANADIAN SUBMARINE PATROL OPERATIONS
AGAINST SOVIET SSBNs, 1983–87

Michael Whitby

On the clear moonlit night of 16 November 1986, the Canadian patrol submarine HMCS *Onondaga* stole warily on the surface, transiting the narrow confines of the Strait of Belle Isle. It was the Cold War, and Soviet shipping was reportedly in the area, breeding vigilance. To disguise his boats' identity, commanding officer Lieutenant-Commander Larry Hickey rigged false masthead lights to resemble a fishing trawler, and to ensure covertness, he eschewed radar, relying on visual navigation. *Onondaga* was on an Operational Surveillance Patrol (OSP). Its destination was the far reaches of the Canadian Atlantic Submarine-area of NATO (CANLANT) south of Greenland; its mission, to intercept Soviet ballistic missile submarines (SSBN) patrolling off North America.

If there is any doubt that *Onondaga* was embarked on a serious operation and not a routine peacetime evolution, one only has to consider Hickey's notations in his night order book. On 17 November he warned his watchkeepers, "Once east of Belle Isle we are susceptible to interception by Soviet submarines." The next day, upon receiving intelligence of the movements of a particular SSBN, he wrote, "Soviet bastards still 500 nm [nautical miles] east!"[1] In an unprecedented move he readied his weapons by flooding a torpedo tube containing a Mark 37 war shot torpedo. The hunt was on.

OSPs were conducted under the strictest secrecy, and, until now, knowledge of them was restricted to a handful of personnel in Maritime

Command (MARCOM). The high level of security was characteristic of both the Cold War and the "silent service," as the submarine community is known, and in keeping with the shroud that still covers the submarine operations of many Cold War navies. In the Canadian case, an unfortunate biproduct of that security is that discussion about the requirement for submarines has been conducted at an almost theoretical level since, except for a few operations in support of other government departments in the early 1990s, there have been few actual examples before the public of what submarines can achieve. Most importantly in the context of this study, few Canadians realize the talent, pride, and flare that Canadian submariners routinely exhibit as they go about their work — or "Doin' the Biz" as they call it.

They have been extremely proficient at what they do, and are well respected by our allies. However, unlike their American, British, and German brethren whose wartime exploits became part of popular lore, Canadian submariners, whose service was only formally established in 1965, had no such operational heritage.[2] OSPs gave Canadian submariners a tangible operational role, and they responded with skill and audacity;

Courtesy Department of National Defence.

HMCS *Ojibwa* running on the surface. Submariners dubbed *Ojibwa* the "Go Boat" because it was very reliable.

the very nature of submarine operations, especially in conventional boats, demands that. It is an important chapter in our naval history and one that deserves to be known.

The early 1980s have been described as the nadir of the Cold War.[3] Fallout from the Soviet invasion of Afghanistan, the aggressive rhetoric of U.S. President Ronald Reagan, the deployment of American intermediate range nuclear missiles to Europe as well as many other flashpoints, ratcheted up tension to make it one of the most dangerous periods of the Cold War. The tumult spilled over into the world's oceans. Amid the largest increase in defence spending in American history, Reagan began funding a 600-ship navy, and announced the aggressive Maritime Strategy, whereby the U.S. Navy (USN) and its Allies planned to take the war at sea to the front doorstep of the Soviet Union. The Soviets, for their part, were seeing the fruits of Admiral Sergei Gorshkov's vision of a blue water navy in the form of powerful surface ships and new generations of nuclear submarines. The latter, especially ballistic missile submarines, absorbed the attention of Canada's maritime forces.[4]

In the early 1980s the Soviets began to withdraw their most powerful strategic missile submarines close to home into so-called "bastions" where they would be under the protective umbrella of air, surface, and undersea assets. However, older Project 667A- and 667B-class SSBNs — known as Yankees and Deltas respectively by NATO — which had shorter-ranged ballistic missiles, were forward deployed so as to be within range of North America. Vice-Admiral J. Andrew Fulton, commander of Maritime Command in the early 1980s, remembered, "I was reminded on a daily basis that the Cold War was not far from our shores. Virtually every day there were four Soviet nuclear-powered Yankee-class ballistic missile submarines operating off North America, three on the east coast (with one usually in the Canadian sector) and one on the west."[5]

Beginning in the 1970s, two or three Yankees occupied what NATO navies dubbed the "Yankee Patrol Box" east of Bermuda. From there, their 16 R-27U missiles — each a range of 3,000 kilometres (km) — could reach targets in the eastern United States and Canada within minutes. These missile boats — "Boomers" to Canadian sailors — sailed from their Northern Fleet bases, penetrated the so-called GIUK Gap,[6] and crossed the Atlantic basin towards Bermuda, which meant they entered or skirted the eastern extremity of the CANLANT zone in the deep water off the Grand Banks.[7] In the 1980s they were joined by newer Delta-class SSBNs. Essentially enlarged Yankees, but far quieter, the four Delta variants' R-29 missiles had a 7,850-kilometre range, which enabled them to occupy more-distant launch stations — in the Northwest Atlantic they typically occupied firing positions in the Labrador Sea. Countering the dangerous Yankee and Delta threat was an important part of NATO ASW strategy and in 1983 MARCOM began to use its three Oberon-class submarines — commonly known as O-boats — in dedicated operations against these targets, giving Canadian submariners their first real opportunity to do the "Biz" in home waters.

Since their acquisition in the 1960s, the O-boats had been employed almost exclusively as "clockwork mice," providing targets for the anti-submarine assets of Canada and its NATO allies. This service, as shown

Author's Collection.

A Soviet Project 667B Delta I SSBN. More than four times the size of an O-boat, a Delta's missiles could wreak devastation on North American targets.

through bitter experience in the Second World War, was critically important as it gave sailors and aircrew the chance to practice against the real thing. All NATO navies allocated submarine time for anti-submarine warfare (ASW) training, but in the Canadian case, the emphasis was such that O-boats were left with limited opportunity to prepare for their own wartime role. Under NATO war plans, at the outbreak of any conflict the O-boats would be deployed into choke points like the GIUK Gap and the Davis Strait to destroy Soviet submarines entering the North Atlantic. As will become evident, submarine versus submarine operations are an exceedingly complex form of warfare, and like other similar military endeavours, required comprehensive training to first attain, and then maintain proficiency. However, apart from sporadic SSXs — submarine versus submarine serials — which typically lasted a day-or-two at most, and large set piece NATO exercises, Canadian submariners had no sustained opportunity to train for their wartime role.

Submariners also chaffed at the restrictive nature of clockwork mouse activity. Although they occasionally had a chance to "attack" their adversaries in the free-play portion of exercises, they otherwise had to manoeuvre within strict parameters: Generally, ASW practitioners wanted a submarine they could find without much difficulty. This grated. As one veteran recalled, "'Provision of target services' did not sit well with a Submarine Service striving to gain a reputation internationally for imaginative, dynamic submarine operation."[8] The only real opportunity to broaden their experience came when they deployed to the United Kingdom.

From the time the O-boats joined the fleet in the 1960s, work-ups had been carried out under the auspices of the Royal Navy (RN).[9] In exchange for these services Canada loaned individual boats to the RN for short periods, during which time they came under British operational control (OPCON). Besides acting as training platforms, they were assigned Cold War missions as if they were British national assets, and taskings included surveillance of Soviet warships. On one occasion HMCS *Onondaga* was ordered to gather intelligence on a new Kara-class cruiser transiting the English Channel, presumably on a similar information gathering mission.

Normally, the intent on operations of this type was to get close under the target's keel — within about a dozen feet from the periscope — to take photographs, record the acoustic signature, and capture electronic emissions. On this occasion the water was too shallow to get underneath but *Onondaga* shadowed the cruiser from about 1,000 yards and recorded valuable data. That these were dicey evolutions was underscored later in the same deployment when *Onondaga* ran into a sea mount while trying to get underneath a Soviet intelligence vessel. With "sharp end" experiences like these, EASTLANT deployments were extremely popular among Canadian submariners. When OSPs brought the chance to carry out operational missions on our side of the Atlantic — a Canadian mission, under Canadian operational control — it provided a real boost to the submarine community.

A decade ago the author received invaluable insights into the leadership dynamic of a submarine when he toured the A-class boat HMS *Alliance* at the RN Submarine Museum at Gosport. The tour was conducted by a retired chief petty officer with some 30 years experience in submarines. Proudly wearing his old uniform, he led the group through the boat, reminiscing about his service and explaining *Alliance*'s complex anatomy in terms of who did what and how. Entering the control room, his voice took on a hushed, reverential tone. Gesturing to the periscopes, he told his audience "In a submarine, the Captain is God. All depends on him."

Those sentiments convey how far more responsibility rested on the CO of a submarine than of other warships. Larry Hickey, who commanded two O-boats and a frigate in the Canadian Navy, explains it this way:

> A submarine Captain is subjected to a considerably more stressful environment in day-to-day business than is the surface ship Commanding Officer. Unlike his destroyer counterpart, the submarine skipper operates his vessel for protracted periods in traditional fashion as the lone wolf, without the support of other ships in company. He also lacks the back up of a command qualified Executive Officer, his Second-in-Command. Cramped conditions,

bad air, and continual physical discomfort make concentration and decision-making difficult. And always lurking in the back of the Submarine Captain's mind is the grim understanding of his vessel's vulnerability. He knows, for example, that the entire crew of a destroyer could instantaneously fall asleep, and the ship would continue to float; if only one or two of his submariners were to snooze, the results could be catastrophic.[10]

To qualify for the rigours of command, Canadian submariners had to pass the four-month Commanding Officers Qualifying Course run by the Royal Navy, "a gruelling baptism of fire, known by the submarine community simply as 'Perisher.'"[11]

Perisher tested the candidates' ability to operate a submarine safely and skilfully in every conceivable type of operation, including attacks against shipping, evasion from ASW forces, surveillance, harbour reconnaissance, mine laying, and the insertion of special forces. Tactical serials were treacherous with the submarine having to track as many as four frigates manoeuvring at high speed in close contact, the candidate taking the boat up to the surface and down to periscope depth, keeping the surface picture clear while making complex mental calculations to develop a firing solution; all while trying to keep the boat safe and covert.

To the uninitiated the tension is probably incomprehensible. According to Hickey for four months "the candidate is placed under a military microscope twenty-four hours per day, whether wide awake and alert or suffering from lack of sleep. Every possible scenario is examined. By the time the course is over, the budding submarine captain will have been pushed to his physical and mental limits." Unlike qualification for surface ship command, where candidates could retake the command board until successful, Perisher was a one-shot, pass or fail proposition. And failure, which could occur at any point, was dramatic: The candidate learned his fate from "Teacher," the officer running the course, and was given a bottle of scotch and immediately whisked off the boat. "Cold, swift and clean," as Hickey described the process. Failure meant you were finished in submarines; success made you part of an exclusive elite. As

American author and submarine enthusiast Tom Clancy points out — seemingly apologetically to American submariners — Perisher graduates were "arguably the world's finest quality submarine captains."[12]

The men that commanded Canadian O-boats were relatively junior officers, in most cases only recently promoted lieutenant-commanders. They were also usually young; Hickey was just 29 when he took over *Onondaga*. Those characteristics, in combination with the boost from having surmounted Perisher, meant they oozed confidence. It would be inaccurate to describe them as cocky or arrogant, although some undoubtedly were, but they were universally bold and aggressive. They never pushed their commands past the point of safety, yet they knew how to get the most out of their boats and sailors. "Daring" is not a word normally associated with a category of naval-type command — Motor Torpedo Boats might be the only other instance — but with O-boat COs it applied as a matter of course.

Although submarine captains bore a heavy burden, it was not strictly a one-man show. The sailors who proudly wore Dolphins also considered themselves part of an elite, and typically displayed solid proficiency in a challenging, technologically complex environment. Submarines are intricate mechanisms, and it took a lot of training and experience to understand the various systems onboard and endure the cramped, uncomfortable conditions.

A chronic problem was that the navy never had enough qualified submarine ratings. Commander Ray Hunt, who led the squadron from January 1978 to August 1981, recalled, "From the first day I arrived in the Submarine Squadron it was apparent that personnel shortages were going to be my biggest challenge. I wasn't worried about operations, because I knew that the people in submarines were professional and very competent — and as good if not better than their NATO colleagues. It was just that I didn't have enough of them...."[13] In particular, there were consistent shortages among the senior technical trades, which meant a lot of shuffling of personnel so that boats could head out on operations fully manned. That increased sea time, which reduced opportunities to attend training courses ashore — i.e., qualify for promotion — and disrupted family life. Moreover, boats often had to embark on patrols with sailors who had yet to qualify for submarines — one sailed with 22, or about a third of the complement. Not only would the "greenhorns" have a tough time handling the challenges thrown at them, but those who had already earned their Dolphins had to bear a greater burden.

In 1915, Rudyard Kipling penned an apt description of the character of submariners and their place with in the Royal Navy of the First World War era. "The submarine," he wrote in *The Fringes of the Fleet*, "has created its own type of officer and man, with language and traditions apart from the rest of the service, and yet at heart, unchangingly of the Service." Seventy years later, Canadian submariners would have embraced those remarks. They considered themselves a group apart, and thought they lay on the fringes of the Canadian fleet.[14] Unhappy at the priority put on the training role and the secondary status it seemed to bring, officers and ratings alike welcomed the opportunity to fulfil a real operational role.

The decision to embark upon OSPs derived from a confluence of factors. First, the O-boats were in the midst of the Submarine Operational Update Program (SOUP), essentially their mid-life modernization. According to a contemporary account, SOUP transformed the boats from "a semi-passive ASW training vessel, to a fully capable offensive underseas weapon platform."[15] Among a number of improvements SOUP boosted the surveillance capability of the O-boats through the fitting of AN/BQG 501 MicroPUFFS passive ranging sonar and the digital Singer-Librascope Submarine Fire Control System. In conjunction with their original Type 2007 fixed linear array and 187c attack sonar, the new systems enabled attack crews to conduct Target Motion Analysis (TMA) on up to four targets simultaneously. As one commentator explained, "using automatic TMA on multiple targets, a submarine commander could form a picture of the underwater and surface activity around the submarine, a sort of equivalent of a radar picture, without giving the submarine's position away by pinging with sonar."[16] Moreover, digital processing helped to classify the increased number of contacts detected by the improved sonar. In combination with O-boats' legendary quietness and long endurance, SOUP transformed the Oberons into potent ASW platforms.

A weakness of that generation of conventional submarines was that their relatively slow submerged speed limited their ability to search large areas of ocean.[17] O-boats could not cover distance quickly and still remain covert; with speed came noise, with noise came counter-detection. Adding to the problem was their need to snort regularly, about every four to six hours depending on the amount of battery power being consumed, which impaired search capability and sonar performance.

Fortunately, they gained their legs through the new Lockheed CP-140 Aurora, which became operational in the early 1980s. Probably the most effective Maritime Patrol Aircraft (MPA) of its generation, the Aurora married the airframe of the P-3 Orion with the avionics package of the USN's new S-3 Viking carrier-borne ASW aircraft. With relatively high speed, long endurance, extensive sensor, and weapons suites, and a crew including four tactical navigators and three electronic sensor operators, Auroras could track the newest Soviet submarines for extensive periods. Shortly after the CP-140s began flying operations, Vice-Admiral Fulton informed Admiral Harry Train USN, Supreme Allied Commander Atlantic, that a team of Auroras had tracked two Soviet SSBNs continuously over three days; after accepting congratulations, he added "and by the way" they had also tracked the USN attack boats (SSN) trailing them. American SSNs were supposed to be too quiet for that, and the look in Train's eyes was apparently one of surprise and consternation.[18]

Canadian submariners had long enjoyed a close relationship with the MPA community, therefore, it is not surprising that the officer serving as senior staff officer (Sea Operations) on Fulton's staff, Commander Keith

Perhaps the most effective guardian of Canada's maritime sovereignty during the Cold War, Lockheed CP-140 Auroras maintained an accurate picture of Soviet activity in the CANLANT zone.

Courtesy Department of National Defence.

Nesbit, grasped the potential of a partnership between modernized O-boats and the new Auroras. Nesbit was highly respected in the submarine community, known for his intellect, vision, and leadership; he was also an accomplished musician, and when CO of *Okanagan* in the mid-1970s he and his officers had coined the infamous *Dolphin Code*, an informal cipher submariners could use to communicate with — really tweak — adversaries during exercises, particularly "skimmers," as they called their surface brethren.[19] Nesbit had long been critical of the propensity of senior officers to view O-boats strictly as training platforms, overlooking their operational capability. He also thought it vital to demonstrate to the Americans that Canada could look after its own area of responsibility. It was critical to be seen to be able to defend our sovereignty, and to Nesbit deploying O-boats on operational patrols was like "putting a chunk of Canada out on station."[20]

There was a final, matter-of-fact reason for sending O-Boats after Soviet SSBNs. Although Auroras could track them there was doubt whether their "lightweight" Mk 46 ASW torpedoes — the same type used by Canadian destroyers and ASW helicopters — could actually destroy Soviet nuclear boats, most of which had durable, double-hulls. On the other hand, the Oberons' "heavy" Mk 37 torpedoes packed far more punch, and, even though they had a well-earned reputation as a temperamental weapon, their warhead was powerful enough to destroy a boomer.[21] The challenge was to get into position to achieve a fire solution. Commander Bob Bush, a respected submariner and veteran of a number of OSPs, believes that Fulton and Nesbit wanted to prove to the Americans that they could get an O-boat into position to kill a SSBN. The little chunk of Canada out on station in the North Atlantic had to have teeth.

Launching OSPs represented a distinct challenge for Maritime Command. In one of his initial planning memos, Nesbit conceded, "because of our boats' somewhat limited experience in this regard (most of which has been obtained from tasking when under British OPCON) and because of MARCOM headquarter's lack of practice at directing/controlling submarines in a fully 'operational' sense, there should be a lot to learn."[22] Under NATO protocol, before each OSP, MARCOM had to earmark a submarine patrol area (SPA) through the Commander Submarines At-lantic — COMSUBLANT — at Norfolk, who oversaw NATO submarine operations in the Atlantic.[23] This reserved an operational area for the boat, including a "moving haven" for the transit, which reduced the risk of mutual interference and collision with other NATO submarines.[24]

At the Maritime Operations Centre (MOC) in Halifax, a small sealed cell of experienced submariners had to be set-up to coordinate each mission. Their job as controllers was to sift intelligence of SSBN movements from SOSUS, MPAs, and other sources, and vector an O-boat to the best position for an interception. Communications procedures also had to be confirmed with the signal establishment at Mill Cove. Security surrounding these preparations was incredibly tight, and outside the controllers and the command team of the submarine, only a handful of senior officers were aware of individual operations. Some COs even chose not to inform their entire crew of their mission.

O-boats were expected to remain covert throughout the entire patrol. This was a challenge since the Soviets habitually positioned their own surveillance assets in the Northwest Atlantic. Research vessels and weather ships could usually be found in the CANLANT zone, and Soviet aircraft routinely probed our air defence systems. Each would be equipped with sensors capable of detecting a surfaced or snorting O-boat. Although not normally equipped with sensors beyond standard commercial radar, the ubiquitous Soviet fishing fleet also had to be avoided. There was also concern that the Soviets used satellites to detect submarine movements, either visually or through thermal or wake detection technology, therefore patrol orders included reference to expected exposure to satellites.

Most germane, however, was the threat of counter-detection by the targets they were pursuing, Soviet SSBNs. Here, O-boats were on fairly safe ground. They were exceedingly quiet; in fact Auroras had trouble tracking them even if they knew their general location. More-over, Soviet passive sonar systems were substandard, and since their boats were also noisier they would have difficulty hearing an O-boat over their own self-generated noise.[25] Because of these shortcomings Soviet COs relied more on active sonar, "pinging" as often as every three hours, but this usually disclosed their location.[26] Given all these factors, if a Canadian O-boat maintained effective quiet routine, the risk of counter-detection was low.

HMCS *Okanagan* embarked on the first OSP in the summer of 1983, under the command of Lieutenant-Commander Bruce MacLean. Under the patrol order, MacLean was instructed to head to the southeast portion of the CANLANT zone about 900 miles from Halifax with the primary objective of "the interception/location of a Yankee class SSBN with subsequent shadowing to the extent possible." The available intelligence report provided three possible "candidates." The secondary objective of the mission was to "BINT," or in laymen's terms, gather basic intelligence, such as visual features, and acoustic and electronic emissions on Soviet surface traffic including the massive space research vessel *Kosmonaut Yuri Gagarin*, which was expected to monitor a French missile test in the mid-Atlantic following a visit to Halifax. His final objectives were to investigate the oil platform *Vinland*, and to make a short operational visit to Argentia, presumably in support of SOSUS research. It was an ambitious program for a 20-day patrol, therefore, MacLean was instructed to transit on the surface as much as possible "to make most of the total time allotted."

Although *Okanagan* had not had the benefit of SOUP — this was the only OSP carried out by a non-modernized boat — it received a FAS 1B narrowband sonar analyzer as a special mission fit. Passive sonar had become the predominant ASW detection system, especially in the context of submarines hunting other submarines. O-boats had both active and passive sets, but since "pinging" could reveal their presence, Canadian submariners took it as a matter of pride never to use active systems on operations. Whereas active sonar causes a return from a transmitted pulse, passive sonar detects sound emitting from the target itself. This falls into two categories: broadband, which includes sound such as water moving over the hull and propeller cavitation; and narrowband, which includes low-frequency noise generated from machinery such as pumps and generators.[27] As ASW analyst Tom Stefanick explains, "Submarines make different kinds and levels of sound at different speeds. When a nuclear-powered submarine is stopped, it must continue to run reactor cooling pumps, generators, and air conditioning. Those generate narrowband spectra that are relatively independent of speed." Besides picking out a submarine from a myriad of ocean noises, narrowband enabled a remarkable degree of classification. "Passive sonar operators," Stefanick continued, "can sometimes identify the nationality and class of an unknown submarine. Unique machinery noises may even permit identification of a particular submarine."[28] Accordingly, NATO ASW forces not only tracked Soviet boomers to determine their location and patrol pat-

Courtesy Department of National Defence.

The cramped clutter of an O-Boat's control room with an officer at the attack periscope. During action stations, as many as 18 sailors crowded into this space.

terns, but also to record their acoustic signatures, which enabled analysts to trace the activity of individual boats. FAS 1B introduced Canadian submariners to this capability, but they never seemed to receive enough training and experience to get the most out of the system. According to a 1986 analysis, FAS 1B "was not generally understood," and there was "general weakness in narrowband theory knowledge in Canadian submarines."[29] Nonetheless, the chance to test drive narrowband technology, placed the O-boats at the forefront of NATO ASW.

Okanagan slipped Jetty 2 at 1220Z hours 30 June. Since a Soviet merchant ship alongside in Halifax witnessed its departure — one wonders why boats did not sail for OSPs during darkness — and the *Yuri Gagarin* and several fishing vessels were in position to monitor the boat as it passed surfaced through the harbour approaches. However, MacLean headed south as if destined for Bermuda before altering eastward to his patrol area. Once on station *Okanagan* patrolled for three days but was unable to detect any SSBN activity. A subsequent analysis concluded that the three Yankees in the Northwest Atlantic were either too distant to prosecute or controllers lacked specific intelligence to cue *Okanagan* into position. Putting himself in the mindset of his opponents, MacLean loitered around the French research vessel *Poincaré*, which was monitoring a missile test, in the hope that Soviet boats might also be interested in the activity, but still came up empty.[30]

On 4 July, controllers changed *Okanagan*'s mission. At 1956Z hours they alerted MacLean to an unusual change in Soviet activity as two intelligence vessels (AGI) had vacated their normal positions off the U.S. eastern seaboard. One of these was the *Kavkaz* (AGI 591), a modern purpose-built AGI usually stationed off the Virginia Capes to monitor naval activity out of Norfolk.[31] MPA surveillance indicated that this valuable intelligence target was heading northeast through the CANLANT zone, therefore, *Okanagan* was tasked to intercept it. Unfortunately, because of inaccurate position reports and communications glitches, the submarine failed to catch *Kavkaz*. At one point, MacLean thought he was within 10 miles of the AGI, however, after later reassessing the information he concluded that it had actually been some 200 miles to the southwest. *Okanagan* completed its operational port visit to Argentia and conducted routine surveillance of the Vinland oil platform before returning to Halifax.

As expected, OSP 1/83 yielded a number of lessons. MacLean and analysts at the Canadian Forces Maritime Warfare Centre (CFMWC), who scrutinized the results of all patrols, were impressed by the capability of the FAS 1B narrowband analyser, especially in terms of monitoring *Okanagan*'s own noise. "By presenting a visual display," MacLean reported, "the entire crew were able to see the effect of such noisy equipment as the movie projector operating in the forends, the main domestic fridge as it started and stopped, the effect of an electrician's ratchet as a battery hatch was opened. The reduction in crew noise was profound and gratifying."

Analysts also recommended that O-boats be fitted with towed acoustic arrays to boost their search capability. This relatively new technology — American SSNs had first deployed it in the early 1970s — encompassed a long thin array lined with passive sensors that was towed behind a submarine.[32] "Tails," as they were dubbed, enhanced narrowband capability exponentially and increased detection ranges to dozens of miles. A Canadian system was being trialled at that time but, in contrast to all other major NATO navies, priority was given to fitting it in destroyers. To submariners, this reflected a lack of understanding by senior officers of the Oberons' ASW capability — as well as an unrealistic assessment of that of destroyers against modern SSNs and SSBNs. It seemed to confirm their place in the pecking order, and struck them as a missed opportunity. As it was, O-boats did not stream tails until the end of the decade by which time OSPs were a thing of the past.[33]

MacLean asserted that 19 days had not been enough for such a mission. "Most of the patrol," he reported, "was spent in surface and snort transit":

Okanagan covered over 2,500 nm and was deployed over 900 nm from Halifax. Although the chance of counter-detection was generally low — making such transits reasonable and effective — the transits disrupted the sonar search and greatly reduced the likelihood of SSBN detection. To conduct an SSBN Narrowband (NB) Search, in a standard SPA such as Ewan[34] would take approximately 10 days; i.e., one circuit at four knots with a NB range of prediction 20 nm each side of the submarine. In other words, the SSBN search problem is massive unless intel or other assets can reduce the search area.

Since a war-stored O-boat could remain at sea for 90 days, lengthening the duration of OSPs presented no real challenge beyond making room for the longer patrol among myriad commitments. But the best way to ensure success, as MacLean suggested, was effective cueing from MPAs and SOSUS.

The commandant of the CFMWC expressed a reluctance to implement "lasting changes" on the basis of one OSP, and concluded, "the only general recommendation made is that we continue these patrols with a view to expanding our experience and ability." The next patrol, OSP 2/83 conducted by Ojibwa from 14 November-6 December 1983, fulfilled that objective.

OSP 2/83 featured several variations from its forerunner, underscoring they were still a work in progress. Most significantly, Ojibwa had undergone the SOUP modernization so it brought added capability to the mission. In terms of taskings, the boat's CO, Lieutenant-Commander N.P. Nicolson, was not only directed to intercept Soviet Yankee-class SSBNs, but also to gather electronic information, or ELINT, on TU-95 RT "Bear" reconnaissance aircraft, monitor the activity of surface vessels, and observe the changeover of two weather ships on semi-permanent station in the North Atlantic. In addition, Ojibwa was instructed to conduct a tracking exercise with the Los Angeles-class SSN USS Atlanta as it transited the CANLANT zone.[35] This wide range of objectives — against air, surface, and sub-surface targets — underscores the copious surveillance capability of a modern submarine.

Ojibwa departed Halifax at 1745Z hours on 14 November, feinting to the southeast before settling on an easterly course. While passing south of Sable Island, Ojibwa monitored emissions from the Soviet research vessel Academik Korolev, satisfying one of its secondary objectives. On 17 November it detected a pair of Bears en route to Cuba that were testing the North American air defence system by flying inside the CANLANT zone. The large ungainly patrol aircraft flew within 5–10 nm of Ojibwa, forcing Nicolson to break-off snorting to reduce the risk of counter-detection. Electronic monitoring indicated that the Bears operated their radar intermittently for a period of 2–4 minutes every 15–20 minutes. Although "BINTing" Soviet air and surface activity was important, the *raison d'etre* of OSPs was to monitor submarine activity. Soon after arriving in its patrol area *Ojibwa* experienced two ASW encounters that not only validated its mission, but also demonstrated the challenges associated with undersea warfare.

At 0100Z hours, 18 November, while *Ojibwa* came around to a course of 047 degrees below the layer[36] in deep water east of the Tail of the Bank, its Type 2007 sonar gained a fleeting contact at about 7000 yards range. The sonar team double-checked the contact with the 187c attack sonar, which found possible turbine whine on the same bearing. After tracking for 15 minutes, Nicolson assessed the contact as a possible submarine.[37] Target Motion Analysis indicated that it was steering 250 degrees at a speed of eight knots. *Ojibwa*'s closest point of approach (CPA) was about 4,000 yards. At 0148Z the contact initiated the telltale manoeuvre of clearing its baffles — circling back to ensure it was not being followed by another submarine lurking behind its propeller cavitation — altering to 120 degrees for five minutes before returning to its original course. *Ojibwa* lost contact at 0158Z and Nicolson elected not to attempt pursuit since the speed required might reveal his presence. Following standard operating procedure Nicolson immediately attempted to report the contact to MARCOM but the gremlins that consistently disrupted ship/shore communications in this part of the Atlantic intervened. *Ojibwa* remained at periscope depth for more than eight hours trying to raise MARCOM and an exasperated Nicolson complained "all conceivable HF [high frequency] frequencies and shore stations have been tried … there is no chance *Ojibwa* has *not been DF'ed.*"[38]

After the patrol Nicolson claimed a definite submarine contact through the following data:

- a quiet, high bearing rate;
- a short detection range (approximately 7,000 yards)
- biological noise on the contact bearing (common around submarines);
- course alterations;
- no visual contacts in conditions of good visibility;
- intermittent 187c high channel contact; and
- whine audible on the stern aspect.

COMSUBLANT, the repository for intelligence of submarine movements, later advised it had no candidates for the contact, "friendly or otherwise." But Nicolson was not deterred, and "strongly considered" that the contact was a SSN, and suggested it might have been a Soviet Project 671 Victor transiting to Cuba to replace another Victor undergoing repair.[39] Others speculate it might have been an Allied boat.

Two days after this incident, *Ojibwa* encountered the bulk carrier *Columbia Liberty* east of the Flemish Cap. With no other contacts evident, Nicolson decided to carry out a simulated attack on the unsuspecting merchant ship. However, as the boat approached the attack team detected anomalies between bearings reported acoustically from sonar and visually from the periscope. Sonar operators "initially considered that 2007 was cutting a strong side lobe, however when *Ojibwa* altered to port at CPA, the 2007 'side lobe' broke fast right at a higher bearing rate (about 20–25 deg/min) than the *Columbia Liberty*." Analysis revealed two contacts, the second at about half the range of the merchant ship and emitting sounds associated with military machinery. Nicolson concluded "it was very likely a submarine travelling on the MV's starboard quarter at close range in order to obtain an acoustic cover." These were known Soviet tactics, especially in areas like the Northwest Atlantic where there was a high probability of detection by SOSUS.[40]

Unfortunately, contact was lost before this could be confirmed. However, four days earlier *Ojibwa* had received intelligence of a Yankee SSBN designated YL-181. Using "furthest on circles and great circle track to the Soviet SSBN patrol station,"[41] Nicolson concluded, "that the contact was YL-181." This estimate seemed accurate, and COMSUBLANT later confirmed it was "not U.S. or known friendly submarine."[42]

It is impossible to verify either of the submarine contacts claimed by *Ojibwa*. This was a recurrent problem of Cold War ASW, since there was no "flaming data" nor usually even sighting reports to confirm "enemy" activity. It was an acoustic war, and submariners and analysts often disagreed on the authenticity of contacts. This was not a new phenomenon. During the Second World War, for example, the RN's U-boat Assessment Committee had often cast aspersions on claims of sunken U-boats, and it was only after Allied and German records were compared decades after the war that the issues were resolved — if they were at all. The problem with Cold War ASW research is that we do not currently have access to the patrol records of our Allies, let alone the Soviets. In the case of OSP 2/83, the situation was obscured farther by glitches in the recording procedure, which prevented sufficient data being gathered for analysis. As a result, the validity of *Ojibwa*'s contacts remains a mystery. Nonetheless, crew members remain convinced both were submarines.

After the planned tracking exercise with USS *Atlanta* failed to come-off, *Ojibwa* spent the last part of its patrol monitoring the changeover of the Soviet weather research vessels *Musson* and *Passat* at Ocean Weather Station Charlie, in the mid-Atlantic 850 miles northeast of St. John's. Except for an engineering emergency, this should have been a routine surveillance evolution. Working from intelligence provided by CP-140s, at 2220Z hours 29 November, *Ojibwa* found the AGOR *Musson* sitting motionless, presumably conducting weather research. *Ojibwa* moved in to about 1,000 yards to gather intelligence but could not get closer because of a high sea state, which exposed the periscope to detection. Nicolson opened range to about 12,500 yards to await the second AGOR, but at 0725Z hours 30 November, heavy smoke choked the motor room, and *Ojibwa* suffered a complete loss of propulsion.

As a post-mission analysis described with considerable understatement, this left the boat in an "unpleasant ship control situation." The boat was submerged, apparently on fire, close to Soviet units. These are precisely the situations a crew trains for, and *Ojibwa*'s reacted with speed and professionalism. While sailors sought the cause of the smoke, Nicolson surfaced and tried to remain covert. ESM confirmed that *Musson*'s radar was emitting continuously, but Nicolson used auxiliary power to keep stern-on to the AGI, reducing *Ojibwa*'s radar profile. In the meantime, engineers found the cause of the propulsion failure, and by 0917Z hours had jury-rigged repairs so that the boat could get underway on the port main motor. But *Ojibwa* was still not out of the woods. Within an hour the "unpleasantness" continued when ESM picked up another Soviet radar to the southeast, which was soon classified as the *Passat*. As Nicolson described in his patrol report, "at 1100Z hrs *Passat* was sighted briefly at 12Kyd [thousand yards]. *Ojibwa* maintained a stern aspect to this closer

AGOR and *Passat* continued North to rendevous with *Musson*. It is considered likely that both *Musson* and *Passat* detected *Ojibwa* on radar but because of the range, stern aspect, lack of lights, high sea state, and poor visibility (frequent rain and hail showers) did not classify *Ojibwa* as a submarine." Nicolson's hunch was probably correct since the AGORs would have relished the opportunity to inspect a surfaced submarine.

Having probably saved the day through his manoeuvring under emergency conditions, Nicolson withdrew from the area and once well clear of Ocean Station Charlie stopped to effect repairs.[43] Engineers quickly had both main motors back on line, and the submarine began its submerged transit to Argentia. It carried out one last surveillance task on its way home when it responded to a flash tasking to take ESM readings on a pair of Bears sniffing around the CANLANT zone just east of St. John's.

There was no doubting the value of OSP 2/83. *Ojibwa* had conducted surveillance on Soviet MPAs, a possible SSBN, an unidentified SSN, and two AGORs. Unhappily, although it had gathered a great deal of useful intelligence most of the taped sonar data could not be analyzed because of equipment or procedural problems. Despite that, analysts were impressed by *Ojibwa*'s record keeping and recommended the data form the basis of a more rigorous operational analysis regime for SSK patrols.[44] Ship/shore communication between *Ojibwa* and Halifax had also been problematic and analysts recommended the boats be fitted with satellite communications systems (SATCOM) to ensure reliable and secure communications. However, this was not realized until the 1990s.

Finally, although *Ojibwa* had encountered two submarines, it had been unable to trail them. Both Nicolson and the CFMWC analysis re-emphasised that boats needed to be permanently fitted with narrowband equipment such as FAS 1B as well as a towed array. OSP 2/83 had proved that O-boats could detect ASW targets but without sophisticated detection and analysis systems, they were unable to standoff at 7,000–10,000 yards like a USN SSN with a tail. Instead, they had to snuggle up to close, white-knuckle range of contacts, increasing the risk of both collision and counter-detection.[45]

When he formulated the plan for OSPs, Commander Nesbit envisioned that "each operationally available boat conduct at least one such patrol annually."[46] That seemed like a reasonable commitment, and would result in no fewer than three patrols a year, with all the accrued benefits. Unfortunately, the small size and training priority accorded the Canadian submarine fleet made that impossible, and 13 months passed before another OSP could be mounted. In 1984, *Ojibwa* was committed to an EASTLANT deployment as well as NATO exercises on both sides of the Atlantic, *Okanagan* was entering its SOUP refit, and *Onondaga* was heading to the U.K. for work-ups. Since knowledge of OSPs was limited to so few, the inability to carry out any of the patrols in 1984 was akin to the philosophical question "If a tree falls in a forest does anyone hear?" We are unable at this point in time to ascertain what the Soviets knew of our submarine operations, but it is safe to assume that they would have been gratified to know there was one less ASW platform to be concerned about. From MARCOM's perspective, they had one less asset to deploy in defence of Canadian waters. The impact of all this is unclear; however, it is evident that in the interregnum between OSPs 2/83 and 1/85 the submarine community attempted to fine-tune the operations. As a result, the operation *Ojibwa* embarked upon in late February 1985, turned out to be the most successful — and certainly the most dramatic — patrol of its kind.

Summarizing the heavy load of exercises and training serials *Ojibwa* had borne in 1984, its commanding officer, Lieutenant-Commander Phil Webster — "Ace" to his colleagues — repeated the hoary adage that operations at sea are typically 99 percent boredom, one percent wild excitement. Although complete patrol records are unavailable, there is enough evidence to apply that maxim to OSP 1/85.[47] After the last minute loading of torpedoes and other supplies, *Ojibwa* departed Halifax on the afternoon of 25 February 1985. Despite the confidence accrued through outstanding performance in NATO exercises in 1984,[48] Webster lamented that *Ojibwa*'s crew did not have the benefit of a dedicated training period before the patrol to shake off the rust that had accumulated over a maintenance and leave period. This was an old lesson, and senior officers subsequently acknowledged, "that rigorous equipment 'shakedown' and significant preparation must precede all patrols of this nature."

Ojibwa was headed to a patrol area in the Labrador Sea southwest of Greenland where Soviet Delta SSBNs regularly occupied firing positions.

Courtesy Captain [Navy] E.P. Webster.

Having to endure tough conditions, submariners grabbed respite when opportunity arose. Here Lieutenant-Commander Phil Webster enjoys "sundowners" on *Ojibwa*'s bridge after the boat ran 33 consecutive days submerged during the NATO exercise TEAMWORK 84.

It was a long transit. Typical for the time of year, the weather was poor and a following sea made snorting difficult. The intelligence Webster received during the initial part of the trip also was not promising and with the prospect of a long boring patrol ahead he tried to catch up on his reading. One of the first books he cracked was Lothar-Günter Buchheim's *Das Boot*, and he recalls the environment described in the classic novel of U-boat warfare was not all that different from what *Ojibwa* was enduring.

Despite the routine nature of the transit there was still work to do. The command team practised BINT procedures and the torpedo crew conducted maintenance checks on the Mk 37s. *Ojibwa* also carried out noise radiation checks with CP-140s that indicated that the boat was running "incredibly quiet." Despite that, Webster had concerns that poor communications discipline ashore and from an MPA may have compromised their location.

After a nine-day transit *Ojibwa* reached its patrol area on 6 March 1985. Although they obtained a number of inconclusive long-range sonar hits there were no other signs of activity, and Webster worried *Ojibwa* might come up empty. The picture improved on 10 March when they received information that a Soviet SSBN, designated LD-010, had been detected moving into the CANLANT zone. As *Ojibwa* awaited cueing, CP-140 Auroras, guided by information from SOSUS, flew constantly, sewing sonobuoy patterns in an attempt to find the boomer. In waters notoriously bad for sonar and with the SSBN likely running deep and slow to reduce its signature, this was an exceedingly difficult task: as one submariner recalled, "it was a very hard place to find a quiet submarine."[49] After four days, however, MPAs localized the contact, classified it as a Delta-class SSBN, and controllers sent *Ojibwa* north to intercept.

Since the 1970s American attack boats had attempted to shadow every Soviet SSBN throughout their patrols. The rationale was brutally simple. In 1985 Secretary of the Navy John Lehman announced that American SSNs intended to attack Soviet missile boats "in the first five minutes of the war."[50] Although this was the first public declaration of the strategy, the Soviets had been aware of it for some time — probably from information provided by the Walker spy ring.[51] In an attempt to preserve their first strike capability, the Northern Fleet began to use its own attack boats to screen their SSBNs. This practice — used by both sides during the Cold War — was known as "delousing," and in the early 1980s the Soviets introduced the new Project 671RTM Victor III class SSN into this high-stakes strategic waltz. Victor IIIs were the most advanced submarine yet produced by the Soviets and they quickly assumed almost mythical status within the NATO ASW community. They could be tracked with great difficulty through the GIUK Gap and other choke points, but once they were in the open Atlantic, as *Ojibwa* discovered, they were extremely elusive.[52]

On 16 March, while *Ojibwa* searched for the Delta, controllers informed Webster that a Victor III was in the immediate area, and, worse still, might be trailing him. The hunter had become the hunted. Webster immediately took his boat deep into the sound convergence layers where sonar achieved best results and, sure enough, soon picked-up a contact. Although initially classified as biological, further investigation indicated it might be a submarine, and this was suddenly substantiated by an active sonar transmission from down the same bearing. Since Soviet submariners often "banged away" on active sonar, this was probably confirmation of their presence. It also signified that *Ojibwa* might have been counterdetected. The next time he went to periscope depth to check communications, Webster received a situation report (sitrep) based on MPA tracking that suggested *Ojibwa* had passed close to the Delta and probably the Victor III as well. At the same time, MARCOM ordered Webster to head south along the projected course of the SSBN. Unsure if they were themselves being followed, *Ojibwa* crept away as quietly as possible.

The next 72 hours brimmed with tension. As *Ojibwa* moved south, Auroras put up a maximum effort, flying around the clock to track the Delta. With SOSUS support they managed to localize the contact, and on St. Patrick's Day afternoon, Webster received the go-ahead to close the Delta for the purpose of gathering acoustic intelligence. It was a long, challenging search. Biological contacts fouled broadband and the SSBN used the standard Soviet tactic of keeping close to the North Atlantic Ridge to mask its signature: Like all O-boat crews involved in OSPs *Ojibwa*'s attack team lamented the lack of sophisticated narrowband equipment. Teamwork between the SSK and MPAs remained almost seamless. When *Ojibwa* had to snort MPAs cued it back to a promising area upon completion.

Finally, *Ojibwa* hit the jackpot. At 0102Z hours on 19 March — the day before it was to begin its return passage to Halifax — the sonar crew gained hits with both 2007 and 137. A firing solution was immediately input into the fire-control system, and Target Motion Analysis tracked the Delta as it conducted a routine turn to clear its stern arc. The big missile boat kept coming and passed so close down the starboard side — Webster estimated under 800 yards — the crew could hear the quiet thumping of machinery as the SSBN slunk by. Webster recalls no real excitement in the boat; the crew just went about their business, quietly and professionally. *Ojibwa* stuck with the Delta throughout the 20th, tailing it from about 2,000 yards, and maintaining a firing solution. Each time they went to snort MPAs brought them back into contact. All the while *Ojibwa* gathered a treasure trove of acoustic intelligence.

After hours of what now seemed like routine shadowing, the situation suddenly became exceedingly tense. When the Delta turned to clear its baffles in the late hours of 20 March, a second contact popped up on sonar, heading the other direction. Webster immediately classified it as the Victor III he had been warned about four days earlier. The "delouser" did its job. Breaking towards the Canadian boat it lit up *Ojibwa* with active sonar. The effect was dramatic. Soviet SSNs used high frequency active sonar that NATO codenamed "Blocks of Wood;" the sound it made on the hull of its target was precisely that of a pair of two-by-fours being slapped crisply together.[53] Now certain he had been detected, Webster faced a difficult situation. His primary responsibility had to be the safety of his boat and he was far from port, so far in fact that if something went wrong his nearest refuge was the U.K., not Halifax.

Moreover, he was manoeuvring in extremely close proximity to two adversaries, one of which was trying to drive him away. Rumours of collisions between NATO and Soviet submarines abounded — current unofficial estimates put the number at as many as 40 incidents[54] — and Webster was determined that *Ojibwa* not join that company. Because he was to begin his homeward passage within hours, and already possessed acoustic data from both contacts, at 2300 hours 20 March, Webster broke off contact. Summarizing the drama in his patrol report, he ruefully noted, "… was counter-detected … and actively prosecuted…. The second submarine was successful in riding off the patrolling unit."

Despite the fact that Webster broke off the operation, *Ojibwa* had conducted the most successful surveillance patrol mounted by an O-boat in Canadian waters. It certainly achieved Commander Nesbit's objective to demonstrate to the Americans that we could look after our own backyard. On its way back to Halifax, COMSUBLANT notified MARCOM and *Ojibwa*, "Your recent ASW prosecutions most impressive and productive. Your efforts have contributed significantly to the LANTFLT ASW picture and have not gone unnoticed."[55] That was about as wide as the celebration got, as OSP 1/85 remained cloaked in secrecy. When *Ojibwa* reached home, the squadron commander mustered the crew — Webster had kept them in the picture — and threatened if anybody uttered a word about the patrol he would cut off a vital part of their anatomy. Likewise, when Vice-Admiral J. Wood, the commander MARCOM, reviewed the patrol with Nesbit and Webster, he said they had better keep the information to themselves.

Post-operation analysis found praise for the "VP/Sub co-op," as well as familiar discussion of communications shortfalls, the failure to forward up-to-date intelligence information, and the fact that O-boats urgently needed satellite navigation (SATNAV) and a towed array. There was also disagreement about the identity of the second contact detected on 20 March. Some analysts thought it might have been an American SSN that was trailing the Delta, and wanted to ward off *Ojibwa*. That could have been the case, but it is not in line with the tactics used by American boats. By this time most SSNs shadowing SSBNs were fitted with towed arrays that enabled them to standoff at about 10,000 yards in deeper water. There was thus no reason for them to get in as close as *Ojibwa* and the other boat. Moreover, with intelligence indicating that a Victor III was in the area, it is likely that Webster's appreciation was correct. If that was the case, and if the Victor had in fact detected *Ojibwa*, and perhaps classified its as an O-boat, then the patrol demonstrated to the Soviets as well as to our allies that we were indeed capable of monitoring submarine activity in our waters. By the standard of the Cold War, that made the patrol an outstanding success.

After the excitement of OSP 1/85 expectations ran high for *Onondaga*'s follow-up in November but as so often happens the result met with disappointment. This was not because of the performance of the submarine; there were simply no contacts to be found; in the words of one analyst, the target "did not cooperate." The target was again Soviet SSBNs but, interestingly, the primary objective assigned to the boat's CO, Lieutenant-Commander J.A.Y. Plante, was "detection of transiting Soviet submarines and trailing *only as far as necessary to record sufficient acoustic data for subsequent analysis.*"[56] This reflected a new degree of caution, and one wonders if senior officers were reluctant to allow boats to get "stuck in" as Webster had done.

OSP 2/85 got off to a rough start when severe weather impeded *Onondaga*'s passage by way of the route south of Sable Island, to the extent that it struggled to maintain pace with its designated moving haven. The patrol area was on the northeast edge of the CANLANT zone in the vicinity of Ocean Station Charlie and the boat was tasked against a specific SSBN, designated L-124. The boomer had been tracked through the GIUK Gap, and on 29 October its position had been fixed south of Iceland on the "traditional YANKEE SSBN transit to the Bermuda operating areas."[57] Unfortunately, MPAs could not track the missile boat, and *Onondaga* spent most of the patrol chasing hither and yon after a ghost. L-124 was ultimately relocated southeast of Bermuda on 14 November — the day before *Onondaga* began its return passage to Halifax — and the track between that position and the one reported on 29 October, indicates that it probably passed close to *Onondaga's* patrol area. The failure to locate L-124 demonstrated just how difficult it was for an O-boat to find a target without the benefit of cueing.

Despite the failure to snare a SSBN, the CFMWC analysis concluded OSP 2/85 "was still an extremely valuable operation." Plante shared that opinion. The intelligence and oceanographic package provided in the days before sailing had "been most helpful in determining appropriate search policies," and the command team had benefited from a comprehensive training program conducted by the submarine squadron. "Consequently," Plante concluded, "ONONDAGA arrived on patrol much better prepared than its predecessors."

Still, blemishes persisted. *Onondaga* sailed with 22 sailors unqualified in submarines, which placed a heavy burden on the rest of the crew; and too much activity had been crammed into the pre-sailing program.[58] The boat also experienced the familiar problems with communications — along with a newly identified one in that the floating wire antenna appeared to attract sea gulls, "which," according to Plante, "would surely give away the submarine's position at anytime a portion of the wire remained floating on the surface." Despite these issues, CFMWC judged OSP 2/85 to be "the best run of the OSP series."

Even as the organization behind OSPs improved, the principal objective of intercepting Soviet SSBNs remained a hit or miss proposition. *Ojibwa* carried out OSP 1/86 in June-July 1986, but the mission was apparently largely uneventful, the only notable events being surveillance of a weather ship occupying Ocean Station Charlie and a tracking exercise with a British SSN.[59] *Ojibwa* enjoyed balmy summer weather, but the next patrol took place in the teeth of severe late autumn gales. In fact, Bob Bush, *Onondaga's* executive officer (XO) for OSP 2/86, recalled that weather was "the main enemy." Nevertheless, the boat fought through the terrible conditions to intercept one SSBN and was attempting to intercept another before forced to break off its patrol.

On previous OSPs, boats had proceeded to their patrol areas by heading eastward from Halifax, but Lieutenant-Commander Hickey decided to go by way of the Gulf of St. Lawrence and the Strait of Belle Isle. O-boats seldom entered the Gulf so Hickey saw this as an opportunity to gain experience in a body of water that may well have to be used in the future. He also proposed conducting port visits to some of the small outports on the Labrador coast on the way home. Hickey recalled, "we probably wouldn't have been able to get alongside anywhere, but just would have anchored in the harbour overnight, then departed the next day with a big maple leaf flying from the masthead. It would have attracted a bit of attention."[60] O-boats had not operated in northern waters since the early 1970s, but the publicity attending such a port visit, accompanied

Courtesy Department of National Defence.

Lieutenant-Commander Larry Hickey, who hunted two SSBNs amid horrendous weather during OSP 2/86.

by some well-crafted subterfuge from the intelligence community, may have persuaded the Soviets that *Onondaga* was returning from a patrol in the Arctic approaches. As it was, the squadron commander, Commander W.J. Sloan, agreed to the new transit route, but not the port visits.

The weather was good when *Onondaga* departed Halifax on 14 November, and Hickey decided to take advantage by initially running on the surface. To protect its identity when the boat crossed the shipping lanes running through the Cabot Strait on the night of 15 November, the *Onondaga*'s crew rigged lights similar to a fishing trawler. Traffic eased after the boat passed north of Corner Brook, but grew as they approached the Strait of Belle Isle. Hickey cautioned watchkeepers to remain alert since Soviet merchant ships were reportedly in the area, and ice also posed a danger. After moving submerged through the approaches to Belle Isle, *Onondaga* surfaced to transit the strait on the night of 16 November, "fully lit as a trawler." *Onondaga* dived when it exited the straits at dawn on 18 November with no evidence it had been detected.

As *Onondaga* transited the strait, controllers informed Hickey that Auroras had begun tracking a SSBN. This was originally identified, presumably by SOSUS, as L-107, a Yankee on passage to the patrol box east of Bermuda, however, new intelligence changed the classification to a Delta designated L-103. This contact had not been the original target of the mission, but it now offered a "chance encounter to *Onondaga*." For next four days the boomer — the "Soviet bastard" Hickey had referred to earlier — absorbed the boat's attention.

Onondaga's original patrol area was at the far edge of the CAN-LANT zone, more than 1,000 nm northeast of the Strait of Belle Isle. The new intelligence indicated that L-103 would be found out even farther therefore MARCOM requested additional water space from the COMSUBLANT. Moreover, *Onondaga* would have to reach its SPA 36 hours earlier than planned so Hickey had to increase the average speed of advance to eight knots, which meant running on the surface at least some of the time. As they ploughed northeast, *Onondaga* observed the same tactical prudence as if at war. It only ran on the surface at night and did not burn navigation lights; snorting was carried out at irregular intervals; and after replenishing batteries the boat went deep to the best listening depth to conduct a sustained acoustic "look-around." When submerged, stern arcs, or "baffles" were cleared at least every 40 minutes, again on an unpredictable cycle. Watchkeepers kept 12,000 yards clear of any contact and made every effort to reduce noise. Unfortunately, a "rub" developed on the port shaft, which meant for the rest of the patrol *Onondaga* could not exceed 6.5 knots submerged without emitting noise that could lead to counter-detection. As they advanced northeast Hickey received continual updates about L-103's progress, and in the early hours of 21 November he warned watchkeepers the SSBN was only 54 miles away: "THIS IS OUR BIG CHANCE" he scrawled across the page of his night order book.

At this point friction chucked a spanner in the works. According to pre-mission arrangements, Hickey thought Aurora support was about to stop; instead, it had actually been extended to allow a full effort against L-103. Unfortunately, Hickey did not receive that information. Not expecting additional cueing, at 0500Z hours on the 21st, with L-103 46 miles away, *Onondaga* went deep to begin an intercept run that would put it across the SSBN's projected path. When *Onondaga* reached that position seven hours later, a careful five-hour search came up empty. In fact, they had been reacting to stale data, some 14 hours out of date. When Hickey went to periscope depth at 1700Z hours he was startled to find an MPA on station, and it gave him an updated position report that put L-103 17 miles to the northeast, heading away.

One can only imagine the frustration in *Onondaga*. Had they known that the MPA was available to provide fresh information they could have been cued right onto the SSBN, snorting as they approached. As it was, by having to conduct a sustained dived search they had run down their battery, which limited tactical alternatives. By this point the weather had also deteriorated, impeding snorting as well as impairing sonar. Moreover, a "flutter" had been discovered in the snort's exhaust system. This was a potentially serious source of noise, and Hickey "considered that the counter-detection opportunity offered to the TOI [Target of Intent] by the exhaust flutter was greater than that of the transient noises associated with surfacing and diving." Thus, at 1829z hours on the 21st, with his battery down to 26 percent, and now also suffering problems with a generator, he surfaced with the intent of closing to within seven miles of L-103, and then diving to resume the search.

Although one post-operational analysis thought Hickey's decisions "prudent," another analyst disagreed. This officer, an experienced CO, thought that Hickey should have double-checked for MPA support before initiating his search. Moreover, he criticized the decision to pursue L-103 on the surface. "Unless the aim is to deliberately offer counter-detection opportunities," he wrote, "to surface or snort in the vicinity of the TOI is not supported. Additionally, a submarine on the surface is without sensors; assuming the TOI is in close proximity, how are sweeps for clearance conducted before diving and how can the dive be conducted quietly?" These points are valid from a theoretical perspective, but given his battery condition Hickey had no choice but to either snort or surface. Given the high sea state, which Hickey thought would mask the sound of diving, and the fact that an MPA was maintaining contact with L-103, this was an occasion when one should defer to the man on the spot, who was acting aggressively to achieve an interception. That said, there is no way to know if L-103, the subject of all this attention, played the role of cat as well as mouse and indeed monitored *Onondaga's* evolutions.

After four and a half hours on the "roof," a MPA signalled *Onondaga* that L-103 was just five miles to the southeast. The airmen also informed Hickey that they would only be on station for another two hours and would not be immediately relieved by another aircraft. Thirty-five minutes later, Hickey submerged in a static dive to reduce noise. Shortly afterwards, sonar crew detected noise down L-103's general bearing, and Hickey called action stations. The contact turned out to be a merchant ship, but sonar briefly held two others, which could not be classified. At 0014Z 23 November Hickey went to periscope depth to get a final report from the MPA, and was informed that L-103 bore 115 degrees at just 3.5 miles, and was tracking on course 240 degrees at five knots. *Onondaga* went deep to find the best sonar conditions, and after searching down the bearing for about 20 minutes, finally detected the Soviet missile boat at 0047Z. The contact remained steady on course 240 degrees as the O-boat approached carefully to within about 1,500 yards. With war shots in each of the six torpedo tubes, Hickey had kept a single tube flooded and equalized ready for action. There was now discussion in the control room concerning the merits of opening the tube's outer door, but the CO decided that might be excessively provocative: "I don't want to start World War III." After running roughly parallel to the Delta, at 0100Z Hickey turned south to compute a Target Motion Analysis but at that moment *Onondaga* lost contact. It could not be reacquired, and at 0120Z, the action team assumed that the target had maintained its course and speed and opened the range to some 9,000 yards. Unfortunately, *Onondaga* could not increase speed to overtake the SSBN because of the noise that would be emitted from the shaft rub, therefore Hickey hovered in the area, hoping L-103 would circle back to the northeast.

Questions linger if *Onondaga* had actually intercepted a Soviet SSBN. Some analysts pointed to navigational discrepancies and, because the on-station MPA and *Onondaga* failed to achieve plot-lock before the interception, there were doubts about the accuracy of their mutual position reports. Yet, it seems to have been acknowledged that *Onondaga*

Courtesy Captain [Navy] L.M. Hickey.

Daring was part of the job description. HMS *Apollo* charges HMS *Walrus* during Larry Hickey's "Perisher." *Apollo* was approximately 1,100 yards — quite close at sea. Hickey would have to take the submarine down to 90 feet to avoid it and the other frigates that may well be "attacking" from other directions.

detected something, and sonar crews recorded tonals associated with machinery noises of a Soviet SSBN. Also, at 0200Z an MPA had monitored a merchant ship in the vicinity trying to raise a Soviet submarine on VHF. Certainly, *Onondaga*'s combat team thought they had intercepted a Soviet boomer. In the words of Bob Bush, "If it wasn't that; what was it?"

Onondaga loitered for several days fruitlessly trying to regain contact with L-103 but on 25 November controllers sent it after another target. This search proved even more frustrating than the one previous. The storm had kicked up into a full-blown North Atlantic gale. *Onondaga* had difficulty maintaining stability at periscope depth and, because of the high sea state, snorting could only be carried out on certain courses. Severe quenching impeded sonar performance and a casing rattle threatened covertness. The crew was tired, and the icy air vented through the boat when it snorted or rode on the surface chilled them to the bone — Bush remembers seeing icicles on the beards of sleeping sailors. Although the boat was neither deaf nor immobile, conditions were far from optimal for a search that ultimately required a lot of time in transit. Adding to the challenges, confused intelligence put the boat and controllers at cross-purposes.

At 1330Z 25 November, reacting to a new contact designated L-110, controllers sent *Onondaga* towards its original patrol position. Because the boomer's identity could not be confirmed they ordered the O-boat "to move southeast of its present position to a point that was considered an optimum holding point for *Onondaga* because the TOI had not been solidly classified Yankee or Delta, and therefore it was not certain where it would enter CANLANT waters." Twenty-four hours later, L-110 was classified as a definite Yankee, and Hickey was directed to continue southeast to straddle its likely deployment route. For 48 hours *Onondaga* laboured towards the new position fighting gales and high seas — the boat was even restless at periscope depth. Meanwhile, MPAs, flying under the same miserable conditions developed a clearer acoustic picture and reclassified the target as a Delta-class SSBN. At 1606Z 28 November, controllers rerouted *Onondaga* back to the "typical Delta Patrol Area" in the northern sector of CANLANT. Again the communications gremlins interceded. High seas made snorting difficult and *Onondaga* "flamed out" several times.[61] Moreover, hydroplane misalignments made it difficult to maintain depth control, disrupting other snorts. As one commentator observed, periscope depth was "a very unfriendly place to be." Hickey took the boat deep to calmer water to repair the hydroplanes, and because of broadcast reception problems in the boat and a computer problem ashore, he did not receive the message changing the identity of the contact and ordering him northward. Two days passed before Hickey figured out he had missed a signal, and inferring from subsequent messages that he had in fact been ordered north, turned the boat around.

Given the lost hours, Hickey thought he would have trouble reaching the intercept point in time. A seven-knot speed of advance would be required but poor snorting conditions — the only effective snorting course was invariably 90 degrees to the track — and the persistent shaft rub made that difficult to attain. As predicted, as *Onondaga* struggled northward the required SOA rose to nine knots on 1 December, "a difficult enough problem even under ideal conditions." Hickey wanted to surface to make up time but controllers would not grant permission. On 2 December the SOA had escalated to 11 knots — *Onondaga*'s actual progress was about 3 — and he complained in his patrol narrative "If only they would allow me to surface I would make it on time and have one day to search for L-110. As it stands now we won't get there until 031300Z which will only give me ten hours to search." This was a typical sharp-end reaction; Hickey wanted to do more but thought controllers were holding him back. For their part, the controllers had their own reasons for not letting Hickey surface as it would denigrate *Onondaga*'s surveillance capability and expose it to counter-detection. Moreover, they had apparently not been informed about the shaft rub that reduced the boat's submerged speed. Hickey eventually took matters into his own hands and surfaced but admitted in his night order book "we can't nail him unless he turns towards." L-110 did not cooperate. Ever persistent, on 3 December Hickey requested a two-day extension to his patrol but when this was turned down, departed for home as scheduled the next day. It appears *Onondaga* only ever came within about 150 miles of the Delta.

OSP 2/86 was subjected to the now familiar post mortem. But there was a subtle change. Apart from the typical communications problems, there was no real discussion about the organization of the operation. Rather, debate focussed primarily on the actions and decisions taken during the actual patrol. This was a clear sign that the command and control organization had matured, and that MARCOM could now carry out submarine surveillance operations as a matter of course.

Two final patrols carried out in 1987 proved unique. In June, *Onondaga* headed out in search of a SSBN; what made the mission different was that the CO, Lieutenant-Commander R.D. Carter, was an officer of the Royal Australian Navy (RAN). Because they both operated O-boats and used the RN for training, including Perisher, the submarine services of the RAN and the Canadian Navy had forged an extremely close relationship. Personnel regularly undertook training with the other service, and exchange officers filled billets on squadron staff. On rare occasions, qualified officers even commanded boats of the other navy. In this instance, the Canadian command pipeline had been disrupted by Perisher failures and other circumstances, and as Ops officer in the Canadian squadron, Carter was spare CO, and thus automatically filled-in when the vacancy occurred. The transition was seamless, and Carter recalls being treated the same as a Canadian, a fact confirmed by *Onondaga*'s XO.[62] Besides gaining fleeting contact with a Delta III SSBN, *Onondaga* had a chance encounter with a new class of AGI, and three-hours of shadowing produced valuable intelligence. Interestingly, when *Onondaga* suffered a generator problem during its outward transit, rather than returning to Halifax and possibly having to scrub the mission, engineers persuaded Carter they could fix the problem. The boat anchored close by the Newfoundland coast under the cover of fog for 22 hours while they made good repairs, allowing the patrol to proceed. To Carter, the incident "clearly demonstrated that Canadian submariners were determined to see through any chance they were given to undertake 'real operational tasks….'"[63]

The second patrol was unusual in that *Okanagan* went up north. O-boats had twice participated in exercises in northern waters in the early 1970s, playing clockwork mouse and conducting acoustic research around ice, but they had never carried out a patrol in Arctic waters. Although O-boats could not safely operate under ice they could guard the approaches to the Arctic in much the same way as they plugged the

GIUK Gap. And, of course, such deployments projected sovereignty. On this mission, *Okanagan's* primary objective was to BINT a Soviet merchant ship exiting Hudson Strait after visiting Churchill, Manitoba. *Okanagan* achieved that objective, and conducted surveillance of Soviet fishing vessels. It came across no SSBNs but thought it might have gained contact with a friendly SSN.[64]

In 1987 Soviet submarine activity in the Northwest Atlantic virtually ceased when Mikhail Gorbachev scaled back Soviet naval operations, including the forward deployment of SSBNs off North America. The operational role of Canada's O-boats did not end; like other naval forces confronting the new post–Cold War era they adjusted to new circumstances. Whereas their targets had previously been boomers and intelligence vessels, they became drug smugglers and fisheries violators. The missions involved the same close range, covert surveillance as OSPs, and that experience paid off at both the seagoing and the command and control levels. After carrying out a successful fisheries patrol in 1994 Larry Hickey noted that it was "a military surveillance operation whose targets of interest just happened to be fishing vessels."[65] Clearly, Canadian submariners were now comfortable carrying out surveillance operations in home waters.

In 1978, the American nuclear attack boat USS *Batfish* shadowed a Soviet Yankee for 50 days, sticking to the boomer throughout virtually its entire patrol. Since information about other Cold War surveillance missions conducted by USN SSNs remains closed, *Batfish's* feat stands as the "gold standard" for submarine ASW.[66] In contrast, Canada's O-boats trailed fewer than a half dozen Soviet nuclear boats for less than a week in total, and in only one instance did they stalk their adversary for more than a few minutes. The difference in success seems staggering, but one must be careful with the comparison. Notwithstanding the enormous advantage in endurance and mobility held by a nuclear-powered submarine like *Batfish*, the USN had decades of experience in submarine operations, involving hundreds of boats and tens of thousands of sailors. In contrast, OSPs represented MARCOM's first experience in running sustained submarine operations. That O-boats appear to have intercepted adversaries on four of the eight missions, and that the command and control organization grew increasingly effective, indicates a level of success that was both tangible and laudatory.

What did the OSP experience mean to the Canadian submarine service and say about its capability? More than anything, OSPs finally gave submariners the opportunity to train properly for their prospective wartime role. Moreover, at this time most of the navy was battling the effects of "rust-out," and the O-boats were one of few platforms actually "doing the biz." That was not lost on submariners, but apart from engendering pride, participation in the missions sharpened their skill. One CO recalls "the OSP experience (in command or in a senior appointment aboard a boat on an OSP), made us better COs. They contributed to the development of boldness, aggressiveness, "stick-to-it-iveness," and a better appreciation of how to drive submarines to the limits."[67] OSPs also showcased the vast potential of the Sub/Air team, with Auroras demonstrating they could cue O-boats into killing distance of SSBNs. The partnership was a true force multiplier, and strengthened MARCOM's overall surveillance capability. As Keith Nesbit recalls, "Surveillance is about building pictures, and we got better at it."[68] That raised Canada's credibility with its allies, particularly the U.S., and emphasised that when MARCOM declared a submarine operating area it had the means to monitor activity in that area (a capability that increased enormously when the O-boats finally received towed arrays in the late 1980s). In terms of sovereignty, the advantages accrued from that recognition are invaluable. Given all this, it is fair to say that OSPs demonstrated the important contribution submarines could make to the defence of Canada. Sadly, until now, only a handful of people were in a position to appreciate that achievement. Keeping Cold War secrets close is sometimes a necessary evil, but in this case it has obscured understanding of the role of submarines,[69] and cost Canadian submariners due recognition for "Doin' the Biz."

NOTES

1. *Onondaga*, Night Order Book, 14–18 November 1986. This study, the first comprehensive look at O-boat operations during the Cold War, is based primarily on Canadian operational documents that remain classified, as well as interviews with some two-dozen former submariners, most of them O-boat COs. It is part of a larger operational study being prepared for the Canadian Maritime Staff. The opinions expressed are strictly those of the author.

2. Some Canadian officers experienced success in command of British submarines during both the First and Second World Wars. See David Perkins, *The Canadian Submarine Service in Review* (St. Catharines: Vanwell, 2000), and Julie Ferguson, *Through a Canadian Periscope* (Toronto: Dundurn, 1995).

3. Norman Friedman, *The Fifty Year War: Conflict, Strategy and the Cold War* (Annapolis: Naval Institute Press, 2000).

4. Norman Polmar, *Soviet Naval Developments* (Annapolis: Naval Institute Press, 1984). This publication is a sanitized version of the U.S. Office of Naval Intelligence's annual report.

5. Vice Admiral J. Andrew Fulton, Autobiographical chapter in Michael Whitby, Richard Gimblett, and Peter Haydon, *The Admirals: Canada's Senior Naval Leadership in the 20th Century* (Toronto: Dundurn, 2006), 328; and Norman Polmar and K.J. Moore, *Cold War Submarines: The Design and Construction of U.S. and Soviet Submarines* (Washington: Brassey's, 2004), 171. Citing research by Russian academics, Polmar and Moore note that beginning in 1971 there were regularly two and as many as four Yankees deployed within missile range of North America in the North Atlantic, as well as one in the eastern Pacific.

6. The GIUK Gap refers to the choke point between Greenland, Iceland, and the United Kingdom.

7. Larry Robideau, "Third Battle of the North Atlantic, 1962–1991," *Cold War Times* (February 2006).

8. Keith Nesbit, "Beneath Canadian Seas," 4. Draft article in author's possession.

9. Many individual Canadian officers and ratings also did exchange tours in British submarines, where they were involved in a wide range of Cold War activities.

10. Larry M. Hickey ms in author's possession, Chap. 7, 1.

11. *Ibid.*

12. Tom Clancy, *Submarine* (New York: Berkley, 1993), 163. The best account of Perisher is Jonathan Crane's, *Submarine* (London: BBC, 1984), 49–106. Americans qualified for command through the Prospective Commanding Officers course, which put as much emphasis on nuclear engineering safety as tactics. The account of the first USN officer to take Perisher is of interest. See, Lieutenant-Commander Stephen Mack, USN, "Perisher: Submarine Command Training in the Royal Navy," *Under Sea Warfare* (Spring 2003), accessed online at www.navy.mil/navydata/cno/ n87/usw/issue_18/perisher.htm

13. R.C. Hunt ms in author's possession, 121.

14. Rudyard Kipling, *On the Fringes of the Fleet* (Garden City: Doubleday, Page & Co., 1915).

15. Thomas Lynch, "Modernizing the Subs: SOUP," in *Canada's Navy* (Calgary: Corvus, 1985), 168–170.

16. Robert Gardner and Norman Friedman, eds., *Navies in the Nuclear Age: Warships Since 1945* (London: Conway, 1993), 71.

17. The top speed of a submerged O-boat was about 16 knots, but at that speed they would have to snort frequently; in contrast the Los Angeles-class SSNs then being introduced into the USN could make more than 30 knots submerged.

18. Whitby, Gimblett and Haydon, *The Admirals*, 328; and Fulton to author.

19. For example, Dolphin 58 translates to, "With sub-killers like you around, I look forward to a long life." The Dolphin Code is still used by submariners of several navies, including the RAN and RN. For a complete list go to *http://www.chebucto.ns.ca/~ac121/soca/code.htm*.

20. Nesbit draft ms, "SMIDS: Submarine ideas ... for a "rationale" paper," in author's possession.

21. The Mk 37 torpedoes used by the O-boats had a 330 pound (lb.) (145 kilogram [kg]) warhead whereas the Mk 46's was 98 lb. (44 kg). In the late 1980s, the O-boats were armed the even more powerful Mk 48 torpedoes.

22. Commander K. Nesbit, "Canadian 'O' Class Submarines — Operational Patrols," 13 October 1982.

23. To ensure effective liaison, since the 1970s a command qualified Canadian submariner has served on COMSUBLANT staff.

24. This not only involved demarking the actual patrol area but also setting a "moving haven" that covered the speed of advance for the transit to and from the patrol area. As a result of these requirements, and other factors, OSPs were tightly scripted, especially in terms of duration. Water Space management is an important aspect of submarine capability, helping to avoid "Blue-on-Blue" encounters. Moreover, since the NATO navies operating submarines inform each other of their demands for water space, they have an idea of overall submarine activity. If a navy does not have a submarine capability it does not receive that information. For more see Captain (N) Phil Webster, "Arctic Sovereignty, Submarine Operations and Water Space Management" *Canadian Naval Review*, Vol. 3, No. 3 (Fall 2007), 14–16.

25. See Norman Friedman, *Seapower and Space: From the Dawn of the Missile Age to Net-Centric Warfare* (London: Chatham, 2000), 200–208; Owen R. Cote, *The Third Battle: Innovation in the U.S. Navy's Silent Cold War Struggle with Soviet Submarines* (Newport: Naval War College Press, 2003), 61;

and Polmar and Moore, 185–187. Although strictly from a USN-U.S.S.R. perspective, Cote is perhaps the best study of Cold War ASW.

26. Polmar and Moore, 173 n 32.

27. Cote, *The Third Battle*, 22–24.

28. Tom Stefanick, *Strategic Antisubmarine Warfare and Naval Strategy* (Lexington: Center for Defense and Disarmament Studies, 1987), 8–9.

29. DCOS Ops, "Patrol Instructions — Operational Surveillance Patrol 1/83," 29 June 1983; and CO *Okanagan*, "Operational Surveillance Patrol 1/83, 30 June 83–19 July 83 Patrol Report," 19 June 1983.

30. The exact position from where the missile test was launched has proved elusive but the missile landed about 400 nm north of the Azores.

31. *Primorye*-class AGIs were based on the *Mayakovsky*-class commercial stern trawlers. Mast arrangements and electronic fits varied but the vessels displaced 3,700 tons full load, with a length of 278 feet, a beam of 46, and a draft of 23 feet. They could make 12 knots, with a range of 10,000 nm at 10 knots. *Jane's Fighting Ships*, 2000–2001.

32. Early arrays were attached to the hull when the submarine left harbour, but later sets were winched in and out of the hull.

33. The surface navy had good success with towed arrays. For example, while trialling the system in June 1984 the destroyer HMCS *Iroquois* tracked a Soviet SSBN at long range east of Bermuda.

34. MARCOM submarine patrol areas were named after Canadian Perisher graduates, in this case Commander R.C. Ewan.

35. DCOS Ops MARCOM HQ, "Patrol Instructions — Operational Surveillance Patrol 2/83," 13 November 1983; and SSO Subs, Summary of Lessons Learned, 24 July 1984.

36. Variations in density and temperature can create pronounced "layers" that can sometimes cause sound to bend or be reflected entirely, allowing submarines to hide at depth.

37. CO *Ojibwa*, Patrol Report; and Interview with Captain (N) Norm Jolin, 1 November 2007. Jolin was XO.

38. Direction finding is a technique for identifying the location and sometimes the source of a radio transmission, in this case by plotting the bearings of *Ojibwa*'s transmissions.

39. CO *Ojibwa*, Patrol Report, 2. In a fascinating incident, on 31 October 1983 a Victor III was found wallowing immobile on the surface 470 miles east of Charleston, SC. U.S. forces then tracked it as it was towed to Cienfuegos, Cuba to repair a damaged propeller. Apparently it had got caught up on the towed array of the frigate USS *McCloy*. Polmar and Moore, 160.

40. Polmar and Moore, 174.

41. This is a technique for estimating the maximum range a target might have advanced from its last known position.

42. CO *Ojibwa*, Patrol Report, Annex C, 2: CFMWC Analysis Annex A, 8.

43. An Aurora over flew the rendezvous but noticed no unusual activity. The MPA also spotted *Ojibwa* on the surface, but in keeping with instructions made no attempt to contact the boat.

44. See for example, CO CFMWC, "Operational Analysis — Operational Surveillance Patrols," 3 April 1984. The CO CFMWC recommended an analysis regime similar to that used for certain MPA missions.

45. Thomas B. Allen, "Run Silent, Run Deep," *Smithsonian* (March 2001), Vol. 31, No. 12, 4.

46. SSO SO MARCOM to Commander Submarine Force U.S. Atlantic Fleet, "Canadian Submarines — Operational Surveillance Patrols," 8 April 1983.

47. The account of OSP 1/85 is based upon SSO Subs Minute, "OSP 1/85," May 1985, and interviews with Captain (N) E.P. Webster (CO), Captain (N) K.G. Nesbit (Retired) (EA Com MARCOM), Commander C.J.D. Soule (XO), and Commander W.C. Irvine (Controller).

48. During the NATO exercise TEAMWORK 84, *Ojibwa* set a record for consecutive days at sea for a Canadian warship (40) — including 34 straight days submerged — that lasted until Op APOLLO. In the amphibious portion of the exercise off Northern Norway, *Ojibwa* gained sonar contact with a Soviet SSN and captured valuable acoustic intelligence.

49. Commander R. Bush to author, 25 October 2007.

50. Cited in Polmar and Moore, 173.

51. Over a 20-year period, Warrant Officer John Walker USN and three others provided the Soviets with intelligence on USN submarine operations, including ciphers and signal traffic. This material would have provided unique insight into USN submarine activity, and perhaps of its allies. See Barron John, *Breaking the Ring: The Bizarre Case of the Family Spy Ring* (New York: Houghton, Mifflin, 1987); and Polmar and Moore, 285.

52. Polmar and Moore, 156–60; and Cote, *The Third Battle*, 69–70. For the deterrence aspects of "delousing" see Harvey M. Sapolsky, "Strategic ASW: Making the Deterrent Work," Massachusetts Institute of Technology, *Breakthroughs* (Spring 2004), 3–7. A useful contemporary discussion of the strategy is Captain J.L. Byron, USN, "No Quarter for Their Boomers," United States Naval Institute *Proceedings* (April 1989), 49–52.

53. The formal name for the sonar was the MGK-100 *Kerch*. Polmar and Moore, 173.

54. Polmar and Moore, 174.

55. CFT 24 to CTF 302, 1550 26 March 1985.

56. CO *Onondaga*, "OSP 2/85 22 October 85 — 21 November 85, Patrol Report,"

21 November 1985. Author's emphasis.

57. CO *Onondaga*, Patrol Report.

58. In the five days before sailing, *Onondaga* took on stores, fuel, and ammunition; completed a Short Work Period; conducted command team training; and opened for visitors to celebrate Submarine Week.

59. Interviews and correspondence with Commander W.C. Irvine and Commander CD Soule, *Ojibwa*'s CO and XO respectively.

60. Captain (N) L.M. Hickey to author, 15 November 2007.

61. "Flame out" refers to a situation where a boat is forced to stop snorting because safety criteria for running engines submerged are being exceeded. This is normally caused by loss of control of the boat at periscope depth because of high sea state or poor trimming.

62. Interviews with Commander Bob Carter, RAN (Retired), and Commander Bob Bush, 20 December 2007.

63. Carter to author, 26 December 2007.

64. *Okanagan*, signal traffic September-October 1987.

65. For a 1992 fisheries patrol by *Ojibwa* off Georges Bank see Sean M. Maloney, "*Canadian Subs Protect Fisheries*," U.S. Naval Institute Proceedings, March 1998, 74–76. For *Okanagan*'s 1994 fisheries patrol on the Grand banks see Commander L.M. Hickey, "The Submarine as a Tool of Maritime Enforcement," *Integrated Coastal Zone Management* (Spring 2000), 118.

66. See Thomas B. Allen, "Run Silent, Run Deep," *Smithsonian* (March 2001), Vol. 31 No. 12, 50–62. As part of the commemoration of the Submarine Centennial, the USN declassified *Batfish*'s report and gave its CO permission to discuss the patrol. The popular account *Blind Man's Bluff* describes a 1969 mission during which the SSN USS *Lapon* trailed a Yankee over a number of weeks. See Sherry Sontag and Chris Drew, *Blind Man's Bluff: The Untold*

Story of American Submarine Espionage (New York: Public Affairs Press, 1998), 121–139.

67. Hickey to author, 24 December 2007.

68. Nesbit to author, 9 January 2008.

69. Likewise, the secrecy surrounding Aurora operations during the Cold War has obscured understanding of the immense value of MPAs to Canadian maritime defence.

10

THE MEDAK POCKET: PROFESSIONAL SOLDIERS' DISCIPLINE AND AGGRESSIVE USE OF THE CAMERA

Lee Windsor

In the new era of military operations where warfighting is mixed closely with humanitarian assistance and brokering truces between feuding groups, information is a weapon system. The "news" is an information battlefield on which commanders will win or loose their mission to impose order amid chaos. In September 1993, Canadian troops with the United Nations Protection Force in Croatia found that when used to convey difficult truths, and if a commander is audacious enough, the international media has decisive power. Ironically, reporters and cameras helped bring an end to an armed showdown between United Nations forces and Croatian troops engaged in carrying out war crimes, but the story of Canada's operation in the Medak Pocket would not come to light until years later.

For many Canadian soldiers the turning point from Cold War–era peacekeeping between sovereign nations to a new era of peace-building within failed or fragile states was the infamous firefight in the Medak Pocket in Croatia in September 1993. The watershed event in Canadian military history that occurred near the small town of Medak and challenged the discipline and skill of 2nd Battalion, Princess Patricia's Canadian Light Infantry was completely unknown to the general public until the story broke in the *Ottawa Citizen* in 1996. After that veterans of the action began to speak, attracting the attention of a handful of journalists and academics. In April 1998, a delegation from 2 PPCLI was heard by the House of Commons Standing Committee on Defence and Veteran's Affairs. Around that time, the Department of National Defence (DND) Directorate of History and Heritage began working behind the scenes to organize a public acknowledgement of the action. The story was finally told loud enough that in December 2002 Governor General Adrienne Clarkson awarded members of the 2 PPCLI Battlegroup the first ever Commander-in-Chief's Unit Commendation for "a military deed of rare, high standard in extremely hazardous circumstances." The award seemed to signal government recognition of a new era for the Canadian Forces.

A PPCLI soldier surveys a recently abandoned village.

Department of National Defence 025-IMG0091.

Before and after the award ceremony, the Medak Pocket action was discussed among soldiers as a landmark example of a sharply increased need to apply deadly force on the new and dangerous type of peace support missions they found themselves conducting after the Cold War. The 1993 firefight was only one instance of Canadian troops exchanging fire with armed groups in accordance with their lawful rules of engagement (ROE) in the former Yugoslavia and elsewhere in that decade. Force was used not just for self-defence, but to enforce ceasefire and disarmament agreements as well as to protect civilian lives directly. Unfortunately, few Canadians seem aware that their armed forces frequently engaged in warlike activity to shut down violent, armed groups in the Balkans, thereby creating the secure environment required for peace to take root. As Canadians struggle with understanding the question of using force to build peace and stability for the people of Afghanistan, it is worth remembering Medak, how it shaped the Canadian Army's understanding of the new challenge of restoring peace in war torn or fragile states, and how the Canadian people missed the sea change.

It may have come from our government's post–Cold War inability to communicate foreign policy goals and associated risks to Canadians and more important, to explain why Canadian Forces personnel should take those risks and use deadly force achieve those goals. Whatever the reason for not telling Canadians about Medak the results were damaging in two ways. The first, as Carol Off's 2004 book *The Ghosts of the Medak Pocket* indicates, was a failure to publicly acknowledge and therefore validate soldiers' combat experience and bearing witness to ethnic cleansing. The effect, Off argues, magnified the impact of post-traumatic stress disorder in some soldiers and created a wider sense of abandonment and shame for a larger number of participants who questioned the value of their efforts.

The second problem of keeping Medak under wraps was to conceal the violent and difficult nature of maintaining order in failed and fragile states in the 1990s. As public debate over Canada's role in Afghanistan heated in 2006, critics bemoaned how using force in the Kandahar area is a departure from traditional Canadian policy and an abandonment of a "peacekeeping" heritage.[1] The popularity of that perception reveals how many Canadians are unaware of what functions their soldiers have performed since 1992 to restore stability, law, and order in places where these conditions do not exist. Even learned Canadians, well-informed about military matters, remain ignorant of the level of discipline, skill, and professionalism the nation's soldiers have demonstrated on complex stability operations. In November 2006, well-known Canadian political and military historian Desmond Morton spoke publicly of his concerns that soldiers in Afghanistan would find it impossible to be equal parts warfighters, conflict negotiators, and peacekeepers.[2] Yet, this is exactly what was asked of, and delivered by, Canadian troops at Medak. The lesson for soldiers here is that while the Government of Canada must obviously always lead efforts to inform the public about policy, commanders on operations requiring the use of force should engage or at least be aware of measures taken to explain their missions to the public at home. To ensure operational success that explanation must mirror the one provided to soldiers conducting the mission.

It is all too easy to find fault with the government's communication effort regarding Canadian peace-building efforts in the former Yugoslavia. However, given that the key CF news-making event in the 1990s was Somalia, public relations failures are perhaps explicable. For many Canadians the Somalia Affair became a symbol of their armed forces in the 1990s. Intense media coverage of a Shidane Arone's murder by Master-Corporal Clayton Matchee; its cover-up by senior bureaucrats and officers at National Defence Headquarters; and a series of subsequent scandals shook public confidence in the nation's military institutions. Negative coverage particularly in the first half of the 1990s created an image of military incompetence and unprofessional conduct, vividly captured in letters to the editor to major newspapers across the country. In recent years that image was balanced with more positive ones of CF personnel protecting the peace in the former Yugoslavia, Africa, East Timor, and Afghanistan. Nevertheless, the spectre of Somalia still lingers in the minds of many both in and out of uniform.

The strong presence of Somalia in the national collective memory is perhaps partly a result of the Report of the Commission of Inquiry into the Canadian deployment to East Africa, revealingly titled *Dishonoured*

Legacy: The Lessons of the Somalia Affair. This report is one of the few publicly accessible, quasi-scholarly accounts of a Canadian military operation in the last decade that is based on an allegedly full appreciation of primary sources. Essentially, the report represents a first draft of Canadian military history since the end of the Cold War. It presented an opportunity to, among other things, show Canadians how peacekeeping was evolving. Instead the report, composed by a commission of two jurists and a senior journalist, only served to lend credibility to public perceptions that the CF in the 1990s were deficient and in danger of collapse. The commissioners claimed that during Operation Deliverance (the mission to Somalia) "systems broke down and organizational discipline crumbled within the Canadian Airborne Battlegroup," and that "planning, training, and overall preparations fell far short of what was required ... We can only hope that Somalia represents the nadir of the fortunes of the Canadian Forces. There seems to be little room to slide lower."[3] The report implies that Canada's military personnel were poorly trained, incompetently led, badly equipped, and often racist. *Dishonoured Legacy* is especially influential as a historical text since it passes criticism

Courtesy Lieutenant-Colonel Holland.

Many PPCLI soldiers felt that their intervention came too late.

of the Somalia operation to all of Canada's military institutions based on an admittedly incomplete investigation of criminal activity and cover-up during the mission of one battlegroup on a foreign deployment.

Obviously, Operation Deliverance was only one of dozens of peace and stability-building missions carried out by Canadian soldiers, sailors, and aircrew since 1992. It is therefore ridiculous to accept the commission's condemnation of CF leadership and professionalism and of the army in particular, without scrutinizing other military activity during the same period. The Balkans are a good place to start. Indeed, Canadian experience in the former Yugoslavia is more representative of the nation's military experience in the 1990s than the rather unusual case of Somalia.

Since 1992 tens of thousands of Canadian military and naval personnel endeavoured to restore peace to the Balkans. They acted as peacekeepers, negotiators, aid workers, and quite often as combat soldiers. Initial examination of a number of specific Canadian actions in the region in 1992–94, including those at Sarajevo, Srebrenica, and the Medak Pocket, contrast with the Somalia Commission's findings about poor leadership and training. What follows is an examination of Canadian Army implementation of the "Medak Pocket Agreement" in 1993 to determine if the nation's armed forces were truly at their "nadir" during the fateful year of the Somalia scandal and to shed light on the CF's role in the new reality of restoring peace and stability in a chaotic world.

In mid-September 1993 United Nations Protection Force (UNPROFOR) soldiers from 2nd Battalion, Princess Patricia's Canadian Light Infantry advanced into the disputed Medak Pocket in southern Croatia with orders to implement the latest cease-fire between Croatian Army troops and Serb irregular forces. 2 PPCLI was reinforced with two mechanized companies of French troops. The Canadians, well schooled in the delicate art of "peacekeeping," discovered their negotiation skills and strict impartiality were not immediately required in the Medak Pocket. Instead they found themselves calling upon their primary warfighting skills when Croatian Army units opened fire with machine guns, mortars, and artillery in an effort to stop the Canadian advance. To complete their assigned mission the Patricias were required to threaten the use of, and ultimately use, deadly force against Croatian units. However, the true test of military professionalism and discipline came after the smoke cleared, when the Croatians backed down and the Canadians immediately reverted to their role as impartial peacekeepers in their dealings with individuals who only moments before had attempted to kill them.

Resolute Canadian and French action came at a time when the UN reputation in Croatia was at a low ebb because of repeated failures to secure the infamous United Nations Protected Areas (UNPAs). Colonel George Oehring, commander of UNPROFOR Sector South, claimed the Patricias "won for the whole mission a credibility and respect that will be long remembered by the opposing parties and much facilitate our future efforts here."[4] For their efforts, 2 PPCLI was awarded a United Nations Force Commander's Commendation from French General Cot, the first of its kind and one of only three awarded in UNPROFOR's history.

The Canadians originally deployed to the former Republic of Yugoslavia to protect a fragile truce, not to impose peace on warring factions locked in a bloody civil war. Until the early 1990s Yugoslavia was a federation consisting of six republics including Croatia, Serbia, Montenegro, Slovenia, Bosnia-Herzegovina, and Macedonia, all similar in language, culture, and custom. Despite the presence of ultra-nationalist movements in each republic, the Yugoslav federation existed harmoniously, earning international acclaim and the privilege of hosting the world at the 1984 Winter Olympics.

The collapse of centralized communist authority in Yugoslavia during the late 1980s brought nationalists in each republic into mainstream politics. In Serbia, Slobodan Milosevic, and in Croatia, Franjo Tudjman, rose to power by destroying the carefully constructed Yugoslav identity in favour of a new nationhood based on blood and religion. In the process, Serbia, most powerful of the six republics, attempted to take control of the crumbling federation. This did not appeal to growing nationalist movements in Croatia and Slovenia, resulting in declarations of independence in 1991, followed closely by a similar move in Bosnia. Croatia and Bosnia contained large numbers of ethnic Serbs, hostile to the federal break-up. Croatian and Bosnian Serbs established paramilitary forces, and two distinctly separate civil wars soon followed.

During the opening months of these wars, the Yugoslav National Army (JNA), on orders from Belgrade, openly intervened to prevent the breakup of the federation. JNA involvement usually meant assisting Serb militias in Croatia and Bosnia. However, the regular army was a mirror of the old federation and thus suffered from the same problems of divided loyalties. Non-Serb officers and senior non-commissioned officers left the JNA to join the new national armies of their home republics. This exodus of non-Serbs destroyed cohesion in the JNA, therefore eliminating the only modern professional military force in Yugoslavia. With no army left to implement its goals and an economy on the verge of collapse, Serbia gradually withdrew from conflicts in Croatia and Bosnia, leaving Serb minorities there to fend for themselves against the newly created Bosnian and Croatian armies. Serb militias acquired weapons, vehicles, and even volunteers from the JNA as it withdrew, while newly created

Croatian soldiers in the aftermath of the fighting.

Courtesy Lieutenant-Colonel Holland.

Croatian and Bosnian forces received equipment from outside sources such as Germany and the United States. However, equipment alone does not build an army. It would take years before the various militias and armed gangs coalesced into professional military forces.

For most of the period between1992–95, the Yugoslav wars of succession were waged by amateurs. When the JNA was removed from the equation, they took with them the normal codes of conduct held by modern professional military officers. Rival militias fired weapons in the vicinity of opposing troops, more often than not, intent on killing civilians. The result was to create a pattern of combat where military casualties were few. The new armies knew how to kill, but not how to wage war against other soldiers properly. Unprotected civilians were a different matter. And so, the objective in these wars was not to defeat the opponent's combat power but to consolidate new ethnic nation-states by killing or driving out those who did not fit.[5]

UNPROFOR entered this storm in 1992, first in Croatia and later in Bosnia. In Croatia, the UN brokered a cease-fire between the new Croatian government in Zagreb and minority Serbs who sought independence from the new state. The peace agreement included establishment of a UN patrolled buffer zone in under chapter 6 of the UN Charter.[6] Both parties welcomed the cease fire, when in fact it held, as an opportunity to build their military capabilities until victory could be assured. This was the environment faced by Canadian soldiers making up UNPROFOR's Canadian Battalion Number 1 (CANBAT 1) in 1993.

The second rotation of CANBAT 1 was based on the 2nd Battalion, Princess Patricia's Canadian Light Infantry. However, of the 875 soldiers making up the battlegroup, only 375 actually came from that unit. One hundred and sixty five came from other regular force units and assignments. The remainder consisted of 385 reserve soldiers who had volunteered from militia units across the Canada. Because highly skilled and experienced regular soldiers were needed in support and technical trade positions within the battlegroup, and combat infantry soldiers in the Canadian Army were in short supply, most of the reservists served in the rifle companies. In fact, reserve soldiers made up 70 percent of rifle company strength during the mission. This included seven out of the 12 platoon commanders who came from militia battalions as Reserve Entry Scheme Officers (RESO).[7]

Reserve augmentation was not new in the Canadian Army, even in 1993. For decades, under-strength regular battalions filled out their ranks with reservists before deploying to Cyprus. Indeed, after much debate in the Canadian defence community, providing regular unit augmentation with individual soldiers became a primary role for the reserve force in the 1990s. Augmentation was particularly vital during the time of immediate post–Cold War conflict proliferation, a corresponding spike in the number and intensity of peace support missions combined with shrinking personnel pools and budgets. This was especially true in 1993 when the army, now known as Land Forces Command, was stretched nearly beyond its means. In that year, it provided two battlegroups to the former Yugoslavia (the other in Bosnia); one to Somalia; and a number of other units, detachments, and individual soldiers to a myriad of missions around the world. Nevertheless the 2 PPCLI Battlegroup in Croatia contained the highest concentration of reserve soldiers on an operational mission to date. The standard of militia performance in a tense and demanding theatre like Croatia remained to be seen.

The 2 PPCLI Battlegroup spent the first three months of 1993 conducting preparation training first in Winnipeg, and later in Fort Ord, California. Much of this time was spent working the large reserve complement up to basic Regular Force standards for section and platoon battle-drills. There was no time to properly exercise companies, let alone the whole battalion.[8] Besides, section and platoon skills were generally all that is required of soldiers manning observation posts on UN peacekeeping duty. No one could know that the 2 PPCLI platoons would be called upon to gel together and go into action as a complete, mechanized infantry battlegroup.

2 PPCLI moved to Croatia at the end of March 1993, replacing 3 PPCLI on what Land Forces Command referred to as Operation *Harmony*. At that time, UNPROFOR's CANBAT 1 was responsible for a UN Protected Area in Sector West, in the northwestern corner of Croatia. It was there that Lieutenant-Colonel James Calvin, commanding the 2 PPCLI Battlegroup, and his troops developed a reputation among the warring parties and their fellow UN contingents for being fair, but tough.

Unlike units from most other international contingents in UNPRO-FOR, Canadian battalions operated with its full complement of warfighting weaponry and equipment. Rifle companies travelled in M-113 armoured personnel carriers (APCs) complete with an armoured cupola offering some protection for crewmen manning the powerful Browning .50 calibre machine gun. The companies also carried along with them C-6 medium machine guns and 84-mm Carl Gustav anti-tank rocket launchers to add to the normal platoon weaponry, which consisted of C-7 automatic rifles and C-9 light machine guns.

Rifle company firepower was amplified by the heavy weapons of Support Company including 81-mm mortars and TOW (Tube-launched, Optically-tracked, Wire-guided) anti-armour guided missiles mounted in armoured turrets aboard purpose-built APCs.[9] Canada was among the first member nations to deploy blue-helmeted soldiers with this kind of firepower when UNPROFOR first deployed to Croatia in 1992. This sort of stance was not initially well received in UN headquarters in New York, where the traditional notion of lightly armed blue-bereted peacekeepers prevailed.[10] However, by 1993, the value of well-armed international troops in the former Yugoslavia, where consent of the warring parties could often evaporate, was well understood.

Once on the ground, 2 PPCLI earned their tough reputation not only with their equipment, but by their demonstrated willingness to use it. Not long after their arrival, the battalion conducted a major defensive exercise in the sector. The exercise was intended partially to complete the battlegroup's collective training and improve force cohesion, but also to demonstrate to the Croats that an attack into the UN Protected Area in Sector West would and could be resisted by the UN.

The Patricias vigorously enforced weapons bans in their area of operations, seizing contraband arms of all types from both warring factions. Lieutenant-Colonel Calvin also, on his own initiative, developed a procedure to deter Croat and Serb patrolling and raiding within the Protected Area. Previously, belligerent soldiers detained by the UN after engaging in such activity would be returned to their own authorities for punishment. Calvin began releasing detainees to the opposing forces with UN civilian police keeping a close eye to ensure punishment was not terminal.[11]

After five months of in-theatre training coupled with hands on practice, the 2 PPCLI Battlegroup became one of the most effective and respected units in all of UNPROFOR. It was for that reason that the new force commander, French Army General Cot, selected them to move to Sector South to undertake one of the more difficult assignments in United Nations peacekeeping history.

By comparison to Sector West, 2 PPCLI's area of responsibility, Sector South, was still a war zone. It was here that Croatian Serbs most fiercely resisted the notion of living under Zagreb's rule. Croatian and Serb troops routinely exchanged small arms, mortar, and artillery fire throughout the vicinity. This steady exchange of fire was punctuated in 1993 by several major Croatian offensives, including Operation Maslencia in January. At Maslencia, French troops guarding the UN Protected Area were forced to abandon their positions when faced with heavy Croatian fire. The French withdrawal allowed advancing Croatian units to occupy the supposedly

Croatian soldiers in the aftermath of the fighting.

Courtesy Lieutenant-Colonel Holland.

demilitarized "zone of separation." These events destroyed Serb confidence in the force mandated to protect them. It also taught the Croatians that a few well-directed bullets and shells would send the blue-helmets packing anytime they wished to remove prying UN eyes.[12]

Nonetheless, by the summer of 1993, both sides were pressured by the international community into adopting a new ceasefire in Sector South known as the "Erdut Agreement." Under its terms Croatian forces would withdraw from much of the ground gained during the Maslencia offensive. The Canadian battlegroup, reinforced with two mechanized French companies brought in from Bosnia and northern Croatia, was ordered to ensure that Croatia followed through with the agreement. General Cot anticipated that the Croatians would be reluctant to withdraw from their hard-won gains. This is why he chose the well-armed and highly effective CANBAT 1 to implement the agreement and restore UN presence in Sector South. Cot expected and even hoped for trouble as he was looking for an opportunity to win back UN credibility lost in January.[13] He would get his wish.

Although Cot expected trouble, he was apparently not aware of the extent to which Croatian forces used the Erdut negotiations to shield preparations for a renewed offensive in Sector South. On 9 September, as lead UN elements moved into the village of Medak, the Croatian 9th Lika Wolves Guards Brigade commenced an assault on the salient section of front known as the Medak Pocket. Intelligence assessments later indicated the Croatians were most likely attempting to push back the frontline so that their operational zone headquarters in the town of Gospic would be out of range of Serb gunners located in the long, narrow Medak salient.[14] They may also have intended to drive a corridor to the Dalmatian coast, or draw attention away from domestic political controversies back in Zagreb.

The Lika Wolves Guards Brigade was well supported with tanks and artillery, including a squadron of former East German Army T-72 main battle tanks, as well as older model Warsaw Pact armour. However, while the Croat force contained all the trappings of a modern mechanized army, it could only apply its combat power in rudimentary fashion. Artillery was used to lay down a simple barrage while the infantry and armour advanced with little coordination or fire and movement. As Croat armour pushed down the main road along the valley between Gospic and Gracac, a Croat light infantry force operating in the mountains to the south moved to close off the Medak Pocket from the opposite direction. The even more poorly organized and equipped Serb defence collapsed under the crude, but effective Croat onslaught.[15]

The Croat preliminary barrage on Serb defences in the Medak Pocket commenced as lead elements of 2 PPCLI were moving up to the front, through the Serb rear area, in preparation to implement the Erdut Agreement. The outbreak of heavy fighting required a rapid and dramatic adjustment to Canadian plans. Trained to react quickly to unexpected developments on a fast-moving battlefield, the Patricias easily managed the adjustment. Forward platoons immediately commenced construction of fortifications to protect against the bombardment. The well-drilled Patricias took advantage of every lull in the barrage to further sandbag and revet positions. It was a good thing they did. Over 500 mortar, field, and medium shells fell in an area the size of Parliament Hill around Lieutenant Tyrone Green's 9 Platoon (Charlie Company) within the village of Medak itself. This did not deter Green and his soldiers from carrying out their newly assigned tasks of gathering intelligence on the developing battle and recording cease-fire violations. It is a tribute to their high-intensity warfighting skills, including a thorough appreciation of the effects of artillery, that only four Canadians were wounded during the shelling.[16] If the Croats expected that their barrage on Serb defences would also drive off the UN, they were wrong.

Serb reinforcements poured into the Medak Pocket from all over Yugoslavia and in two days managed to stop the Croatian advance cold, but not before the 10-kilometre long and five-kilometre wide salient had been pinched out and the front line straightened, roughly 3,000 metres northwest of Medak. Fighting raged on in a bitter stalemate for two more days until Serb artillery opened fire on the Croatian city of Karlovac, and then launched a FROG long-range missile into a Zagreb suburb. Serb retaliation coupled with growing pressure from the international community was enough to convince President Tudjman to abandon the offensive and withdraw his forces to their pre–9 September start line.[17] A verbal agreement to that effect was signed and became the "Medak Pocket

Agreement" on 13 September. It would be up to the reinforced Canadian battlegroup to ensure all parties complied with the new terms.

Up to this point, 2 PPCLI had been passive, if direct participants, in the Medak Pocket action. That quickly changed. At 1630 hours, on 14 September 1993, Lieutenant-Colonel Calvin held an Orders Group (O Group) with his subordinate officers and NCOs to review plans for the coming operation. The new withdrawal agreement was to be implemented in four phases. The first step of occupying Serbian frontline positions would be made by 2 PPCLI's Charlie Company and one French company on 15 September. Phase 2 would see Charlie Company, under the watchful eyes of the anti-armour platoon, establish a crossing point in the no man's land between the opposing armies on the main paved road running the length of the valley floor. In phase 3, Delta Company and a second French company from FREBAT 3 (French Battalion 3) would move along the road, through the secure crossing point and on to occupy the forward Croatian positions. 2 PPCLI's Reconnaissance Platoon and the battalion tactical headquarters would follow Delta Company into the pocket. The last step would be to oversee the Croatian withdrawal to their pre-9 September positions thereby completing the separation of forces and establishing a new demilitarized zone. Alpha and Bravo Companies, 2 PPCLI, just arrived in the area from Sector West, would secure the remainder of the CANBAT 1 area of responsibility during the operation. Unfortunately, the Canadians would have to do without their 81-mm mortar platoon. Since the unit was due to rotate home in a few weeks, the tubes had already been shipped back to Canada.[18]

In the hours before the operation, General Cot personally flew into the area to speak to Lieutenant-Colonel Calvin, essentially taking overall command and eliminating the link to Sector South headquarters in Knin. Too much was riding on the coming events to have any delay in the reporting chain or any misunderstanding about what was to happen. The UNPROFOR commander reminded Calvin of how vital it was that his battlegroup succeed in order to restore UN credibility. Cot also indicated that details of the Medak Pocket Agreement would not likely be transmitted from Zagreb down to the frontline Croatian soldiers soon to be encountered. General Cot strongly implied that force may have to be used to ensure their compliance with the agreement. He reminded Calvin that the UN rules of engagement allowed the blue-helmeted Canadian and French troops to return fire in kind if they or their mandate were threatened.[19] The mission was clear and the stage set.

The M-113 armoured personnel carriers of Charlie Company rolled forward on 15 September on schedule. Not long after setting off, Lieutenant Green's 9 Platoon came under small arms and machine-gun fire from the Croatian lines. At first it appeared that General Cot was right about the Croat frontline units not being advised that the Canadians were coming. The solution to this problem seemed obvious. Get the white-painted armoured vehicles out in the open where there would be no mistake that the movement was UNPROFOR advancing, rather than a Serb counterattack.

With large blue UN flags were fixed to radio antennas, the carriers were driven out of a tree line into the open. This brought an increase in Croat fire, including heavy machine gun, rocket propelled grenades and 20-mm anti-aircraft gunfire. It was now obvious that the Croatians had no intention of letting the Canadians advance. All along the Charlie and FREBAT 1 Company front, the blue helmets halted in whatever defensive positions they could find, roughly along the former Serb line. For the next 15 hours, the Croatians shot it out with Canadian and French troops.[20] Interestingly enough, of all the weapons used against the advancing UN troops; the deadly T-72 tanks known to be in the area did not make an appearance. Perhaps Croat officers were aware of the potency of the TOW anti-armour missile system, especially when operated by Canadian crews, and were unwilling to risk their precious new vehicles.

What happened in those tracer filled hours was not exactly a battle, at least not by the standards of Western armies that are accustomed to attacking positions with fire and movement. There were no infantry assaults or sweeping tank thrusts to seize ground held by the UN. That is not how war is waged in the Balkans. Ground combat in the former Yugoslavia consisted of both sides attempting to make opposing positions untenable by bring maximum fire to bear. Conversely, as soon as a position became too dangerous to hold because of accurate and sustained fire, it was abandoned. Any movement that involved placing troops in the open was avoided. Weapons were plentiful in the region but soldiers, especially of the trained variety, were not. This way of war may also be a vestige of Tito's guerrilla military doctrine that formed the basis of the old Yugoslav National Army in which many officers and NCOs on both sides had served.

By Balkan standards then, the Medak firefight was indeed a battle. It surely seemed that way to Sergeant Rod Dearing's section of 7 Platoon on Charlie Company's right flank in the village of Licki Citluk. It was there that some of the heaviest firing took place, often at ranges of 150 metres. At one point in the evening Croat mortars and 20-mm automatic-cannons went to work on the Canadian trench line. Croat infantry tried repeatedly to flank Dearing's section, but each time they were driven off by Canadian rifle and machine-gun fire directed by a Starlight telescopic night vision sight.[21] In the early hours of 16 September, when Croat troops made one last attempt to push out the Patricias, Private Scott LeBlanc leapt out of his trench blazing away at the attackers with his belt-fed C-9 light machine gun. Leblanc's audacious act was apparently enough to convince the Croats that these Canadians were not about to give ground and that it was time to pull back.[22] Regardless of the fact that this was supposed to be a traditional UN peacekeeping mission, or of how this action compares to larger battles in Canadian military history, for the riflemen of Charlie Company, it was war. It is worth noting that five of Dearing's soldiers fighting that tiny war were reservists, including LeBlanc.

Over on the UNPROFOR right, the French company was having better luck. Each of their mechanized platoons was equipped with one VAB infantry fighting vehicle mounting a 20-mm auto-cannon in an armoured turret. When hostile fire was returned with this powerful and accurate weapon, Croat troops were less inclined to offer resistance.[23]

The firefights lasted all night and early into the next morning. During the night, Colonel J.O.M. "Mike" Maisonneuve, UNPROFOR's chief operations officer, arrived from Zagreb in an effort to talk down the Croatians. Eventually, Maisonneuve, Lieutenant-Colonel Calvin, and a senior UN Military Observer drove down the main road to meet with the local Croat commander. Operational Zone Commander General Rahim Ademi, rough equivalent to a NATO corps commander, agreed to the meeting and let the Canadians delegation pass through the lines to his headquarters in Gospic. After much heated discussion, Ademi agreed not resist phase 2 and that the Canadians could establish their crossing point that night without Croatian interference. Phase 3 could commence at 1200 hours the following day when Delta Company would pass through the crossing point to move into the Croatian trench line.[24] During the night, Major Dan Drew and his Delta Company headquarters moved up the road to the crossing point. The remainder of the company would join him in the morning for their 1200 hours departure time.

The Patricias rose to a horrifying sight on the morning of 16 September. Smoke could be seen rising from several villages behind Croatian lines. Explosions and an occasional burst of automatic rifle fire could also be heard. It suddenly became clear why the Croatians resisted the Canadian advance. Those villages were inhabited predominantly by Serbs and Croatian Special Police were not yet finished ethnically cleansing them.

Calvin clamoured for action and immediately recalled Colonel Maisonneuve to meet again with General Ademi. Unfortunately, with only four widely separated companies and no supporting tanks or artillery, Calvin's force had no chance in a frontal attack against the entire Croatian 9th Brigade with its tanks and heavy guns. Even if the Canadians did have the strength, it was far beyond the scope of UNPROFOR's mandate to deliver a full attack. Returning aimed fire and defending against aggression was palatable to the UN in 1993 but launching an outright assault was at that time in the evolution of peace-building was out of the question. Therefore, the Canadians could do little but sit back and wait for the 1200 hours timing. As they waited they listened helplessly to the explosions and shooting and imagined what was happening to the Serb civilians to their front. Years later those sounds and that feeling of helplessness continues to haunt many of them.

Finally noon arrived and Delta Company rolled ahead mounted in their M-113 armoured personnel carriers and accompanied by several TOW anti-armour vehicles. They no sooner started down the road in column before they ran into a Croatian roadblock. To the left of the road sat a modern and deadly T-72 main battle tank, a gift from Germany. On the right side of the road, two towed anti-tank guns and a bank of Sagger anti-tank missiles took aim at the Canadian column. A company

Courtesy Lieutenant-Colonel Holland.

The reason for the delay became abundantly apparent to the Canadians once they advanced beyond the roadblocks — ethnic cleansing.

of Croatian infantry, protected by a hastily laid minefield, completed the obstacle. The senior Croatian officer on the barrier refused Major Drew's demand that his company be allowed to pass. Weapons on both sides were made ready for action. This tense Mexican standoff lasted over an hour. Throughout the standoff, the well-trained and highly disciplined Canadian riflemen maintained their cool while the Croats grew increasingly uneasy. Essentially the resolute and stern-faced Canadians began to stare down the Croatians manning the roadblock.[25]

During the tension, Lieutenant-Colonel Calvin arrived on the scene. He argued heatedly with the ranking Croat officer, Brigadier-General Mezic.[26] Mezic was General Ademi's senior liaison officer. His presence at the road block indicated that the Operational Zone commander had no intention of keeping his word. In fact, Mezic was stalling to give Croatian Special Police the time they needed to destroy evidence of murder and ethnic cleansing.

Shortly after 1300 hours, Calvin took a gamble to break the deadlock and avoid a bloody point-blank shootout in the middle of the road. Some

20 international journalists accompanied Delta Company, all seeking to cover the story of the Croatia's latest invasion of the Serbian Krajina. It was time to bring them into action. Calvin called the media crews to the front of the column for a press conference, complete with cameras, in front of the roadblock. He explained to reporters what the Croatian special police were doing on the other side of the barricade and had the cameras film the Croatian's obvious interference with UN efforts to make peace.

The cameras broke the increasingly shaky Croat resolve. By 1330 hours, Delta Company was on the move. Calvin's imaginative ploy was too late to stop the ethnic cleansing of Serb villages in the Medak Pocket, but it did allow the blue-helmets to reach most of the villages before all traces of Croatian atrocities could be erased.[27] Unfortunately, the battlegroup was held up again later in the afternoon, this time by senior UN officials who insisted on sticking to the rigid time table for advancing into the pocket. That timetable did not take into account that with every wasted minute, more evidence was destroyed. It was not until 17 September that UNPROFOR soldiers occupied the whole area.

The next few days were the most difficult for Canadian soldiers involved in the Medak Pocket operation. Their job was now, along with civilian police officers and UN medical officers, to sweep the area for signs of ethnic cleansing. The task was enormous. Each and every building in the Medak Pocket had been levelled to the ground. Truck loads of firewood had been brought in to build intense fires among the wooden buildings to ensure large timbers burned to ash and could not be re-used. Brick and concrete buildings and foundations were broken down with explosives and anti-tank mines. The Croatians completed their task by killing most livestock in the area. That act was the small-arms firing heard on 16 September. The dead animals were dumped, mixed with oil, into wells to make them unusable for Serbs entertaining any thought of return.[28]

Sixteen Serb bodies were found scattered in hidden locations and the ground littered with rubber surgical gloves. Calvin and his soldiers believed the gloves indicated that most bodies of Serbs shot in the open were transported elsewhere. The Canadians figured that the bodies recovered belonged to a handful of those discovered hiding in basements or in the woods whose bodies were left behind in haste. This analysis was corroborated when a mass grave containing over 50 bodies was later located in the vicinity. The bodies recovered in the Pocket itself included those of two young women found in a basement. They were apparently tied up, shot, and then doused with gasoline and burned. When found, the bodies were still hot enough to melt plastic body bags. These girls were apparently used for "entertainment." At another location, an elderly Serb woman had been found shot four times in the head, execution style.

Some veterans of the operation still carry with them a deep sense that they should have done more to stop the killing. During a CBC Television interview just after the 2002 award ceremony, Master-Corporal Philip Tobicoe lamented that he felt his unit arrived "kind of late" and their inability to stop the destruction on that final morning "really affected" him. However, members of the 2 PPCLI Battlegroup can take some comfort knowing that the sounds they heard on 16 September were not those of people being murdered but of animals being shot and foundations being demolished. Bodies found at the scene were badly decomposed indicating they were shot some considerable time earlier, probably when Croat

Courtesy Lieutenant-Colonel Holland.

The discovery of mass graves.

special police followed advancing troops into the pocket not long after 9 September and before the 15 September "battle" with the Canadians.[29]

Although the job of gathering war crimes evidence may have been the most difficult for the Canadians, it was of critical importance. The Medak Pocket provided the world with the first hard evidence that Serbia, although probably the largest, was not the sole perpetrator of ethnic cleansing in the Balkans. This evidence weighed heavily at a time when international intervention against Serbia, which would have sacrificed UN impartiality the region, was under consideration. News of the atrocities provoked a strong rebuke from the international community that doubtlessly improved Croatian military behaviour, perhaps at the behest of their American advisors. On a legal level, meticulous Canadian procedures for sweeping and recording evidence became the standard template for use in UNPROFOR, subsequently providing a degree of deterrence to those who feared being called to account for war crimes. Evidence gathered at Medak was eventually used by the International Criminal Tribunal for the Former Yugoslavia to indict Croatian officers implicated in the massacres, including General Ademi. These judicial proceedings were vital to the re-establishment of rule of law, good governance, and longer term peace in the region.

At the more practical level of maintaining stability in Croatia, Canadian action at Medak earned back some of the respect for the United Nations lost at Maslencia. Canadian Colonel George Oehring took over command of Sector South short days after the shootout and investigation. Oehring was in a better position that anyone to feel the effects of Medak. He wrote:

> Medak restored UNPROFOR's credibility resulting in renewed dialogue leading to a local informal cease-fire in November, a more formal and wider one at Christmas, and a "bilateral", universal cease-fire signed in Zagreb on 29 March, 1994. Everybody hated us in September 1993. I was stoned and threatened during my first trip to Zadar to meet the Croat commander there. Medak changed all this. The Serbs, right up to my departure a year later, would spontaneously mention the

resolute fairness of the Canadians at Medak, while the
Croats, although grudgingly at first, came to respect the
Canadians in Sector South.[30]

Unfortunately Medak could not completely wipe away the memory
of Maslencia. The Canadians may have documented Croat war crimes
near Medak, but they had not the mandate or the firepower to stop them,
adding to the Serb's sense of insecurity.[31] The international peacekeeping
community was not unified or willing in 1993 to take resolute steps to stop
ethnic cleansing, especially against the vilified Serbs. Even when crimes
were perpetrated by Serbs, it took several much larger massacres around
the world before the international community unified and mustered
the political will to intervene in Kosovo in 1999. Meanwhile, fears in
the Krajina were born out in 1995. By then the Croatian Army, with
military aid, training, and staff support from the United States, was ready
to solve the Serb Krajina "problem" with military means. In May 1995,
new and improved Croatian forces launched Operation Flash followed
by Operation Storm in August. These powerful, U.S.-directed offensives
overwhelmed weak Serb resistance as well as international community
resolve to continue protecting the Krajina. Indeed, the presence of the
Serb enclave in Croatia was a barrier to convincing the former warring
parties to agree to the 1995 U.S.-brokered "Dayton Accord." That accord
paved the way for a NATO-facilitated peace in Bosnia in 1996.

However, Jim Calvin and his soldiers can take pride in the knowledge
that they set a standard by doing everything within their means to
keep order in Croatia. Routine loss of civilian life in Sector South from
continual exchanges of fire along the line of contact came to an end when
the Medak operation restored the UN zone of separation there. Stability
was more or less maintained in the area until international deal-making
and the final 1995 offensives made the mission operationally suicidal
and diplomatically pointless to continue. At the tactical level, the joint
Canadian-French operation at Medak marked the beginning of new
period of using international military forces for conflict resolution and
humanitarian intervention. The Canadian battlegroup possessed a high
degree of combat power and a demonstrated willingness to use it. Calvin

and his soldiers also understood and proved how powerful a deterrent the court of international public opinion can be when the media spotlight is placed on actions of armed groups seeking to take advantage of the weak in places like the former Yugoslavia.

Unfortunately, most other contingents in UNPROFOR were totally unprepared in regards to equipment, training, and political will to engage in the types of action carried out by the Canadians. Medak therefore offers a striking example of the need of unity of action on peace and stability building operations, both politically and militarily. No matter how disciplined, well-equipped, and effective the Canadian portion of an international force might be, it must act with similarly equipped forces as part of a coherent multinational diplomatic and reconstruction plan to succeed. Thankfully, events in the former Yugoslavia, after the 1996 deployment of NATO's implementation and stabilization forces (IFOR and SFOR), and then in Afghanistan, with NATO's International Security and Assistance Force, indicate that the lessons of Medak are turning into policy, if slowly.

Analysis of activities engaged in by Canadian troops at Medak also offers an alternative view to the conclusions of the Somalia Report. Operations in UNPROFOR's Sector South demanded the full range of capabilities possessed by Canadian soldiers, from fortification construction, marksmanship, and mechanized mobile combat to negotiation and basic crime-scene investigation techniques. In all these categories, Canadian military leadership and training in the Medak Pocket was of the highest standard. Contrary to the findings of the Somalia Inquiry, the Canadian Army in 1993 contained dedicated, skilled, and well-disciplined professional soldiers. These troops were led by competent, educated, and highly capable officers and senior NCOs. Medak made it clear that an institution capable of producing soldiers who could perform well in the difficult and constantly evolving conditions at Medak was probably not as close to collapse as the Somalia commissioners thought. The greatest tragedy for Canada is that so few Canadians have any knowledge of this story or much else of the Canadian experience in the former Yugoslavia. As a result most are ill-equipped to understand or make informed contributions to the debate over current and future missions that require the careful application of force to restore peace, order, and the rule of law.

NOTES

1. W. Andy Knight, "Canada Abandons Its Role as UN Peacekeeper," *Edmonton Journal*, 16 April 2006.

2. Desmond Morton, "In Afghan Fields the Poppies Blow," 6th Annual Dominick Graham Lecture on War and Society, University of New Brunswick, 15 November 2006.

3. Commission of Inquiry into the Deployment of Canadian Forces to Somalia, *Dishonoured Legacy: The Lessons of the Somalia Affair* (Ottawa: 1997), xxix.

4. Memorandum, Colonel G. Oehring to UNPROFOR Deputy Force Commander Major-General J.A. MacGinnis, 1 October, 1993.

5. Overview of Yugoslav break-up based on UN Reports and print media analysis conducted while author served as CF operations analyst for Conference of Defence Associations Institute, 1996–98. For more information on the topic see: Susan L. Woodward, *Balkan Tragedy: Chaos and Dissolution After the Cold War* (Washington: Brookings Institution, 1995); and *The United Nations and the Situation in the Former Yugoslavia* (New York: UN Dept. of Public Information, 1995).

6. Troops deployed under chapter 6 of the *United Nations Charter* are mandated to impartially support peaceful resolution of disputes between parties, as opposed to deployments under chapter 7, which allows the use of force to restore international peace and security.

7. Interview with now Colonel J. Calvin, Kingston 1997. Reserve combat arms officers enrolled in the RESO program received training that was virtually identical to that given to their regular force counterparts up to platoon/troop command level.

8. Interview with Colonel J. Calvin, Kingston 1997.

9. War Diary, 2 PPCLI, Operation Harmony Rotation 3, March-October, 1993.

10. Lewis MacKenzie, *Peacekeeper: The Road to Sarajevo* (Vancouver: Douglas & McIntyre, 1993).

11. Major Dawn M. Hewitt, USAF, *From Ottawa to Sarajevo: Canadian Peacekeepers in the Balkans* (Kingston: 1998), 55–57.

12. Interview with Colonel G. Oehring (Retired), Kingston 1997.

13. Interview with Colonel J. Calvin, Kingston 1997; and Medak Pocket Hearing, Standing Committee on Defence and Veterans Affairs (SCONDVA), 1998.

14. UNPROFOR Intelligence Summary, W.D. 2 PPCLI, September 1993.

15. Interview with Colonel J. Calvin, Kingston 1997.

16. SCONDVA Hearing.

17. Colonel J.O. Michel Maisonneuve, "Unity of Action in ex-Yugoslavia," *Defence Associations National Network News* (Winter 1995–96).

18. War Diary, 2 PPCLI, Medak Pocket After-Action Report, 1993 Section 5.

19. SCONDVA Hearing.

20. War Diary, 2 PPCLI, Medak Report.

21. Hewitt, *From Ottawa to Sarajevo*, 64.

22. SCONDVA Hearing.

23. Interview with Colonel J. Calvin, Kingston 1997.

24. *Ibid.*, 1997.

25. *Ibid.*,

26. War Diary, 2 PPCLI Medak Report.

27. SCONDVA Hearing.

28. War Diary, 2 PPCLI, Medak Report.

29. Interview with Colonel J. Calvin, Kingston 1997.

30. Letter from Colonel G. Oehring to Minister of National Defence, December 1996.

31. "It was impossible to have any meeting or negotiations with the Serbs without having (Op Maslencia) discussed ad nauseam." War Diary, 1 PPCLI, End Tour Report Op Harmony, Rotation 4, October 1994.

11

NO SMALL ACTION: OPERATION MEDUSA, PANJWAYI, AFGHANISTAN

Bernd Horn

The oppressive heat and relative calm of the September Afghan morning betrayed the undercurrent of tension that permeated the surroundings of a non-descript white school house complex in Panjwayi, Kandahar Province in southern Afghanistan. Hidden away in bunkers and fortified buildings was a group of fanatical Taliban fighters who tightened up the slack on their triggers as they nervously eyed the Canadian vehicles that were cautiously approaching. Equally, the soldiers from "C" Company, 1st Battalion, The Royal Canadian Regiment Battle Group (1 RCR BG) were tense as they rolled their vehicles towards the suspected enemy position. In a split second, the hot relatively quiet countryside erupted in a fusillade of noise, explosions, and death. The fight was on.

What became known as Operation Medusa was a major offensive conducted by the International Security Assistance Force (ISAF) with assistance from the Afghan National Army (ANA), from 1–17 September 2006. Their objective was to establish government control over an area of Kandahar Province centered on the district of Panjwayi, approximately 30 kilometres from Kandahar City, the birthplace and heartland of the Taliban. In essence, it was an enemy stronghold. NATO's intent was to destroy or capture the insurgents that had dug-in to fight. Initially the campaign design followed a phased approach of engaging the local leaders first to attempt to minimize the level of death and destruction and then to apply superior and precise combat power. By 2 September 2006,

The infamous White School House in the village of Bayenzi.

it was apparent that combat was inevitable. The brunt of this combat fell to the Canadians.

The scope of the actual problem, however, had been long in brewing. By the spring of 2006, Canada had been in Afghanistan for four and a half years. Within a month of the tragic terrorist attack on the Twin Towers of the World Trade Centre in New York, on 11 September 2001, the Canadian government announced it would support the American Operation Enduring Freedom, the attack on the Taliban regime in Afghanistan, by launching Operation Apollo. This entailed the deployment of a Naval Task Group, as well as the dispatch of elite special operations forces (SOF) soldiers from Joint Task Force 2.[1] In addition, a Canadian battle group based on the 3rd Battalion, the Princess Patricia's Canadian Light Infantry was deployed on 1 February 2002, to support American operations in the Kandahar area.[2]

Throughout the next six months, in support of the American initiatives to destroy Taliban and Al Qaeda forces, Canadian SOF and members from

3 PPCLI conducted combat operations with their American counterparts in the Tergul Mountain range in the Sha-I-Kot valley in Eastern Afghanistan, as well as in the Gardez area. By late July 2002, these ground forces had been redeployed to Canada.[3]

However, Canadian ground participation in Afghanistan quickly resumed. In July 2003, close to 2,000 troops were dispatched to Kabul, as part of Operation Athena, to assist the NATO ISAF mission, which was tasked with providing security in the Kabul area and reinforcing the Afghan Transitional Authority.[4] Over five successive six-month rotations, Canadian troops conducted foot patrols and surveillance tasks that established a presence and capability within the ISAF area of responsibility. These tasks also generated intelligence and situational awareness. In addition, Canadian soldiers assisted and facilitated the rebuilding of the democratic process in Afghanistan. Operation Athena officially ended on 18 October 2005, with the withdrawal of the remaining Canadian sub-unit, the reconnaissance squadron from the Kabul area.[5]

But Canada was not leaving Afghanistan. Rather it was redefining its contribution as part of Stage 3 ISAF expansion into Afghanistan. As such, Canada took responsibility for a Provincial Reconstruction Team (PRT) in Kandahar.[6] Equally important, starting in February 2006, Canada contributed an infantry battle group of approximately 1,000 soldiers to work with the American forces to conduct stabilization and combat operations throughout Kandahar Province. The American forces were still operating under the framework of Operation Enduring Freedom (OEF) and the introduction of the Canadian battle group became part of the transition from the U.S. OEF framework to the ISAF Stage 3 transition of NATO control of Coalition forces in Afghanistan.[7] This new evolution of the mission was called Operation Archer.

Subsequently, under Operation Archer, it fell to the 1st Battalion, the PPCLI (1 PPCLI) or Task Force (TF) Orion as its commanding officer Lieutenant-Colonel Ian Hope titled it, to conduct the combat tasks in Kandahar Province.[8] Their mission read, benignly enough, "Task Force Orion will assist Afghans in the establishment of good governance, security and stability, and reconstruction in the province of Kandahar during Op Archer Rotation (Roto) 1 in order to help extend the legitimacy and credibility of the Government of Afghanistan throughout the Islamic Republic of Afghanistan and at the same time help to establish conditions necessary for NATO Stage 3 expansion."[9]

As such, it was Lieutenant-Colonel Hope's intent for the Battle Group to become an extension of the efforts being exerted by the PRT. He pushed his sub-units out into independent forward operating bases (FOBs) located in areas that would allow them to work with Afghan National Security Forces (ANSF) and district leaders to improve governance, security and socio-economic conditions in key districts of the province. Hope instructed his TF elements to convince village, district, and provincial leaders to implement Government of Afghanistan (GOA) initiatives. The Battle Group (BG) committed itself to this "3D" (Development, Diplomacy, and Defence) whole of government approach.

Their tour began quietly, almost too quietly, with many of the troops complaining that they had not yet "closed with the enemy." The young soldiers craved action — they wanted to see combat and the endless patrolling and leader engagements became rather mundane to many. However, as the adage goes, "be careful of what you wish for." As winter turned to spring, the traditional Afghan campaign season began and TF Orion initiated what would be a long series of events leading to a cataclysmic encounter between Canadian and Taliban forces in the killing fields of Panjwayi.

The surge in activity became clearly apparent in June 2006, when it became evident that the steady increase in Taliban activity was indicative of a full blown offensive. Consequently, 1 PPCLI BG now focused its energies on security operations, specifically to find, fix, and destroy the enemy. Hope deployed his manoeuvre forces in a dispersed, dynamic, and flexible manner. They lived among the Afghans to gain their trust and to keep the Taliban off-balance. The Task Force leaders used coalition intelligence and sensors to try and pinpoint the enemy. They also used human intelligence (HUMINT) gathered from local nationals.[10] All of this information, distilled with intuition, shaped the decisions Hope and his subordinate commanders made in regard to finding the enemy. Once the enemy was located, they attempted "to manoeuvre into that district quietly under the cover of darkness, using deception, and — as much as possible — isolate the village by using thin blocking and cut off forces." The CO explained, "We would conduct manoeuvre (cordon and searches) and fires (show of force with artillery or 25-mm fire) to produce enemy ICOM [communication intercept] chatter, and from this ICOM chatter (or HUMINT from local nationals), we would attempt to vector in upon the enemy locations." However, in the end, Hope conceded, "finding him [the enemy] was almost always a result of advance-to-contact in the close country where he hid and was confirmed by the exchange of fire at close quarters."[11] He added:

> We trained ourselves to hold and fix the enemy with whatever we could bring in, as close as 100 metres. We resisted the tendency to withdraw back to our last safe place. But, finishing the enemy was difficult. They [Taliban] were very good at slipping away. You could drop as much ordnance as you wanted but in the end to finish the enemy you had to walk the ground — it was always a close quarter fight.[12]

Not surprisingly, TF Orion conducted many operations in Kandahar Province. "We were the 'fire battalion' for the brigade," quipped Captain Kevin Barry, "We would be sent out to put down a contact somewhere and would do it and then another fire would start up somewhere else and we would be sent there."[13] But ominously, the "troops-in-contact" (TICs) in the Pashmul area took on a ferocity that was foreboding.

Operation Mountain Thrust, mounted between 15 May and 31 July 2006, started the showdown. "Operation Mountain Thrust," explained Lieutenant-Colonel Shane Schreiber, the assistant chief of staff of the Multinational Brigade Headquarters (MNB HQ), "was [intended] to defeat the Taliban in their traditional areas." The scope of the mission he lamented, "was like digging a hole in the ocean — it was difficult to secure an area. Once an area was secure we hoped that the ANA would [continue to] secure it — but once we left the Taliban filled back in."[14] Moreover, not only did the Taliban slip back in, but they did so in increasing numbers.

Between May and June there was an alarming increase in the number of TICs. In addition, the Taliban began to confiscate cell phones from local nationals as a counter-intelligence measure. They also established plans for setting up checkpoints and moving into Kandahar City itself. On 30 June 2006, the Task Force received reports indicating that the Taliban were issuing night letters asking Afghan locals to leave the Panjwayi and Zhari areas immediately as Taliban elements were planning to engage GoA forces and Canadian Forces elements.

The state of chaos and violence reached such levels that by June 2006 the Senlis Council reported, "In Kandahar, Canadian troops are fighting increasingly deadly counterinsurgency operations under Operation Enduring Freedom against the resurgent Taliban." The Council added, "Kandahar now is a war zone, with suicide bombings, rocket attacks, ambushes and repeated outbreaks of open warfare, resulting in numerous Canadian fatalities and many more injuries."[15] They concluded, "Kandahar is a province at war: there is no peace to keep."[16] Statistics backed their assertions. By June 2006, there was a "600% increase in violent attacks in the last six months, and terrorism is now a pressing concern in Kandahar; the majority of terror attacks in Afghanistan occur in Kandahar and bordering provinces."[17]

In July, in the face of the increasing Taliban presence and activity, Lieutenant-Colonel Hope developed a concept of operations in Pashmul to "disrupt the Taliban in Zhari District through concentration of combat power and isolation and clearance of objective Puma in the vicinity of the village of Pashmul." He explained, "The clearance of Puma will be conducted by deliberate cordon and searches of areas assessed to contain Taliban and/or their caches based on previous intelligence and current HUMINT gained by Afghan National Security Forces partnered with TF Orion for this operation."[18]

The Taliban, however, refused to go quietly. "As we arrived [7 July 2006] closer to the objective area [Pashmul] we saw the women and children pouring out of the town," described Captain Andrew Charchuk, the forward observation officer for "C" Coy Group, 1 PPCLI. "Not a good sign," he added, explaining "we pushed on and about 3 kilometres from our intended line of departure to start the operation [at around 0030 hours] we were ambushed by Taliban fighters." He continued, "I saw about 20 RPGs [rocket propelled grenades] all bursting in the air over the LAVs. It was an unreal scene to describe. There was no doubt we were in a big fight."[19]

That contact initiated a larger sequence of events. The Task Force fought hard in the 50 degree Celsius heat in a running battle that lasted for days. As embedded reporter Christie Blatchford summarized, "July was a daily diet of long battles that went on for hours and stretched the battle group thin over 600 kilometres in seven separate districts over some of the most treacherous terrain in Afghanistan."[20]

By August intelligence reports continued to paint a picture of ongoing Taliban activity, namely key leader engagements and increasing TICs, all of which indicated that the enemy was massing forces in the Panjwayi district. The Taliban focus on the area was not hard to understand. Panjwayi has always been critically important to them because it is a fertile, densely populated, and economically lucrative area. It has also been the traditional staging area for attacks against Kandahar City, and an area for resupply for troops staging in Zhari district.

As well, Kandahar province and its capital, Kandahar City, have always interested the Taliban because the region has consistently maintained a kind of autonomy from any of the various central governments in Kabul. It is also the second largest province in Afghanistan located in the harsh, barren, desert environment of the volatile southeastern corner of the country. It is bounded on the north and northeast by the mountainous Uruzgan and Zabul provinces and in the west by Helmand, and it shares a porous 402 kilometre long border with the Pakistan province of Baluchistan. Kandahar City, is situated at the junction of Afghanistan's main highways and is the major southern link to Pakistan. In fact, the highway system passes from Spin Boldak on the Pakistan border, through Kandahar City to Kabul. Moreover, Kandahar was the birthplace and continues to be the heartland of the Taliban itself.

Kandahar had become a centre of gravity for the Government of Afghanistan, the Coalition, and the Taliban, in the fight for the confidence and support of Afghans. As Lieutenant-Colonel Schreiber explained, "[We] began to develop Afghan development zones (ADZ) to create a secure bubble around a nucleus where we could push resources and redevelopment (i.e., ink spot method)"[21] These efforts were all part of the governance, security, and reconstruction strategy for rebuilding a modern Afghanistan. Conversely, for the Taliban, victory in Kandahar Province would discredit the GoA and coalition forces in the eyes of Afghans. Consequently, "We were convinced that the Taliban were massing in Panjwayi to establish a permanent base of operations there, with a view to attacking Kandahar City," confirmed Lieutenant-Colonel Ian Hope.[22]

And the Talibes were intent on winning. "The Taliban emptied Quetta and other centres to conduct offensive operations in Regional Command (RC) South in 2006," confided Schreiber, "It was a window of opportunity for them as we focused on elections and the handover from U.S. control in Kandahar to NATO control as part of Stage 3 expansion."[23] The American and NATO focus on these activities provided the Taliban with an ideal opportunity to achieve success. "Our intelligence," revealed Lieutenant-Colonel Schreiber, "estimated that they [Taliban] brought in, as a minimum, 12,000 foot soldiers."[24]

In early August continuing reports of major enemy activity and massing of troops triggered yet another coalition foray into the area. On 3 August 2006, Lieutenant-Colonel Hope and his Battle Group found themselves in the Pashmul / Panjwayi area once again.

The day started ominously when, in the inky darkness of predawn, the lead assault platoon snaked its way silently using thermal sights through a wadi towards its objective, a bazaar comprised of eight to 12 buildings. Suddenly, shattering the early morning calm, the assault platoon opened a concentrated fire when they identified Taliban fighters in early warning positions a scant 150 metres from their vehicles. As they rolled forward in their Light Armoured Vehicle IIIs (LAV IIIs), the lead vehicle struck a pressure-plate-activated improvised explosive device (IED) killing two of the soldiers inside. Evidence indicated that a minimum of three additional IEDs, half buried in the soft ground, covered the restricted axis of advance which led to a narrow bridge, which in turn was surrounded by fighting positions. Furthermore, the severely canalized terrain included thick mud walls on either side of the narrow road. To make matters worse, the walls had loop holes in them from which the enemy could fire in multiple directions without exposing themselves. In addition, numerous irrigation ditches (four to six) feet deep and most covered with grass) provided even more cover for the enemy.

The Task Force plan was amended and a dismounted approach in conjunction with ANSF was undertaken. Quickly, TF Orion soldiers advanced and seized a schoolhouse. Unconsciously, however, they had sprung a Taliban trap. The Canadian soldiers soon found themselves hammered from three sides as the Taliban quickly tried to seize the opportunity to kill and capture them. "You know, I wouldn't say it was farmers dropping their shovels by the way they operated," reminisced Master-Corporal Matthew Parson, "they knew tactics, they knew how to get on our flanks, they knew how to use fire and manoeuvre." Parsons concluded, "They were smart, they were a smart crew."[25]

The fight became desperate: One soldier described it "as a well-planned ambush." He recounted how stealthy Taliban forces formed a horseshoe around Canadian troops holed up in a tiny schoolhouse surrounded by land mines, then launched a volley of rocket-propelled grenades towards them. When he poked his head out of a doorway, a grenade swished by him and scorched his forearm. He then turned to watch the grenade strike a wall, the ensuing spray of shrapnel killing three of his comrades. "They were too organized," asserted the soldier, "we had to pull back."[26]

Another participant, Sergeant Patrick Towers, later acknowledged that the Taliban were determined to win and fought bravely. "I underestimated them because I figured them to be just a bunch of farmers that pick up AK-47s but they employ tactics, they have training, and what blew me away was later, when we swept their ambush positions, they had depth to their positions, cut-offs with machine guns, anti-tank positions — all dug-in, as well as a casualty collection point." He concluded, "They were well trained and they can employ tactics." Towers concluded, "They're certainly not just a bunch of dirt farmers."[27] Sergeant Towers was not the only one to have underestimated the enemy. The Taliban, conceded Brigadier-General David Fraser, the ISAF MNB commander, "was more sophisticated at what he was doing than we had originally thought."[28]

As the situation went from desperate to precarious, even the seriously wounded fired their weapons to hold back the advancing Taliban.

Lieutenant-Colonel Hope pushed fresh troops forward. All braved the fire to assist their comrades. An American B-1 Bomber, aware of the desperate situation below, appeared out of no where and buzzed the objective at a mere 500 feet. This air support and the assistance of French Mirage fighter jets turned the tide and returned the initiative to the Canadians. However, with light fading and the absence of any ANSF troops to hold the ground once taken, Hope decided to pull back. He also realized that the Taliban had returned in strength and it had now become a larger operation, beyond his unit, to dislodge them.[29] The concept of Operation Medusa was born in the heat, death, and destruction of the 3 August battle.

Brigadier-General Fraser pondered the problem. Fraser believed Panjwayi was going to be the Taliban's "major fight for the summer." He explained, "the third of August was the defining day that we knew exactly what we were facing, and what the enemy wanted to do, the enemy's intent."[30] In Fraser's estimation, the enemy's intent "was to isolate Kandahar City, not directly but indirectly, to demonstrate the weakness and the inability of the national Government to come after them with a conventional force."[31] He stated, "This also indicated to us that the Taliban were actually progressing with the evolution of their own operations to the next stage[32] where they thought they were capable enough to go and challenge the national government and coalition forces in a conventional manner."[33] He added, "We also assessed that their intent was to engage the international community in a battle of attrition on ground of their tactical choosing to cause as many casualties as they could to attack our centre of gravity (i.e., domestic public support)."[34] Fraser concluded that the Taliban plan "was designed to defeat us from a "political will" point of view; to illustrate weakness in the Government of Afghanistan and thereby set the stage where the Taliban could attack the city and defeat not only the provincial government there but also attack the national government in Afghanistan in a fairly sophisticated and substantive way."[35] As a result, Fraser briefed his plan to Lieutenant-General David Richards, the British commander then in charge of NATO's forces in Afghanistan at NATO headquarters. "I said this is a fight we can't lose," remembered Fraser, "This is the main, main fight."[36]

To defeat their wily foe, Fraser's staff developed what they thought would be an effective plan. The MNB mission was to defeat the Taliban in Pashmul to set the conditions for the establishment of the Kandahar ADZ. Fraser's intent was to disrupt the Taliban in the district, achieve security for the local population and freedom of manoeuvre for aid agencies, complete Quick Impact Projects (QIPs) to achieve rapid reconstruction, and subsequently develop the region's governance and economic capacity. His scheme of manoeuvre involved four phases:

1. Shape the battlefield to disrupt Taliban forces through the conduct of leadership engagements; brigade manoeuvre and the intensive application of air and indirect fires (e.g., fighter aircraft, Spectre C-130 gunships, artillery);

2. Conduct operations (i.e., decisive strike; link-up; and secure AO) to clear enemy out of Pashmul/ Panjwayi;

3. Exploit success to the West of Panjwayi to create a secure zone for the ADZ; and

4. Conduct stabilization operations and reconstruction to support the return of the region's population and their security.[37]

Not surprisingly, the Taliban were not about to make it easy. Their build-up and posture directly challenged the GoA and NATO forces in a truly conventional manner. The enemy operated in teams of roughly platoon equivalent size (i.e., 20–30 fighters) over which effective command and control was maintained. As they had already shown, and would further confirm, they were sophisticated enough to conduct tactical reliefs in place and syncronized attacks against their opponents. Their defences were prepared as strong points, which made extensive use of natural and man-made obstacles, and all had interlocking arcs of direct fire with small arms, RPGs, and recoilless rifles. Their indirect fire from mortars was responsive and well coordinated. They placed many obstacles on roads, making extensive use of pressure plate IEDs (in one area five such devices were found in a 50-metre span of road leading into a Taliban defensive position). Finally, they widened the existing canal with light equipment so that it could act as a tank trap.

The Taliban's fieldcraft was also excellent. Trench lines were well prepared by hand and superbly concealed to evade detection by ground and airborne ISR (intelligence, surveillance, reconnaissance) assets. Trenches were tied into thick mud walls that proved extremely resilient against both direct fire weapons (i.e., 25-mm cannon and small arms) and C4 explosives. In fact, they had developed a sophisticated strongpoint replete with entrenchments that resembled a Soviet defensive position. Communications trenches were dug to connect the larger trench system and bunkers. Lieutenant-Colonel Schreiber concluded, "[the Taliban] had a battalion defensive position fully dug in with complex robust command and control capability with mutually supporting positions and advanced surveillance and early warning."[38]

But their physical preparations were not all. The Taliban were highly motivated and fought in place. Their fire discipline was strictly imposed in order to draw coalition forces into their kill zones and they aggressively launched counterattacks from the flanks with small mobile teams to attack the depth of assaulting forces. Finally, their gunnery, "particularly with the SPG [73-mm/82-mm recoilless rifle] was good resulting in the defeat of a LAV III and support vehicles during one assault."[39]

Undeniably, the Taliban had chosen their ground well. Beyond the fortifications they had built, the natural lay of the land worked in their favour. Pashmul was a green belt with thick vegetation. Seven foot high marijuana fields hid movement and masked the thermal imagery of the LAV.[40]

The imposing challenges facing the attacker due both to natural terrain and the tenacity and preparation of the enemy required careful preparation. Brigadier-General Fraser explained, "A lot of effort was devoted in Phase 2 to building up, assembling the enablers and forces we required, as well as the logistical support." He added, "In addition, we attempted to lure the Taliban out so we could determine their exact size, location and engage them." His intent was not to launch Phase 3, the actual ground attack until "we decided we were ready and the Taliban were severely weakened."[41]

Having determined the Taliban's intent, Fraser was focused on controlling the conduct and tempo of the battle. He explained:

> So I made an assessment and I thought, "okay, they've gone conventional, this is their intent, so how do we defeat their intent." Well, I decided that we will defeat their intent by putting our forces all around them and we will wait them out. You see, they wanted us to get into a battle of attrition, to slug it out, to try and clear them out of that complex terrain where they have all the advantages of a well dug-in and protected force — where our technological superiority could be nullified. I directed that we would wait them out. I reversed the roles on them. The Taliban went conventional and ISAF went unconventional. I decided that we would manoeuvre, feint and slap a cordon around them. We would engage them in a battle of attrition, but it would be on our terms, namely a battle of attrition through joint fires.
>
> We anticipated that the enemy had two courses of action. One was that they would just continue to move around and we would continue to attack them. The second enemy course of action, the most dangerous, was if they attacked. This is what they did — they continually challenged us on the fringes of the terrain that they held and fortified. Nonetheless, I wanted to wait for two to three weeks, all the while hammering them with fires and then eventually when I thought the time was right, when the enemy was physically and psychologically weak, then go in and seize the objective areas we had identified in the Pashmul area.[42]

And so, Fraser deployed his forces around the objective area to provide as much containment as he could. The containment force maintained a dynamic disposition in order to provoke the enemy to move inside the "circle so we could shape the battle and advantageously engage the enemy."[43] Coalition forces also dropped psychological pamphlets to warn and encourage non-combatants/civilians and less fanatical enemy personnel to vacate the area. "For the three weeks before we launched Operation Medusa, we talked to and gave money to every village leader in the area," revealed Fraser, "In exchange, we asked them to get rid of the Taliban." He conceded, "We had limited success."[44]

Brigadier-General Fraser briefed General Richards on the plan for Operation Medusa. In turn, the ISAF commander confirmed to Fraser that Operation Medusa was the ISAF main effort. In fact, he went even further and pronounced that Operation Medusa was actually the "NATO main effort."[45] This assurance, however, was of little help. Coalition forces were spread thinly around the cordon. Despite the rhetoric at the highest levels of NATO regarding the importance of the looming battle, the action would be a largely Canadian fight. The Americans and British were already engaged in combat elsewhere in Afghanistan and were hard-pressed to assist, although they did what they could. Overall, the Europeans failed their allies and refused to participate. The Dutch declined to assist in the actual combat but did take over a FOB and outposts on Highway 1, which freed up additional Canadian resources that were fed into the battle.

Brigadier-General Fraser lamented, "The national caveats in NATO are killing me, they are really killing me." He noted, "We found out what NATO could not do. We simply couldn't get everyone we needed." He observed, "The Germans wouldn't come down here; the French company weren't allowed to come down here; and I couldn't get the Italians." He added, "We did get the Portuguese to come into the Kandahar Airfield to help out with static security tasks but most NATO countries came out with national caveats that precluded them from assisting us in actually fighting in Pashmul." As one senior Canadian officer later described of Operation Medusa, "we were basically told you're on your fucking own for a while."[46]

The lack of allied participation was not only frustrating, it was also shocking considering what was at stake. As Fraser elaborated:

> The idea of failing here [i.e., not defeating the Taliban
> in Pashmul] was unacceptable. You want to talk about

pressure, this was about a city [Kandahar City], a country, an alliance, and Canada was right in the middle of it, both from a battle group and from a brigade point of view. The battle was everything and failure was not an option. This was not just an attack; it was not just an operational fight; it was a NATO fight, it was everything and the more that we got into this fight, the more the pink cards — the un-stated national caveats started to creep into it. The more we got into the fight, the more we found that this was exactly what NATO was built for. This was almost Cold War-like type of fighting. It was conventional fighting. But not everyone was prepared to participate.[47]

The fight, however, no longer rested with Hope and TF Orion. Their tour was quickly coming to an end and by early August they were already conducting a relief in place (RIP) with the 1 RCR BG or Task Force 3–06 as it was officially termed.[48] At 1600 hours, 19 August 2006, a small ceremony, the Transfer of Command Authority (TOCA) was taking place at Kandahar Airfield (KAF) between Lieutenant-Colonel Hope and Lieutenant-Colonel Omer Lavoie, the CO of TF 3–06. Within hours of the TOCA, before Operation Medusa could even be launched and with portions of his force having only been in theatre for a few weeks, Lavoie was fighting his first major battle.[49]

Reports from locals pointed to a continuation of the infiltration of insurgent fighters, as well as new leaders, into the Panjwayi district. More troublesome were reports that a large portion of the reinforcements moving into Pashmul were assessed as the more experienced Taliban fighters from out of area who were likely augmented by foreign fighters. They continued to reinforce their defensive positions in Pashmul but also began conducting noticeably more and better-coordinated attacks. They also demonstrated a large improvement in their use of fire and movement and their ability to coordinate and concentrate their fires. The insurgents began to conduct almost daily ambushes along major routes targeting ISAF and ANSF elements.

Courtesy Omer Lavoie.

Lieutenant-Colonel Omer Lavoie, CO TF 3–06.

The new task force reacted quickly and pushed out its companies to monitor enemy activity. "A" Coy, 1 RCR BG was deployed to the dominating high ground at Ma'Sum Ghar to observe the enemy. They arrived at approximately 1730–1800 hours, on 19 August 2006 and linked up with the Afghan National Police (ANP). This activity initiated a prompt response from the enemy. At approximately 1845 hours, with the TOCA ceremony barely finished, the Taliban launched a major assault against the Baazar-E-Panjwayi District Centre. "I had not anticipated," conceded Lavoie, "having my first command combat experience within hours of transfer of command authority."[50] Nonetheless, an estimated 300–500 insurgents armed with small arms and RPGs and using disciplined section fire and movement, began to manoeuvre to over-run the ANP and "A" Coy positions on Ma'Sum Ghar. Their assault entailed dismounted coordinated attacks from the three directions.

The enemy was engaged at a distance of 3,000 metres but they pushed on relentlessly. In the growing darkness, "A" Coy found it increasingly difficult to differentiate the enemy that was swarming over the adjacent peaks as they captured observation posts (OPs) from the ANP, who were quickly abandoning their positions. Major Mike Wright, the officer commanding "A" Company explained, "our first clue that the ANP no longer had control of the high feature was when we had the RPGs fired at us [from there]."[51]

The assaulting enemy was tenacious. The fight had lasted over three hours when "A" Coy pulled off the feature in darkness and under contact. They could no longer secure their position and were running low on ammunition and therefore, decided to pull back to more defensible ground to resupply and regroup. Within hours they were pushed back into the fight. In the end, however, the defence of the outer perimeter had blunted the attack against the ANP headquarters inside Baazar-E-Panjwayi. Coalition battle damage assessment indicated that approximately 80–100 insurgents were killed. In fact, local security forces recovered the bodies of at least 37 insurgents, a remarkable feat in itself as the Taliban were always meticulous in policing the battlefield so as not to leave any indication of their losses.

In the aftermath of the attack, events had reinforced once again that the Taliban build-up in the Panjwayi/Pashmul region represented a significant threat to ISAF and ANSF movement along Highway 1. In addition, it presented a formidable obstacle to the establishment of the Kandahar ADZ. Not surprisingly, the upcoming Operation Medusa took on an even greater importance.

Having beaten off the Taliban attack, Lavoie now focused his task force on the approaching mission. However, he still had to ensure the Taliban were kept in check until he was ready to launch Operation Medusa. As such, between 22–29 August, his Task Force undertook deterrence patrolling to prevent the Taliban from attacking the district centre. Lavoie gave formal orders on 27 August 2006. "TF Kandahar [designation of TF 3–06 for the operation]," he detailed, "will secure Pashmul in order to set the conditions for the Kandahar ADZ."[52] The CO outlined that he intended to achieve his mission by denying the enemy freedom of movement or action within the Panjwayi-Zhari-Kandahar-Argandab greenbelt, which had historically served as a significant sanctuary and transit route in past efforts to seize Kandahar City.

The operation was to be a joint ANSF/ISAF initiative, with the ANSF leading wherever possible. Lavoie explained, "The key to success of this operation lies in our ability to match our strengths against enemy weaknesses in order to constantly disrupt his decision cycle and prevent his C2 [command and control] assets from being able to react to our manoeuvre." As such, he directed that the Battle Group would "make maximum use of joint fires, ISR [intelligence, surveillance and reconnaissance], EW [electronic warfare] superior direct firepower capability, mobility and C2 to dominate the three-dimensional battle space and overwhelm an enemy capable of operating on only one plane of the battlefield."[53]

Lieutenant-Colonel Lavoie planned on deceiving the enemy into believing that a major assault was imminent on their lines of communication, as well as on their command and control nodes. He hoped to achieve this by advancing aggressively from east to west on two separate axes with two respective balanced company group (Coy Gp) teams — one advancing from the north and the other from the south. The plan was premised on the notion that once the Taliban understood that their critical vulnerabilities were being threatened by a major ground force, they would mass to defend themselves. This would allow ISAF assets to destroy them using precision fire from close air support (CAS), aviation, and artillery.

The precursor to the operation began on 1 September, when the Coy Gps moved to waiting areas located close to their objectives and conducted battle procedure in preparation for their opening roles. "B" and "C" Coy Gps were responsible for conducting feints north and south of Pashmul respectively with a view to drawing the enemy out of their defensive positions. Concurrently, because of the nature of the threat and terrain, "A" Coy Gp was to isolate Baazar-E-Panjwayi to provide flank protection to "C" Coy Gp. If successful in their actions, the enemy would be pummelled and annihilated by precision-guided munitions and indirect fire.[54]

The following day, 2 September 2006, at 0530 hours, TF Kandahar manoeuvred deployed elements into battle positions centred on enemy objectives in Panjwayi/Pashmul. "C" Coy, under command of Major Matthew Sprague was responsible for seizing Ma'Sum Ghar. They did so without incident arriving on the objective at 0600 hours, which was the intended "H-Hour."[55] By 0615 hours, Sprague radioed his higher HQ and declared that there was "no pattern of life across the river."[56] By 0630 hours air and artillery assets began to engage targets of opportunity. Inexplicably Brigade HQ cancelled a planned air strike on a number of known or suspected Taliban command and control nodes. Nonetheless, "C" Coy Gp joined the shooting gallery and engaged Taliban defensive positions from their commanding position on the heights of Ma'Sum Ghar.

As the operation began to unfold the initial impression was deceiving. Lieutenant-Colonel Lavoie received reports that there were no Taliban in Panjwayi. In addition, civilian women and children, reassured by the ANSF/ISAF presence, remained in their compounds. In Pashmul, coalition situation reports indicated that "23 of 25 TB [Taliban] in cemetery were KIA [killed in action]."[57] TF Kandahar HQ noted, "since operations have commenced, 80 TB have been detained by ANSF forces and it is assessed that 250 insurgents in the Objective area have been killed or wounded."[58] Despite these reports, the CO held his manoeuvre elements firm in their current battle positions. According to the Brigade plan the enemy was to be hammered for another 48 hours.

Despite the indirect fire being hurled at the enemy, Lieutenant-Colonel Lavoie faced a daunting situation. He was facing a numerically superior enemy who was well entrenched in complex terrain. However, Lavoie was not overly concerned. "Even though they [Taliban] had a 6–1 manpower ratio over us," revealed Lavoie, "they could never bring their superiority in numbers to bear or concentrate their force." Lavoie fought them by exploiting the electronic spectrum. Through his ISTAR capability he could often adjust to Taliban manoeuvres and react in such a way so as to disrupt their decision cycle. For instance, through unmanned aerial vehicles (UAVs) he could watch them manoeuvre to form an ambush, "which I could then counteract by firing hellfire missiles into that ambush site, followed by artillery." Furthermore, through their situational dominance the coalition forces could detect the enemy massing on mountaintops, or moving to a specific road junction and before the Taliban even reached their destination they would be bombarded with artillery. Consequently, asserted Lavoie, "we were able to keep just ahead of their decision cycle and prevent them from getting within ours and as a result we could normally outmaneuver them."[59]

At this point, not surprisingly, the CO was confident with the progress of the operation. Given that the enemy fighters were fixed within the Coalition cordon, though it was a very thin, loose noose, ISAF and the ANSF could now pummel the Taliban into submission. "Once that area was seized and the enemy was hemmed in from the north and the south, [the intent was] to continue to engage the enemy for the next three days with primarily offensive air support, as well as artillery and direct fire, in order to, from my perspective," explained Lavoie, "determine where the enemy actually was, and to degrade the enemy's ability to fight before we actually committed the main force into the attack."[60]

However, the absence of any major enemy action or movement created impressions of weakness in the eyes of some coalition leadership. They wondered whether the enemy had been destroyed or effectively weakened, or if they simply refused to take the bait, choosing to remain safely hunkered down in their prepared positions?

The MNB commander, Brigadier-General Fraser, visited the forward Coy Gp in the early afternoon on 2 September at Ma'Sum Ghar and decided that the Task Force would cross the Argahndab River without delay. "C" Coy Gp had already cleared two lanes from their battle positions on Ma'Sum Ghar down to the river. They had taken their bulldozers and ploughed two widely separated lanes through the grape fields directly to the river flood plain. With these preparations already in place, at 1400 hours, the officer commanding "C" Coy, his engineer detachment and a security platoon conducted a reconnaissance to map out possible crossing points.

"I drove up and down the river bed," recalled Sprague, "still thinking we would have two and a half days of bombardment in accordance with the plan so we could do this [assault river crossing] in a deliberate fashion." He added, "No one had been down to the river yet — it was not an issue of getting across, but rather getting a foothold on the other side." Sprague further explained, "The enemy side of the river was steep and heavily covered with brush."[61] It became evident that the only clear flat crossing point was alongside the main road directly in line with the famous white school complex in the village of Bayenzi, which caused so much grief for TF Orion a month prior during the desperate combat of 3 August.[62]

"This was the ground the enemy had chosen to defend," acknowledged Fraser, "[Objective] Rugby [the approximate area around the school complex] was where we assessed that the Taliban wanted us to fight them. That was their main battleground." The Brigade commander elaborated, "Their whole defence was structured to have us coming across the Arghandab River in the south and fight into Rugby." He added, "And the schoolhouse was the area in the centre, where there were big killing fields to the east and the north."[63] Surprisingly, this also became the ground ISAF agreed to fight on.

Fraser ordered Sprague to push the security platoon across the river and leave them on the far side. "I was unhappy with this," acknowledged Sprague since they would be isolated in terrain that the Coalition did not control, without a complete understanding of the size or location of the enemy force. The CO, Lieutenant-Colonel Lavoie, was successful in arguing that there was no tactical advantage to leaving a platoon exposed on the edge of enemy territory and they were withdrawn as darkness fell.

But during the middle of the night both the CO and OC were completely surprised by the ensuing orders from Fraser. "At midnight I heard we had to cross the river," recalled a perplexed Major Sprague.[64] The Brigade commander ordered the Task Force to conduct an assault river crossing at 0200 hours. Hard words were exchanged and Lavoie pushed back, concerned at the change in plan and lack of preparation. In essence, despite an apparently successful day of bombardment and cursory recce of the river, there were just too many unknowns. The crossing point was not marked; they had no data on flow rate or depth of the river; and, most important, they had little information on the enemy's disposition. Faced with these obstacles, Fraser relented and agreed to a first light attack.

Based on the pushed timelines, "C" Coy Gp had no choice but to use the only existing crossing point which led into the killing fields that the Brigade commander had previously described. On 3 September 2006, at 0445 hours, engineer elements crept out to clear the route soon to be used by the infantry. A slight delay was experienced because of the darkness and the necessity to wait for the air support package. Sprague recalled, "I gave combat team orders on the fly over the radio." He lamented, "half of the combat team wasn't even with me at 0545 hours." The orders for the attack were basically "single file, order of march and follow me," stated the OC.[65] At 0620 hours, the leading elements of "C" Coy Gp crossed the Arghandab River under cover of A-10 "Thunderbolt" and B2 fighter bomber aircraft.

At first, events unfolded well. "We crossed and got into a descent defensive posture and established a good foothold," explained Sprague, "we were in a half circle with 8 Platoon facing West, 7 Platoon facing North, the ANA and their American embedded training team (ETT) team facing northeast and the engineer Zettlemeyer and bulldozer and other support elements in the flat area behind us."[66] To Lieutenant Jeremy Hiltz, the 8 Platoon commander, the whole scene upon crossing was eerie — the landscape was completely still. "We knew deep down inside," he revealed, "we knew they [Taliban] were there ... but its still quiet and there's no indication that anything's wrong, except that guys are looking at each other, there's that feeling."[67]

To get through to the suspected enemy positions, however, "C" Coy Gp had to traverse a farmer's field that had been ploughed out. They also had to breach a series of ditches and berms. The ditches were approximately three to four feet deep and about eight feet wide in the middle of a huge marijuana field. The engineers took the dirt from the berms and simply filled in the ditches to make crossing points. Sprague sent 8 Platoon, dismounted, to clear some buildings on his left flank. He sent the ANA, also dismounted, off to his right flank to keep an eye on the main road. Then, shortly before 0800 hours, he sent 7 Platoon, mounted in their LAV IIIs, straight up the middle through the breach. "Initially," conceded Sprague, "We all thought this is too easy."[68]

Indeed, the enemy had not been idle. A variety of surveillance assets, as well as the deployed troops, began to report on Taliban activities in response to the assault. Groups of 10–15 insurgents were reported moving about and occupying three to five man ambush positions that overlooked IEDs planted on the route leading to the enemy position. These targets were continuously engaged. In fact, it became clear that there were a lot more enemy and that "C" Coy Gp had stirred up a hornet's nest.

Courtesy 1 RCR BG.

Canadian LAV IIIs operating in lush Arghandab terrain.

As 7 Platoon, or call-sign (CS) 31, emerged on the other side of the breach, they found themselves in the middle of a marijuana field. There was an eerie calm as the 7 Platoon LAVs pushed through the gap and took up an extended line facing the white school house complex approximately 50 metres away. The platoon second-in-command, Warrant Officer Rick Nolan, pulled up his LUVW (light utility vehicle wheel), the German manufactured *Gelaendenwagen*, more commonly referred to as the "G" Wagon, and took up his position.

The enemy displayed remarkable fire discipline. They allowed the Canadians to approach extremely close before they opened fire. When they did, it was with devastating effect. "It was dead quiet," remembered Master-Corporal Allan Johnson commanding CS 31A, a LAV III. Then he saw an enemy jump up on a roof and "all hell broke loose." Without warning, 7 Platoon was enveloped in fire from three directions. "The entire area just lit up," described Johnson, "We were taking fire from at least two sides, maybe three, with everything they had."[69]

The "C" Coy soldiers were ensnared in a horseshoe ambush. The engineer LAV was hit first, by a recoilless rifle round that killed Sergeant

Stachnik. The gunner and crew commander were left with minor shrapnel wounds. Both were leaning forward to look through their gun sights when the round came whistling in just missing them by inches. The round slammed into the LAV turret ring and sprayed shrapnel throughout the back of the LAV. Sergeant Stachnik was mortally wounded in the neck. The explosion also destroyed the radios so neither the OC, nor the platoon commander knew what had happened to their engineer call sign.

Shortly thereafter, Warrant Officer Nolan's "G" Wagon suffered a catastrophic hit. An RPG slammed into the unarmoured vehicle penetrating the passenger windshield. Nolan died instantly and the remainder of the occupants were severely shaken. Corporal Richard Furoy, a medic, was sitting directly behind Nolan. "Everything in the world came down on us and then, whoomp, the G-Wagon went black," recalled Furoy. "I sort of lost consciousness," he explained, "[but] I could still feel the spray of gunfire; I could feel the concussion of the rounds inside my chest, but I couldn't hear anything."[70] Corporal Sean Teal, remembered, "we sat there for a few minutes, we were joking around … then just a flash followed by a big burst of heat, the big crush. And then everything went black."[71]

Meanwhile, the entire platoon was hammered by small arms and RPG fire. Every weapon available fired in return, but no-one could see their antagonists. "The whole time," complained Private Mike O'Rourke, "you couldn't see a thing, you couldn't see any movement, nothing."[72] The marijuana plants were so high that the gunners in the turrets could not even see any targets. The barrels of the 25-mm chain guns soon glowed with heat. Many jammed because of the incessant firing. The pintle mounted machine guns soon ran short on ammunition. Even the Zettlemeyer bulldozer to the rear was quickly hit with an enemy 82-mm recoilless rifle and put out of action. "It was total chaos," remembered engineer Warrant Officer Roger Perreault.[73] Not surprisingly, it quickly became a fight for survival.

At the same time that 7 Platoon was engulfed in fire, 8 Platoon was fighting through a group of buildings on the left flank. Master-Corporal Ward Engley's section dismounted to secure a large ditch. "All of a sudden the whole world exploded around us," recalled Engley. RPGs, mortars, small arms, and machine-gun fire, seemingly coming from all directions, slashed the air. Nevertheless, the 1 RCR soldiers made their way to clear the complex array of compounds and buildings. They were required to go back and clear out buildings that had already been cleaned out because the compounds had so many passages and tunnels that enabled the enemy to use their greater knowledge of the terrain to re-infiltrate previously cleared areas. Adding to the problems of the 8 Platoon soldiers were malfunctioning grenades, which forced the troops to use their M72 66-mm rocket launchers to clear buildings. A door would be kicked in and the M72 tube punched into the room and fired. The effect of the blast and concussion gave the soldiers bursting into the room the necessary edge.

The ANA were also heavily engaged. The ANA seemed fearless. Initially trailing behind "C" Coy, as soon as the Taliban ambush erupted, the ANA troops "ran past us with their kit firing on the run," described Sergeant Donovan Crawford with admiration. "They raced up without hesitation," he added.[74] Lieutenant Ray Corby added, "they [ANA] are quick, aggressive and eager."[75]

At one point, it seemed that luck was simply not with "C" Coy Gp. A French Mirage jet zoomed in to deliver badly needed air support but for some inexplicable reason the 1,000-pound global positioning system (GPS)-guided bomb went off course and landed 20 feet from Sprague and his men. Sprague recalled, "the entire firefight stopped as everyone watched this bomb bounce towards us." He recalled, "I thought we're fucked now." Corporal Rodney Grubb reminisced, "In the middle of all this chaos, we see this big, black fuck-off bomb coming towards us." He added, "it was like a big, black steel football. It hit the ground and bounced and bounced and bounced." Grubb hit the ground and concluded, "okay, we're done."[76] Fortuitously, the bomb never went off.[77]

As the recovery of vehicles began, the firefight intensified and "C" Coy continued to be plagued by mishaps. The tow vehicle, a G-Wagon, detailed to recover Nolan's G-Wagon missed the breach and fell into the ditch. After two and a half hours of attempting to recover it, Sprague made the call to blow in place (BIP), destroy the vehicle to deny any advantage to the enemy. Work was also underway to recover the engineer LAV that had been struck by the 82-mm recoilless rifle when the unconscious driver came to and drove the damaged vehicle out.

Not so fortunate was CS 31B, another LAV. As the platoon tried to withdraw from the trap it found itself in the driver backed into a ditch. Like a beached whale, the LAV was stranded and unable to move. Half suspended, its wheels were spinning wildly in the air. It now became a preferred target for the enemy and RPG rounds sailed in, a number of them finding the target. The back door was hit rendering it useless. Other rounds smacked into the vehicle — its armour saving those inside. Ten or more soldiers were in the overcrowded LAV, which also held the body of Warrant Officer Nolan. They now had to make their exit through the escape hatch. One at a time they left the vehicle to dash to the closest piece of shelter and provide covering fire for the next individual to run the enemy's gauntlet of fire. Because of the circumstances, the body of the platoon warrant was initially left behind.

As the fight raged, 9 Platoon, located in a firebase position on Ma'Sum Ghar, was frustrated at their lack of ability to fully support their sister platoons. "We called in for a reference," explained Sergeant Jamie Walsh, "so one of the sections threw out white smoke and told us everything east of the white smoke was friendly, everything west was enemy. So we just used the white smoke as a reference point and just started hammering everything, trying to keep their [Taliban] heads down to let [call sign] 31 recover their casualties and be able to pull off the position."[78]

Major Matthew Sprague realized that there was not much more he could do so he directed more fire forward and calmly organized the withdrawal of his forces, ensuring that both the casualties and disabled vehicles were recovered. Warrant Officer Frank Mellish established a casualty collection point (CCP) behind the now disabled Zettlemeyer in a hollow in the ground. When Mellish discovered that the body of his best friend was still in the stranded vehicle he grabbed Private Will Cushley to assist him retrieve the corpse. Before they could move an 82-mm recoilless rifle round slammed into the casualty collection point spraying the area with hot molten shrapnel. Mellish and Cushley were mortally wounded.

The withdrawal continued and all the wounded and dead were pulled from the bloody field of battle. All the stranded vehicles that could not be recovered were "BIP'd" by close air support. The attempted assault on the enemy positions had been costly. The task force suffered eight wounded and four killed.

"How more people weren't killed," pondered Sprague, "I don't know."[79] He asserted, "This wasn't some one-hour firefight we were in — we were fucking fighting for our lives, for seven hours."[80] Private Daniel Roasti asked the same question. "I'm convinced someone was watching over us," he stated, "The amount of bullets that were flying, I just don't know why some of us are still here."[81]

By 1700 hours, 3 September, ISAF's intelligence assessed, "the enemy believe that they are winning, and their morale is assessed as high." In fact, the Taliban quickly claimed victory following the withdrawal of "C" Coy back to their battle positions on Ma'Sum Ghar. Moreover, despite the loss of a significant numbers of Taliban fighters, the Coalition intelligence concluded that it did not have a demoralizing affect on those who remained. In fact, the defence of Pashmul became a rallying point for the local Taliban insurgents and they began pushing reinforcements into the area and remanning many of the abandoned ambush positions.

The change in the original coalition plan created a great deal of dissension within the ranks. Many of the participants could not understand why things were "rushed" and why the additional 48 hours of bombardment were not permitted. Retrospectively, they argued that this would have weakened the enemy physically and psychologically and provided more time to map out the enemy's strength and disposition.

Lieutenant-Colonel Lavoie was never given a reason for the change in plan but he suspected that the initial success, specifically how easily "C" Coy Gp had seized Panjwayi, had created a false impression in the higher headquarters. Originally, "everyone was expecting a real fight, but it never materialized," stated Lavoie. "We rolled through the village unopposed, seized the high features [Ma'Sum Ghar and Ma'ar Ghar], isolated the village and then started pounding the enemy on the other side," explained the CO. He believed this unmitigated victory created the impression there was an opportunity to exploit. "They wanted to rush it through," stated Lavoie, "so I asked what happened to the original timelines." He described how each layer of leadership is continuously pushing for results on the ground. A now seasoned Lavoie concluded,

"Now, I just say no — I learned my lesson the hard way at the beginning of the operation."[82]

Lavoie was not so far wrong. Brigadier-General Fraser conceded, "I would say there was a tremendous amount of pressure from ISAF to 'get it done!'"[83] However, he disagreed with the soldiers' criticisms. "You don't fight a plan," he explained, "you fight the enemy guided by a plan." He added, "the enemy also has a vote and if you ignore the enemy you will lose."[84] By 2 September Fraser believed the situation was changing and he felt it opportune to attack. In short, he felt there was nothing to be gained by waiting another 48 hours. "I knew a lot of the enemy were there," he acknowledged:

> But, you know, you do two more days of bombardment, how many do you kill? How do you know that? You guess. No matter if you went in on the 2nd, 3rd, 4th, 5th or 6th, guess what ladies and gentlemen? It is a difficult thing to cross a river and to go into a main defensive area where the Taliban were waiting and wanted to fight on. It would have been gut-wrenching, whatever day was picked to go across the river.[85]

Lieutenant-Colonel Schreiber revealed another catalyst. By the night of 2 September, local nationals were reporting that the Taliban were actually abandoning their positions — that they were running away. "The locals said they're [Taliban] abandoning their positions, they're leaving. And [we knew] they [Taliban] could get out, because they had covered routes in and out, so we had to rely on local reports."[86] As soon as ISAF headquarters received this information pressure began immediately to act. The ISAF deputy commander (security) pushed the brigade. Schreiber described the ISAF sentiment as one of "They're [Taliban] leaving, you're [MNB] letting them out of the bag," An overwhelming concern by everyone was that the Taliban would escape and then the coalition would have to fight them again some other place. Therefore, the deputy commander (security) directed, "the Taliban are leaving, so you got to get in there and get after them."[87] General Richards agreed. And as a result, as Schreiber remembered, "we started to get a significant amount of pressure to get in there and to actually find out what was going on, on Objective Rugby.[88]

Regardless of the debacle of 3 September, seemingly in light of the pressure from higher, the Brigade commander ordered the task force to try again the following morning. The plan was to try and draw the enemy out by feinting more to the south, forcing the Taliban to react and leave their fortified positions. Then, as per the original plan, the enemy could be annihilated with coalition air, aviation, and indirect fire.

Reveille for "C" Coy Gp on 4 September was 0530 hours. They were to launch an hour later. They followed their normal routine — ablutions and burning garbage. Then disaster struck. "I knew immediately what happened," remembered Sprague, "you can't mistake that noise." The A-10 was called in to attack an enemy position identified by a small fire.

Courtesy 1 RCR BG.

A Taliban fortified entrenchment in Panjwayi.

When the responding pilot popped-up over Ma'Sum Ghar, he spotted the burning garbage on Battle Position 301 and became briefly disorientated. Before he realized his error, he unleashed a partial burst of deadly fire from his seven-barrelled 30-mm Gatling gun killing former Olympic athlete Private Mark Graham and wounding 35 others, including the "C" Coy Gp OC.[89] "The first rounds hit about 10 metres behind me," Corporal Jordache Young recalled, "We saw flashes and looked back — it was mass devastation."[90] Sergeant Brent Crellin stated, "There were sparks in the dust, like the sparklers you wave on Canada Day." He continued, "And then we heard the burp of the gun and then we felt sick."[91]

The latest calamity to hit "C" Coy Gp was disastrous. Having lost most of its command structure and almost a third of its strength, it was now combat ineffective. "Twenty minutes away from an assault river crossing and Omer [Lieutenant-Colonel Lavoie] lost half a company," recounted Fraser, "We delayed 24 hours but at the end of the day we had to get it done."[92]

A pause was now required to regroup and plan out the next steps. What was left of "C" Coy Gp was sent back to the Kandahar Airfield to regroup and send off their dead. They returned to Ma'Sum Ghar on 6 September 2006, to rejoin the fight. General Rick Hillier, the CDS at the time, summed up "C" Coy's resilience:

> [Labour Day Weekend 2006,] On that terrible week-end, they lost a company commander in action, lost a company sergeant-major, lost one out of three platoon commanders, lost all three platoon warrant officers, one wounded, two killed, lost five section commanders out of nine and lost all of the sections' second in command master-corporals — a total of 40-plus wounded and five killed in a 48-hour period. They all stepped. A young sergeant promoted to sergeant last July became the company sergeant-major. Young master-corporals became platoon commanders and platoon second-in-commands. And young soldiers became section commanders and they carried on the operation and the fight against the Tali-

ban that gave NATO such an incredible boost right at the start of the mission. Now, if that's not a Canadian epic ... I don't know what is.[93]

By the time "C" Coy returned a new battle plan had taken form. First, on 6 September Brigadier-General Fraser requested tanks from General Hillier because his forces were facing a dug-in enemy.[94] Second, the emphasis was shifted from the South to the Northern flank, onto the shoulders of "B" Coy Group. Up until this time "B" Coy had largely sat out the action and had only sporadic and limited fire fights with Taliban forces. They were now the primary effort.

Before launching the second assault, however, Brigadier-General Fraser had to reform his brigade. First he created Task Force Grizzly, which consisted of the remainder of "C" Coy combined with an American rifle company, as well as the American national command element, which became the TF HQ.[95] "Based on the results of our first probe [on 3 September], it became clear that I needed to adjust," explained Fraser,

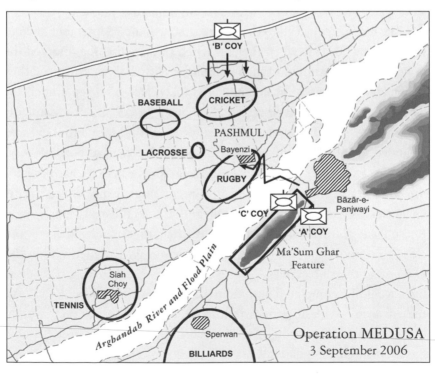

Operation MEDUSA
3 September 2006

adding that "the enemy had focused on where he thought we were going to cross the Arghandab River from the south." Quite simply, the ground the coalition had attacked "was key terrain tactically for the Taliban and they had reinforced and defended the northern shore of the Arghandab River," with tenacity and resilience.[96]

At the start of the second assault on 6 September, once the redeployment was complete, Fraser ordered Lieutenant-Colonel Lavoie and his Task Force to deliberately put pressure on the enemy to force the Taliban to react. Instead of the Canadians continuing to move into ground of the enemy's choosing, Fraser now wanted to force the Taliban to react to their choice of terrain. Simultaneously, Fraser ordered Task Force 31, which consisted of U.S. Special Forces and an Afghan Kandak (battalion/unit) with its U.S. Embedded Training Team to move north into Sperwan Ghar at the same time as the 1 RCR BG started moving from the north, clearing towards the Arghandab River. Fraser also had special operations forces operating in the Reg Desert to interdict any reinforcements coming from, or retreating enemy attempting to escape to, Pakistan. The intent was to clear the ground step by step and capture or destroy as many Taliban as possible.

The renewed push started, as already stated, on 6 September 2006 in the north by "B" Coy when they breached the tree line that marked the divide between friendly and enemy territory. With the breach in place, they systematically began to push South. Two days later, on 8 September, "B" Coy, which had now linked up with Mohawk 6 (a U.S. infantry company — "A" Coy, 2nd Battalion, 4th Regiment, 10th Mountain Division, mounted in HUMVEEs), was now in forward defensive positions and began to create lanes and breaches in the grape fields to be used as run-ups for the LAV IIIs. Both companies increasingly experienced enemy engagements as they slowly exerted pressure southwards. Each night Recce Platoon would plot out the route. Then, preceded by artillery and close air support, the rifle companies would engage the enemy and seize and secure their objectives. As one objective was secured, a passage of lines would be completed and the next assault element would continue the advance. "With all arms working together and under the constant umbrella of air cover," noted the TF 3–06 CO, "my BG advanced towards Pashmul and the Arghandab River."[97]

Courtesy Graeme Smith.

Soldiers from "B" Coy wait for smoke to clear before assaulting an enemy compound.

The 1 RCR BG was now hitting its stride. Two days later on 10 September 2006, "B" Coy seized the northern half of Objective Cricket setting the conditions for Mohawk 6 to move through them and capture the southern portion of Objective Cricket the following day. Throughout, TF Grizzly conducted feints to the south to fix the enemy on Objective Rugby. "Task Force Grizzly was doing a great job keeping the enemy preoccupied in the south while TF 3–06 just cleared down from the north," lauded the Brigade commander. "Intelligence was telling us, despite the attack and heavy bombardments, we were actually seeing fighters who were risking staying in place," revealed Fraser. Nonetheless, he conceded, "The [enemy] command and control was still very effective and still pressing very hard for the fighters to keep on going, even though they were taking a pounding."[98]

Meanwhile, as the operation unfolded, Task Force 31 was heavily engaged in Sperwan Ghar in a fight that lasted over three days. Despite severe opposition, Task Force 31 was prevailing. "The enemy was just dumping on them," described Fraser adding that "the Taliban [in this

Courtesy Graeme Smith.

"B" Coy soldiers clearing a compound during their push into Objective Rugby.

location] were coming across the intervening ground in convoys of trucks, dumping off 5 to 10 guys from each truck, all who just unloaded and attacked Task Force 31's position." Fraser acknowledged, "It became a turkey shoot. In one night, I think they killed between 100 to 200 Taliban, it was a phenomenal shoot."[99]

At the same time, TF Grizzly was also meeting with success. As a result of the changing dynamic on the battlefield, "we made the decision to press really hard," explained Fraser. He added:

> I mean, it's a feeling in a battle — you can feel the battle when you got the enemy. Its something you cannot teach, you just got to know when to push. Our forces got to that stage. You read the intelligence; you read what the soldiers were doing on the field; and then you just realize it — okay, it's time to push. And we went out there and we pushed because the enemy was starting to pull back, even though we were not in any great strength there.[100]

On 11 September 2006, with Objective Cricket captured and the engineers beginning to improve the routes for better manoeuvre, Brigadier-General Fraser pushed Task Force Grizzly, with the remainder of "C" Coy, north across the across Arghandab River. "So I said, okay, we got something really big in Siah Choy and in Sperwan Ghar, and there is little pressure coming out of the main stronghold, so I pushed TF 3–06 to get down and take our main objective, which we called Rugby, in Panjwayi," he explained, "At the same time I told Task Force Grizzly to get across the Arghandab River get into the eastern side of Rugby and roll up the Taliban position from the flank, realizing that the Taliban would then collapse."[101]

As always the plan did not unfold so easily. TF Grizzly struggled to get across the river. Reinforced with ANP they finally managed to gain a foothold. The MNB commander then pressed the TF commander to get "Charles" Company (minus), supported by elements of ISTAR (intelligence, surveillance, target acquisition, reconnaissance) squadron, across the river. This too was done against "medium" enemy resistance. Once TF

Courtesy 1 RCR BG.

Aerial view of the 3 September battle. The white school house complex can be seen in the middle of the photograph.

Grizzly gained lodgement into the enemy trench line, Fraser ordered, "TF 3–06 [in the North] to push hard and link-up with TF Grizzly because once we had the momentum going and the Taliban started to fall back, I just wanted to keep the pressure on."[102]

By 12 September, Mohawk 6 had pushed onto Objective Lacrosse. Concurrently, "A" Coy, 1 RCR BG was preparing to move onto the eastern portion of Objective Rugby. The enemy seemed to be dispersing. The troops found well-constructed entrenchments but they were abandoned. "It looked like they were prepared for a fight," explained Major Geoff Abthorpe, "B" Coy commander, but I think over the last few days they lost their gumption to fight and they pulled out before we showed up."[103] At 1400 hours, "B" Coy, 1 RCR BG seized Rugby centre. Both companies hunkered down for the night to set the conditions for Mohawk 6 to take Rugby West at first light the next morning. Once completed, this would allow for the link-up of TF Kandahar (TF 3–06/1 RCR BG) and TF Grizzly. It would also permit the engineers to clear routes and compounds found with unexploded ordnance, bunker, and tunnel complexes.

By 13 September NATO estimated that it now controlled 65 percent of the objective territory.[104] Coalition intelligence assessed that the insurgents in the Panjwayi/Zhari area had withdrawn west or had stored their weapons and remained in the region. Those fighters not from the area had exfiltrated west along the Arghandab River valley or through Arghandab district off to the north. The following day, 14 September, at first light, Mohawk 6 seized Objective Rugby West. They met no enemy resistance.

Brigadier-General Fraser explained, "At that stage of the game, we had great pressure on the enemy — we were coming from the north, from the south and from the southeast." He elaborated:

> We had three task forces that moved in with significant pressure. Lieutenant-Colonel Lavoie and his 1 RCR BG linked up with TF Grizzly, which was pushing towards them from the southeast to the northwest. Meanwhile, the moment Sperwan Ghar was secured by Task Force 31, I ordered them to push to Siah Choy. We thought we were going to have a huge fight in Siah Choy based

on our experience and the Taliban tenacity at Sperwan Ghar, which was just staggering. As a result, I told the other two Task Forces to just stand by because the main effort that morning was going to be Task Force 31 and their push to Siah Choy. I allotted them priority on artillery, aviation and everything else.[105]

Remarkably, TF 31 seized Siah Choy without firing a shot. The Taliban had fled. At that point, Fraser pushed his brigade to exploit — he ordered all to move into Phase 3 of Operation Medusa. "Now you have the enemy on the run and now is the time to take the ground," concluded the Brigade commander. Fraser explained, "And, I wanted TF 3–06 to take that ground because of what they lost there — they took some heavy casualties and I mean for them, there was psychological value in that terrain." He added, "In fact, I was there when "Charles" Company actually took it and I was so happy that they were the ones who went across and seized the ground — I thought, 'you took it, no one else did, you guys did it' and that was another reason why I assigned them to TF Grizzly in the south — this was important for that company because it came at a high cost."[106]

In the end, Fraser assessed, "after all that pressure, after all that time, the enemy just collapsed and they went to ground."[107] The conditions for the Brigade to move from Phase 3 (exploitation) to Phase 4 (reconstruction) was the creation of a secured area of operations in the Pashmul district. As the situation remained fluid, exact dispositions took time to sort out. Nonetheless, ISAF now placed an emphasis on returning the civilian population and creating freedom of action for the GoA and development agencies in order to set the necessary preconditions for the establishment of the Kandahar Advanced Development Zone.

Once again a phased approach was taken. In fact, a three-stage plan was developed. The first stage entailed restoring security through the visible employment of ANSF throughout the area with RC(S) forces in support. It was also to be the commencement of an enduring ANA/ANP presence in the Pashmul/Panjwayi area. The next stage called for resettlement. In coordination with the Disaster Management Committee and key district leaders, along with the UN and appropriate civil agencies,

Brigadier-General Fraser (middle) meets with two of his task force commanders to assess the progress of Operation Medusa.

ISAF forces were earmarked to assist with the return of the civilian population to the area. Finally, the third and last stage of Operation Medusa was the development piece where the larger and more enduring projects targeted for long term development would be started. The end state to Operation Medusa was described as being achieved when "the people of Afghanistan have freedom of movement along Highway 1, the villagers of Pashmul and greater Zhari have returned to their villages and the Taliban have been denied freedom of action in the vicinity of the Kandahar ADZ."[108]

By 15 September 2006, the various task forces began pushing their presence further out from their original objective areas. Although there were no enemy engagements, locals were observed fleeing the area, which normally portends no good fortune. However, in this case there was no combat. At the same time, the GoA and ISAF began radio and television broadcasts to encourage locals to return to their homes, explaining that the fighting had stopped. By 16 September some of the task forces such as Mohawk 6 were redeployed to KAF. The next day, 1

RCR BG began to rotate its companies through KAF for rest and refit, maintaining two company groups on security and clearance operations in the AOR.

It seemed that by 17 September 2006, Operation Medusa, aside from the non-kinetic Phase 4 reconstruction phase, was over. The MNB, but particularly 1 RCR BG that bore the brunt of the fighting in the Pashmul area, had indeed defeated the Taliban. The cost, however, was not inconsequential. In total, the Canadians had lost five killed and approximately 40 wounded. The fact that Canada bore the brunt of the fighting was not hard to discern. One reporter noted, "Canadians are getting killed at a rate five times the average for NATO and U.S. forces in Afghanistan, where Canada's soldiers have suffered more than one-quarter of the combat deaths in Afghanistan [in 2006].[109]

The impact of the victory, however, was hailed as a monumental success. A NATO statement was swiftly broadcast announcing the victory:

> NATO launched its largest ever combat operation, against a well-prepared and determined enemy. It was fought to the south west of Kandahar City, in the Panshwaye and Zhari districts. It was here that the Taliban filtered in large numbers of insurgents in to first taken and then, far more significantly, hold the area. It was a trial of strength that will have a lasting effect both militarily and on the hearts and minds of the Afghan people.[110]

Another NATO missive declared, "The operation has met its initial aims by dealing a severe blow to the leadership and forces of the extremists so that they are no longer a cohesive force and have had to dispense after suffering important losses."[111] A political official was less restrained. He remarked that Operation Medusa, "wiped the floor with the Taliban."[112]

Not surprisingly, NATO leadership used the success to push select messages. General James L. Jones, commander of Allied Command Operations cooed, "It has been necessary to fight in this instance to achieve the required effect. Importantly it has proved that NATO will not shirk from taking robust action where necessary and especially given the level of insurgent activity."[113] Similarly, ISAF commander, Lieutenant-General David Richards, boasted:

> Operation Medusa has been a significant success and clearly shows the capability that Afghan, NATO and Coalition forces have when they operate together. I always said that I would be robust when necessary, and that is what I have done. The Taliban had no choice but to leave … Having created a secure environment in the area, it is now time for the real work to start. Without security, there can be no reconstruction and development. Without reconstruction and development there can be no long-lasting security.[114]

According to Lieutenant-General Richards, Operation Medusa was a key battle against the Taliban insurgency. "If Kandahar fell," he explained, "and it was reasonably close run last year, it did not matter how well the Dutch did in Uruzgan or how well the British did in Helmand. Their two provinces would also, as night followed day, have failed because we would have lost the consent of the Pashtun people because of the totemic importance of Kandahar."[115]

The Afghan government also hailed the success of Operation Medusa. Provincial Governor Assadullah Khalid stated on 17 September 2006, "Six nations fought side by side to inflict significant casualties on the entrenched insurgent forces, who could have avoided this sad loss of life by reconciling with the legitimate Afghan government."[116]

He added, "The ability of the Taliban to stay and fight in groups is finished. The enemy has been crushed."[117]

The largely Canadian action did not go unheralded by its national command either. The CDS, General Rick Hillier, asserted, "Afghan ministers will tell you that operation [Medusa] saved Afghanistan." He explained, "If Kandahar had been encircled, if Highway 1 had been shut down and if the Panjwayi had been held by the Taliban, the government in Kabul would have fallen."[118] Brigadier-General Fraser simply added, "It was one of the hardest things we've done for a very long time. Canada led the operation,

NATO's biggest one ever, and successfully defeated the Taliban in this area. Canada did what was right and the cost was not insignificant."[119]

In more private settings the MNB commander was more unrestrained. "The ISAF commander was ecstatic," Fraser revealed, "He [Richards] just could not believe what we were able to accomplish." Fraser elaborated, "He was enthusiastic, I mean psychologically, what our troops did was impressive. They saved the city of Kandahar, arguably saved the country and they saved the alliance. They proved that NATO could fight as a coalition.[120] The MNB commander concluded, "We defeated the Taliban with only four casualties [killed]. Then the Taliban tried to bug out one night. Not many made it out. We saved the city, and in so doing, saved the country."[121]

NATO's initial assessment claimed 512 Taliban were killed and 136 captured.[122]

Lieutenant-Colonel Schreiber stated, "it is a conservative estimate that the Taliban suffered 1,500 casualties (1,000 wounded, 500 dead)."[123] Brigadier-General Fraser's assessment was similar."We think we probably killed about 300 to 400 and captured 136, which includes the death of approximately five senior commanders on the ground." He added, "that's a significant defeat, the worst defeat the Taliban ever experienced in probably 40 years according to the Afghan Minister of Defence."[124]

The effects of Operation Medusa seemed impressive. "Casualties from roadside bombs and suicide attacks have fallen from 245 in September to 29 for the first two weeks of November," boasted British Brigadier-General Richard Nugee, "and soldiers in Panjwayi have started an $8m reconstruction drive."[125] The assessment, however, is subjective. The local Aghans had a completely different perspective. "The bombing and the fighting destroyed our mosque, our homes and our vineyards," said one farmer. "The Taliban are gone, bus so is most everything else."[126]

Similarly, the longer term assessment is more difficult to discern. Brigadier-General Fraser explained:

> So, when the enemy left we knew we had won this fight. However, we also realized that they would evolve. We knew the enemy would go back, they would go to ground

for a bit [disperse and regroup in safe areas] and that they would do an after action review, after which they would come back at us in a far more sophisticated and dangerous way. They always do, they always adapt. The only question we had was how long was it going to take them to replace their leaders and how long was it going to take for them to come back at us again and what form would it take. When they did come back at us, they did so very quickly. They hit us with suicide attacks, IEDs and ambushes. So was it a surprise? No. Are they more dangerous now? Yes.[127]

An official Canadian report agreed. "It is expected that the kinetic effects of OP Medusa will be transitory," it stated, "The TB [Taliban] has demonstrated that they are adept at infiltrating fighters into the region and it is expected that enemy force numbers will be replenished in the coming months. Consequently, there is no belief that the TB movement has been defeated in Kandahar province, nor in RC (S).... Ironically, there is some unofficial suggestion that the TB will enter into a more dangerous posture reverting back to terrorist tactics involving the use of suicide bombers and IEDs to inflict casualties on ISAF forces."[128]

Nonetheless, Lieutenant-Colonel Omer Lavoie and his Task Force rolled into Phase IV of Operation Medusa after having defeated the entrenched Taliban forces in a bitter struggle. But, Lavoie was not misled by what he and his soldiers accomplished. "Phase IV of Operation Medusa, reconstruction, is the most important," he commented, "that will actually defeat vice just killing the enemy."[129]

In the end, regardless of long term assessment the immediate success of Operation Medusa at the time was both critical to the government of Afghanistan and to the NATO alliance. In the humble words of Major Marty Lipcsey, the deputy commanding officer of TF 3–06, "it was quite a battle."[130] The brunt of that epic struggle, however, was born by the tenacious soldiers the 1 RCR Battle Group. Lavoie's assessment that "The soldiers under my command have proven their courage and determination time and time again," is not based on false pride. As American secretary of state Condoleezza Rice asserted, "[the Taliban] have learned a tough lesson that the Canadians are fierce fighters."[131] In the hot, inhospitable terrain of Panjwayi, Canadian soldiers once again proved their tenacity and courage in what can easily be termed not a small action.

NOTES

1. The Naval Task Force consisted of two frigates, a destroyer, a supply ship, and Sea King helicopters with over 1,000 personnel. An additional frigate from the West Coast, HMCS Vancouver, also integrated into a U.S. carrier battle group. The Canadian commitment also authorized more than 100 Canadian Forces personnel who were serving on exchange programs in the United States and with other allied military forces to participate in any operations conducted by their host units in response to the recent terrorist attack.

2. Lieutenant-Colonel Pat Stogran was the commanding officer. During their six months in Afghanistan, 3 PPCLI Battle Group performed tasks ranging from airfield security to combat operations.

3. The Taliban government in Kabul fell 13 November 2001, and multinational forces took control of the Taliban homeland of Kandahar on 7 December 2001. Nonetheless, Canadian air, sea, and SOF elements remained to support the Coalition force efforts.

4. The International Security Assistance Force is a United Nations-mandated operation, but NATO led. It was authorized by United Nations Security Council Resolutions (UNSCRs) 1386, 1413, 1444, and 1510. UNSCR 1386 (20 December 2001), as well as UNSCR 1413, authorize ISAF to operate under chapter 7 of the UN Charter (peace-enforcing). Furthermore, under UNSCR 1444 (27 November 2002) the role of ISAF remained to assist in the maintenance of security and to help the Afghan Transitional Authority (Afghan TA) and the initial activities of the United Nations in Kabul and its environs — nowhere else. However, UNSCR 1510 (13 October 2003) authorized the expansion of the ISAF mandate beyond the original provision of security in the Kabul area into the rest of Afghanistan. The

first ISAF troops deployed as a multinational force (without Canadian participation) initially under British command on 4 January 2002.

5. The last Canadian material assets were moved and shipped to Kandahar on 29 November 2005 and Camp Julien was officially handed over to the Afghan Ministry of Defence.

6. The PRT brings together elements from the Canadian Forces, the Department of Foreign Affairs and International Trade, the Canadian International Development Agency, and the Royal Canadian Mounted Police in an effort to reinforce the authority of the Afghan government by assisting in stabilization and development in the Kandahar region.

7. NATO took control of ISAF in 2003. Since then it expanded to the North in 2004 (Stage 1), to the west in 2005 (Stage 2) and its plan to move to the south (Stage 3) transpired in 2005–06.

8. The 1 PPCLI Battle Group consisted of 1 PPCLI, a tactical unmanned aerial vehicle (TUAV) troop, an HSS, company, a forward support group (FSG), and the Kandahar Provincial Reconstruction team. Hope stated that he chose the name Orion to give everyone a common identifier. "I chose Orion from the constellation — representing the mythical Greek hunter of mountain beasts — that I knew blessed the Afghan skies, so that our soldiers might look up and seeing it, feel part of a larger entity, enduring and meaningful." Ian Hope, "Reflections on Afghanistan: Commanding Task Force Orion," in Bernd Horn, ed., *In Harm's Way. The Buck Stops Here: Senior Officers on Operations* (Kingston: CDA Press, 2007), 212.

9. "1st Battalion Princess Patricia's Canadian Light Infantry Battle Group (Task Force Orion) — Operational Summary," 12 August 2006; and Hope, "Reflections on Afghanistan," 212. Hope stated, "Our tasks were multifarious, divided into three broad categories: governance, security and reconstruction."

10. Despite all the sensors and HUMINT, Hope noted that he "never had more than 20 percent of the information. Most often not even that much." Lieutenant-Colonel Ian Hope, presentation — Canadian Infantry Association Annual General Meeting, 25 May 2007.

11. Hope, "Reflections on Afghanistan," 216–17.

12. Hope, presentation, 25 May 2007.

13. Captain Kevin Barry, TF Orion QRF commander, 1 CMBG briefing, 22 January 2007.

14. Lieutenant-Colonel Shane Schreiber, ACOS, Multinational Brigade HQ, 1 CMBG briefing, 22 January 2007.

15. The SENLIS Council, *Canada in Kandahar: No Peace to Keep. A Case Study of the Military Coalitions in Southern Afghanistan*, London, June 2006, v.

16. *Ibid.*, xi.

17. *Ibid.*, 31.

18. "Brigade and Battle Group Operations — Kandahar and Helmand — July 2006," CO's PPT presentation. ANSF consisted of the ANA, Afghan National Police, and border forces.

19. Captain Andrew Charchuk, "'Contact C' A Forward Observation Officer with Task Force Orion," *The Canadian Army Journal*, Vol. 10, No. 2, Summer 2007, 25.

20. Christie Blatchford, *Fifteen Days* (Toronto: Doubleday Canada, 2007), 13.

21. Schreiber, 1 CMBG briefing, 22 January 2007.

22. Lieutenant-Colonel Ian Hope, *Dancing with the Dushman: Command Imperatives for the Counter-Insurgency Fight in Afghanistan* (Kingston: CDA Press, 2008).

23. Schreiber, 1 CMBG briefing, 22 January 2007.

24. *Ibid.*

25. Interview with author, 24 January 2007.

26. Terry Pedwell, "Taliban 'Were Too Organized,'" *Canadian Press*, 4 August 2006.

27. Interview with author, 24 January 2007.

28. Interview with author, 21 October 2006. The interview has been captured in full in Brigadier-General David Fraser, "No Small Victory: Insights of the Commander of Combined Task Force Aegis on Operation Medusa," in Colonel Bernd Horn, ed., *In Harms Way. The Buck Stops Here: Operational Perspectives of Senior Military Leaders* (Kingston: CDA Press, 2007), 243–256.

29. Hope, *Dancing with the Dushman.*

30. Blatchford, 250.

31. Interview with author, 21 October 2006.

32. This refers to the Maoist model of insurgency: Phase 1 — Strategic Defence: Focus on survival and building support. Bases are established, local leaders are recruited, cellular networks and parallel governments created; Phase 2 — Strategic Stalemate: Guerrilla warfare ensues. Insurgents focus on separating population from government; Phase 3 — Strategic Offensive: Insurgents feel they have superior strength and move to conventional operations to destroy government capability.

33. Interview with author, 21 October 2006.

34. *Ibid.*

35. *Ibid.*

36. Blatchford, 251.

37. Interview Brigadier-General David Fraser with author, 21 October 2006.

38. Schreiber, 1 CMBG briefing, 22 January 2007.

39. Memo, Director Army Training to Commander Land Force Development Training System, "Tactical Reconnaissance Report — Training Assessment OP Archer Rotation 3," 21 September 2006, 3. SPG refers to the Soviet designation Stankovyy Protivotankovyy Granatamet or, literal translation, mounted anti-tank grenade launcher. In NATO terminology it refers to a anti-tank recoilless rifle.

40. General Rick Hillier, the CDS at the time, explained in an interview, "The challenge is that marijuana plants absorb energy, heat very readily. It's very difficult to penetrate them with thermal devices ... And as a result you really have to be careful that the Taliban don't dodge in and out of those marijuana forests. We tried burning them with white phosphorous — it didn't work. We tried burning them with diesel — it didn't work. The plants are so full of water right now ... that we simply couldn't burn them. A couple of brown plants on the edges of some of those [forests] did catch on fire. But a section of soldiers that was downwind from that had some ill effects and decided that was probably not the right course of action." CNN.Com, "Canada Troops Battle 10-Foot Afghan Marijuana Plants," *http:www.cnn.com/2006/WORLD/Americas/10/12/Canada.troops. marijuana.reut/index.html* (accessed 13 October 2006).

41. Interview with author, 21 October 2006.

42. *Ibid.*

43. *Ibid.*

44. Janice Gross Stein, *The Unexpected War. Canada in Kandahar* (Toronto: Viking, 2007), 219.

45. Brigadier-General David Fraser Interview with author, 21 October 2006. This in itself didn't solve any problems for the Canadians. Although one would think that if the ISAF commander approves and supports the plan, and the operation has become NATO's main effort, then the MNB commander should receive the necessary support. However, that is not

necessarily the case because NATO does not own the enablers, which for the most part are still owned by their contributing countries and here in Afghanistan, largely the enablers that are required are aviation, air, and ISR (Intelligence, Surveillance and Reconnaissance) platforms, which are still American or British, and, to some degree in this theatre, Dutch. As a result, it became necessary to convince those countries that Operation Medusa or the MNB are the main effort. Fraser explained, "And if they are reluctant, NATO doesn't even necessarily have the hammer to direct, for sake of example, the British to provide this and the Americans to provide that. As a result, there was a lot of begging. I know that the Multinational Brigade and even the commander of ISAF had to go and do a lot of grovelling and bartering to get the required assets shifted over to our operation. And the effect it had on me though was that the enablers that did become available had restrictions on them. For instance I was told, okay you can have these things for x-amount of days, but then they're being shifted back to whatever region again."

46. Situation Briefing, Senior CF officer, NDHQ, 5 June 2007. General Egon Ramms, the commander of JFC Brunssum, lamented on 6 June 2007, "The European perception is that there is an ISAF mission and an OEF mission. According to European politicians ISAF does stabilization and OEF fights."

47. Interview with author, 21 October 2006. Because of the inability of NATO countries to "pony up" troops, Fraser had to become creative. He explained, "I had to constitute the appropriate force because I was short of soldiers. As a result, the British and the Dutch sent troops that were able to take over certain outposts and garrisons, which in turn freed-up the Canadian troops from TF 3–06 (i.e., 1 RCR Battle Group) so that they could concentrate themselves in Pashmul to conduct the actual offensive. In addition, I asked for Task Force 31 (American Special Forces) if they could go and conduct operations to our south-west near Sperwan. That way I could concentrate my forces on the main effort in the Pashmul area. Interview with author, 21 October 2006.

48. Captain Ryan Jurkoskie stated: "I felt that we left an unresolved situation for other people to deal with ... Op Medusa should have been our battle

group, we knew the battle space, we knew the fucking area, we'd been patrolling through there day in and day out, decisions were made again for all the right reasons but tactically I think, anyways, in my opinion we were too dogmatic in the ingress and egress of our troops and the timelines associated with it rather than tactical fighting and where we had a two month learning curve prior to our first firefight, we had two months to shake ourselves out, their first firefight was in their RIP [relief in place], like holy fuck." Interview with author, 24 January 2007.

49. The 1 RCR/1 PPCLI RIP occurred from 24 July to 24 August. During their tour 1 PPCLI BG conducted: 128 Shuras/leadership engagements; 29 operations; 23 combined operations with ANSF; 646 total patrols; and 291 joint patrols with ANSF. They also participated in 15 intensive fire fights and 100 plus troops in contact. They were the target of 67 small-arms attacks; 59 RPG attacks; 33 rocket attacks; 16 mortar attacks; and 25 IED attacks. They captured 39 detainees, inflicted four confirmed and 181 estimated enemy wounded in action (WIA), and 26 confirmed and 213 estimated enemy killed in action (KIA). They themselves suffered 19 KIA and 76 WIA. "1st Battalion Princess Patricia's Canadian Light Infantry Battle Group (Task Force Orion) — Operational Summary," 12 August 2006

50. Commander's Entry, TF 3–06 War Diary, 19–31 August 2006.

51. Interview with author, 13 October 2006.

52. Details of TF 3–06 operations are from an amalgam of extracts from the BG War Diary and operations documents, interviews and press releases.

53. Interview with author, 13 October 2006.

54. The concept was that once the enemy had been heavily attrited, through the sustained employment of joint fires, they would be forced to withdraw using their exfiltration routes to the South near Siah Choy where they would interdicted by SOF elements and completely destroyed. Manoeuvre was actually initiated earlier than initially planned because of the window of availability for key enablers such as the Predator Unmanned Aerial Vehicle, which were required for Operation Mountain Fury in Regional Command

East (RC (E)) which was running concurrently with Operation Medusa. Memo, Director Army Training to Commander Land Force Development Training System, "Tactical Reconnaissance Report — Training Assessment OP Archer Rotation 3," 21 September 2006, 4.

55. "H-Hour" is the designated time given for coordination of movement and fires for all engaged forces for any given operation.

56. Interview with author, 19 November 2007.

57. TF Kandahar narratives, 2 September 2006.

58. *Ibid.*

59. Interview with author, 8 October 2006.

60. As quoted in Adam Day, "Operation Medusa: The Battle for Panjwai. Part I, The Charge of Charles Company," *Legion Magazine, http://www.legion-magazine.com/features/militarymatters/07–09.asp* (accessed September/ October 2007).

61. Interview with author, 19 November 2007.

62. The school was built in 2004 with funds from the U.S. Commander's Emergency Reconstruction Program (CERP).

63. As quoted in Day, "Operation Medusa: The Battle for Panjwai."

64. Interview with author, 19 November 2007.

65. *Ibid.*

66. *Ibid.*

67. Christie Blatchford, "Did he abandon his troops?" *Globe and Mail,* 29 December 2006, *www.theglobeandmail.com/servlet/story/RTGAM.20061229. wxafghan-blatch29B* (accessed 30 December 2006).

68. Interview with author, 19 November 2007.

69. Mitch Potter, "The Story of C Company," The Star, 30 September 2006. *http://www.thestar.com/NASApp/cs/contentserver?pagename=thestar* (accessed 27 October 2006).

70. *Ibid.*

71. Interview with author, 14 October 2006.

72. *Ibid.*

73. Interview with author, 19 October 2006.

74. Interview with author, 14 October 2006.

75. *Ibid.*

76. Potter, "The Story of C Company."

77. To this date there is no explanation. Two theories exist. One — it was a dud. Two — once the bomb went off its GPS track its arming device shut off. Sprague opined, "we had lots of bad luck that day, but we also had lots of good luck as well." The aircraft has also been both described as a French Mirage and an American aircraft of unknown type.

78. Interview with author, 14 October 2006.

79. Interview with author, 19 November 2007.

80. As quoted in Blatchford, *Fifteen Days*, 256.

81. Potter, "The Story of C Company."

82. Interview with author, 8 October 2006.

83. Interview with author, 21 October 2006.

84. *Ibid.*

85. As quoted in Day, "Operation Medusa: The Battle for Panjwai."

86. Interview with author, 18 October 2006.

87. *Ibid.*

88. *Ibid.*

89. One of the wounded described: "When I close my eyes, I also see the morning after Panjwayi. Sparks, smoke, fire…. then the burp of the main gun of the A-10. I remember the feeling of panic as I crawled for my weapon and PPE, thinking we were under attack. I can still feel the burning on my legs and back, the shock of thinking my legs were gone. I can see the faces of the injured … the twice wounded soldiers of Charles. I see the face of the soldier who saved my life by applying tourniquets to my legs and stopping the bleeding from my back and arm." Anonymous Post — *Army. ca* — "Dealing With Being Home from Kandahar," TF 3–06 BG Notable News — 22 October 2006.

90. Brian Hutchinson, "C Company Shoulders Heavy Burden Fighting Taliban," *Times Colonist (Victoria)*, 12 November 2006, A8.

91. Potter, "The Story of C Company."

92. Brigadier-General David Fraser, presentation — Canadian Infantry Association Annual General Meeting, 25 May 2007.

93. General Rick Hillier, speech at Conference of Defence Associates Seminar, Ottawa, 15 February 2007.

94. VCDS, NDHQ briefing, 8 May 2007. The first tanks arrived 3 October 2006.

95. TF Grizzly was commanded by American Lieutenant-Colonel Steve Williams. "He was a warrior, a smart determined, aggressive, outstanding officer," commented Fraser. "I gave him a bunch of forces, I told him, that's

your sector and here's your mission," explained Fraser, "what I want you to do is to fix the enemy in Rugby and make them think that we are, you are, a whole task force." Interview with author, 21 October 2006.

96. *Ibid.*

97. Commander's Entry, TF Kandahar War Diary, period 1–30 September 2006.

98. Interview with author, 21 October 2006.

99. *Ibid.*

100. *Ibid.*

101. *Ibid.*

102. *Ibid.*

103. Canadian Press, "Path of Little Resistance," *The Kingston Whig-Standard*, 12 September 2006, 10.

104. Les Perreaux, "Afghan Battle Enters Final Phase," *The Kingston-Whig Standard*, 13 September 2006, 11.

105. Interview with author, 21 October 2006.

106. *Ibid.*

107. *Ibid.*

108. See endnote 52.

109. Paul Koring and Graeme Smith, "The Afghan Mission — Canadian Deaths Underscore PM's Plea to NATO," *Globe and Mail*, 28 November 2006, A1.

110. Podcast — "Audio Report by Mark Laity, NATO's Civilian Spokesman in Afghanistan," NATO Speeches 22 November 06 — NATO Library

online, *http://www.nato.int/docu/speech/2006/s060922b.htm* (accessed 26 November 2006).

111. NATO — Allied Command Operations — SHAPTE News, "ISAF Concludes Operation Medusa in Southern Afghanistan," 17 September 2006, *http://www.nato.int/shape/news/206/09/060917a.htm* (accessed 24 November 2006).

112. "Operation Medusa Foiled Taliban Plans, NATO Commander Says," 20 September 2006, *http://london.usembassy.gov/afghn187.html* (accessed 26 Septmber 2006).

113. NATO — Allied Command Operations — SHAPTE News, "ISAF concludes Operaton Medusa in Southern Afghanistan," 17 September 2006, *http://www.nato.int/shape/news/206/09/060917a.htm* (accessed 24 November 2006).

114. "Aid Arriving in Panjwayi Following Taliban Defeat," *ISAF News*, Issue No. 116, 1.

115. House of Commons Defence Committee, *U.K. Operations in Afghanistan. Thirteenth Report of Session 2006–07* (London: The Stationary Office Ltd, 18 July 2007), 16.

116. David McKeeby, "NATO's Operation Medusa Pushing Taliban from Southern Kandahar," 18 September 2006, *http://usinfo.state.gov/xarchives/display.html?p=washfile-english&y=2006&m=September&cx=2006091816 051idybeckcm0.9616358* (accessed 26 Septmber 2006).

117. CTV news staff, "Operation Medusa a 'Significant' Success: NATO," 17 September 2006, *http://www.ctv.ca/servlet/ArticleNews/story/CTVNews/20060917/suicide_bomb_060917/20060917/* (accessed 24 November 2006).

118. Paul Koring, "The Afghan Mission — A Thin Canadian Line Holds in Kandahar," *Globe and Mail*, 6 December 2006, A26.

119. Mitch Potter, "General Frets About Home Front," Middle East Bureau, 1 October 2006.

120. Interview with author, 21 October 2006.

121. Quoted in Stein, *The Unexpected War*, 219.

122. CTV news staff, "Operation Medusa."

123. Schreiber, 1 CMBG briefing, 22 January 2007. General James Jones stated number of killed about 1,000 "but if you said 1,500 it wouldn't surprise me." "Operation Medusa Foiled Taliban Plans, NATO Commander Says," 20 September 2006, *http://usinfo.state.gov/xarchives/display.html?p=washfile-english&y=2006&m=September&cx=20060920172756adtbbed0.444072* (accessed 24 November 2006). Journalists reported, "NATO commanders maintain that Taliban have been on the 'back foot' since Op Medusa, a battle which killed more than 1,000 insurgents." Declan Walsh and Richard Norton-Taylor, "UN Chief: NATO Cannot Defeat Taliban by Force," *The Guardian Weekend*, 18 November 2006, 1.

124. Interview with author, 21 October 2006.

125. Declan Walsh, Richard Norton-Taylor, and Julian Borger, "From soft hats to hard facts in battle to beat Taliban," *The Guardian*, 18 November 2006, 5.

126. CTV news staff, "Operation Medusa."

127. Interview with author, 21 October 2006.

128. Memo, Director Army Training to Commander Land Force Development Training System, "Tactical Reconnaissance Report — Training Assessment OP Archer Rotation 3," 21 September 2006, 5.

129. Interview with Lieutenant-Colonel Lavoie, 13 October 2006.

130. Interview with author, 20 October 2006.

131. Michael Tutton, "Rice Gives Nod to Military," *The Kingston-Whig Standard*, 13 September 2006, 11.

12

OPERATION INTIZAAR ZMAREY: THE BATTLE OF ARGHANDAB, 30 OCTOBER–1 NOVEMBER, 2007

Sean Maloney

Canada's war in Afghanistan has produced many company and battalion-level fights but without a historical framework, it can be difficult to assess their relative importance. The Battle of Arghandab, however, is a clear cut case of success in a war fraught with the normally high-level of ambiguity endemic to any counterinsurgency campaign. Conducted over three days in the autumn of 2007, a Canadian-led multinational effort blocked a major Taliban move to dominate key physical and, more important, psychological terrain in Kandahar City. The enemy bid for control of Arghandab district could have had catastrophic operational consequences for NATO's International Security Assistance Force in the fight against the Taliban, not to mention long-term ramifications for the alliance efforts in the region.

At the tactical level, the brunt of the battle was fought in complex terrain and borne by a dismounted Canadian infantry company, "B" Company from the 3rd Battalion, The Royal 22nd Regiment (3 R22R), working alongside an Afghan National Army infantry company and supported on a number of levels by other coalition and Canadian forces.

Within decision making circles, the perceived political problems with employing Quebecois troops in combat, the potential for casualties, and the potential loss of political support for the Canadian government, loomed large in the background during this particular deployment. This added (and unnecessary) strategic pressure paradoxically makes the

Battle of Arghandab even more important historically for Canada. The objectives of Operation Intizaar Zmarey were achieved without a single Canadian death.

SETTING THE STAGE: ARGHANDAB DISTRICT

"Christening the ground" is a time-honoured tradition in Canadian battle procedure. An observer must have in the mind's eye an accurate idea of where a battle is fought to understand why it was fought. In this case, Arghandab is a rural district northwest of Kandahar City. It is one of several "green zones" surrounding the city, areas that have access to irrigation along the rivers and areas that are agriculturally and thus economically prosperous. All of these green zones are significant to military commanders, insurgents, and counterinsurgents alike. They provide cover in an otherwise arid, desert-like mountainous environment. They sit astride or next to the four major roads leading into Kandahar City. Domination of all or some of the green zones permits a force to dominate the city or at least interfere with commercial, civilian, and military movements throughout the region. Kandahar City is the primary commercial, transport, governance, and religious hub of southern Afghanistan. Its seizure is sine qua non for control of the region.

Any traveller in Arghandab, especially one moving along route GREEN LIGHT, the main southwest-northeast road north of the river, would notice that the terrain is different from the vineyard trenches of the more familiar Zharey and Panjwayi districts that Canadians have fought in since 2006. A "Coyote" (light-armoured reconnaissance vehicle) crew commander taking a patrol down GREEN LIGHT would see brown, dusty hills with virtually no cover off to his left for a considerable distance. The contested district of Khakriz lies over those hills. To his right, there is flat but cluttered ground populated with orchards and scrub interspersed with several hundred family compounds. Each house is a rabbit warren of irregular rooms and is a natural fortress surrounded with a wall or walls and linked by trails that only a motorcycle can go down. The crew commander might glimpse the Arghandab River three kilometres away.

If the river isn't in full flood, it is strewn with rocks with channels of water flowing down it. As such, it is classed as a wadi, which acts as a highway of sorts, though it is seasonally dependent. The wadi is about 500 metres wide and completely open,

Along the road, a traveller would pass by family compounds and walled fields, some right up to the road itself, forming significant built-up defiles. Five kilometres down the road from Highway 1, there are the towns of Jelawur, Hajji Kodayraham, and Tabin, the commercial centres with markets and services. Stopping at a checkpoint in Adihira, a gunner traversing his turret, which houses his 25-mm cannon, can make out the district centre four kilometres away to the east, across the river, with an incongruous cylindrical building with cell phone advertising perched on the side the hill next to an elaborate shrine. To the north about 20 kilometres away is the Dala Dam, built in the 1950s. It commands the flow of water to Arghandab and the districts to the southwest. North of Dala Dam is Shah Wali Kot district, which, like its neighbour Khakriz, is contested by the enemy. Kandahar City itself is less than five kilometres from Arghandab through the hills as the crow flies.

Arghandab is also key ethnic, and therefore political, terrain. All counterinsurgency campaigns emphasize the role of the population, which is itself as much a battleground as geographical features. Arghandab is dominated by the Alokozai tribe and, up to early 2007 was led by a charismatic and respected leader, Mullah Naqib. As long as Mullah Naqib was in charge of Arghandab, the coalition forces did not have to divert scarce resources to garrison it. Mullah Naqib's militia and police were capable of handling any Taliban threat and were generally able to keep the enemy at bay on their own.

On 9 March 2007, Mullah Naqib was subjected to an assassination attempt. Badly wounded, he withdrew from Afghanistan to recuperate, but his sons were killed and the possibility of a power vacuum or even internecine tribal conflict loomed large. Militias and police in Afghanistan are leadership-dependent and the possibility that the Taliban were deliberately trying to destabilize Arghandab district was discussed among the Task Force Kandahar Staff as early as June 2007. When Mullah Naqib died on 12 October rumours circulated that it was only a matter of time before the Taliban arrived to exploit the situation. As a result, Coyote armoured vehicles from 12 Régiment blindé du Canada (12 RBC) Reconnaissance Squadron were sent to patrol in Arghandab district as a precautionary measure.

INDICATORS AND PLANS: 12 OCTOBER–29 OCTOBER 2007

Contrary to assertions from individual observers and aid agencies in Kandahar,[2] Canada's Task Force Kandahar (TFK) was closely monitoring the situation after Naqib's death. The All-Source Intelligence Centre (ASIC) went onto a heightened alert status on 12 October and established a number of indicators in and around Arghandab district. If a sequence or combination of them were triggered by enemy movements or actions, the planning staff would swing into action and develop a contingency plan to counter the enemy move. Brigadier-General Guy Laroche, TFK commander, and Lieutenant-Colonel Alain Gauthier, the battle group commander, and their staffs agreed by 20 October on a number of decision points that linked the indicators with specific responses.

If the enemy massed outside Arghandab district, this would be detected and dealt with using a combination of special operations forces, unmanned aerial vehicles, and air power before they moved in. However, a more complicated scenario was the possibility of infiltration, either singly or in small groups, over a protracted period. Such a move could not be pre-empted using the other tools and could only be dealt with once the enemy embarked on a detectable course of action. Brigadier-General Laroche determined that the primary trigger point would centre on a enemy threat to the Arghandab district centre, the symbolic seat of power in the area and located next to the main road leading over the hills into Kandahar City.

The Taliban weren't exactly subtle in their approach. One of the commanders selected to carry out operations against Arghandab initiated a cell phone intimidation campaign against the district chief of police telling him and his men to get out, that the Taliban were coming, and if the police did not leave that they would be slaughtered. The police chief taunted them back: "If you come as friends, don't come," he retorted. "If you come as enemies we'll kick you out."

Another key monitoring tool was the Kandahar Provincial Reconstruction Team led by Lieutenant-Colonel Bob Chamberlain. The PRT deployed a Civil-Military Cooperation (CIMIC) representative, Master Warrant Officer Michel Pelletier, regularly to Arghandab district. Other development and aid contacts, established through the Department of Foreign Affairs and Canadian International Development Agency (DFAIT) representatives at the PRT, were additional venues for situational awareness. Until the enemy made an overt move, however, there could be no effective response.

The cell phone network in Kandahar province had expanded geometrically since the fall of the anti-technology Taliban in 2001–02. People with little or no apparent means, in the most remote locations imaginable, seemed to all have cell phones by 2007. When the Taliban entered Arghandab district, a wave of panic ran through the population in the area, and it spread rapidly among the half-million citizens of Kandahar City. This cascading wave of panicky cell phone calls, coupled with the sight of carloads of Arghandabians fleeing the district panicked non-governmental organizations (NGO) and United Nations aid work-

Department of National Defence, Negative Ar2007-T080-13.

Members of the Operational Mentor and Liaison Team and the Provincial Reconstruction Team working with 2nd Kandak on the northern axes advance on Objective "J."

ers who then reported through their communications systems to superiors in Kabul that the enemy was at the gates. The media also contributed to the panic. Families with relatives in Pakistan received calls telling them to get out of Kandahar City before it fell. One family on the east side of the city even cancelled an elaborate wedding on the strength of a couple of cell phone calls.

The situation within the district itself was confused. The police checkpoint at Jelawur was attacked and its forces scattered. The locals called several police agencies in Kandahar City to report enemy movements; these agencies in turn informed the Governor, Asadullah Khalid, who was pressuring ISAF to intervene. The commander of the Afghan National Auxiliary Police (ANAP)[3] in the district, Abdul Hakim Jan, was in Kabul at the time. He phoned his militia and ordered them to engage the Taliban as soon as possible. The subsequent abortive attack resulted in three wounded police, who retreated in the face of significant firepower. Two Royal Air Force (RAF) Harrier GR-7 ground support aircraft were brought in and conducted a low-level show of force. These moves may have forced the Taliban commanders to delay their assault on the district centre.

The problem for Task Force Kandahar was the possibility that the Arghandab move might be designed to distract the attention of the coalition forces away from the Zharey and Panjwayi districts to the southwest where substantial ground was being made in retaking key communities from Taliban control. The clincher came on the morning of 29 October when a delegation of leaders from Arghandab presented themselves to Brigadier-General Laroche and formally requested help in ejecting the Taliban.

By 1200 hours, Laroche, part of his staff and the district elders deployed to the district centre on a recce. An hour later, battle procedure started for the 3 R22eR battle group. Radio orders were given at 1700 hours and in time the battle group quick reaction force, which amounted to a LAV-III platoon and some surveillance assets, arrived at the district centre. At approximately 1800 hours, an American Police Mentoring Team (PMT) in its armoured HUMMV vehicles, accompanying 120 ANP and their leader General Saquib, deployed around the district centre and along the east bank of the river in a screen. The 12 RBC Recce Squadron sent a troop of Coyote vehicles to secure the road junction of Highway 1 and route GREEN LIGHT, which would serve as a possible staging area.

A coordination meeting was held two hours later at Forward Operating Base Wilson over in Zharey district with all the principle Canadian and Afghan commanders, including Lieutenant-Colonel Shareen Shah of the 2nd Kandak, an Afghan National Army infantry battalion operating in Zharey district. Analysis of the enemy's strength concluded that there were between 100 and 300 Taliban in what became called "The Box." The general plan was to establish blocks to the north and east, screen the west, and then drive an Afghan infantry company and a Canadian infantry company along route GREEN LIGHT — Afghans to the left of the road, Canadians to the right — like a plunger into a syringe. At the same time, however, the battle group was still responsible for control of the Zharey and Panjwayi districts. As a result, the entire infantry battalion could not be made available.

Indeed, it appears in retrospect that the Taliban sought to coordinate its actions in Arghandab district with supporting operations in Zharey district. A Taliban unit operating near Howze-e Madad prepared to block

Courtesy Sean M. Maloney.

The Quick Reaction Force was deployed to the Arghandab District Centre as the first indicators were tripped.

the vital Highway 1 east-west route and draw off reinforcements. Pre-emptive manoeuvring by the Canadian operational mentoring and liaison team (OMLT) and 2nd Kandak deterred this action for the duration of Operation Intizaar Zmarey and this and other enemy operations were not mounted in Zharey district.

The ANP with the PMT were already to the east of the river, so the manoeuvre issue revolved around establishing blocks to the north and the screen to the west. Part of an American Special Forces task force, TF-32, was available but since it didn't belong to ISAF, it took some time to sort out where and how it could be used. Ideally TF-32 elements would handle the northern block. Lieutenant-Colonel Gauthier decided to use a combination of Recce Squadron Coyotes and Leopard 2 A6M main battle tanks from "C" Squadron, a composite tank squadron led by The Lord Strathcona's Horse (Royal Canadians), to handle the western screen. This force would watch in both directions-first to support the infantry company as it advanced, but also to prevent any enemy reinforcements coming down from Khakriz district. The Afghan infantry company, transported in Ford Ranger pickups and working closely with the Canadian OMLT, was augmented with an engineer troop mounted in LAV IIIs. Orders went out at 2200 hours. "X" Battery, 5e Régiment Artillerie Léger du Canada (5 RALC) prepared a M-777 155-mm gun detachment to support the operation from a forward RMA.

Lieutenant-Colonel Gauthier's scheme of manoeuvre, dictated by the terrain, meant that the mechanized infantry company would have to operate dismounted. Major David Abboud, Officer Commanding "B" Company, assessed his forces. A combination of the rotating leave policy and static protection tasks meant that "B" Company could muster 58 personnel or three platoons with two sections each. Two of these platoons were led by Warrant Officers St Germain and Royer because the platoon leaders were on leave. When the crews of the LAV IIIs were subtracted, this brought the number of infantry dismounts down to 52 individuals. A small number of combat engineers from 53 Escadron de campagne were added but "B" Company would have to mount the operation at reduced strength. Major Abboud decided to use his company headquarters, 15 soldiers, as a small manoeuvre group fro provide him additional flexibility and capability.

Intelligence on the size of the Taliban force remained sketchy, though better information was coming in. The ISTAR (Intelligence, Surveillance, Target Acquisition, Reconnaissance) apparatus identified three Taliban commanders and each was thought to control between 30 to 50 insurgents, plus support augmentees, all in all around 200 enemy.

The battle group's initial planners, using 1:50,000 maps, which didn't provide a lot of detail (one maze-like area was simply labelled "numerous ditches"), hastily identified compound areas called "A," "B," "C," and so on, essentially blobs on the map. Two hours before the company deployed from FOB Wilson, however, Abboud received more detailed imagery. The generalized blobs became sharper clusters of compounds and were relabelled A-1, B-1, B-2, and so forth. His team had less then an hour to rename and learn all the control measures before departing.

DAY 1: 30 OCTOBER 2007

Preliminary moves took place starting around 0200 hours. With the 2nd Kandak and the OMLT massing at the road junction, "B" Company passed through, into Kandahar City and made its way to the Arghandab district centre, down the hill and into the wadi, opposite Objective "A" around 0530 hours. The troops dismounted from the LAV IIIs. The intent was to use the Zulu vehicles[4] to move along the wadi parallel with the advance and provide fire support if possible. There was substantial gunfire to the north as the police and their American mentors engaged the Taliban with harassing fire.

The Afghan infantry company and the OMLT mentors arrived at Objective "H" around 0730 hours, where the retreating population warned them that the enemy was in a compound complex up the road (designated Objective "J"). The Afghans even snagged a lone, unaware Taliban and detained him for questioning.

The first troops from "B" Company into Objective "A" found fleeing civilians, shocked people moving southwest in groups of 15 to 20. A detailed clearance of Objective "A," completed at 1100 hours, produced nothing. The next objectives, B-1 and B-2, were approached tactically and

Leopard 2 A6M tanks from "C" Squadron provided the screen on the left flank as the 2nd Kandak and the OMLT cleared the compound complexes along Route GREEN LIGHT.

Department of National Defence, Negative Ar2007-z042-05.

quietly, with the company tactical headquarters and 3 Platoon deployed to seize B-1 and, 1 and 4 Platoons responsible for securing objective B-2. Abboud was surprised to find a lone man in B-1 who was happy to see the Canadians and told them the enemy was 300 metres away. He was even willing to show "B" Company where they were located.

That compound complex, designated C-2, was located across an 200-metre open field. Abboud had the company's C-6 and C-9 machine guns set up to cover the approach, but then when the company tactical headquarters turned a corner in a maze of compounds that made up objective B-1, they surprised an insurgent. He was wearing a black tactical vest, had dark brown uniform pants and top, a long black beard, and an AK-47. The enemy had observation posts, but their men were languid in the heat of the day. Shots were fired and the fight was on.

The company tactical headquarters and 3 Platoon were then engaged from the compounds in C-2, mostly with PKM machine-gun fire, but soon after the Taliban fired an endless amount of rocket-propelled-grenade rounds at B-1, a total of about 25 shots all with their distinctive two bangs-the first when fired and the second when detonated. The enemy lofted the RPG rounds in an arc in an attempt to use plunging fire.

Platoons 2 and 3, hearing the firing, pushed hard into and through the B-2 compounds and emerged south of objective B-1. Royer and St Germain had clear shots and good fields of fire, so they engaged the C-2 objective from their direction.

This firefight lasted about two hours, with the Van Doos (R22eR soldiers) moving back and forth along walls and on compound roofs, getting better firing positions. All the while RPG rounds rained down on them and they returned fire with their C-7A1 assault rifles, 203-mm grenade launchers, and C-6 and C-9 machine guns. Soon the volume of enemy fire made it clear that objective C-2 was a major Taliban position.

The Taliban then tried to manoeuvre and flank objective B-1 to the north with a 12-man group. The company tactical headquarters and 4 Platoon caught the movement through the orchards and walls and put a high volume of fire down. The forward observation officer was by now in contact with the two M-777 artillery pieces. Two fire missions blasted the Taliban group, the rounds cashing down and permanently eliminating it from the order of battle.

Department of National Defence, Negative Ar2007-z049-13.

Recce Squadron Coyotes secured advance routes, provided long-range surveillance, and patrolled Arghandab District once it was secured.

Not long after, the Taliban commander in C-2 tried another flanking move, this time to the south to the right side of the compounds in B-2. Unfortunately for this group of insurgents, the Zulu LAV IIIs in the wadi detected the movement. The 25-mm cannons, with their distinctive "Boom-boom-boom" three-round bursts, forced the enemy to take cover. The forward observation officer with the LAV IIIs then called in another fire mission from "X" Battery, again eliminating the flanking force as a threat.

This enemy was no rag-tag force of Jezail-wielding farmers from the hills, as some commentators in the Canadian media portray them. They had distinctive uniforms, heavy weapons, and a command and control hierarchy. When surprised on their flank, they manoeuvred. They fought in place and did not wantonly withdraw. This was not hit-and-run warfare in the hill but a classic Fighting in Built Up Areas (FIBUA) battle. Experienced and probably professionally-trained, they were also not aging Mujahideen from the 1980s. It is possible some were foreign fighters, but this remains unclear.

Under normal conditions, airpower would have been called in and the compounds in Objective C-2 would have been obliterated using several 1,000-pound Guided Bomb Units (GBUs) dropped from Harrier, A-10 or Mirage aircraft. The fact that Arghandab was a friendly district and had suffered little battle damage throughout the course of the war played a role in limiting how coalition firepower was employed with the deliberate aim of reducing collateral damage.

The fact that the enemy wasn't withdrawing from Objective C-2 piqued the interest of the planning and intelligence staff back in the Provincial Operations Centre (POC) at Kandahar Airfield. They directed a Sperwer Tactical Unmanned Aerial Vehicle (TUAV) and later an MQ-1 Predator to take a look at what was going on in depth behind the C-2 compound complexes. Much-maligned, loud, unarmed, and not as sexy as the MQ-1 Predator or the MQ-9 Reaper UAVs, the Sperwer still carried a respectable sensor package. One eye was better than none. In due course observers located what looked like a meeting of enemy personnel, about a platoon's worth, clustered around a commander who was giving them instructions. Two U.S. Air Force (USAF) F-15 Eagles

Soldiers from "B" Company, 3 R22eR engage the enemy in Objective "C."

were orbiting the battlefield and, once the airspace was de-conflicted by the POC staff, one aircraft was cleared to engage the concentration with a 500-pound GBU. At least 15 Taliban were fragmented by the blast. The only collateral damage was to the mud wall they were leaning against.

"B" Company had contact for the rest of the day in the vicinity of Objective C-2. Two soldiers were wounded with RPG fragments to the face and legs-but continued to fight nonetheless. Meanwhile, on the second axis of advance, the Afghan National Army company made good time and cleared the compound complexes in Objectives "G" and "H" without incident. A troop of Leopard 2A6Ms and a troop of Coyote surveillance and recce vehicles moved along the west flank in parallel fashion, turrets traversed in all directions when a forward observation officer confirmed that a section of Taliban with anti-tank weapons was manoeuvring to engage the tanks. A fire mission from the M-777's finished off that group.

When the ANA troops tried to move into Objective "J," however, the Taliban opened up with a high volume of small arms fire. The ANA lieutenant leading the attack was killed outright and the attack stalled and became an exchange of fire, with the ANA troops engaging in an RPG dual with the Taliban, while 53 Escadron's LAV IIIs provided fire support. Throughout the afternoon it proved difficult to push the enemy out from Objective "J" without employing tank fire or air support. The ANA finally brought up mortars and lobbed several rounds at the enemy positions in the compounds.

Lieutenant-Colonel Gauthier was confronted with a problem as the sun waned. "B" Company's advance and that of 2nd Kandak were asymmetrical. His concern was that the enemy, who had demonstrated a level of tactical sophistication, might try to exploit the widening gap at night either to harass or assault either company, or the enemy might exfiltrate through the gap and get away into Zhari district. He ordered Major Abboud to halt and establish observation posts for the night.

At the same time, Lieutenant-Colonel Shareen Shah from 2nd Kandak was deploying another infantry company to back up the one at Objective "J" and he was figuring out how to bring in his third company. The Afghan National Police also wanted to be involved in the next day's operations. The U.S. Police Mentoring Team had by this time moved north on the east side of the river in part because there were delays in getting TF-32 into position up near the Dala Dam. Eager to get into the action, the PMT engaged the Taliban with 203-mm grenade fire along the river but sustained several wounded ANP officers during the night.

"B" Company didn't get much sleep. The temperature, usually 25 degrees Celsius during the day, dropped at night down to 0 degrees. Each soldier was already loaded down (personal protection gear, weapons, ammunition, water, and food), in some cases carrying 160 kilograms. Moreover, they had been sweating all day. At night, some became nearly hypothermic. At this point, the medics treated six orthopedic injuries, turned ankles, strained backs, plus the two wounded by shrapnel.

Resupply was complicated by the lack of navigable roads, so the Zulu LAV IIIs moved as close as they could along the wadi. In fact, 50 percent of each platoon's vehicles moved through 800 metres of uncleared (the possibility of mines was very real), complex terrain down to the wadi, and back to the positions to resupply depleted stocks, particularly ammunition and water. Major Abboud also decided to move a LAV-III platoon back to the Arghandab district centre. There the nine crewmen parked the vehicles, and came back to fight dismounted.

A variety of ISTAR resources were deployed that night to watch for enemy movement, but nothing was seen. The enemy understood, by 2007, how capable the coalition forces were in this realm and limited their movements to covered routes.

The Taliban commanders, however, were stunned by the rapidity of the coalition response and by their own losses on the first day, estimated to be 15 dead and 50 wounded (many of whom would later die). Furthermore, their command and control was breaking down (it was possible that leaders were killed in the airstrike) and fear was palpable in the enemy camp. Their leaders were unsure what to do — stay and fight or withdraw. They contacted their higher commanders and asked for reinforcements. The senior Taliban commanders subsequently tried to muster support for the Arghandab effort from Taliban groups located as far away as Helmand province and in Pakistan.

DAY 2: 31 OCTOBER 2007

As dawn broke on Day 2, "B" Company's plan was to move onto the Objective C-1 complex. The idea was to convince the enemy they were about to be outflanked, thus forcing them to disengage or, if the weren't thinking, drive them towards the wadi, and into the 25-mm guns of the Zulu LAV IIIs. The 2nd Kandak was up bright and early, moving at strength into Objective "J," which they proceeded to clear thoroughly during the morning. ISTAR assets detected a section of insurgents heading north, who subsequently split up individually and went in separate directions. Another Taliban section detected heading north away from the river was engaged with artillery fire before it could "starburst," killing an estimated seven enemy.

Once the companies were symmetrical on both axis of advance, "B" Company prepared to move on Objective C-1 around 1400 hours. 2 Platoon and the company tactical headquarters struck out for the compounds-and then ran into the enemy, who engaged at 100-metres range with harassing fire from the C-1 compounds. Lieutenant-Colonel Gauthier instructed "B" Company to get into the C-2 complex as quickly as possible and back off of Objective C-1.

The Sperwer TUAV spotted enemy movement behind these objective areas and then two AH-64 Apache attack helicopters arrived on station to support the effort. One of the machines fired a Hellfire missile against a mud wall on Objective C-2 to "rattle the cage" of any occupants. There was no reaction and "B" Company started to methodically search the compound complexes. The search was slow going; there was concern that the enemy may have laid anti-personnel mines or left booby traps behind so that by night fall only 60 percent of Objective C-2 had been examined.

On the northern axis, the Afghan force prepared to assault into Objective "I." The Leopard 2 tanks and engineer LAV IIIs manoeuvred to form a firebase to the northwest, while the 2nd Kandak and the OMLT prepared to rush the compounds. This move was delayed because it was getting dark. Two bewildered enemy wandering around the area were detained. Another Taliban section was spotted moving among several compounds, but the fleeting target couldn't be engaged with artillery, so the AH-64 Apaches were asked to hunt them down. The attack helicopters had no luck finding them in the built up area. As the force moved into the compounds south of Jelawur, a short sharp firefight broke out, leaving two Taliban dead.

The Afghan Kandak and "B" Company consolidated in three locations for the night and conducted resupply. There were no engagements that night.

DAY 3: 1 NOVEMBER 2007

"B" Company cleared the other 40 percent of the Objective C-2 compounds throughout the morning. A local national, who stayed behind and hid, emerged and told the soldiers that the enemy was placing IEDs or mines on some of the routes. The combat engineers conducted a recce and discovered an IED between C-2 and the wadi. On careful examination, two other IED sites were located, again on routes leading to the wadi. It appeared as though the weapons were laid back on the first night in anticipation of an ANP/PMT attack across the wadi. When that didn't materialize, the IEDs were left in place. The clearance effort, conducted by combat engineers, took an hour. The enemy clearly anticipated a mounted attack and planned accordingly. Once again, a dismounted operation had caught the Taliban by surprise and dislocated them.

The "B" Company platoons moved on to Objective C-3 and cleared it as well. Major Abboud then sent a platoon back to Objective C-1, just in case the enemy surreptitiously reoccupied it during the night. Again, no contact. Lieutenant-Colonel Gauthier believed that the enemy had exfiltrated and so he sped up the advance. "B" Company moved on to the "D" series of objectives and was surprised to find local nationals who were returning. Almost all had been informed by cell phone that it was safe to return to their homes, that the enemy had left. On encountering the Canadians, the hospitality component of Pashtunwali[5] came into effect and the platoons were invited to move into the houses and bed down in the compounds by overjoyed Arghandabians.

The Afghan army and OMLT assault on Objective "I" were conducted but there was no resistance. ISTAR surveillance at this time picked up what amounted to an enemy evacuation of the Jelawur and Chalgoa communities. The enemy, apparently, was dispirited over the loss of leadership and the unwillingness of other Taliban commanders in the region to reinforce the Arghandab effort. They withdrew from the field, split up into small groups or individuals, buried or concealed their weapons, and left. Lieutenant-Colonel Gauthier continued to accelerate his advance, so "B" Company moved forward to Objective "D," and the ANA company to Objective "K" once the ongoing clearances were completed in their present locations. The Canadians and Afghans were by this time running out of district as they headed north and the terrain tapered between the hills and the river. The rest of the day was spent methodically searching the remaining objective compounds. There was no enemy contact.

ENDGAME: 2 NOVEMBER 2007

The 2nd Kandak supported by the ANP moved on to Jelawur in a massive show of force as the district population flowed back in, while "B" Company cleared the last objectives in D-2, E-1, and E-2. There was an atmosphere of jubilation not only in the district, but in Kandahar City as well. When "B" Company was reunited with its LAV IIIs, they drove out of the district and back to FOB Wilson with cheering crowds lining the roads, something not seen in Kandahar after any previous operation. The Taliban left behind a surprise in the form of a lone suicide bomber. Before he could detonate his vest, however, the locals in Tabi-e Sofia prevented him from doing so and turned him over to the ANP. On 4 November, a Taliban IED team that infiltrated the area succeeded in disabling a Leopard 2 tank that was supporting Recce Squadron in maintaining a presence in the district. However, without the forces to follow up, the Taliban action amounted to nothing. By January 2008, the district shura was more interested in electricity and irrigation issues than security matters.

After the action, there was some finger-pointing by local officials and "Monday-morning quarterbacking" by other locally-based commentators who were upset that the enemy "got away" or somehow outwitted Task Force Kandahar during their exfiltration and were not destroyed in detail. The reality of the situation is that the terrain is porous and not all the necessary blocking forces were in place throughout the course of the battle. Moreover, the sad reality is, if insurgents divest themselves of weapons and equipment, they can easily blend in with the returning population and escape individually. None of this should detract from the most important effect of the operation — the enemy did not retain any control over Arghandab district or its population. They retreated to areas of the province that do not matter, areas that consist of rock and sand, that are difficult to resupply from Pakistan in the face of other coalition forces' operations in Regional Command (South), and areas with small population bases that offer fewer recruits. In addition, the elimination of experienced leaders will have a cumulative effect on those Taliban cells that took place in this operation and indeed these effects have been felt throughout the Regional Command (South) area. The really telling aspect is that the other Taliban commanders in adjacent areas and even provinces declined to join the fight for Arghandab when it became evident the Taliban force was in trouble.

The ability of 150 to 200 enemy to generate panic in a city with a population of half-a-million inhabitants, whether deliberately or inadvertently, was astounding. Could this have been prevented? The answer is yes, but only by a concentrated and concerted information campaign and only when it is recognized by the coalition forces that such panic is spreading like wildfire.

As such, the action in Arghandab district proved to be a critical one in the overall history of the campaign. The vital nature of the district, its proximity to Kandahar City, and, most important, the fact that the enemy was unable to gain a foothold in the community let alone control it are stark indicators of success. The Canadian-led operation was mounted extremely quickly, used methods unanticipated by the Taliban, and thoroughly dislocated them psychologically, in contrast to the more deliberate set-piece actions conducted in Zhari district back in 2006. The geographical and psychological aspects of Operation Intizaar Zmarey need to be understood especially by counterinsurgency practitioners operating in Afghanistan.

NOTES

1. This chapter is for the most part based on a series of interviews conducted in-theatre in Kandahar by the author two months after the operation with the primary Canadian command and planning personnel; Major Dave Abboud and his staff; members of the Kandahar Provincial Reconstruction Team; and Afghan personnel. Certain details relating to intelligence sources have been blurred and the code names of all route control measures and geographical identifiers have been altered for operational security considerations.

2. One Westerner with romantic and emotional attachments to the Alokozai tribe asserted to many Afghan officials and international aid workers in Kandahar City that "Canada" (not just TFK or ISAF) had been surprised by Taliban infiltration of Arghandab, thus the belief that Canada's response was needlessly slow gained credence in the media and within the population.

3. The ANAP are essentially an auxiliary militia and are different from the Afghan National Police or ANP. The ANAP was an experiment, which was intended to be disbanded; however, in 2007 the ANAP was still in place in Arghandab.

4. Zulu vehicles are those which have unloaded their infantry soldiers but are still operated by their vehicle crews.

5. Pashtunwali is the tribal code of the Pashtuns that emphasizes hospitality to guests and blood debts with enemies.

Department of National Defence, Negative Is2007–0588.

Soldiers from "B" Company, 3 R22eR, engage the enemy in Objective "C."

CONTRIBUTORS

MAJOR, DR. ANDREW B. GODEFROY is an historian and strategic analyst with the Canadian Army as well as the editor of the *Canadian Army Journal*. He holds a PhD in War Studies from the Royal Military College of Canada (RMC) and has authored over a dozen studies on the Canadian Army in the First World War. Andrew is now researching and writing a definitive biography of Sir Arthur Currie.

MAJOR JOHN R. GRODZINSKI teaches history at RMC, where he is also a doctoral candidate in the war studies program. His areas of interest include North America wars and warfare from 1608 to 1815, particularly the War of 1812. His other academic fields of interests are the Napoleonic Wars, specializing in British operations in the Iberian Peninsula, and the development of smooth bore weaponry. John also regularly leads battlefield tours to Seven Years' War and War of 1812 sites and is also editor of the online *War of 1812 Magazine*, available through the Napoleon Series website.

COLONEL, DR. BERND HORN is an experienced infantry officer who is now serving as the deputy commander of Canadian Special Operations Forces Command. He has command experience at the sub-unit and unit level and was the officer commanding 3 Commando, the Canadian Airborne Regiment, from 1993–1995 and the commanding officer of the 1st Battalion, The Royal Canadian Regiment from 2001–03. He is also an adjunct professor of history at RMC. He has authored, co-authored, edited, and co-edited over 25 books and many articles on military affairs and military history.

WILLIAM JOHNSTON is a historian with the Directorate of History and Heritage, Department of National Defence. He is the co-author of official histories of the Royal Canadian Air Force and the Royal Canadian Navy and the author of *A War of Patrols: Canadian Army Operations in Korea.*

DR. SEAN M. MALONEY is the historical advisor to the chief of the Land Staff and is the Army's historian for the Afghanistan mission. He has travelled to Afghanistan regularly since 2003 to observe operations in the field and is the author of many books and other writings dealing with the war in that country.

DR. KEN REYNOLDS is the assistant Canadian Forces heritage officer with DHH. After graduating with his doctorate from McGill University he spent several years as a freelance researcher and writer with DND, other government departments, and various non-governmental organizations. He joined DHH in his current position in 2003. Among other duties at DHH, he works on the casualty identification team that investigates military remains found on various Canadian battlefields. As such he played a small role in the efforts to identify Private Herbert Peterson, 49th Battalion, Canadian Expeditionary Force, killed during the trench raid of 8–9 June 1917.

MICHAEL WHITBY is senior naval historian at DHH. He has published widely on 20th Century naval history. As well as being co-author of the two-part official operational history of the Royal Canadian Navy in the Second World War — *No Higher Purpose* and *A Blue Water Navy*, his edited volumes include *Commanding Canadians: The Second World War Diaries of A.F.C. Layard* (University of British Columbia Press 2005), and *The Admirals: Canada's Senior Naval Leadership in the 20th Century* (Dundurn Press, 2006).

DR. LEE WINDSOR is deputy director of the University of New Brunswick's Gregg Centre for the Study of War and Society. He is an historian specializing in the Canadian Army from Confederation to the present. His primary interests include the 1943–45 Italian Campaign and post-Cold War "peace and stability" operations from the former Yugoslavia to Afghanistan. He is a former member of the CF Reserve, having served with the 8th Canadian Hussars and the West Nova Scotia Regiment.

MICHEL WYCZYNSKI is a senior archivist with Library and Archives Canada. He has authored and co-authored many books and articles on Canadian military history and is an acknowledged expert on the Canadian Airborne experience.

INDEX